LEGAL SECRETS

LEGAL SECRETS

Equality and Efficiency in the Common Law

KIM LANE SCHEPPELE

The University of Chicago Press
Chicago and London

KIM LANE SCHEPPELE is assistant professor of political science, assistant research scientist in the Institute for Public Policy Studies, and adjunct assistant professor of law at the University of Michigan. She is coauthor of *Crime and Punishment: Changing Attitudes in America* and is cofounder of the Conference Group on Jurisprudence and Public Law.

Cover illustration:
Les Gens de Justice (#32 of the series, Delteil 1368)
Honore Daumier
French, 1808-1879
Lithograph
Caption: "Laizzez dire un peu de mal de vous. . .," 1847
Babcock Bequest
Courtesy, Museum of Fine Arts, Boston

The University of Chicago Press, Chicago 60637
The University of Chicago Press, Ltd., London
© 1988 by The University of Chicago
All rights reserved. Published 1988
Printed in the United States of America

97 96 95 94 93 92 91 90 89 88   54321

LIBRARY OF CONGRESS CATALOGING-IN-PUBLICATION DATA

Scheppele, Kim Lane, 1953–
    Legal secrets.

    Bibliography: p.
    Includes index.
    1. Jurisprudence. 2. Economics. 3. Contracts.
4. Secrecy—Law and legislation—United States.
I. Title.
K487.E3S34   1988   340'.1   88-1283
ISBN 0-226-73778-0
ISBN 0-226-73779-9 (pbk.)

Contents

CONTENTS

Preface

An old Irish story recounts the experience of a traveler who stopped in a countryside pub to ask for directions to Dublin. The pubkeeper scratched his head, thought a minute, and said with all sincerity, "Well, if I were going to Dublin, I certainly wouldn't start from here."

Though we may be unwilling to admit it, a good deal of scholarship probably starts from the intellectual equivalent of the countryside pub. We set out from unlikely places on major journeys, asking directions of those who haven't been where we are going and can't imagine why we want to go where we're heading.

I have written a book about jurisprudence and social theory, about law and economics, about moral philosophy and legal interpretation, about the sociology of knowledge. But the project started when I worked in survey research and mathematical sociology. If there is nary a number or equation in this book, it is because in the end the subject matter couldn't have absorbed it without serious distortion (not that I didn't try at first). During a long journey, I learned much about a different culture, the culture of law.

The culture of law can be found at an intellectual crossroads where an autonomous legal tradition is open to the traffic of neighboring disciplines in the social sciences and the humanities. Social theory and moral philosophy have always bordered on the law. Social theory may fairly be said to have developed out of jurisprudential concerns in the nineteenth century (Weber, Simmel, Durkheim, and Marx were all trained as lawyers), and moral philosophy has been a close cousin of legal theory for much longer than that. History itself has a long history in legal culture. In recent years, the economic analysis of law has had a major influence on legal thinking, and now, with the appointment of many of its most distinguished practitioners to the federal bench, it has worked its way into actual judging. The hermeneutic tendencies of literary and cultural criticism have been to-ing and fro-ing with the law of late, too, and recently the rush of concern for legal interpretation has increased the immigration of new ideas from these quarters into legal method.

This book takes advantage of these disciplinary connections. Like the cubists, who took the traditional idea of perspective in art and superimposed on one canvas the results of seeing from many different points of view, I have taken the ideas and methods of different disciplines and superimposed them in these pages. By intellectual orientation, then, I am a theoretical cubist. I have used an interpretive analysis of legal opinions drawn with a rigorous sampling procedure from nineteenth- and twentieth-century legal doctrine to figure out whether a normative theory in the contractarian tradition (which proceeds from a Simmelian vision of social interaction) is a better description of the law than a normative theory associated with contemporary microeconomics. Like the cubists in art, I hope that the result is not a jumble of conflicting images, but rather a new sort of picture with a coherence of its own.

Writing is a solitary activity, but scholarship is not. I have been very fortunate in having a large number of friends, colleagues, and institutions who have helped this book along in many ways, and who have aided and abetted the migration of my interests, ideas, and abilities.

This book started as a dissertation in the Department of Sociology at the University of Chicago, and I owe much to the department's traditions and its tolerance of multidisciplinary work. I am also grateful to the University of Chicago Law School, which provided a surprisingly encouraging welcome to an interloper and a heretic. In the Department of Political Science at Chicago, the ongoing seminar in ethics run by Brian Barry and Russell Hardin showed me the force of normative argument. Friends and teachers all around the University of Chicago have made that institution a very special and exciting place for me.

In the early stages, Bob Schmitz strongly influenced the direction of the project, pushing me toward doing serious economics. Rebecca Adams, Joan Merlo, and Bruce Stephenson supplied much moral support. Jim Zuehl showed me how to find my way around the law.

The members of my dissertation committee provided a stimulating atmosphere for intellectual growth and I hope the positive influence of each of them is evident in these pages:

James Coleman, chair of the committee, began as a skeptic and ended as a friend—and this is much better than the other way around.

A good advisor allows a student to be someone other than the advisor's intellectual shadow, and the numerous points of difference between us in this text reveal how good an advisor Jim has been, though they may not reveal how much of my intellectual development I owe to him.

Arthur Stinchcombe helped me write the book I wanted to write rather than the one he would have written. His sociological imagination is sharp, sure, and shared freely, even if his oral sentences don't always have enough verbs in them. Art is unerringly wise and a valuable friend.

Judge Richard Posner, a master intellectual jouster, taught me how to argue with lawyers and has, in a fair-minded way, challenged and improved my ideas at every stage. I regret that I have not changed his mind, but I have appreciated his willingness to listen nonetheless.

Edward Shils impressed upon me the lasting value of tradition in social theory and the importance of clear prose. If this book isn't the exploration in the history of Western civilization that he would have wanted, it is certainly not his fault.

I particularly appreciate the fact that my committee members let me become an intellectual adult in their midst without reminding me of my awkward intellectual adolescence.

Bucknell University, where I taught sociology for four years, provided the institutional resources and incentives to get the dissertation written. Wendell Smith, Dan Quinlan, and Michael Suarez supplied personal encouragement and important intellectual challenges. Yvonne Wetzel typed an early version of the manuscript with exemplary efficiency and good humor.

The Center for the Social Sciences at Columbia University in the person of Jonathan Cole arranged for me to work in Columbia's law library on periodic pilgrimages, and the staff of the law library at Dickinson Law School provided a home for my research between visits to New York.

Much of the actual writing was done while I was a visiting scholar at the Yale Law School. Stan Wheeler kindly arranged for my stay at Yale. Lane West-Newman, visiting from the University of Auckland, was an essential intellectual companion during my time in New Haven, and it is hard to imagine the manuscript ever getting written were it not for her enthusiastic support and willingness to listen to endless oral drafts. Harriet Fraad made the world safe for writing and taught me a great deal about strength, creativity, and justice.

The focus of the book shifted enormously once I arrived at the University of Michigan. Partly this was my response to having switched my home base from sociology to political science and partly it was a reaction to the intellectual challenges to my work posed by Don Herzog and Will Harris. Don, both in person and by computer mail, pressed me on ideas I took to be self-evident and showed me how they weren't. He also read multiple drafts of the whole manuscript and made detailed and probing criticisms. Will and I traded talking texts and iterated interpretations. I learned from both Don and Will that theory may not make things simpler.

The Department of Political Science at Michigan has provided a most hospitable work setting, and my associations with the Department of Sociology, the Institute for Public Policy Studies, and the Michigan Law School have enriched my experience here. This project has especially benefited from discussions with Mark Brandon, Becky Eisenberg, John Finn, Leo Katz, Rick Lempert, Larry Mohr, and Fred Schauer. John Chamberlin was extremely helpful in working through the mathematical dimensions of the material on fraud with me for a separate paper.

Many people have commented on all or part of the manuscript. Jim Gordley and Russell Hardin provided detailed comments on the penultimate draft of the whole book. Robert Post's comments assisted me in rethinking both what is now chapter 1 and part 4 and what once was but no longer is chapter 2. Part 3 benefited from being presented in seminars at the University of Chicago, Georgetown, and Michigan law schools, and I am grateful to many participants in these seminars for raising important issues. Chapter 5 was improved by comments from John Brigham, Michael Moore, Jennifer Nedelsky, Patricia Overby, and Fred Schauer. Chapter 14 was presented at seminars in the sociology departments at the University of Chicago and Northwestern University and in the Department of Politics at Princeton University. Comments from participants in these sessions, as well as comments from Brian Simpson, helped this chapter along considerably. Becky Eisenberg and Leo Katz made wise suggestions about the preface.

Bits and pieces of this book, some now only footnotes, were presented at the meetings of the American Sociological Association, the American Political Science Association, and the Law and Society Association between 1978 and 1986. I am grateful to these organizations for providing helpful audiences. I am also grateful to James Buchanan's 1986 seminar at the Center for Public Choice of George Mason University (sponsored by the Liberty Fund) for consolidating my commitments to contractarianism.

Jeremy Waldron was an important presence during the last year of this book's evolution, and his critical comments on chapter 4 transformed it in substantial ways. Our joint work on contractarianism sharpened my thoughts considerably on the subject.

Several people have seen this project through from beginning (or near beginning) to end, and as that process has taken the better part of a decade, they have become friends and intellectual companions for the long haul:

Carol Heimer kept asking resonant-frequency questions and pointing out places where things were going to be a good deal harder than I thought. She is, so far as I can tell, almost always right.

Michael Brown provided critical moral support in strategic locations throughout the writing process and was particularly helpful in getting me to finish—several times.

Karol Soltan has been closer to this project than anyone, following its intellectual course through many twists and turns. Our joint work on methodology and on authority has advanced my thinking a great deal, and being able to talk with one person about jurisprudence, social theory, public choice, economics, moral philosophy, political economy, and constitutionalism has made my intellectual life much less fragmented than it otherwise would have been. Karol was often the scout, going ahead and telling me what intellectual treasures could be found in neighboring disciplines. His patient intelligence, sure insight, and deep friendship kept a long and arduous journey on course.

My parents, still puzzled by what I have been doing all these years, have provided a background against which I could take risks— and for this and everything else I thank them.

Many of those thanked will not be able to say that their contributions resulted in a changed manuscript. The extensive comments I received from such a diverse array of people often conflicted so that almost every suggestion was countered by an equal and opposing suggestion. If I have not taken all the good advice offered me, I can only say that to have incorporated all the comments would have introduced untold inconsistencies and multiplied the pages beyond bounds. I am sure that the flaws that remain in this book would have been both corrected and magnified if only I had been able to heed all the advice I received.

The process of writing this book has taught me that intellectual projects are never really finished. One just stops.

ONE
Framing Secrecy

CHAPTER ONE

The Sociology of Secrecy

THIS IS A BOOK ABOUT secrets. It examines the way in which Anglo-American legal culture discusses and regulates secrets. Law is, among other things, an institution where the unspeakable is spoken, where the details of situations and lives are made public, and where the dominant normative forces of a culture are brought to bear on the raw materials of human life. Law is, in short, one of the few places in social life where one can see the magic and the devastation wrought by secrets. In the chapters that follow, I examine the legal description and justification of secrecy.

This is also a book about economics. Lawyers increasingly have been learning to talk about law in the language of economics since "law and economics" has become a regular feature of the law school curriculum. Much of law and economics purports to be a positive theory of law, asserting that judges in many areas of law actually decide cases in a way that maximizes economic efficiency.[1] In examining what secrets count as legal secrets, I ask whether these secrets are also efficient secrets, whether the way legal language describes and justifies secrets can be squared with what lawyer/economists say is ideal. I will argue that, whatever else law and economics may be, it is not a descriptively accurate positive account of law.

Finally, this is also a book about law and legal theory. It develops a way of thinking about law that extends beyond the boundaries of the empirical case of secrecy and beyond the boundaries of an economic

---

1. Richard A. Posner's enormously successful casebook, *The Economic Analysis of Law*, 3d ed. (Boston: Little, Brown, 1986), recently issued in its third edition, describes the "Chicago school" version of law and economics. It is this approach that I take on in the present book. The maximization of efficiency is, for Posner, achieved through the maximization of wealth, a position that he defends in *The Economics of Justice* (Boston: Harvard University Press, 1981), part I: "Justice and Efficiency."

theory of law—and it does this in two ways. First, the book makes a methodological point about how law ought to be studied. The stories law tells about what is and what ought to be provide a modern mythology, narratives that describe and justify. The way these legal narratives are accomplished—the way what is, in the world, blends imperceptibly into what ought to be, in law—illuminates how descriptions of fact reveal what is valued. An interesting question to ask in legal theory is how we conceive the relation between the "is" of the empirical world (the facts) and the "ought" of law (the rules). This raises an interpretive question, asking how judges should find meaning in legal texts, meanings that make sense of abstract norms in the context of particular instances.[2] I will argue that the facts of particular disputes and the rules of texts that are called on as resources in resolving the particular disputes provide constraints on each other. The process of legal interpretation can be seen as the mutual construction of facts and rules.

Second, the book develops a theory about what we might expect, in a democratic regime, the content of the law to be if law is to attract obedience and not simply impose its threats of punishment on an unwilling populace. Those who study politics have puzzled over the countermajoritarian tendencies of courts, wondering how it is possible to justify the presence of institutions that protect minorities against the momentum of the majority will in a democratic culture. But democracy does not have to mean that numbers alone justify political action. Democracy may instead be a commitment to a certain sort of political justification, justification that relies on the consent of the governed. And this consent does not have to be of the Gallup Poll variety but may instead be what rational argument, starting from certain shared premises, commits us to. In short, it may be possible to see, as a positive matter, the law as the repository of the results of rational argument generated in an effort to attract consent. Where the law fails to mount a plausible case for such consent, it may be open to criticism for failing to justify its own rules.

Our story begins with secrecy.

2. The recent explosion of literature on this subject has focused primarily on constitutional interpretation. See "Symposium on Interpretation," *Southern California Law Review* 58, Nos. 1 & 2 (1985); Walter Murphy, James Fleming, and William F. Harris II, *American Constitutional Interpretation* (Mineola, NY: Foundation Press, 1986); Ronald Dworkin, *Law's Empire* (Cambridge, MA: Harvard University Press, 1986); and Robert Cover, "Foreword: Nomos and Narrative," *Harvard Law Review* 97: 4–68 (1984). But there is an interpretive tradition in the common law, one that includes such works as Karl Llewellyn, *The Common Law Tradition: Deciding Appeals* (Boston: Little, Brown, 1940);

The Trails of Five Secrets

By the time a secret is discussed in a public, legal setting, it no longer exists as a secret. But the trails in memory that secrets leave reveal the distances they have traveled, the force of their passage, the gashes they have left in the ongoing order of things. The creation and destruction of human social relationships are linked to secrets shared and secrets betrayed.

Secrets have a dual character. They constitute large parts of the social world by creating alliances and divisions, social spaces that are shared and those that are partitioned off from others. We know our friends by what they tell us, our enemies by what they do not. The creation and maintenance of secrecy shapes the social world around us by establishing insiders and outsiders, groups of "us" and "them."

But secrets are also used as tools of power, wrenching advantage from the unknowing actions of others. What we don't know often *does* hurt us—and serves to benefit others who kept us in the dark. Secrets provide the unobservable weapons of the devious. So while secrets enable the social world to be partitioned and individualized, making the expression of individual autonomy in the construction of the social world possible, they also serve as staging grounds for the deployment of power, assaults on the very autonomy that they constitute.

We can see this in a series of examples.

IN AUGUST 1935, JOHN B. FULLER was hired to teach German at DePaul University in Chicago for the 1935–36 school year.[3] With a Ph.D. from the University of Chicago and eight years of teaching experience, Fuller met with the immediate approval of Father O'Connell, then dean and soon to be president of the Catholic college. But before classes began that fall, Fuller received a letter, indicating that the college would not be needing his services.

Through an elaborate network of Catholic contacts, DePaul had learned that John B. Fuller was in fact the former Father Bernard Fuller, who had once been ordained to the priesthood and had served as a priest at Techny, a Catholic community near Chicago, from 1912 until 1927. In 1927, the former Father Fuller had apparently gone off to Greece, from which news of his death returned shortly thereafter. A requiem high mass had been held for him.

Arthur Goodhart, "On Finding the *Ratio Decidendi* of a Case," *Yale Law Journal* 40: 161–183 (1930); and Edward Levi, *An Introduction to Legal Reasoning* (Chicago: University of Chicago Press, 1949).

    3. *Fuller v. DePaul University*, 293 Ill. App. 261, 12 N.E.2d 213 (1938).

The former Father Fuller had in fact started a new life, but not just in the spiritual sense. Changing his name to John B. Fuller, the former priest was found to be "not dead, but . . . teaching at Amherst College."[4] He had broken his perpetual vows of poverty, chastity, and obedience and had married Anna Kuber in Buffalo, New York. He and his wife had two children, and the former Father Fuller became a fugitive from the faith.

After Fuller filed a lawsuit for breach of contract, DePaul University claimed that Fuller's initial secret was illegitimate, amounting to fraud. The university argued it had been misled since it never would have hired him had it known his secret. With an apostate priest on the faculty, the university contended, irremediable damage would be done; all the nuns and priests currently on the faculty would leave. Fuller, for his part, claimed that the information was a well-kept secret and that no harm would come to the university if they just did not publicize the information.

The Illinois Appellate Court approved the university's action in firing Fuller. By withholding clearly relevant information that he knew would be important to the DePaul, he had led them into doing something that they regretted. Moreover,

> the experience of hundreds of years past has shown that a teacher, to be qualified to perform his duties, must possess such a character that he may be a good example to pupils and create character in them. The teacher must be honest and honorable, not performing his duties under the cloak of honesty, but genuine, and beyond suspicion as to his character. The defendant, DePaul University, is surrounded by an unusual religious atmosphere, and to have injected plaintiff, an apostate priest, into this world would have been disastrous.[5]

Fuller's secret, the court said, amounted to fraud.

VERY EARLY ON THE MORNING of 19 February 1815, Hector Organ paid a visit to Francis Girault, an agent of Peter Laidlaw and Company in New Orleans.[6] During their brief conversation over the sale of tobacco, Girault asked Organ whether he had heard any news. Fighting in the War of 1812 had flared up again and people were anxious to learn

4. 293 Ill. App. 261, 265 (1938).
5. 293 Ill. App. 261, 269 (1938).
6. *Laidlaw v. Organ*, 15 U.S. (2 Wheat.) 178 (1817). The opinion itself is uncomfortably sketchy on some of the critical facts, and so the account of the circumstances surrounding the case is taken from Gulian Verplanck, *An Essay on the Doctrine of Contracts:*

whatever they could. Organ responded rather vaguely and then bought more than sixty tons of tobacco from Girault. Later that day, Girault seized the tobacco that had already been delivered to Organ, claiming he had been defrauded. The dispute between Organ and the Peter Laidlaw Company raised the issue of legal secrets for the first time in the U.S. Supreme Court.

Before Organ bought the tobacco, he had heard of the signing of the Treaty of Ghent, ending the war and, more important for the tobacco trade, ending the naval blockade of New Orleans. As long as the port had been blocked, tobacco and cotton sales had been depressed and merchants were selling these goods at very low prices. News of the treaty caused prices to rise by 30–50 percent in one day, and Organ, keeping his exclusive information secret, was able to make a substantial profit on the sixty tons of tobacco he purchased from the ignorant Girault.

Organ had heard the news from three American merchants who happened to be sailing with the British fleet at the time that the fleet heard the news of the treaty. The treaty apparently surprised everyone, since fighting had been particularly heavy at that time and no one expected such a rapid settlement. By 8 A.M. on the morning of 19 February, word of the treaty was being circulated in handbills prepared by one of the merchants who had sailed with the British fleet; but Organ's deal had already been wrapped up. Girault, for his part, claimed that Organ should have revealed his secret at the time of sale and further claimed that Organ's reticence amounted to fraud.

The Supreme Court, asked to decide whether this secret was fraudulent, indicated that withholding the information was acceptable:

> The question in this case is, whether the intelligence of extrinsic circumstances, which might influence the price of the commodity, and which was exclusively within the knowledge of the vendee, ought to have been communicated by him to the vendor? The court is of the opinion that he was not bound to communicate it. It would be difficult to circumscribe the contrary doctrine within proper limits, where the means of intelligence are equally open to both parties. But at the same time, each party must take care not to say or do anything tending to impose upon the other.[7]

Being an Inquiry How Contracts Are Affected in Law and Morals by Concealment, Error or Inadequate Price (New York: G. & C. Caruill, 1825). Verplanck was an observer at the time and was appalled enough at the outcome to devote a book to the issues raised by this case.

7. 15 U.S. (2 Wheat.) 178, 195 (1817).

Since the exact words Organ said at the time of the sale were unclear, the Court remanded the case with instructions for the lower court to inquire into Organ's truthfulness. Had Organ lied, he would not have prevailed. But if Organ had merely kept secret what he knew, the Laidlaw Company would lose the profits that the war's end brought. Organ's secret was a legally permissible secret.

IN THE 1940s THE POWELL STATION Water Company in Powell Station, Tennessee, had the odd practice of turning off the water to the residences it served at 7 P.M. each evening and turning it on again at 7 A.M.[8] each morning; between those hours, no water could be had. The Evans family owned one of the affected residences, and they decided to sell their house. The Simmons family bought the house for $6,000 and were quite surprised when they moved in to find the house was waterless half the time. The scarcity of water made the property worth at least $2,000 less than they had paid.

The Simmonses immediately took the problem up with the Evanses, who responded by saying, "We did not tell you because we knew that you would not buy the property if we told you about the water being off half the time."[9] Having got this admission, the Simmonses sued to rescind the contract of sale on the house, claiming that they had been defrauded.

The court agreed that this was fraud and that the Evanses should have told the Simmonses about the water because ordinary inspection would not have revealed the problem. Moreover,

> Complainants in the exercise of ordinary care would not be required to make a night inspection in order to ascertain whether the water situation with reference to this residence was different from what it was during the day. A person of ordinary prudence would not have the remotest idea that there would be any difference, for such difference is so extraordinarily unusual as not to be anticipated. Nor were complainants called upon in the exercise of ordinary care to go to the people in the community or to the utility which furnished this water and inquire whether the water situation with reference to this residence was different from what it appeared. The fact that there was a difference at night from that which appeared to be the fact during the day was so entirely contrary to ordinary experience as to make such inquiry more or less ridiculous.[10]

8. *Simmons v. Evans,* 185 Tenn. 282, 206 S.W.2d 295 (1947).
9. 185 Tenn. 282, 284.
10. 185 Tenn. 282, 286–287.

The court believed that a secret whose existence was so unexpected had to be disclosed.

ON 27 OCTOBER 1969, Prosenjit Poddar killed Tatiana Tarasoff. But the awful event was not entirely without warning. During the course of outpatient therapy with Dr. Lawrence Moore, a psychologist employed by the University of California hospital in Berkeley, Poddar had indicated that he wanted to kill Tarasoff, his former girlfriend, when she returned from a summer in Brazil. Moore was sufficiently concerned that Poddar would actually try something that he attempted, but failed, to have Poddar committed for observation in a mental hospital. Shortly after this attempt, Tarasoff was murdered and her parents sued the University of California. They claimed that the university, through its doctors, should have warned their daughter of the impending danger.[11]

Contending that the secrecy maintained in psychotherapeutic relationships was essential to their success, the university and Moore argued that they did not have to notify Tarasoff of this threat against her life. The court acknowledged this by stating:

> We realize that the open and confidential character of psychotherapeutic dialogue encourages patients to express threats of violence, few of which are ever executed. Certainly a therapist should not be encouraged routinely to reveal such threats; such disclosures could seriously disrupt the patient's relationship with his therapist and with the persons threatened. To the contrary, the therapist's obligation to his patient require that he not dislose a confidence unless such disclosure is necessary to avert danger to others.[12]

But here, the court decided, there was reason to expect that violence was likely. Moore would not have sought to commit Poddar if this were not the case. But although the attempt to commit Poddar was unsuccessful, this did not discharge Moore's obligations. He had a further duty to warn Tarasoff of the threat on her life. Poddar's secret had to be disclosed.

BECAUSE THEIR MARRIAGE WAS FALLING APART, Dr. Jane Doe, a university professor, and her husband entered therapy together. They

---

11. *Tarasoff v. Regents of the University of California*, 17 C.3d 425, 131 Cal. Rptr. 14, 551 P.2d 334 (1976).

12. 17 C.3d 425, 441.

consulted Dr. Joan Roe,[13] a psychiatrist with several decades of experience. After they had confided a wide range of very personal information to Dr. Roe, Dr. Doe left therapy.

Eight years after her treatment ended, Dr. Doe discovered that Dr. Roe was publishing a book that used the life stories of Dr. Doe and her husband as a case history. After attempting but failing to stop publication, Dr. Doe sued for invasion of privacy when the book, "a book which reported verbatim and extensively the patients' thoughts, feelings and emotions, their sexual and other fantasies and biographies, their most intimate personal relationships and the disintegration of their marriage,"[14] appeared.

Dr. Roe's defense was that while in therapy Dr. Doe had consented to the publication of her case history. But the court found that this was highly unlikely. Instead, the court focused on the nature of a relationship between a patient and psychiatrist:

> Every patient, and particularly every patient undergoing psychoanalysis, has . . . a right to privacy. Under what circumstances can a person be expected to reveal sexual fantasies, infantile memories, passions of hate and love, one's most intimate relations with one's spouse and others except upon the inferential agreement that such confessions will be forever entombed in the psychiatrist's memory, never to be revealed during the psychiatrist's lifetime or thereafter?[15]

The court concluded, on the basis of a theory of implied contract, that the relation of trust established between patient and therapist required that the therapist not publish the patient's secrets.

THESE FIVE SECRETS REVEAL BOTH the tensions and the variety in conflicting claims to knowledge. In the first three stories, Fuller, Organ, and the Evanses kept their secrets in order to complete a deal that would not otherwise have taken place. In each of these cases, those from whom the secret was kept claimed later that they should have been told. The secret-keepers were able to get something that they wanted by hiding information that the targets would have thought relevant,

13. In the report of this case, *Doe v. Roe,* 93 Misc. 2d 201, 400 N.Y.S.2d 668 (1977), obviously fictitious names are used for both the plaintiff and defendant. Cases such as these raise interesting problems; when the lawsuit itself may generate as much if not more publicity than the disclosure complained of, filing a privacy action may serve to undermine the claim made in the suit. The use of pseudonyms enables the lawsuit to proceed without further spreading the information about a specific individual.
14. 93 Misc. 2d 201, 204 (1977).
15. 93 Misc. 2d 201, 201 (1977).

thereby gaining at the latters' expense. Despite the structural similarities in the three cases, however, Organ's secret was acceptable while the secrets of Fuller and the Evanses were not.

In these cases, we might ask, whose claim is more compelling? Should the person who is keeping the secret be permitted to operate without having to disclose unique knowledge—or should the targets of secrets be informed before they act at their peril? Should we expect innocent individuals to find out for themselves—or should we require disclosure by those in the know?

In stark form, disputes over secrets like these present all-or-nothing problems. Either the secret-keepers, hiding relevant information from ignorant others, are allowed to prevail as they please—or the targets of the secrets, being able to demand knowledge, can thwart them. In such cases, the information at issue can be thought of as a strategic secret. Strategic secrets are kept for the purpose of influencing the actions or feelings of others. Withholding information about one's discreditable past, about a significant peace treaty that affects the likelihood of foreign trade, or about the dry spells in one's house provides leverage for the secret-keeper to influence the innocent other. The secret-keeper withholds information in order to achieve some desired goal; therefore, the secret can be considered part of a strategy.

In the last two of the five cases considered above, the secret involved three parties rather than two. The subject of the secret was not the one whose action in disclosing to third parties was at issue; in both cases, the subject confided in someone else who then claimed to be able either to reveal the information over the subject's objection or to hide it in the interests of the subject. These cases explore whether confidants can or should reveal others' secrets. One secret was found acceptable and the other was not.

In these two cases, the question, again, is, which claim is more compelling? Should individuals be allowed to retain control over information that they have confided in others—or can those in whom they have confided reveal the information in particular circumstances?

Poddar's secret was clearly a strategic one; if his former lover had found out, he would not have been able to accomplish his evil plan. But Doe's secret is of a different character. It may be called a private secret. Private secrets are pieces of information that are withheld not to influence others but because the secret-keeper feels that the information is not relevant, is none of the other's business, or gains its symbolic significance because it is not shared. Much of what is withheld in the name of privacy consists in information that cannot be used for strategic purposes. It is information that usually has a special value for the person hiding it, a value that it does not have in the same sense for others. One guards private secrets from other people not because one is trying to hide something that would be useful if these others knew but because this information anchors one's sense of identity. While the motivation behind the strategic secret consists first and foremost in controlling other people, the motivation behind the private secret consists in the construction and preservation of an internal and/or selectively shared symbolic life.

In both two-party (direct) and three-party (serial) secrets, the clash of claims is evident. Sometimes courts allow secrets to remain hidden; other times, disclosure is permitted. Organ could hide news of the treaty while Fuller could not hide his mutiny from the priesthood and the Evanses could not hide their water problems from the buyers of their house. Doe could hide her sexual fantasies while Poddar could not hide his fantasies of killing. Why the courts allow some secrets to be kept but require (or at least do not punish) revelations of other secrets is the subject of much of this book.

Before analyzing in more detail the types of secrets and the social circumstances in which they are found, it would be best to examine what secrets in general are.

The Concept of Secrecy

In this book, I will use the following concept of secrecy:

> A secret is a piece of information that is intentionally withheld by one or more social actor(s) from one or more other social actor(s).

There are several features of this definition that are important to note:

1. Secrecy is a property of information, the property that it is withheld from others. It is not a property of individuals or groups. Thus, when we speak about secret societies, for example, we refer to organizations about which the distribution of information is limited. It is not, properly speaking, the society that is secret; it is the information about the existence, membership, or purpose of the society that is restricted. Our everyday language represents a shorthand; wherever the word secret appears, the term information or knowledge is always implied.[16]

---

16. This definition may appear to include much of what we think of as privacy, such as information about oneself that one hides from others. But I wish to reserve the term privacy to represent not a property of information but a property of individuals. Privacy is a state of the individual that can be achieved through withdrawal from others,

2. Another important feature of the definition of a secret is that the information in question is intentionally withheld. Mere observation of the failure to transmit information is not enough to establish secrecy. This is an intentional, not strictly a behavioral, definition. People may forget, think they already have revealed the information, or intend to transmit the information eventually when the opportunity arises. When we observe that knowledge is uniquely in the possession of a particular person, however, we cannot conclude that this information is necessarily a secret. The requirement that a secret be an intentional[17] withholding means that there must be a self-conscious and identifiable motivation for keeping someone else in the dark about something in particular.

The intentionality of secrecy is crucial to the present study for two reasons. First, we might think of the unequal distribution of knowledge in a particular society as the result of a series of forces operating at the same time. People may not know something for a variety of reasons. There may be psychological factors at work affecting what people may know. They may forget, fail to perceive, misunderstand, or distort the information they receive. In addition, there is an economic consideration: people may not be able to afford to acquire information. The technology may fail, leaving people without information to which they would otherwise have access. In short, people may not know something for a variety of reasons that do not indicate

---

through keeping information about oneself away from others, through retaining control over the demands on one's self. Privacy is a condition in which individuals can, temporarily at least, free themselves from the demands and expectations of others. Secrecy is one of the methods that an individual may use to attain this condition. But privacy and secrecy describe different entities. Secrecy describes information, and privacy describes individuals. (I am indebted to Robert Schmitz for first suggesting this line of thought.) In the present work, then, secrecy will be the primary focus, since the purpose is to shed light on the withholding of information, not on all of the other methods that individuals use to escape from the control of others, although the two concerns are clearly related.

17. The way in which "intentional" is used here generally parallels the usage of that term in G. E. M. Anscombe, *Intentions,* 2d ed. (Ithaca, NY: Cornell University Press, 1976), §47. Intentional accounts "are all descriptions which go beyond physics," describing "what *further* they [actors] are doing *in* doing something" (p. 86). To say someone is doing something *because* or *in order to* is to give an intentional account. But this usage differs from Anscombe in that Anscombe does not require that the actors themselves be aware of the relation between their actions and the consequences, while my usage assumes that actors will be able, when pressed, to give an account of their secret-keeping. Since the law generally requires that people be able give reasons (at least after the fact) for their actions if they are to claim or defend against a legal action, it seems reasonable to suppose that an intentional account in a legal theory would consider that the subject's reasons be self-conscious and capable of explication.

that someone else is keeping a secret from them. By saying that a secret is a piece of information intentionally withheld by particular individuals, we can limit our inquiry to those cases in which knowledge is being used as a social resource in the achievement of particular goals.

Second, highlighting intentionality enables us to see secrecy as a rational process, in the sense that we may expect people to be able to recognize that they are withholding information from others and to give reasons why they are doing this. Purely behavioral accounts either find reasons irrelevant or reduce reasons to speech actions, analyzable as behavior. Seeing secrecy as intentional withholding of information both allows reasons to be seen as causes of social action and requires that an analysis of secrecy consider the subjective dimension of social life.

3. This definition of a secret, with its emphasis on one person withholding information from another, stresses that secrets are always located in particular social contexts. Speaking of secrecy in general misses a critical point, that secrecy always occurs against an important backdrop of particular social relations. In the limiting case, one person who knows something may choose to withhold the information from everyone, regardless of their relationship to her. In these cases, the secret is absolute and does not serve to create special communities of knowledge. More frequently, however, people engage in selective disclosure; for example, one may confide in a lover what one would never tell one's boss.

The patterns of selective disclosure shape the contours of the social world. To say that national defense information is secret, for example, implies that it is secret *from* some particular others. Generally, this information is withheld from the enemy;[18] but it is also withheld from the vast majority of those who are allegedly being defended. This reveals a fear that the more people there are who know the information, the more likely the information is to be spread to those who should not know. The permeability of networks and a distrust of the population are revealed by this pattern of distribution. Multiple communities of "us" and "them" are created, leading not only to a strain in communication between potentially warring states

18. Although this is not always true, as Michael E. Brown has pointed out. He recounted a story of a friend of his in graduate school, a friend working on a paper about the CIA. He needed to know the number of people employed by the CIA who worked out of the Langley, Virginia, headquarters. A call directed to the CIA produced no answer; a call to the State Department also produced the response that the information was secret. Exasperated, he finally called the Soviet embassy. It gave him the information.

but also to an isolation of the military and national security communities both from other policymakers and from the general public. The audience or audiences for the secret help us to understand how the secret functions as a social resource.

Information may be secret even if it is being consciously withheld in only *one* social context. The *degree* of secrecy may be specified by examining the number and quality of different contexts in which the information flow is intentionally blocked. When information is shared in one context and restricted in another, we can begin to see differences in types of social relations (who is "us" and who is "them"?) and in the relation of the information in question to the strategic purposes of the secret-keeper (how is the secret being used?).

4. The term "actor" has been used instead of "person" so that groups can be considered as creators and targets of secrecy. Collectivities of all kinds seek, create, transmit, and withhold information just as individuals do. Some may object that there are conceptual problems that arise in treating corporate entities as actors like individuals, problems with, for example, determining the intentionality required for our definition.

We may say that withholding information is intentional when a decision has been made by some authoritative group within the organization or by some authorized agent of the group. But there may be *unauthorized* leaks of information (by, for example, whistle-blowers), leaks that impair secrecy but that cannot be said to be an intentional release of information on the part of the corporate actor. The general point to be made is that one cannot infer from the revelation of information possessed by a corporate actor that this disclosure is intended by the organization. In addition, one cannot infer from the withholding of information that secrecy exists. A corporate actor's failure to reveal information may mean that the information has been "forgotten" (deleted from the files, lost somewhere in the organization, sitting under a pile of papers on someone's desk). Although there may be some areas where referring to the knowledge of a corporate actor may be a bit strained, corporations clearly engage in strategic manipulation of information and thus fall within our orbit of study.

FROM OUR SIMPLE DEFINITION OF secrecy, then, several important features of the phenomenon can be illuminated. First, secrecy is a property of the information, a property that indicates its level of availability to others. Second, secrecy may not be bestowed on information accidentally; it must result from an intentional decision. Third, secrecy is defined in terms of its social context, specified by the identification of the concealer(s) and the target(s). And, finally, both those who maintain secrets and those who are excluded by them may be either individuals or groups.

Forms of Secrecy

Although the secret is a simple sort of social device, entailing only the withholding of information by one person from another, it can take on a variety of different forms[19] as social contexts become more elaborated. These forms, as we will see in the next section, shape the sorts of normative claims people can make for the keeping and disclosing of secrets. They also reveal the way in which secrets construct social relations, bringing some people together while pushing others apart.

There are three major forms of secrets to which all other forms may be reduced:[20]

1. In the *direct secret* there are two actors, A and B, who can be either individuals or groups. A is keeping from B a secret that B wants to know;[21] for example, a defense secret the United States keeps from the Soviet Union would be a direct secret.

2. In the *serial secret* A shares her secret with B and a third actor, C, wants to acquire A's secret from B;[22] for example, if the United States revealed one of its defense secrets to Great Britain, Great Britain would possess a serial secret as against Soviet attempts to find out by going to Great Britain rather than to the United States.

3. In the *collective* or *shared secret* A and B jointly create a secret and C wants to find out the secret from either A or B;[23] for example, if the United States and Great Britain shared a common defense secret, they would possess a collective secret as against Soviet attempts to acquire it from either of them.

19. The term "form" here is used to identify abstract configurations of social actors. This "formal" analysis borrows much in spirit, although not in the actual categories used, from Georg Simmel, "The Secret and the Secret Society," in Kurt Wolff, ed., *The Sociology of George Simmel* (New York: Free Press, 1950), pp. 307–376.

20. This is not to say that *all* theoretically interesting information about secrets is captured in these categories. The motivations for keeping secrets, for example, are left out of this schema. But, as a matter of social form (when social form is taken to mean the structure of the relationships among actors), other sorts of social configurations collapse into these three.

21. B may be an individual, a group, or a set of unrelated individuals.

22. If C wants to acquire the secret directly from A, then this situation collapses into the direct-secret case.

23. If A and B share a secret with a larger group, this secret is formally identical. It is the ability of any one person to defect from a jointly created secret that is at the core of collective secrets.

Table 1.1   The Distribution of Secrets in Dyads and Triads

	Type of Secret		
	Direct	Serial	Collective
Parties involved	A to B (Dyad)	B to C (Triad)	A or B to C (Triad)
Activity			
Reveals information	Disclosure	Betrayal	Leak
Hides information	Simple secret	Secondhand secret	Conspiracy

Note: A, B, and C are three social actors. The information in question starts as A's secret, and, in direct secrets, A chooses to disclose or not disclose the secret to B. In serial secrets, B must decide whether to disclose A's secrets to C, and, in collective secrets, either A or B may reveal secrets jointly created by A and B to C.

    In each of the three cases, the secret-keeper can act in one of two ways:

    1. The secret-keeper can reveal the information. This action has different implications across the three forms of secrets. A can tell B the direct secret, resulting in *disclosure*. B can tell C the serial secret, making A feel a *betrayal*. Finally, either A or B can reveal the collective secret to C, creating a *leak*.

    2. The secret-keeper can hide the information. If A hides the direct secret from B, this is a *simple secret*. If B hides the serial secret from C, this is a *secondhand secret*. If A or B withhold the collective secret from C, this creates a *conspiracy*.[24]

    The types of secrets outlined above can be seen more clearly in table 1.1.

Justifications for Secrets

People can give an enormous variety of justifications for keeping or requiring revelation of particular secrets. A justification, as the term is used here, is a form of normative argument; giving a justification makes at least a plausible case for a particular "should" proposition. By examining the sorts of justifications that people can offer in situations involving secrets, we can see how different social contexts give rise to clashes of normative arguments.

---

    24. Many of the ordinary-language terms that may be used to describe these sorts of secrets have pejorative overtones. It is hard to imagine beneficial conspiracies. Betrayals also have their emotional baggage, as, in some circles, do leaks. The terms are meant here in a morally neutral sense. None of these secrets can be presumed at the outset to be prima facie good or evil. Serious claims can usually be made for each side of each sort of secret, as we will see later.

In all three forms of secrets, the key normative question is whether A (in the direct or collective case) and/or B (in the serial or collective case) are allowed to claim that they can keep their information secret. The *direct secret* poses the issue of A's duties to B. The *serial secret* frames the problem of B's duties to A in the face of a potential obligation to C. The *collective secret* questions the extent to which A's and B's obligations to each other can overcome any duties to C.

Each of the six types of secrets that we have identified has its own universe of justifications that might arise:

1. *Justifications for disclosure.*—When A reveals a secret to B, A may do so because B has made a convincing argument that she should know. A may also have disclosed the secret because he felt the need to unburden himself. But no matter what the reason for the initial disclosure, A may later discover that he would rather that B not know this information. A may claim that he is injured by B's possession of the former secret and try to claim that B now should not know. This sort of situation arises in law when criminal suspects want to retract confessions or when relations between the A's and the B's of the world turn sour and the previously shared secrets become potentially harmful to A,[25] as happens frequently between employer and former employee in trade-secret cases. Knowledge being what it is, repossession is impossible. A may claim that B's possession of the information now harms A and that A should be able to prevent B from using the information to A's detriment. B, in turn, may claim that A's initial disclosure was voluntary and that any later restriction on the information is therefore invalid.

2. *Justifications for betrayal.*—If A has revealed a secret to B, the circumstance may arise where B voluntarily discloses A's secret to C.

---

25. It is interesting to note in this regard that people may make themselves vulnerable to others in two ways. They may make themselves physically vulnerable by abandoning traditional defenses such as weapons, locks, clothes, or barriers. These physical defenses usually can be reinstated when a relationship turns ugly, as long as no permanent physical damage has been done. But people may make themselves psychically vulnerable (and maybe physically vulnerable also) by abandoning defenses created by personal secrets. By disclosing secrets, one opens up to others and becomes vulnerable to their knowledge and manipulation. Unlike physical defenses, which can be rebuilt, the defense of secrecy can never be reclaimed. One cannot make someone else forget what one has told them: any attempt to do so will probably fix the information more firmly in the other's memory. When the relationship in which the confidence was exposed changes, people often later want to retract what they once voluntarily disclosed. Although it may seem that disclosing a secret creates less risk of harm than allowing oneself to be physically vulnerable, this is a decidedly short-term view. Physical invulnerability often can be reclaimed. The exclusive possession of knowledge cannot be.

In these cases, C may either be a specific person or C may be a large group (the general public, for instance). B generally claims that A's secret really belongs to B—or at least no longer uniquely belongs to A—and that B should be able to do with that information whatever B wants. A's justification for wanting B to keep the secret, however, is that, since the information was A's to begin with, A should therefore be able to restrict B's ability to distribute the information further. A is claiming not only the right to keep a secret but also the right to restrict B's actions so that B will keep the secret also. The most common sorts of legal cases presenting this justification involve the mass media, for example, when A claims that B's publication of personal details about A violates A's privacy. Other cases include debt collections, for example, when A is in debt to B and B reveals this fact to some C (A's employer, for instance) in an effort to encourage A to pay up. The *Doe* case described above is another example of such a situation.

   3. *Justifications for leaks.*—If A and B share a jointly constructed secret, either A or B might disclose the secret to C without the approval of the other.[26] The remaining secret-keeper may claim that the secret should not have been unilaterally revealed to another because the secret is a joint product, not an individual one. Often, these sorts of disclosures destroy the relationship that created the secret, and the remaining secret-keeper might claim that the disclosures caused harm because they ended the alliance. But the discloser might argue that the knowledge was for each to use and that the secret-keeper cannot prevent the discloser from telling others or from leaving alliances that no longer benefit the discloser. Trade-secret cases where the inventor takes her own invention with her on leaving employment and termination-of-employment cases where the employee has leaked information and been fired as a result often present justifications like these.

   4. *Justifications for simple secrets.*—When A keeps a secret from B, B may often claim that she should be told. B may have asked A directly and A refused to disclose the secret, or B may not have even known to ask; for example, in *Laidlaw* Girault did not know that Organ knew about a treaty, but he, like everyone else in the tobacco trade, knew that such a treaty was possible and that it would be very important when it occurred. Fuller's secret about his former status as a priest and the Evans's secret about the lack of water in the house may have come as total surprises to those from whom the secret was kept. In all of these cases, A may claim a property right, if the information is likely to be

---

26. If A and B jointly reveal the secret to C, then this collapses into the simpler case of a direct secret and disclosure.

commercially useful (as in *Laidlaw*) or A may claim a privacy right, if the information pertains to A (as in cases where A refuses to answer nosy questions on an employment application). A's may also claim that B's should have to look for the information themselves and not have to acquire it through A's disclosure (as in *Simmons*). But the B's often claim fraud; they claim they are being fooled by A's silence; they claim a right to know. Legal issues involving this sort of problem come up frequently in fraud and nondisclosure cases, where after a deal has been completed, one party discovers he has been had. They also come up in face-to-face privacy cases, where A claims that B has no right to intrude.

5. *Justifications for secondhand secrets.*—In these cases, A tells B a secret and then C wants to find out the secret from B. B hides the information. B is caught between A's justifications for why B should not reveal the secret and C's justifications for why B should reveal it. C's in these cases, like the B's in the shallow-secret cases, claim a right to know, particularly when they can show that they have a compelling interest in the information. B's maintain that their affiliation with and obligation to the A's makes the disclosure an unwarranted intrusion on the relationship between A and B. These sorts of cases arise most frequently in law as confidential relationship cases, where doctors or social workers or priests or journalists claim that their patients or clients or parishioners or sources have confided in them with the enforceable understanding that the professional will not disclose this information. The psychiatrist in *Tarasoff* tried to avoid revealing the information because he felt an obligation to his client to keep the information secret. The psychiatrist in *Doe* obviously felt no such obligation, although Doe (and later the court) thought she should.

6. *Justifications for conspiracy.*—In this situation A and B share a jointly constructed secret that they together withhold from C. The justifications in this situation are very similar to those in the secondhand-secret cases, with one addition. Because the secrets were jointly created, A and B each have a direct interest in the secret. C, in trying to get the secret from either A or B, tries to split them apart by forcing revelation of common information.[27] Again, C claims some right to know. For A and B, the conspiracy is a combination of the simple secret and the secondhand secret, because both a personal and a joint interest can be claimed. Legal cases that present these sorts of

---

27. Georg Simmel ("The Triad," in Wolff, pp. 154–162) analyzes this sort of social configuration as the *tertius gaudens*, the third party who takes advantage of splits between the other two.

justifications often fall under the heading of privileges, such as the husband-wife privilege. One cannot be made to testify against the other, partly because each reveals him- or herself in so doing and also partly because such disclosure would destroy the relationship.

To THIS DISCUSSION OF JUSTIFICATIONS, one complicating element must be added. Sometimes the targets of the secret know about the potential existence of a secret, even though they do not know the content of the secret itself. Laidlaw's agent, for example, clearly suspected that there might be a treaty; otherwise he would not have asked Organ whether he had heard any news. Laidlaw's agent just did not know whether the treaty had been signed. When the target suspects that there might be a secret, we find *shallow secrets*. When the target is completely in the dark, never imagining that relevant information might be had, we find *deep secrets*. The Simmonses, for example, never thought to ask the Evanses whether the water was turned on all the time. The simple secret, secondhand secret, and conspiracy all have shallow and deep forms. The depth of a secret affects the sorts of justifications that can be made by those left out of the secret.

If someone knows that a secret exists, making this a shallow secret, she can ask for the information directly and claim that her direct questions should be answered. As in the card game Go Fish, where players ask whether their opponents have particular cards in their hands and where they can capture these cards if they guess correctly, people who ask direct questions can claim that the whole negotiation process, like the game, is undermined if their skill in asking questions is not rewarded. With shallow secrets, however, the secret-keeper can claim that the targets at least know that they are deciding with the risk of ignorance. Keepers of shallow secrets may be able to claim that the targets should search for the information rather than expect to have it handed to them outright.

The deep secret allows the targets to make stronger justifications against the secret-keepers. If the targets have no idea that the information exists, let alone what the information consists of, then the targets have a more forceful case that the secret amounts to fraud. The targets cannot protect themselves against information they cannot imagine, and so the secret-keeper can always gain advantage at the expense of the target.[28] But the deep-secret-keepers may claim that they have

---

28. If the targets of the deep secret never find out what hit them, they cannot bring legal action against the deep-secret-keeper. Any disincentives that the law provides only work if the secret is *eventually* discovered. If the deep-secret-keeper is rational, self-

property rights in the information and do not have to reveal it to those who do not know.

In legal disputes, these sorts of justifications are made explicit and courts must decide among them. Who is to prevail in a particular case? On what basis should the decision rest? Which secrets are like others—and which justify a different treatment? The way in which courts frame and resolve these disputes reveals not only the role knowledge plays in society but also the way in which legal facts and legal rules are joined.

A Note on Lies and Half-Truths

In common usage, lying generally means not telling the truth. But the purpose in not telling the truth is often the attempt to keep a secret.[29] The lie in these instances, then, is only a more complicated form of secret, one involving not only the withholding of information but the substitution of some other information. In other words, a lie is often a secret with a story on top. Once one uncovers a lie, then, one must still uncover a secret before the hidden knowledge is revealed.

The half-truth is also related to the secret. It is accomplished by the partial revelation of the secret itself. Its effectiveness in hiding the secret comes from the fact that appearing to reveal the secret (while hiding certain clarifying portions) makes others think they know all there is to know. But knowing part of a secret can lead to different sorts of inferences about the true state of affairs than knowing the whole secret. One may selectively reveal true information and do it in such a way that the overall impression is misleading. This is the essence of the

interested, and believes that the chances of being discovered are very small, large legal penalties will fail to deter this sort of activity.

29. This idea was clear to Simmel, who noted that "the lie consists in the fact that the liar hides his true idea from others" ("The Secret and the Secret Society," p. 312). But Sissela Bok, who has written a book on the subject of lying (*Lying: Moral Choice in Public and Private Life* [New York: Pantheon, 1978]) and another on the subject of secrecy (*Secrets: On the Ethics of Concealment and Revelation* [New York: Pantheon, 1982]), sees the relationship between the secret and the lie differently: "Lies are part of the arsenal used to guard and invade secrecy; and secrecy allows lies to go undiscovered and to build up" (*Secrets,* p. xv). There may be other motivations for telling lies; the compulsive liar may not have any particular secret to hide. But generally, lies, by purporting to be true, substitute for other information, which is true. Erving Goffman refers to the lie not as a falsehood but as a "self-disbelieved" statement (*Strategic Interaction* [Philadelphia: University of Pennsylvania Press, 1969], p. 7.) The fact that the teller thinks that the information is false is the essence of a lie; information that the teller believes is true but that turns out to be false is not a lie when it is told as believed.

half-truth. At the same time that true facts are being given out, the impression being created is false.

The half-truth shares with the lie the inaccuracy of the final impression. But it shares with the secret the use of withholding as the means of accomplishing this. Both the lie and the half-truth, then, can be seen as types of secrets. The motivating force for many lies and half-truths is the desire to maintain a secret. Both the lie and the half-truth hide secrets by aggressively forwarding a version of the knowledge that is hidden. The lie substitutes false information while the half-truth selectively reveals the truth. In both cases, the final impression masks the existence of the secret as well as the content of the secret itself.

Secrets and the Social Distribution of Knowledge

The secret is the social mechanism through which the interests and intentions of particular social actors, making decisions in their daily lives, become translated into inequalities in knowledge. Of course there are other sources of this inequality also; psychological, economic, and technological constraints may operate even when there are no decisions to restrict information. But the secret is significant precisely because it is the means through which the social distribution of knowledge is shaped by the translation of individual, intentional actions into larger social patterns.

Knowledge may not be power, Bacon's aphorism notwithstanding, but it is often important in the accumulation and exercise of power. Shared knowledge by no means guarantees consensus, but it is hard to imagine any common culture or any surviving society without it. What one doesn't know may not hurt one—but, then again, it might. The social distribution of knowledge permeates social relations from the most intimate to the most impersonal,[30] and much of what we think of as social structure grows out of the patterns of hidden and revealed knowledge.

The conflicting justifications over secrecy present difficult decisions for courts. At stake may be something as personal as an individual sense of privacy or as public as the fair operation of markets. How courts choose among the conflicting justifications people give for keeping or disclosing secrets is our subject in the rest of the book.

---

30. In fact, intimacy and impersonality themselves may be defined in terms of the quality and quantity of shared knowledge that particular relationships and collectivities possess.

Chapter Two

The Economic Analysis of Secrecy

An Economic Hypothesis

WHAT SECRETS SHOULD BE LEGAL secrets? The economic analysis of law provides a way to think about an answer to this question. In particular, it offers "the hypothesis that the common law is best explained as if the judges were trying to maximize economic welfare." [1]

Briefly summarized, the economic theory of law argues that American law in general, and the common law in particular, receives a good deal of its underlying unity from the common concern with promoting the efficient use of scarce resources. This concern with efficiency can be seen in an attempt by the law to ensure that goods wind up in their highest valued uses, to provide incentives for productive activities to be undertaken at the lowest social cost, to discourage losses generally by assigning responsibility to those in the best position to prevent them, and to encourage investment in socially valuable activities. [2]

Whether people should be allowed to withhold information can be seen, at least at first pass, as an economic question: Does secrecy promote the efficient use of scarce resources? Does secrecy encourage the production of valuable information? Does secrecy interfere with the operation of efficient markets? To answer these questions, we need to explore the economics of information.

---

1. Richard A. Posner, *The Economics of Justice* (Cambridge, MA: Harvard University Press, 1981), p. 4.

2. A useful general text in this area can be found in Richard A. Posner, *The Economic Analysis of Law*, 3d ed. (Boston: Little, Brown, 1986). But the ambiguities in the notion of efficiency that is so central for the economic analysts of law are made clear in Jules Coleman, "Efficiency, Utility and Wealth Maximization," *Hofstra Law Review* 8: 509–551 (1980).

The Economics of Information: An Overview

Information in economics is a bit like Peter Sellers in a Pink Panther movie. It reappears frequently with a new identity, ready to play a wholly different role. While multiple identities may be amusing in the movies, they create havoc with formal theory. The economics of information, where the most highly developed general mathematical theory is deployed to reach the least generalizable results in all of economics, reveals the dilemmas of theoretical schizophrenia. My focus in this section will be on the role of information in decision making and on the way economic theory conceives of this role.[3]

Information in Individual Decisions

Information plays a dual role in rational choice theory. On one hand, it is a precondition of choice. That is, one needs a certain amount of information in order to be able to imagine one's alternatives, to understand enough of their implications to be able to distinguish among them, and to assess which one would best realize one's aims. All of this requires quite a lot of knowledge, and, generally speaking, the more the better. On the other hand, knowledge is itself an object of choice; that is, one can choose whether to acquire more information. Whether one decides to acquire more information depends not only on what one already knows, but on one's estimates of the chances that more knowledge will improve the decision enough to be worth one's effort. Generally speaking in such a situation, the less additional knowledge one needs, the better. This simple observation, that one needs knowledge to choose but that one can also choose to acquire knowledge, is at the heart of much theoretical confusion.

If we think about how much knowledge we need to function in daily life, the magnitude of the problem becomes clearer. Ethnomethodologists have devoted considerable attention to the discovery of background knowledge, which, as it turns out, is an elaborate system of perceptions and rules. Just walking down the street successfully (that is, getting where one wants to go without committing major social gaffes such as walking into people) requires highly sophisticated, almost theoretical, knowledge about how to recognize when people are walking together so one does not attempt to walk between them, how to pass people without making them think that one intends to join

---

3. To put it differently, one might say that I am engaged in exploring that generalization of microeconomic theory called rational choice theory. Macroeconomic issues in the economics of information will not be touched on here.

them, how to communicate one's intended direction without communicating that one wants to start a conversation.[4] More complex social tasks involving conscious decisions, such as deciding whether to buy one's first house, require even more detailed and specialized knowledge. In fact, before one even knows what questions to ask in a specific case, one needs to know quite a lot about how houses are different from apartments, how to locate information about available houses, how to think about financing options, and whether one has enough money to even start thinking about such a move.[5] Before the idea of decision making begins to make sense in a concrete case, then, we must first posit that the decision maker has at least *some* knowledge both about the general shape of the decision problem (such as *that* a decision might be made and what the chief options are) and about the sorts of considerations that might matter in distinguishing among the options. A theory of decision making must always presuppose some initial distribution of crucial information.

If we begin by thinking of the difficulty an individual faces in acquiring all the relevant information needed to make a particular decision (assuming the individual knows enough to get this far in conceiving the problem), we immediately see that knowledge, like most other economic goods, is often subject to the law of declining marginal utility. In other words, the more knowledge one has about a particular decision, the less each additional increment is worth.[6] One does not need every last shred of information to make a sensible choice. At some point, each additional piece of information will be worth less and less. A rational decision maker would stop looking for information when the value of each additional piece of information drops below the expected value of the information to the decision in question.

4. A. Lincoln Ryave and James N. Schenkein's study, "Notes on the Art of Walking," in Roy Turner, ed., *Ethnomethodology* (London: Penguin Books, 1974), details even more difficulties in this apparently simple task. See also Harold Garfinkel, *Studies in Ethnomethology* (New York: Prentice-Hall, 1969).

5. It is precisely in areas such as this, where high-stakes purchases are being made with potentially ignorant parties, that specialized information brokers such as real estate agents or market analysts or consumer reporting services set up shop. One can trade in valuable information if it is sufficiently costly to acquire that individuals may not want to gather it on their own and if it has a large enough market to spread the costs of acquiring the information over those who might find it useful.

6. This assumes that one is acquiring information *to be able to do something in particular* with it. If one is acquiring knowledge to have the knowledge for its own sake, then this sort of instrumental analysis does not apply, although economists might speak of a taste for knowledge that one sets out to satisfy, subject to the usual budget constraints.

The difficulty the rational decision maker faces in this situation is how to know when such a point has been reached. After all, if one does not know the information yet, how can one know how much it will be worth? One way to think about this problem is to imagine that an individual gathering information is sampling from a distribution of relevant knowledge. Each piece of information provides not only a clue about what a decision ought to be but also a hint about the shape of the distribution of knowledge from which that information was selected.[7] If, for example, one is trying to buy a car, the price of that car will be a critical piece of information. The rational buyer will engage in comparison shopping, pricing the same car at a number of different dealerships. But it will not be rational for the buyer to call every dealership in the country, or even every dealership in the state, before settling on one in particular. Instead, the rational buyer will sample prices until she gets a good sense of what the likely range is. At some point, the costs of getting additional prices will exceed the likely savings to be gained by getting a lower price.

This apparently simple problem, where one estimates the shape of the distribution of knowledge while gathering information about the decision itself, has generated much interest in optimal stopping rules.[8] At what point should one stop looking and just make a decision? How should one sensibly evaluate the information a search produces? Because individuals are quite susceptible to information overload,[9] they are, in practice, only ever *approximately* rational. They cannot process all the information that might be relevant to a decision, even if it were gathered. Instead of selecting the best possible global result (which requires a great deal of information about all the options and all of their attributes), rational individuals (and organizations) often choose the first option that exceeds a threshold level, economizing as a result on the amount of information needed to make a good-enough decision.[10] Choosing a good-enough rather than best solution is one way around the problem of information overload.

---

7. This was one insight provided by George Stigler's justly acclaimed paper, "The Economics of Information" (*Journal of Political Economy* 69: 213–225 [1961]).

8. On optimal stopping rules, see Leo Breiman, "Stopping Rule Problems," in Edwin F. Beckenbach, ed., *Applied Combinatorial Mathematics* (New York: Wiley, 1964); Y. S. Chow, H. Robbins, and D. Siegmund, *Great Expectations: The Theory of Optimal Stopping* (New York: Houghton-Mufflin, 1971); and A. N. Shiryayev, *Optimal Stopping Rules* (New York: Springer, 1978).

9. They remember on average seven things at a time (plus or minus two). See George Miller, "The Magic Number Seven Plus or Minus Two," *Psychological Review* 68: 81–97 (1956).

10. This is called satisficing, and it is at the heart of much of the work by Herbert

One may also cope with the potential overload of information and with the difficulty of searching for just the right insight by using pieces of information that, while not perfect, correlate well with the ideal—but more complex and hard-to-find—information one really wants. These pieces of information, serving as proxies for the real information one wants to know, are called signals.[11] If, for example, an employer is looking for an employee with just the right set of talents, the employer might advertise widely and interview every person who applies. This process would take a lot of time, time spent in gathering much detailed information about particular individuals. The employer might save a lot of this time by restricting the applicant pool to just those people who possess the signals that are likely to correlate highly with the skills required for the job. Requiring that applicants have a college education would limit the search, although it would no doubt exclude some well-qualified high school graduates.[12] But the chances of finding qualified people might, in the employers' view, be much higher in a pool of the more educated. The problem with signals is that they are often noisy; that is, they do not correlate perfectly with the attributes one is looking for. They can be, in individual instances, inaccurate even when they are, on average, accurate.

We have seen that many choices are made not with perfect information but rather with varying degrees of uncertainty.[13] Choices to acquire information are themselves invariably made with imperfect information. While it may be rational for people to stop looking for information before they find everything they possibly could, the decisions made with imperfect information may not always lead to optimal results, which might have occurred if more had been known. Information about transactions themselves, one large component of trans-

---

Simon. For a collection of Simon's major pieces on this problem, see *Models of Bounded Rationality: Behavioral Economics and Business Organizations,* vol. 2 (Cambridge, MA: MIT Press, 1982).

11. See, for example, Michael Spence, "Job Market Signalling," *Quarterly Journal of Economics* 87: 355–374 (1973).

12. In fact, it would be difficult under this regime for bright high school graduates to indicate that they were not representative of their statistical class. In markets where signals are widely used or where critical information is revealed only through experience, information inconsistent with the signals is hard to communicate. This is the problem posed by George Akerlof's article, "The Market for Lemons: Quality Uncertainty and the Market Mechanism" (*Quarterly Journal of Economics* 84: 488–500 [1970]).

13. One of the early perceptive discussions of the problems of uncertainty can be found in Frank Knight, *Risk, Uncertainty and Profit* (Chicago: University of Chicago Press, 1971).

action costs, is particularly likely to produce markets that do not have efficient distributions of scarce resources.[14]

The Production of Knowledge

So far in our discussion, we have presumed that the information in question already exists (at least probabilistically) and that the only question at issue is whether a particular individual will search to find it. But often the relevant economic question is how to encourage the production of the knowledge in the first place. Scientific knowledge, for example, is generally the product of much time and effort. It is expensive to produce. Whether rational actors will engage in the production of costly information depends on whether they can recoup enough of the benefits the knowledge brings to make the search worth their while.

Knowledge, however, has the two critical properties of a public good, jointness of supply and impossibility of exclusion.[15] One person's consumption of knowledge does not "use up" that knowledge in the sense of making it unavailable to others (although it may make the knowledge less valuable in certain commercial contexts). Moreover, once knowledge has been made public it is very difficult for one person to prevent another's use of it. These two attributes make the benefits of producing the good in the first place hard for the producer to appropriate. This reduces the incentives to produce public goods, and so there is a tendency for public goods to be underproduced.

In the case of knowledge, granting property rights in the *use* of information provides one way out of the public-goods dilemma. If the producers of valuable knowledge can appropriate the benefits by excluding others from using it, a more tractable approach than trying to prevent others from *knowing* it, then incentives will be created for the production of knowledge. This is essentially what the patent system does. By granting a property right that enables the inventor to exclude others from using the invention, the law provides incentives for pro-

14. Ronald Coase ("The Problem of Social Cost," *Journal of Law and Economics* 3: 1–44 [1960]) concludes that in the absence of transaction costs goods are transferred to higher-valuing uses. In the presence of transaction costs, all bets that markets will generate efficient results without intervention are off.

15. The theory of public goods began with Paul Samuelson, "The Pure Theory of Public Expenditure," *Review of Economics and Statistics* 36: 387–389 (1954). See Russell Hardin, *Collective Action* (Baltimore: Johns Hopkins Press, 1982), pp. 17–20 for an exceptionally clear discussion of the defining characteristics of public goods.

duction. But the patent is granted in exchange for the inventor's publication of the information so that others can build on the knowledge that went into the invention,[16] thereby eliminating wasteful duplication.

Granting property rights in the realm of information may appear to be exactly the way to establish the proper incentives; the problem is that such property rights do too good a job. Ideally, one would prefer that such valuable knowledge only be produced once; but a regime of property rights in a context where producers keep their progress secret until they can claim a property right means that much duplicated research will occur. This creates more investment in the production of information than would be warranted under an efficient regime of rules, and it is not clear how to escape from this dilemma.[17]

Some duplicated production may be a good thing, because, in addition to all these other dilemmas, knowledge is expensive to move around.[18] Unless it is in the form of a very compact signal—such as a price, which (when it is working properly) conveys a lot of information about the supply of and demand for a particular good—knowledge will sometimes be cheaper to reproduce than to transport. Property rights may create inefficiencies by creating incentives for transportation when rediscovery may be cheaper. In addition, a great part of our knowledge is "local knowledge,"[19] knowledge that is generated by pursuits that are sensitive to time and place. This knowledge is not only expensive to move around, but it may be distorted in the process because its ability to convey meaning may not be separable from the experience giving rise to it.[20]

As this brief review of the economics of information literature has revealed, problems of inadequate knowledge pervade economic mod-

---

16. If the real contribution made in a patent is not the specific, tangible, patentable invention but the knowledge itself, then the patent system may not provide the requisite legal protection to establish incentives. Making the information public so that others may use it for further research may be exactly what the inventor wants to prevent.

17. See Jack Hirschleifer, "Where Are We Now in the Theory of Information?" *American Economic Review* 63: 31–39 (1973) for a discussion of this problem.

18. Friedrich A. Hayek, in "The Uses of Knowledge in Society" (*American Economic Review* 35: 519–530 [1945]), used this observation to make a forceful argument against central planning. This argument has been made in new form more recently by Thomas Sowell, *Knowledge and Decisions* (New York: Basic Books, 1980).

19. To borrow Clifford Geertz's expressive phrase; see "Local Knowledge: Fact and Law in Comparative Perspective," in *Local Knowledge* (New York: Basic Books, 1983), pp. 167–234.

20. Hayek, in "The Uses of Knowledge in Society," also noted this phenomenon.

els. Knowledge is necessary before we can decide what knowledge we need. The public-goods qualities of knowledge make special incentives (property rights in the *use* of information) necessary if we are to ensure its production, but these special incentives also may result in the overproduction of knowledge. And all of these things go on at once. The issues introduced in this section provide a basis for sorting through conflicting claims over legal secrets, and, as we will see in the sections that follow, the economic analysis of law on the subject of secrecy has borrowed heavily from this literature.

The Law and Economics of Secrecy

If legal rules about secret-keeping were economically optimal, what would we expect them to be? This is the question that law and economics might ask in its positive mode.[21]

To the economist interested in testing economic theory against the data of the law, the first step is to come up with a set of causal laws that will predict how courts have resolved these problems.[22] These causal laws specify which facts one needs to observe before certain particular consequences follow. The general formula "Under factual circumstance A expect legal rule X, and under factual circumstance B expect legal rule Y" may serve as a model for this sort of activity.

Two extended treatments of the optimal legal rules about secret-keeping have been developed by Chicago-school theorists. Anthony Kronman's article on nondisclosure and fraud[23] and Richard Posner's

---

21. Of course, law and economics, especially the Chicago-school variety, has its normative side also. I will argue later in the book that the positive and normative perspectives of Chicago-school law and economics are not so easily separable. But in this section, I describe the accounts that Chicago-school theorists have given when they claim to be discussing what the law is rather than what it ought to be.

22. Generally, the methodology of positive economics (to borrow the title of Milton Friedman's famous article, "The Methodology of Positive Economics," in *Essays in Positive Economics* [Chicago: University of Chicago Press, 1953], pp. 3–34) is positivism. "In bald summary of the line handed out to beginners," say Frank Hahn and Martin Hollis, "a natural law is a regularity in nature holding in specifiable conditions; we have detected one when we have a well enough confirmed theory; a theory is a set of logically linked, high-order generalizations; the only test of a theory is the success of its predictions; prediction and explanation are two sides of the same and only coin, in that explaining a fact is finding another from which it could have been predicted" ("Introduction," in *Philosophy and Economic Theory* [Oxford: Oxford University Press, 1979], pp. 1–2).

23. Anthony Kronman, "Mistake, Disclosure, Information and the Law of Contracts," *Journal of Legal Studies* 7: 1–34 (1978). I have described Kronman as a Chicago-school law-and-economics person because at the time that he wrote this arti-

writings on privacy and business secrets[24] offer a positive framework for thinking about which secrets should be legal secrets.

Kronman on Nondisclosure

Secrets commonly occur in business transactions. A sells a widget to B, knowing about the widget's hidden (usually bad) qualities. Does A have to reveal them?[25] If B knows of some particularly good (but hidden) qualities of the widget, does B have to inform A?[26] Can A apply for a job or an insurance policy and hide information B would find relevant?[27] These sorts of issues raise legal questions about when nondisclosure can be seen as fraudulent. Anthony Kronman develops an economic theory for cases such as these.[28]

The puzzle Kronman tries to solve can be seen by contrasting the *Laidlaw* (War of 1812), *Fuller* (apostate priest), and *Simmons* (no night water) cases from chapter 1. Why is it that the law requires, in some situations, that secret-keepers divulge their information while in other situations they do not have to? Hector Organ did not have to tell Laidlaw's agent that the war had ended, although it radically influenced the going price of tobacco. But John Fuller had to tell a potential employer, DePaul University, that he had once been a priest, and the Evanses had to tell the Simmonses about the unusual water conditions. How can we use economic theory to predict when legal opinions will require disclosure?

---

cle, he was teaching at Chicago and working closely with Richard Posner and William Landes. He has since gone to the Yale Law School, largely abandoned law and economics, and set off on a different path. But his article on nondisclosure and fraud remains important in the law-and-economics literature. It was even cited, albeit critically, by the *Restatement (Second) of Contracts*, § 161, Comment d, as a source of theory on this problem.

24. Posner's initial article about privacy, "The Right of Privacy" (*Georgia Law Review* 12: 393–422 [1978]), focused primarily on privacy as secrecy, although it also tried to assess the economic logic of other areas of the privacy tort. Another essay ("Privacy, Secrecy and Reputation," *Buffalo Law Review* 28: 1–55 [1979]) dealt with privacy and reputation, and yet another ("The Uncertain Protection of Privacy by the Supreme Court," *Supreme Court Review* 1979: 173–216 [1980]) with the Supreme Court's analysis of privacy. All of these essays were gathered and codified in part III of the *Economics of Justice*.

25. This is the issue in *Simmons v. Evans*, 185 Tenn. 282, 206 S.W.2d 295 (1947), discussed in chapter 1.

26. This is the problem raised by *Laidlaw v. Organ*, 15 U.S. (2 Wheat.) 178 (1817), discussed in chapter 1.

27. This is the problem encountered in *Fuller v. DePaul University*, 293 Ill. App. 261, 12 N.E.2d 213 (1938), discussed in chapter 1.

28. Kronman, "Mistake, Disclosure, Information and the Law of Contracts."

Kronman argues that courts distinguish between information that is acquired as the result of deliberate effort and information that is acquired casually as a by-product of other activity: "As it is used here, the term 'deliberately acquired information' means information whose acquisition entails costs which would not have been incurred but for the likelihood, however great, that the information in question would actually be produced. . . . If the costs incurred in acquiring the information . . . would have been incurred in any case—that is, whether or not the information was forthcoming—the information may be said to have been casually acquired." [29] In other words, if one explicitly goes out looking for information and engages in activities that one would not have engaged in unless one were looking for that information, then it is deliberately acquired. If one stumbles on information in the course of doing something one would have done anyway, then it is casually acquired.

Since deliberately acquiring information is something that people can choose *not* to do, people may be tempted not to produce it if they cannot reap the benefits of the information they have discovered. This would be, from an economic point of view, an unhappy occurrence, since "allocative efficiency [ensuring that resources wind up in their most valued uses] is promoted by getting information of changed circumstances to the market as quickly as possible." [30] Kronman argues that if the law is really concerned with promoting economic efficiency, then it should develop incentives for this information to be produced. In light of our review, in the previous section, of the economics of information, this should sound familiar.

Incentives of this sort are generally provided through the assignment of property rights. If one can claim a property right in something one has created, then one can exclude others from the use of that thing, appropriating the value oneself. In the case of knowledge deliberately acquired, Kronman argues, giving people property rights in this information (that is, not requiring them to give it away through forced disclosure) would provide an incentive to invest in this socially productive activity of searching. Such incentives would not be necessary in the case of casually acquired information, since resources are not being expended just in order to produce it and hence no curtailment of the production of this sort of information would result if disclosure were required. Economic theory, according to Kronman, would predict that the law would *not* require disclosure of deliberately acquired

29. Ibid., p. 13.
30. Ibid.

information but *would* require disclosure of casually acquired information.

This theory would have no trouble with the decision in *Fuller*. Information about one's past is rarely the result of a deliberate search, and so, under Kronman's theory, it should be disclosed. Nor would there be any difficulty with the decision in *Simmons*, where knowledge of the water condition was a by-product of living in the house. The case that Kronman uses in the greatest detail to illustrate his argument is *Laidlaw*, and he immediately runs into a problem. The Supreme Court allowed Laidlaw to keep his secret even though there is absolutely no evidence that Laidlaw acquired his information after a deliberate search. If anything, the sketchy evidence leads to the opposite conclusion; the Treaty of Ghent was so unexpected to everyone in New Orleans that a deliberate search for the information would have been folly (or, in economic terms, the expected costs would have exceeded the expected benefits). In addition, it is clear that Hector Organ was not himself the merchant who invested his time and effort traveling with the British fleet. It is more likely that Organ was an acquaintance of the brother of one of the American merchants on board and that (unless one subscribes to the view that one cultivates aquaintances solely for the purpose of acquiring information and that one would not otherwise have friends) Organ's acquiring the information was in all probability accidental, however fortunate it may have been.

Kronman acknowledges this and uses the case to add one important qualification to his theory. He argues that courts do not look in detail at whether the information *in the particular case* was deliberately or casually acquired; rather, courts tend to require disclosure in cases where most information *of the type at issue* is casually acquired. Disclosure is not required in those situations that, *in general,* tend to involve information that is the product of a deliberate search. The reason for this qualification is, again, an economic one: it would be prohibitively expensive in terms of both time and effort for the courts to make an individual determination of this fact in every case.[31] One might also argue that, from an economic point of view, there need only be an *incentive* to acquire this sort of information to get the right economic result. If the law wants to encourage the production of valuable but costly information, then it should award property rights

---

31. For a discussion of this sort of "administrative-costs" rationale, see Posner, *Economic Analysis of Law,* 3d ed. chap. 21, "Civil and Criminal Procedure."

in that sort of information even when, in a particular case, such information is fortuitously acquired.[32]

To get the right economic result, Kronman goes on to argue, one needs also to limit the amount of casually acquired information that is subject to required disclosure. If people were required to disclose all their casually acquired information before finalizing an agreement, they would take a long time, an inefficiently long time, in reaching these agreements. Requiring disclosure of obvious things, for example, would be inefficient because it would hinder transactions that would promote the transfer of goods to their most valued uses. Since the law is striving for efficiency, no disclosure is required in those special cases where the information is obvious.[33]

Kronman's argument rests entirely on that part of the economics of information that is concerned with incentives for the production of valuable information. In so doing, it ignores the lessons of the other branches of the economics of information, such as the inefficient consequences that follow individual decisions made without critical information. The claims made by targets of secrets in the shallow- and deep-secret cases of chapter 1—that is, that they, the targets, have a right to know—are not treated by Kronman, although they are not necessarily beyond the boundaries of economic analysis. To address them, an economic analysis of these cases needs to acknowledge that there can be bad economic consequences that result from secrets that injure innocent transacting partners. In the next chapter, I will present

32. Just such an argument was made by William Landes during a workshop that I gave on this topic at the University of Chicago Law School in November 1985.

33. To some extent, Kronman's exception for obvious information contradicts the thrust of the main argument. In the main argument, efficiency was promoted by getting information to the markets as quickly as possible so that goods could more rapidly reach their most valued uses. This required incentives, property rights in information, and so secrets were permitted when those incentives were necessary to get the information produced and used. In the "obviousness" cases, efficiency is promoted by making agreements without undue burden on the negotiating parties. Efficiency here requires *lowering* unbearable transaction costs, while in the first instance efficiency required *increasing* transactions costs. If people know that other people will be allowed to keep secret deliberately acquired information, then the potential targets of secrets will adjust their behavior accordingly, if they are rational. Either ignorant parties will engage in duplicate research (which might be considered to be socially wasteful because there is an overinvestment of resources in producing knowledge) or they will spend much effort trying to screen transaction partners for honesty and openness. Either way, transaction costs in a system that permits secrecy are bound to increase. The argument here—that is, that one must keep transaction costs low—is not entirely consistent with Kronman's earlier argument.

such a theory. But first we will examine Richard Posner's theory of privacy.

Posner on Privacy

Privacy law has been given its most extended economic analysis by Richard Posner,[34] and his approach has generated a great deal of discussion in the legal community.[35] For Posner, privacy is conceived in terms of property rights in information. If one has a right to privacy, then what one has is ownership of information about oneself. A right to privacy, according to Posner, implies that one has the right to exclude others from knowing about oneself and the right to prevent others from using information about oneself. An absence of such a right would imply that others can claim the right to possess such information.

Although Posner's theory of privacy deals with many aspects of that multifaceted term,[36] we will here consider only Posner's discussion of privacy as it implicates secrecy. To facilitate discussion of Posner's somewhat complex argument about privacy as secrecy, we will divide his observations into three sections: (1) privacy of individuals, (2) privacy of corporations, and (3) privacy of conversations. In each of these three areas, Posner has a somewhat different sort of argument.

The Privacy of Individuals. Posner's discussion of the privacy rights of individuals begins with the assumption that people want to keep information about themselves secret so that they can manipulate the impressions that other people have about them. This makes cases in privacy very much like the cases in nondisclosure/fraud that Kronman analyzes. In both privacy and nondisclosure/fraud cases, Posner

34. The discussion here generally follows the codification of Posner's writings on the subject, presented in part III of the *Economics of Justice.*

35. The entire Spring 1978 issue of the *Georgia Law Review* is devoted to Posner's first article on the subject and to various commentaries upon it. In addition, the December 1980 issue of the *Journal of Legal Studies* was entirely filled with articles about the economics of privacy, articles clearly inspired by the Posnerian approach.

36. In tort law, privacy is generally thought of as an umbrella term covering four different torts: (1) intrusion on a person's seclusion or solitude, (2) public disclosure of embarrassing private facts about an individual, (3) publicity that places someone in a false light in the public eye, and (4) appropriation of a person's name or likeness for the advantage of another. See William L. Prosser, "Privacy," *California Law Review* 48: 383–423 (1960). Only the public-disclosure-of-private-facts actions generally deal with the legitimacy of secrets.

would claim, we find primarily strategic secrets, secrets that are withheld in order to get someone else to act in a particular way:

> Even the strongest defenders of privacy describe an individual's right to privacy as the right to "control information about him," and it is only fair to add that this may be information concerning past or present criminal activity, or moral conduct at variance with the individual's professed moral standards, and that often the motive for concealment is to mislead those with whom he transacts. Other private information, while not discreditable in a moral sense, would if revealed correct misapprehensions that the individual is trying to exploit, as when a worker conceals a serious health problem from his employer, or a prospective husband conceals his sterility from his fiancee. It is not clear why society should assign property rights in such information to the individual to whom the information pertains; the common law . . . generally does not.[37]

Although there may be some information that individuals may want to hide that is not at variance with their public image, this sort of hiding for hiding's sake is not common, according to Posner: "Few people have a *general* reticence that makes them want to conceal non-discrediting personal information. Anyone who has sat next to a stranger on an airplane or a ski lift knows the delight most people take in talking about themselves to complete strangers. Reticence is more likely in speaking to friends, relatives, acquaintances, or business associates who might use a personal disclosure to gain an advantage (or avoid being disadvantaged) in a business or social transaction."[38] Although the social scientist may quibble with the representativeness of a sample of airplane passengers and skiers (the class bias, for example, might be significant), the empirical claim is clear even if not entirely convincing. If the motivation for hiding information is generally to deceive, then Posner's claim that privacy is like fraud is understandable.

Posner claims that there is no good economic reason for allowing people to possess property rights in discreditable information about themselves, any more than there is reason to permit fraud in the sale of goods. Both sorts of fraud tend to lead to less-than-optimal transactions, on the view that transaction costs in these sorts of exchanges are

---

37. Posner, *Economics of Justice,* p. 233, refs. omitted.
38. Ibid., p. 234.

high. Following Coase,[39] one can see that the high transaction costs may thwart beneficial trades and produce inefficient distributions of scarce resources. As a result, Posner argues that the law should assign property rights in discreditable information away from the person to whom the information pertains or, as Posner puts it, away from the "possessor of guilty secrets."[40]

On the other hand, when information is not discreditable and would not result in such misimpressions being given, Posner claims that a privacy right would do no economic harm: "To be sure, some private information that people desire to conceal is not discreditable. In our culture, for example, most people do not like to be seen naked, quite apart from any discreditable fact that such observation might reveal. Since this reticence, unlike concealment of discreditable facts, is not a source of social costs, and since transaction costs are low, there is an economic case for assigning the property right in this area of private information to the individual; and this is what the law does."[41]

At the heart of Posner's discussion of personal privacy, then, is a distinction between discreditable and nondiscreditable information. If the information is discreditable and would serve to correct misperceptions, then the law should not assign the property right to the individual. But if the information is not discreditable, then the individual should be given the property right in such information. That is, the property rights should be assigned in this way if, as Posner suggests, the law embodies an economic logic.[42]

To the objection that individuals would be unfairly shunned if all potentially discreditable information were publicly available, Posner responds with the argument made famous by Gary Becker's work on discrimination.[43] If decision makers are rational, the argument goes, "irrational shunning will be weeded out over time."[44] In other words, when people respond to discreditable information (for example, past criminal records, homosexuality, a childhood full of suicide attempts) in such a way that it plays a major negative role in their decisions to befriend, hire, marry, or trust someone and when these decisions then

39. Coase, "The Problem of Social Cost."
40. Posner, *Economics of Justice,* p. 233.
41. Ibid., p. 234.
42. *Doe v. Roe,* 93 Misc. 2d 201, 400 N.Y.S. 2d 668 (1977), discussed in chapter 1, does not seem to square with Posner's analysis, however, since, although the information at issue was perceived by the former patient of the publishing psychiatrist as being at least in part discreditable, the patient still was able to win.
43. Gary Becker, *The Economics of Discrimination,* 2d ed. (Chicago: University of Chicago Press, 1971).
44. Posner, *Economics of Justice,* p. 235.

turn out to be wrong (that is, the information is really not a very good predictor of that person's future conduct), then these decision makers will be disadvantaged relative to those who did not act on that information. There are "opportunity costs" in irrational shunning. So, although there may be some short-term disadvantages for those about whom information is first disclosed, an efficient market system will eventually discount that information if it is not in fact relevant to any predictions about future behavior. At that point, people will stop wanting to know that information, and it might then make sense to assign the property rights in that information to the person to whom the information pertains, since transaction costs are now lower. Someone who still wants that information may then bargain on an individual basis with the person who claims the privacy right.

Privacy of Corporations. Although the common law does not allow corporations to claim a right of privacy, trade secrecy seems to cover the same ground. Trade secrets can be thought of as "personal" secrets about a corporation. Posner examines trade secrets as though they were a variant of privacy.[45]

Posner again begins his analysis with an assumption about the sort of information that corporations generally want to withhold. He assumes that corporations primarily want to conceal information that is the product of substantial investment. Because the sort of information natural persons and corporate actors want to withhold is different, Posner claims, the legal protection for each should differ as well. He writes: "The purpose of a property right, or of according legal protection to secrecy as a surrogate for an explicit property right, is to create an incentive to invest in the creation of information. Where information is not the product of significant investment, the case for protection is weakened. This is an important consideration in drawing the line between socially desirable and fraudulent nondisclosure."[46] If this argument is familiar, it is partly because Posner cites Kronman in support of this point. The general argument is that, unless one gives to people property rights in the work that they have done, there will be insufficient incentives for investment in the production of that thing. Apparently this argument does not affect the claims for personal pri-

45. This way of thinking about trade secrets is not unusual. In *Kewanee Oil Co. v. Bicron Corp.*, 416 U.S. 470, 94 S. Ct. 1870, 40 L. Ed. 2d 315 (1974), former Chief Justice Burger wrote: "A most fundamental human right, that of privacy, is threatened when industrial espionage is condoned or it made profitable" (94 S. Ct. 1879, 1889). Trade secrets are, in the former Chief Justice's view, a form of commercial privacy.
46. Posner, *Economics of Justice*, p. 244.

vacy, because there is presumably little investment in the production of discreditable facts about oneself anyway. What one learns about oneself, at least in Posner's view, is rarely the result of a great deal of investment. It is rather like Kronman's "casually acquired" information, which is a by-product of other activities rather than the object of investigation. Because Posner argues that corporations do tend to invest in the production of information (through corporate research and development or through development over time of particularly efficient or effective ways of accomplishing tasks) and because individuals generally do not, Posner would claim that there is a greater economic rationale for granting a right to privacy to corporations than there is for granting it to individuals. This corporate right to privacy, Posner claims, the common law has actually encouraged, through protection of trade secrets.

Privacy of Communication. Posner's analysis of privacy of communications is not nearly as detailed as his analysis of the other areas, but it is consistent with his other observations about privacy. Once again, Posner starts with an assumption about the most common empirical instance of privacy of communications. He assumes that B wants to tell C something about A,[47] particularly something discreditable about A. In short, Posner takes as his typical case the situation where B is saying nasty (but true) things about A to C, behind A's back. He assumes that if A is able to overhear B saying these nasty (but true) things, B will be deterred from saying them because presumably B will not want to upset A.

But given Posner's earlier argument that discreditable information should receive no legal protection, it should not be surprising that here again Posner claims that the forwarding of discreditable information should be encouraged.[48] Posner argues in favor of granting a right to privacy in conversations, because then discreditable information about individuals will be more likely to spread. This will, in Posner's view, produce more-knowledgeable transacting partners who will

---

47. In Posner's text (*Economics of Justice*, pp. 245–246) A, B, and C also are used to represent the three actors in his discussion; but his A, B, and C represent actors different than our A, B, and C. The usage in the text here is consistent with the usage in the present book, as explained in chapter 1.

48. Posner's theory would account, then, for why the psychiatrist should have revealed Poddar's intentions to kill Tatiana Tarasoff. See *Tarasoff v. Regents of the University of California*, 17 C.3d 425, 131 Cal. Rptr. 14, 551 P.2d 334 (1976). On this economic view discreditable information about Poddar was information that Poddar had no right to withhold. And since Poddar could not claim the right to withhold the information, his psychiatrist could not claim that right either.

each be less able to defraud the other. If, as Posner suggests, the law has an underlying economic argument, then it should permit privacy of conversations.

Overview of Posner's Theory of Privacy. In some respects, Posner's theory looks like Kronman's. Property rights are assigned when individuals would not otherwise have incentives to produce valuable information. But Posner's analysis also goes beyond Kronman's, because many of the situations in which privacy claims arise do not have the problem of potential underproduction of information at their core. Information about oneself is probably information one will learn anyway, even if there is no property right. So the analysis needs to go beyond the incentives-to-produce problem.

Posner starts to consider the costs when individuals who do not have all the relevant information start to make potentially disastrous decisions. The role of information in individual decisions features prominently. Posner's theory takes seriously the economic claim that the efficiency of markets (including friendship, marriage, and employment markets) is increased when individuals who make decisions in these markets have all the relevant information.

Efficient Secrets

The analyses provided by Kronman and Posner together provide a coherent view of the economics of secrecy. When secrets are necessary to ensure the production of information in the first place, the law should, if it values efficiency, grant property rights to provide incentives for the production of valuable knowledge. When the information would be produced anyway, efficiency requires that relevant knowledge be made available to those who might otherwise make disastrous decisions without it. In this economic analysis, information about individuals is indistinguishable from information about goods one buys and sells. The person who hides information about her discreditable past is treated just like the person who hides information about her defective car or house. There is no good economic reason to distinguish privacy from fraud, since both involve secrets that may interfere with the efficient operation of markets.

The Chicago-school economic theory takes into account both lines of the economic analysis of information presented earlier in the chapter. The information necessary for important decisions needs to be made available to the rational actor if she is to make good decisions, subject to the limitation that some information might be withheld when its publicity would interfere with its production. But neither Kronman nor Posner takes seriously the analysis of secrecy presented in chapter 1. As was noted there, secrecy clearly has a strategic character. One withholds information *from* particular other people in particular social contexts. Others react accordingly. In the next chapter, I develop a theory of legitimate secrets that takes into account the strategic nature of secrecy.

CHAPTER THREE

Secrecy and Strategy

Strategic Uses of Information

IF SECRECY IS STRATEGIC, HOW are we to make sense of the rational search for information? For the knowledge problems we considered in chapter 2, we assumed that the world did not change in response to our getting to know it. Things were "out there," and either we might have learned about them or we might not have. But when one is trying to learn about the potential actions of rational others, the world of knowledge becomes reactive.[1] What we do may affect what others do, just as what they do affects us. Our knowledge cannot be certain because we cannot predict the actions of others, especially when what they do is dependent on what we do and especially when what we and they are doing is hiding information from each other or probing to find out another's secrets. The problem is circular.

The uncertainty in attempting to figure out what others are going to do may come from several sources, which have been elaborated in the literature on game theory.[2] We may not know how the other person conceives of the decision problem. We may not know the other's preference orderings or payoffs. We may not know the other person's taste for risk—or her estimate of what we might do and how that affects what she might do. We may know all of these things and

---

1. See Carol Heimer, *Reactive Risk and Rational Action* (Berkeley: University of California Press, 1985) for a discussion of the way in which social actors may cope with reactive risk.

2. Thomas C. Schelling's *The Strategy of Conflict* (Oxford: Oxford University Press, 1960) and *Micromotives and Macrobehavior* (New York: Norton, 1978), as well as Howard Raiffa's *The Art and Science of Negotiation* (Cambridge, MA: Harvard University Press, 1982), are good nontechnical introductions to these problems. R. Duncan Luce and Howard Raiffa, *Games and Decisions* (New York: Wiley, 1957) provides a more technical starting point.

still not know what the other person may do because the structure of the problem may be such that the best thing she can do is to choose strategies at random from a weighted set.

These problems are qualitatively different from the sources of uncertainty we examined in the previous chapter. What each person gets depends on what the other person does, and both sides may have varying degrees of ignorance. Even when both parties know everything—the structure of the problem, the nature of the both parties' payoffs—there may still be some question of what to do, the most famous problem of this sort being the Prisoner's Dilemma.[3] In the Prisoner's Dilemma, the rational solution for each actor taken individually turns out to be a very bad solution for the pair.[4] The uncertainty is structural and reactive. What makes sense for each person to do depends on what the other person does. And what each guesses the other person will do influences what each chooses for herself.

Secrecy problems are necessarily strategic in this sense. As shown by the conceptual framework presented in chapter 1, secrets always occur in specific social settings, being withheld by one (presumably rational) actor from specific other (presumably rational) actors. These other actors may adjust their behavior accordingly, acting with suspicion or withholding information in return. They may also go on acting in blissful ignorance, at least until the secret strikes home. When a secret is "successful" (that is, when it succeeds in keeping the information from the target until after the target has acted to benefit the secret-keeper), the target's fortunes are often dramatically affected.

3. Russell Hardin's description of the Prisoner's Dilemma (*Collective Action* [Baltimore: Johns Hopkins University Press, 1982], pp. 2–3) is particularly clear: "The Prisoner's Dilemma gets its name from the story of two prisoners who are separately interrogated. Naturally, there is insufficient evidence to convict them of the crime that the police suspect them of having committed. Unless they confess, the worst conviction they risk is for illegal possession of firearms, for which they would each be sentenced to a year in jail. But the police and the prosecuting attorney are devious, and they offer each prisoner the following deal: you can turn state's witness to help us put your partner away for ten years, and we'll let you off free. The only hitch is that, if both of you confess, we'll convict both of you of armed robbery and ask the judge for a lenient sentence of only six years for each of you. To confess or not to confess—that is your dilemma. If you are narrowly self-interested, you are better off confessing no matter what your partner does. Since you both must see the issue this way, you may both spend six years in jail. But if you could act together as a group with a single mind, you would act in the group's interest and hold out so that you would both spend only a year in jail. If, however, you reason from the fallacy of composition [that individually rational actions necessarily add up to a collectively rational result] while your partner acts from self-interest, you will rest ten years in jail. It would be a painful lesson in logic."
4. Or for the collective, if the game is being played with more than two actors.

Because disputes over secrets are strategic, it would seem at the outset that a theory that systematically ignored strategic implications (as the Chicago-school economic analysis of law does) would not be able to produce an adequate account of their resolution. A's payoffs are affected by B's actions, which are in turn affected by A's behavior toward B. A theory that grows out of a strategic analysis might have a better chance of helping us to understand legal rules.

To develop a theory that can serve as an alternative to the economic analysis of law discussed in the preceding chapters, I will proceed in two stages. First, I want to get a more accurate description of the social settings in which secrets arise. Developing a game-theoretic view of secrecy is essential to this effort. Then, in the next chapter, I will develop a normative theory, a version of contractarianism, that enables us to see which outcome should be chosen by courts in deciding strategically framed disputes if the values implicit in the normative theory are also embedded in the law.

The Social Context of Strategic Secrets

We need first to describe the sorts of strategic circumstances in which secrets are likely to be kept. Strategic secrets are not the whole of secrecy; they are only those secrets withheld with the particular motivation of altering the actions or feelings of others. Because strategic secrets are not ends in themselves but instead are means used to realize other ends, one can ask whether it is rational for individuals to keep them.[5] For rational individuals to engage in strategic secrecy, three things must be true about the social environment in which the concealer and the target are located:

1. The interests of the concealer and the target of the secret must not be completely coincident. We can see why this condition would be necessary from the literature on game theory. In games where the actors' interests are identical,[6] the only way that the parties can fail to

5. This is not to say that secrecy can be understood only from a rational choice perspective. The notes about privacy and private secrets in chapter 1 should indicate that there is more to the notion of secrecy, particularly when the secrets are about oneself and are kept as ends in themselves, than a rational choice analysis can capture. Later in this chapter, we will analyze these sorts of secrets as well.

6. These are generally discussed under the title of coordination games. In these games, the players have identical preference orderings among the solutions. When there is a clear ordering of these preferences and full information, the games are trivial, because rational actors will always reach the jointly preferred solution. There is no conflict of interest because each achieves her maximum payoff under exactly the same circumstances as the other does. The games become more interesting when there are ties among the

reach their jointly preferred outcome is through a failure to communicate. It will therefore be in the interests of all concerned to forward all relevant information that they might possess. In a game with this sort of structure, strategic secrets are not useful to any of the parties.

To take the opposite extreme—that is, zero-sum or constant-sum games without a single, stable solution (called a saddle point)—the essence of a successful strategy is often secrecy. One person's gain is another's loss; but if one actor finds out what another is doing, she can take advantage of this knowledge and win. In these games, no one solution is the optimal one all the time. The only way one can hope to maximize one's payoffs is to keep secret at each play of the game exactly which strategy one is going to use that time.[7] The inability to keep a secret will quickly translate into an inability to do well in the game. We can see from this that divergent interests provide a necessary but not sufficient condition for strategic secrets.[8]

---

player's preferences and when each one of a set of possible options is equally preferred. In such a situation two players, to achieve the jointly optimal outcome, have to coordinate their choices. If they are forbidden to communicate (a sort of imposed secrecy) and if each gets the maximum payoff only if the other chooses the same option, as the typical example in the literature would have it, then the optimal outcome is not a sure bet. But there is no reason why the actors who are playing this game would ever impose such a condition. This is why strategic secrets would not happen under such circumstances. See Schelling, *Strategy of Conflict*, pp. 54–58, for a more thorough discussion of this point. Also see Kim Lane Scheppele and Karol Edward Soltan, "The Authority of Alternatives," in J. Roland Pennock and John W. Chapman eds., *NOMOS XXVI: Authority Revisited* (New York: New York University Press, 1987), pp. 169–200, for a coordination-game approach to the study of authority.

7. In these games, rational players choose among the alternatives by drawing randomly from a solution set. The solution set contains the alternatives in proportions determined by the structure of the payoffs, so that, although at any given play of the game the exact strategy to be followed by each party is determined by chance, the overall mix of strategies follows a predictable pattern. For this strategy to work, however, it has to be impossible for one's opponent to tell with any certainty what one is going to do in advance. If one's opponent figures this out, then she can always gain advantage.

8. It should be noted that there are a number of gamelike situations in which the reverse of secrecy is essential to gaining advantage. These are the games in which "commitment" (Schelling, *Strategy of Conflict*, pp. 24–30) is likely to work. Commitment involves announcing one's strategy in advance and letting others adjust. Of course, to pull this off, it helps to have a reputation for stubbornness. In asymmetric coordination games (where it is in actors' interests to agree but each available point of agreement benefits one more than the other) and, sometimes, in Prisoners' Dilemma games (where actors find that they fail to achieve jointly optimal results if they each pursue a maximizing strategy but leave themselves vulnerable to attack if they attempt to cooperate), one can gain an advantage by publicity—that is, by announcing that one is opting for the maximizing strategy. This ability to use commitment as a strategy rests on the noncommitting actor's dependence on the committing actor's choice.

But do the interests of the actors need to be completely divergent? The answer is no. In mixed-motive games, where there are some shared interests and some divergent interests, opportunity to take advantage of special knowledge of an opponent's moves often arises. It is also possible, by withholding information about one's own intended move or about one's preferences (if it is not a game with full information about preferences), to gain advantage here as well.[9]

What the literature on game theory tells us is that, as soon as the parties' interests start to diverge, there is often (although not always) an opportunity to use asymmetric information to the detriment of the ignorant actor. If the parties' interests are completely coincident, then strategic secrecy has no value.

2. There must be an asymmetry of *relevant* information that the secret-keeper knows is relevant. The information being kept secret must be knowledge that the target of the secret would take into account if it were known; otherwise a secret would have no effect. In addition, not only must the information be relevant to the target of the secret, but the secret-keeper must know it is relevant to the target of the secret. This implies that the secret-keeper must know enough about the decisions and decision processes of the target of the secret to know what information would, if withheld, influence the target's decisions in the desired fashion. In some cases, of course, this will be obvious; anyone about to sell many tons of tobacco will find it relevant that the naval blockade of the local port has ended.[10] In other cases, it will involve knowing more subtle things about another's preferences. The apostate priest probably knew better than anyone just how much his past would matter to a Catholic university.[11] Generally, the more one knows about another's preferences, the more successful one is likely to be at determining which secrets can be used as strategic secrets. One can become vulnerable to another person when that person knows the sort of information one values the most and knows when to hide it to gain advantage.

3. The secret-keeper's payoffs must be dependent on the choices of the target of the secret; but the reverse need not be true. Clearly, it is not in a rational secret-keeper's interest to withhold information (especially when this withholding entails costs of some kind) unless there

---

9. See Raiffa's *Art and Science of Negotiation* for a useful review of these situations. In circumstances that generate the possibility of advantage from secret-keeping, the patterns are not so clear in these cases.

10. *Laidlaw v. Organ*, 15 U.S. (2 Wheat.) 178 (1817), discussed in chapter 1.

11. *Fuller v. DePaul University*, 293 Ill. App. 261, 12 N.E.2d 213 (1938); discussed in chapter 1.

can be gain from this activity. There must be some action or attitude that the target of the secret can take that would benefit the secret-keeper. In other words, it is the dependence of the secret-keeper on the target's decisions that gives rise to the motivation for creating strategic secrets. If there were nothing that the target of the secret could do to make the secret-keeper better off (or nothing the target could do to keep the secret-keeper from being worse off), then the secret-keeper would have no incentive to resort to the use of a strategic secret.

It is usually, although not necessarily, the case that the secret-keeper's actions or attitudes will have some impact on the target's payoffs as well. This is certainly the case in those situations where the secret-keeper is capable of inflicting harm on the target of the secret. But secret-keepers may wish to control the activities of the target of the secrets, and there may be no reciprocal wish or ability on the part of the target of the secrets. The minimum requirement for a strategic secret is that the secret-keeper's payoffs must depend on the target's choices, but the reverse need not be true. To put it differently, A (the secret-keeper) must prefer some of B's alternatives to others and B may (but need not) prefer some of A's alternatives to others. When A's payoffs are not contingent on B's actions, there will be no incentive to use a strategic secret.

Strategic secrets, then, will only occur when the interests of the actors involved are not perfectly coincident, when there is an asymmetry of relevant information that the secret-keeper knows will be important to the target, and when something the target can do or refrain from doing would affect the well-being of the secret-keeper.

The Costs of Secret-Keeping in a Reactive World

In the general case, a theory of strategic secrecy would predict that a secret-keeper would withhold information from the target of the secret when the above three conditions held and when the secret-keeper stood to gain more than lose in such activity. We can expect that, as with other economic goods, actors will invest in withholding information up to the point at which the marginal cost of withholding information equals the expected marginal return on that investment.

Generally, the benefits of secrecy are easy for the secret-keeper to determine. But the costs are more elusive, in part because they are reactive. In computing the costs of secrecy, a rational secret-keeper would consider two aspects of the long-term relationship between the secret-keeper and the target, aspects that reveal the strategic nature of the problem:

1. *Risk.*—Success of the secret is risky. If A is withholding information from B in order to get B to do X, then the secret will be considered to have been successful when B does not find out the secret before doing X. Both the tobacco trader who hides news of the peace treaty until the deal is struck and the house sellers who hide information of the regular interruptions in the water flow to their house have accomplished a successful secret.[12] Four factors influence the ability to keep a successful strategic secret: (*a*) the existing distribution of information, (*b*) the density of the information network, (*c*) the length of time the secret must be kept, and (*d*) the search behavior of the target of the secret. The more sources of information, the denser the network, the longer the secret must be kept, and the more inquisitive the target, the more risk there is that the secret will fail.

The existing distribution of information refers to the number of other sources of the information. In general, it is harder to keep something secret when it is "common knowledge" than when it is known only by the secret-keeper. Unless a person is an exceptionally bad secret-keeper who gives away the presence of a secret with awkwardness, tenseness, and inconsistencies, it is generally harder to hide the day's headlines than one's own inner thoughts. By this analysis, Organ would have had a harder time keeping the secret about the peace treaty than Poddar would have had keeping his dangerous intentions secret from his intended murder victim.[13] The likelihood that a strategic secret will be found out is usually a function of the number of available sources of the information: one is more likely to be successful at keeping a secret when one has sole possession of it. But keeping information limited in distribution can entail significant costs above and beyond keeping the secret hidden from a particular target. To increase the chances of success one must hide it from many more people than just the target.

For most information of value, sole possession is the exception rather than the rule. At this point, the density of the information network comes in. If one is not the sole possessor of the information, then one's likelihood of managing a successful secret depends on

---

12. On the tobacco trade, see *Laidlaw v. Organ,* and, on the waterless house, see *Simmons v. Evans,* 185 Tenn. 282, 206 S.W.2d 295 (1947); both are discussed in chapter 1.

13. See *Laidlaw v. Organ,* and, on Poddar's secret, see *Tarasoff v. Regents of the University of California,* 17 C.3d 425, 131 Cal. Rptr. 14, 551 P.2d 334 (1976).

whether the information network is dense or diffuse. If the secret-keeper and the target of the secret are in a dense network, then others who know the secret may reveal it to the target before the secret is successful; for example, Fuller's ability to keep secret his previous life as a priest was greatly limited by the fact that the Catholic community in and around Chicago was very tightly knit,[14] and, ultimately, it was just this denseness of the network that led to the secret being discovered before he began to teach at DePaul University. In contrast, when the social network is diffuse (that is, when those with whom the secret-keeper is in social contract—and who may, as a result, know the information—are not in close social contact with the target of the secret), the chances for a successful strategic secret are much greater. Poddar's ability to keep his dangerous intentions from Tarasoff may have been strengthened by the fact that the couple had broken up and were no longer seeing the same set of friends anymore.[15] In a dense information network, the chances that someone will give away the secret are greater than they are in a diffuse network. To be successful at keeping a secret in a dense network, one must go to greater lengths to ensure that the secret is kept. This can increase the costs of keeping secrets.

The length of time the secret must be kept also influences its success. Generally, the longer the secret must be hidden, the more likely the target is to find out, assuming that there are some other sources of the information. If the secret can be exploited quickly, then the number of other sources of information and the density of the information network do not matter as much. When the secret must be hidden for awhile, the first two factors mentioned are more likely to work against the successful secret.

When the target of the secret is particularly inquisitive, the riskiness of the secret is greater. Secret-keepers do not simply hide information in a passive world. The activity of the target may influence the incentives secret-keepers have for hiding information. Had Laidlaw's agent inquired more closely of Organ just what information he had, the deal might not have gone through. Had the agent had a reputation for suspiciousness, Organ might not have even tried to hide the secret.[16] The strategic environment clearly affects the costs of keeping secrets.

14. *Fuller v. DePaul University.*
15. *Tarasoff v. Regents of the University of California.*
16. *Laidlaw v. Organ.*

All four of these factors taken together indicate that secrets are usually kept with some risk. One does not always know whether one will be successful. Therefore, the simple cost-benefit calculation that might be made in advance of keeping a secret must consider the risk of discovery. The risk is clearly dependent on some things within the secret-keeper's control, but controlling the number of other sources of information, the density of the information network, the length of time the secret is kept, or the inquisitiveness of the other party can be quite difficult. The costs of keeping the secret in the first place may not be very high, but, in a reactive world, the costs of policing this decision may be prohibitive.

2. *Retaliation.*—Since it is generally the case that people do not like being kept in the dark about something that matters to them, later discovery that important knowledge was withheld will sometimes activate retaliation. If the target and the secret-keeper still have intertwined payoffs at the time of the discovery, and if this interdependence is such that the target can exploit it, then the secret-keeper may find that decisions that were once being taken by the target of the secret in the secret-keeper's interest may be repealed or altered. If the target can command a substantial threat of punishment against the secret-keeper at some point in the future after the secret is discovered, then the secret-keeper may find it less desirable to withhold information in the first place. The threat of retaliation in the future if the strategic secret is discovered can take one of two forms: the target of the secret may (*a*) be engaged in an ongoing relationship with the secret-keeper and have opportunities to act against the secret-keeper's interests in the future or (*b*) invoke legal rules or social norms that activate a social process of punishment or restitution.

The costs of keeping secrets will be lower for those who plan one-shot transactions with the target of the secret than for those who intend to engage in a long-term relationship. The Evanses may have deceived the Simmonses more readily because they did not expect to be dealing with the Simmonses again.[17] Of course, even when the circumstances have not been secret the targets may retaliate when they are taken advantage of, but secrecy limits the time available for retaliation. If the secret becomes known after the relationship ends, then opportunities for retaliation are minimized. Generally, the longer the relationship between secret-keeper and target is expected to last, the more likely it is that the secret-keeper faces discovery and retaliation. Costs of se-

17. *Simmons v. Evans.*

crecy are increased in long-term relationships in which the target of the secret possesses control over some resources of importance to the secret-keeper over the long haul.[18]

The availability of legal sanctions may greatly influence the calculation also. When the parties do not have a continuing relationship such that the disadvantaged party can retaliate within the context of the relationship, the disadvantaged party is relatively helpless—unless, of course, there is a system of legal rules and/or social norms that can be activated in a larger social context to punish the transgressors. If those who find themselves at the wrong end of a secret can call on the legal system to enforce their claim of unfair advantage, then the helplessness of actors in one-shot transactions can be reduced.[19] Legal rules or social norms against secret-keeping, then, create disincentives for withholding information in short-term relationships, by influencing the ability of otherwise helpless targets to retaliate. The structure of legal rules may become part of the decision process it is regulating.

THE PICTURE JUST SKETCHED INDICATES when we might expect secrecy to occur if it followed a strategic logic. Individuals, operating in a reactive world and trying their best to estimate the costs and benefits of strategic behavior would be led to keep strategic secrets in particular sorts of contexts. Strategic secrets appear when the parties have divergent interests, when information known by only one party is relevant (and known to be relevant) to decisions of the other, and when the secret-keeper's welfare is a function of the target's choices. But risk and the potential for retaliation present significant disincentives under certain circumstances. All these calculations might be significantly altered, however, by the presence of legal norms that would have the effect of increasing the costs of secret-keeping whenever secrets were

18. In some ways, the analysis just presented parallels that of Michael Darby and Edi Karni in "Free Competition and the Optimal Amount of Fraud" (*Journal of Law and Economics* 13: 67–88 [1973]). They examine the behavior of firms deciding to engage in fraud. When clients or customers engage in an ongoing relationship with the firm, there is less incentive for the firm to engage in fraud because discovery of the fraud would jeopardize any future income that the firm hopes to realize from that particular customer. Similarly, if the firm is a going concern with every expectation of maintaining itself far into the future, fraud can be quite shortsighted. Every firm depends on the goodwill of potential customers for its continued survival. The practice of fraud, if discovered, can threaten this. Thus ongoing relationships (or, in the terms used above, continuing interdependent benefits) tend to reduce the level of fraud (or secrecy) practiced in a particular relationship.

19. It appears to be no accident that the majority of secrecy cases that come before courts involve one-shot, high-value transactions in which the target of the secret controls little of importance to the secret-keeper.

forbidden in law. The availability of legal rules not only influences the ability to retaliate; it also significantly affects whether people keep secrets in the first place. A theory that attempts to account for legal rules should ask, first, which rules it would make sense for a society to adopt and, second, whether American law seems to have produced those rules.

TWO
Developing a New Jurisprudence

CHAPTER FOUR

A Contractarian Theory of Law

WHAT LEGAL RULES WOULD IT be right for a society to adopt? In answering this question, we could take one of two approaches. One would be to ask what is right in general—that is, to identify a timeless, placeless moral view that, if legal systems got it right, would make all law the same. If we discovered that the law embodied such a view so that individual legal rules mirrored this moral structure, then we would have found empirical support for the idea of natural law.[1]

But there is no reason to suppose that any particular legal system has, in fact, gotten the answers to moral questions right in this sense.[2] A few observations show why:

1. There is extraordinary divergence in the moral universes implicit in the world's legal systems[3] (although there is also substantial

---

1. For those who still equate natural law theory with someone like Aquinas, natural law theories are often identified with theocratic formulations about law. See St. Thomas Aquinas, *Summa Theologica* (New York: Benziger, 1947), Questions 90–97. But natural law theories may be based on other conceptions of the good. For contemporary examples, see John Finnis, *Natural Law and Natural Rights* (Oxford: Oxford University Press, 1980); and Michael Moore, "Moral Reality," *Wisconsin Law Review* 1982: 1061–1156 (1982) and "A Natural Law Theory of Interpretation," *Southern California Law Review* 58: 277–398 (1985). Only the theocratic formulations, ironically enough, have made the rather bold claim that the law created by humans here on earth in fact embodies the right. Other natural law theorists want to distinguish between positive law and natural law and certainly never would claim that a theory of the good gives one a decent description of law as we know it.

2. This is particularly true if one holds the view that the idea of "the right" makes no sense unless one asks further, In what social context for what sort of problem? Don Herzog has mischievously wondered aloud whether "the right" is any more comprehensible than "the blue" or "the big." For a sense of his brand of pragmatism, see Don Herzog, *Without Foundations* (Ithaca, NY: Cornell University Press, 1985).

3. The enormous literature in legal anthropology supports this claim. See, for example, in the classical literature on this point, Bronislaw Malinowski, *Crime and Custom*

agreement about such things as murder, and these have often been the basis for empirical natural law claims). While this does not argue against any *one* of them embodying the right, legal systems *in general* cannot be said to manage to make law right. Even the claim that American or English law has some deep connection with a transcendent morality based in Anglo-American ethical theory ignores the pervasive legal evolution we still witness, the substantial pockets of injustice that passed for rightness in the past, and the continuing debate over which legal rules best capture a moral point of view.

2. In our own legal system, and undoubtedly in others, there are some things that we might want to say are morally wrong (such as not going to the aid of people in need) that are not illegal and other things that we would want to say have little place in a moral theory (such as driving on the right-hand side of the road) for which one may be punished when one runs afoul of the legal provision. So moral and legal provisions do not perfectly overlap. That does not mean that, in those instances where they do, there cannot be some correspondence. But, in cases where morality leaves out what the law would put in, a theory of morality that could provide an ethical basis for legal rules would provide a very partial account of actual law. And when morality includes what the law leaves out, law would provide only a partial indicator of morality. One would need a theory of morality complete enough to separate those parts of law that have moral content from those parts of law that do not and to explain why some moral provisions should not be legal rules.

3. There is no clear mechanism through which morality would infuse the positive law. Unless judges or legislators have some particular wisdom, or unless, as has been suggested by the economic analysts of law, there is some evolutionary process through which the law

---

in Savage Society (London: Routledge and Kegan Paul, 1926); Lloyd Fallers, *Law Without Precedent* (Chicago: University of Chicago Press, 1969); E. Adamson Hoebel, *The Law of Primitive Man: A Study in Comparative Dynamics* (Cambridge, MA: Harvard University Press, 1954); and E. E. Evans-Pritchard, *The Nuer* (Oxford: Oxford University Press, 1940) for a variety of very different systems of substantive and procedural law. See also Clifford Geertz, "Local Knowledge: Fact and Law in Comparative Perspective," in *Local Knowledge: Further Essays in Interpretive Anthropology* (New York: Basic Books, 1983) for a perceptive discussion of how legal concepts often entail moral judgments and are part of a wider culture that gives them meaning. It is hard to imagine, from Geertz's description, how one can make sense of morally informed legal concepts without considering the specific details of time and place. For a philosopher's account of relativity and moral judgment, see J. L. Mackie, *Ethics: Inventing Right and Wrong.* (New York: Penguin, 1977), pp. 36–38.

comes to approximate more and more closely the ideal,[4] law would seem to develop in response more to social pressures, as various interests compete for ascendancy, than to moral pressures.

But it may be (and here is where the second strain of normative argument comes in) that social pressures *do* embody normative pressures of a particular kind. Certainly we do not want to claim that, because law is unlikely to embody a transcendent moral vision, it is unlikely to be informed by any moral sense at all. Here again, experience and observation would show this to be silly. Law is sometimes praised for having—and sometimes criticized for failing to have—a sense of justice, as if it were expected to. Many people, when pressed to justify their own decisions, rely on legal terms and concepts to account for what they have done. The language of "shoulds" and "oughts" is used in good faith in legal settings. While it may be unrealistic to expect legal rules in any particular system of law to correspond to a particular abstract moral vision, it may be quite reasonable to expect them to correspond to *some* sense of morality. In particular, the law may embody the norms of a specific culture in a particular time and place.[5]

How are we to conceive of these norms? Clearly, within a particular society, many normative systems may exist side by side, in competition or in some patterned relation of alternation or of dominance and submission. The normative system embedded in law may be either chosen from among them or developed by finding a deeper structure that they share. A legal system may translate "ought" into "is" by articulating this deeper structure. In a democratic polity, where legitimacy of rule is founded on consent of the governed, the law *should* reflect this deeper normative structure, if one can be found.

And here is where the claims of right in a particular social context and a more general sense of "the right" can be reconciled. We can develop an abstract moral theory that argues that law *should* corre-

4. See John C. Goodman, "An Economic Theory of the Evolution of the Common Law," *Journal of Legal Studies* 7: 393–406 (1978); Paul Rubin, "Why Is the Common Law Efficient?" *Journal of Legal Studies* 6: 51–64 (1977); and R. P. Terrebone, "A Strictly Evolutionary Model of the Common Law," *Journal of Legal Studies* 10: 397–407 (1981). Even on the basis of these theorists' own accounts of the evolution of law, one would have to presume that, in all those areas of law where the rules were still inefficient, there were potential litigants who could afford the costs of litigating over and over until the rule were changed to an efficient one.

5. This view is widely held among anthropologists. See Paul Bohannan, "The Differing Realms of the Law," *American Anthropologist* 67: 33–42 (1965) for the classic statement of this position and Stanley Diamond, "The Rule of Law versus the Order of Custom," *Social Research* 38: 42–72 (1973) for the classic critique.

spond to a particular society's "deep conventionalist"[6] moral views. We can argue that it is right in general to adopt a legal system that would count as right in a particular political context.

Consent as a Basis for Legal Morality

Moral philosophers typically ground systems of ethics in a particular foundational principle.[7] Thus, a moral judgment may be right because it corresponds to the will of God, because it results in the greatest happiness for the greatest number, or because the principle underlying the judgment may be universalized without contradiction. Social scientists typically are uncomfortable with such foundational principles, since it is difficult to imagine any such principle that would succeed either in justifying or in making sense of moral practices across a wide array of cultures and historical moments. Foundational principles look suspiciously like some particular elite's sense of what would serve its interests, dressed up to look neutral.[8] Or foundational principles simply do not make sense when considered outside their cultural tradition.[9]

But to get a general moral theory one does not need to appeal to a moral principle that ignores features of culture. The principle "When in X, do as the X-ians do" (to generalize from the case of Rome) may be abstract, but one can hardly say that it ignores features of a culture. Whatever counts as typical local practice is what one should do. So, there is no necessary contradiction between being sensitive to the features of local culture and working from a general moral principle.

What sort of principle would it make sense to adopt as the basis of

---

6. The term is used by Moore in "A Natural Law Theory of Interpretation" to describe interpretive theories that rely for a moral foundation on the principles inherent in the deep structure of institutional norms and practices and not on some independent theory of moral reality.

7. The pragmatists constitute a major exception here. See, for example, William James, *Pragmatism: A New Name for Some Old Ways of Thinking* and *The Meaning of Truth: A Sequel to Pragmatism* (Cambridge, MA: Harvard University Press, 1975).

8. This view is particularly prevalent among Marxists. See Hugh Collins, *Marxism and Law* (Oxford: Oxford University Press, 1984) for a sensitive review and commentary on a variety of these sorts of arguments. Recently, advocates of Critical Legal Studies have argued the same thing. See, for example, Roberto Mangabeira Unger, *The Critical Legal Studies Movement* (Cambridge: Harvard University Press, 1986); Duncan Kennedy, "The Structure of Blackstone's *Commentaries*," *Buffalo Law Review* 28: 205–256 (1979); and the articles collected in David Kairys, ed., *The Politics of Law* (New York: Pantheon, 1982).

9. The complexity of legal culture and legal concepts can be seen in Geertz, "Local Knowledge."

a moral theory of law? Developing a moral theory of law is not the same as developing a general moral theory. Law has the effect of being enforced against violators with serious consequences, and a theory that indicated which things were normally objectionable would not settle the question of whether someone should be legally punished for doing such things. Moral judgments should not necessarily be legal judgments. The moral view that people should attend church would become oppressive if legally enforced. And the view that virtues are good things to have does not imply that we ought to be legally obligated to acquire them. A moral theory of law should justify not only legal rules but also their application.

When, then, can we say that law may legitimately be enforced? Or, to put the question a bit differently, when does a person have an obligation to obey the law such that the law could be legitimately enforced against her if she disobeyed? One obvious answer is that the law may be legitimately enforced against deviants if the law serves the general good. But why would that give the person against whom it is enforced any particular *obligation* to obey the law when she does not find that it promotes *her* welfare and when she might disagree with that particular conception of the general good? Clearly, the threat of punishment would provide some reason for obeying it anyway, but, in Hart's well-known formulation,[10] the person then would feel more obliged than obligated to obey. Pointing out the social pressure behind the law is hardly the way to establish a moral obligation.

If the law is to be legitimately enforced against an individual, then it has to be capable of justification *to that individual*. This is not the same as saying that law has to be generally thought right by a majority or that it has to be shown to make people, on average, better off. Law, in its distinctive form, operates in individual cases, when particular plaintiffs and particular defendants face off in court. The enforcement of law must be explained in these individual cases, not just in the grand design of an overall social plan, though the law surely embodies this too. What makes law legitimate, and not just efficient or orderly, is its ability to incorporate those values and arguments that the losing side in a legal case would recognize as appropriate, even when that person finds herself losing as a result of their application.

Law must be capable of justification to the losing parties while also being true to the moral traditions of a community and to the aspirational character of the community's political order. In societies

10. H. L. A. Hart, *The Concept of Law* (Oxford: Oxford University Press, 1961), pp. 85–86.

whose traditional and aspirational values include individual autonomy, a legal system that failed to provide justifications to specific
individuals would fail to meet this standard. The legal compulsion of
church attendance in the United States, for example, would be felt as
oppressive *not* because many people would disagree with the underlying moral view that church attendance is a good thing; rather, the
oppressiveness would be felt as a result of the *state* compelling *religious*
activity. The political ideal of personal liberty—which goes deep in the
tradition of American politics, both in the historical struggle for independence and in the ongoing articulation of the aspirations of the
population—limits this infusion of a *particular* brand of morality, particularly religious morality, into law. What is right for a particular
polity to do is a function of both the political traditions and the political
aspirations of the community. The divergence between legal norms
and moral norms can be understood by sorting out the traditions and
aspirations of a particular society.

This does not mean that societies are necessarily tied to particular
readings or single-right-answer views of their traditions or aspirations.[11] Both traditions and aspirations may be contested. In fact,
given the internal diversity of most societies, it would be surprising if
they were not. But not all versions of a society's moral sense are going
to fit comfortably against culturally available readings of past and
future, and this will limit the range of possible constructions of present
legal rules. Within that range, enormous fights can certainly be found
and there may not seem to be much general agreement. But the fact of
disagreement does not of itself necessarily operate as a sign that traditions and aspirations are unimportant or that morality has dropped out
of law. Disagreement can be read as a battle between competing stories
of how to get from a society's past to its future, and the different
readings of tradition and aspiration are critical in this process of cultural storytelling. Law is one setting where those competing stories are
made explicit and judged and where values gain ascendancy as particular stories come to be viewed as more genuine than others. These
stories must be comprehensible and genuine for the losers in the legal
process, however, or else they have failed the aspirations that have
given rise to them.

In democracies generally, the idea of individual efficacy in the
determination of life choices and chances runs very deep. What sense

11. In the next chapter, we will explore the interpretive character of legal decision
making and the way in which different parties' constructions of facts influence the interpretive enterprise.

would having a vote make without the corresponding beliefs in both the desirability of self-governance and the importance of accountability of political regimes? Of course, having the right to vote does not mean one's individual choices will be the same as the collective result, but underlying the idea of voting is the deeper thought that an individual's consent to the forms of political life and the procedures of policy-making legitimizes the operation of politics. If an individual has agreed to be governed by a particular political order, then, within the boundaries of that consent, that political order may operate legitimately with respect to that individual. Consent, in effect, makes possible the later justification of an application of law. A legal system that operates in a democracy on the principle of consent finds legitimacy in enforcing its laws. But this is all very sketchy. Let us look at this problem a bit more formally.

How Consent Works

We will begin by assuming that we want to know which values a legal system in a democracy ought to contain and that a good democracy is one that lives up to its own ideals.[12] Democratic regimes share the ideal that government shall only proceed by the consent of the governed. In fact, a regime that does *not* take this consent seriously disqualifies itself as a democracy. The rules that people consent to be governed by are, in a democratic regime, the legitimate rules for that regime to adopt. Each democratic society may have a different set of rules, but they might all be equally legitimate if they are based on some underlying basis of consent.

But what does consent require? Surely, if we used some Gallup Poll sense of consent, where individuals are asked at the moment that something becomes a public issue how they personally feel about it, we would not get very far. After all, why would people want to be governed by legal rules under which they know that they are going to lose in a particular dispute that has arisen at a particular time? The two parties to a lawsuit are unlikely to agree to any single set of rules because at the moment of dispute almost any rule will appear to favor one side or the other. And people will not want to lose. Law is most active precisely when people do not agree—and so, asking people to

---

12. The choice of regime type has already been made prior to any consideration of the moral frame in this argument, so the moral status of the democratic regime itself remains unexamined in this view. The moral argument that I am developing is contingent on the separate argument that democracy is a good thing. But I will leave that project to others.

consent to the rules by which they want to be governed at the time of the dispute (in the same way that we ask for popular attitudes at the sign of each impending crisis) is unlikely to produce any agreement on the rules at all.[13] And then we are left with the specter of the law imposing answers on unconsenting citizens in virtually every lawsuit. This means either that law can never live up to a democratic ideal, or that there is no deeper structure that would generate consent, or that there is something wrong with this notion of consent in the first place.

The obvious place to start is with the idea of consent. Contemporary contractarian moral theories[14] do not use a public-opinion sense of what consent means. The question consent raises is not what someone would *like* to have happen given her current state of affairs. Clearly, people would, if they were rational, reason that they would want those outcomes that were best for themselves. But we would not call this *moral reasoning*. Instead, moral theories ask what people would favor if they were making an attempt to be impartial. The play of individual self-interest that is present at the moment of crisis (in our case, at the moment of a trial) overwhelms any inclination of the parties involved to be impartial, and, if the concern is to develop a set of legal rules that people would agree to be governed by no matter what is likely to happen, one needs to ask the parties before they know what they have at stake in a particular dispute. When people answer from an impartial perspective—that is, when they consider in an even-handed way the competing claims that can be made on all sides and when they are not stacking the legal deck in their own favor—they are more likely to produce impartial laws. So, we should use a sense of consent that requires that people agree to the legal rules of the regime when their self-interest is not engaged.

What does the idea of impartiality commit us to?[15] At a first pass, we might say that the idea of impartiality is captured by the metaphor of putting oneself in another's shoes or by the idea of the Golden Rule: to do unto others what we would have them do unto us. But we will

13. In fact, survey researchers often look to maximize variance in responses, by the very questions that they ask. The ideal survey question is one that splits the population evenly among the response categories, providing more variance for researchers to explain and providing more adequate data for statistical models where much of the interesting information is captured in the variance. The approach outlined here looks to maximize consensus. The study of norms is not easily framed in terms of statistical models, *not* because the relevant attributes cannot be counted but because the sorts of models that emphasize variance do not capture the core of the issue.

14. For example, John Rawls, *A Theory of Justice* (Cambridge, MA: Harvard University Press, 1971).

15. I am indebted to Jeremy Waldron for suggesting the argument that follows.

always find in lawsuits that the various parties will think differently—after all, if two people have perfectly coincident interests, what are they doing in court? What do we do then? We might adopt one of two well-known strategies for thinking about this subject. One is the position forwarded by R. M. Hare, a view that demands that one put oneself, in turn, in the shoes of each person affected by a moral rule. After doing this, "when I have been the round of all the affected parties, and come back in my own person, to make an impartial moral judgment giving equal weight to the interests of all parties, what can I possibly do except advocate that course which will, taken all in all, least frustrate the desires which I have imagined myself having? But this . . . is to maximize satisfactions." [16] Hare's position leads to utilitarianism as a way of solving the problem of the diversity and conflict of interests. This is the moral view implicit in the economic analysis of law, protestations by Richard Posner[17] notwithstanding. Impartiality is produced out of a cacophony of interests by merging all conflicting points of view into one, adding them up, and then trying to find that rule that gives the biggest total or the highest average.

The other possibility is to proceed from a contractarian position. Instead of asking in turn what each person would prefer and trying to figure out which solution would maximize the satisfaction of as many preferences as possible, a contractarian might say that this misses the point of what it is to be a person: we are not everyone in turn or everyone all at once but rather somebody all the time. Given that we will have to live our lives as specific individuals, we might well worry about how each individual is treated in the social arrangements that result from moral choice. If we do not know which somebody we will be, it makes sense that we would focus on the position of the person we would least want to be, to make that position the best we can manage to arrange in the event that things turn out for the worst. That is the basis of Rawls's difference principle, but it is also an answer to the impartiality problem. When we have to choose among various social arrangements, we should take the point of view of those who stand to lose. Those rules that will attract the consent of the least well off are preferred to those that cannot—and, since all will have the same incentives to worry about the potential for disaster hidden in the allocation of social positions, the consent of all should follow.

16. R. M. Hare, *Freedom and Reason* (Oxford: Oxford University Press, 1963), p. 123.

17. Richard A. Posner, *The Economics of Justice* (Cambridge, MA: Harvard University Press, 1981), part I.

Those Who Choose

But who are these people who are consenting? In Rawls's scheme, these people were stripped of all knowledge about who they would be in the society beyond what he called the "original position" of social choice. In addition, while people in the original position knew a few facts about the social world in general, they knew nothing either about their conception of the good or about the political or economic organization of their society. These restrictions, while they may make sense when one is choosing the background institutions that control life chances, seem quite out of place in a theory of law.[18] The content of particular legal rules and even the decision about which laws to have in the first place are dependent on the sorts of institutional choices rational deciders would select at the outset. Those choosing a regime of laws should know about the structure of the society they are to live in (even though they do not know their own self-interest in particular cases), because laws themselves generally contain as contingent facts descriptions of the social world. For law to have meaning, these descriptions must correspond to the social world in which the actors live.

Some laws may be drafted without these sorts of contingent descriptions; for example, a general prohibition against murder, found in almost all cultures, does not require detailed descriptions of particular social arrangements, which are likely to vary from society to society. But legal rules about property, for example, depend quite heavily on the particular sort of property regime the society has adopted.[19] If a conception of property does not involve some sort of exclusive ownership, a prohibition against theft is unlikely to mean much. So, beyond a small handful of examples, law requires fairly detailed descriptions of the parts of the social world on which the normative judgment is contingent. If those choosing legal rules do not know enough about the society to accomplish the descriptions necessary for the activation of legal rules, they are unlikely to develop much of a legal system at all. It may be that those parts of law that do not involve descriptions of social arrangements (primarily those areas in-

18. Rawls adopts this view in developing his four-stage model of the moral constitution of political institutions. At each stage, the amount of knowledge available to those behind the veil is increased so that sensible and increasingly specific choices can be made about a constitution, about laws, and about how the laws are to be applied in specific cases.

19. See Jeremy Waldron, "What is Private Property?" *Oxford Journal of Legal Studies* 5: 313–349 (1985) for a discussion of the ways in which different regimes of property ownership may vary.

volving harm to human beings) are most likely to be candidates for explanation in a natural law theory. But if we are interested in both the sorts of legal rules that govern relations among people and the sorts of organizational forms they produce, those choosing the rules need to know the political, social, and economic organization of the society in which they will live.

Of course, law does not just reflect and promote particular social arrangements; it also may *constitute* them in the first place. The structure of American government, for example, is created by the Constitution, being brought into existence in a particular form by the words that the Framers used to describe the new institutions. Other laws have this constituting effect as well: corporations are brought into existence in their charters (which have legal force) and even voting is made possible by a set of laws regulating elections. So, the choice of laws can also be seen as a choice of which sorts of social arrangements a particular society will have—and not just as a reflection of arrangements currently in existence. Either way, the design of laws requires knowing a lot both about the society into which these rules will be an intervention and about the people who will live in the midst of these rules.

This means that, for a particular democracy, it will be relevant to ask what real people, freed from the bias of any particular self-interest, would actually, in fact, agree to, given this deeper sense of consent. Bringing their knowledge of the particular society with them into the decision process, these people would not necessarily decide what was right in some timeless, placeless sense but would instead do the best they could to be impartial, given the relevant backdrop, the moral norms, and political aspirations of their culture. They would decide what is right in the context of their particular social arrangements. In a democracy, where the consent of the governed provides the basis of authority of the regime, it matters that the values *of that population* and not those of some hypothetical one are embedded in the law. As an empirical matter, we would want to look for situations in which non-self-interested individuals consented to determine the local morality of legal rules.[20] Absent evidence of real consent, we should examine what this population *would* do, if they could choose in a non–self-interested way. This may require some tricky inference from available evidence, but in the absence of more detailed information it may be the best we can do.

20. In some ways, this is exactly what a jury does.

Scope of Consent: Holistic or Piecemeal

We still need to ask what sort of thing people are consenting *to*. There are two main alternatives. One is to argue, as Rawls does, that a contractarian stance involves evaluating the entire structure of political institutions, taken as a package. We might call this the holistic approach. Rawls discusses basically just societies that, though they may have individual laws that are objectionable, have, in general outline, most of the features of a just political order. The consent Rawls cares most about is the consent to the basic structure. The lack of contractual underpinnings of individual laws does not, for Rawls, make a legal system or a political system unjust.

The holistic approach is perfectly reasonable when the question is the choice of fundamental principles of justice or the choice of the basic design of political institutions. It is even a reasonable approach to take in the design of legal institutions more specifically, because, if one is engineering a system from the ground up, one wants to do the best one can with the basic structure. The details can be fixed up later or can be compensated for by institutions that provide a buffer against their effects.

But the holistic approach does not work as well when, given a basic structure, one tries to figure out what a particular law should be. It would be a bad legislator or judge indeed who, when given the opportunity to choose between an individual rule that passed contractarian muster and one that did not, chose the one that did not. The most morally responsible thing for an individual lawmaker to do is to choose the best alternative available. This means adopting a piecemeal approach to the evaluation of legal rules. Of course, if the basic structure is unjust, then there is no reason for legislators or judges to accept the confines of the choice situation itself and the most morally correct thing to do may be to change the basic structure. But within a basically just system, individual legislators and judges should choose the legal rule that, standing alone, is the best legal rule they can choose.

In fact, within a basically just system, deciding within the constraints provided by the role of judge or legislator is likely to be quite important to the maintenance of legitimacy of political institutions. The judge who invents laws out of thin air or the legislator who adjudicates specific disputes may be undermining the basic structure that gives effect to the deeper meaning of consent.

A contractarian theory of law, then, may consider the justifiability of legal rules taken one by one, provided that it is primarily a theory of legislative and judicial choice within a basically just political structure and not a theory of the basic structure of the legal institutions themselves. A contractarian theory of judging should examine whether the particular rule a judge has chosen has a reasonable contractarian justification of its own.

Negative and Positive Contractarianism

Consent may operate more decisively in telling us what the legal rules should *not* be than in telling us what the laws *should* be; that is, it may be easier to tell which laws would be *rejected* by the sort of people we have been talking about than it would be to tell precisely on which single rule they would agree.[21] The failures of consent identify situations in which the individuals so situated would find their positions intolerable.

For example, it would be hard to tell a contractarian story about why people who thought they might be *anyone* in a society would ever agree to a regime of slavery. A regime of slavery would, for one thing, undermine the condition that gives contractarianism its moral force in the first place—that is, the condition that individuals be allowed to make important choices about how they will lead their lives. Of course, any commitment (to buy a house, to take a job) results in constraints on liberty; one is no longer free to do whatever one likes. But the restrictions in these circumstances are usually limited in scope and temporary, while slavery is all-encompassing and permanent. Moreover, it is reasonable to assume that people would agree to some restrictions on liberty, if those restrictions actually enhanced liberty in other ways; the limitation on the number of times we can each vote in national elections may look like a restriction on liberty, but the vote would not mean much without this condition. In fact, the restrictions on voting open up a sphere within which it is possible to exercise one's ability to choose, a sphere that, without the restrictions, would otherwise not exist.[22] Slavery does not have this advantage. Consent to a permanent, all-encompassing absence of efficacious choice over areas very important to one's life without receiving any benefit or opening up of new possibilities is highly unlikely. Laws allowing slavery would

---

21. This distinction between rules that people would reject and those that they would accept in an ideal choice situation is made by T. M. Scanlon, "Contractarianism and Utilitarianism," in Amartya Sen and Bernard Williams, eds., *Utilitarianism and Beyond* (Cambridge: Cambridge University Press, 1982.), pp. 103–128.

22. Jeremy Waldron suggested this example.

clearly fail on consent grounds, as (for the same reasons) would laws allowing individuals to be sacrificed for greater social gain.

But the power of negative contractarianism does not mean that agreement on a single positive rule to the exclusion of others is likely to happen. It may be that there are several rules that would be acceptable from a contractarian point of view, depending on the twists and turns of particular arguments. While it is clearly offensive to enforce laws that people would have rejected had they been explicitly asked about them before their self-interest was engaged, it is not offensive to enforce one law among several acceptable versions that people would have consented to, given the choice. The availability of *multiple* rules that may be justified in contractarian terms does not count against a contractarian theory of law so long as the theory is capable of ruling out some alternatives and therefore has some real bite. In fact, the availability of *several* justifiable rules makes possible the exercise of democratic decision making (even majority rule) among this set of alternatives. As long as the rules themselves meet the test of not being rejected on the basis of negative contractarian arguments, then a choice from the set of alternatives remaining may be based on other principles like majoritarianism or efficiency.

From these general arguments on contractarianism, then, we can at least say that in a democratic society it is wrong to impose on people rules to which they would not agree. The contractarian judge or legislator should choose that legal rule in each individual case that is the best among the available alternatives. We are now ready to ask what sorts of rules, in the common-law secrecy cases, people would consent to and judges should select.

Direct Secrets

In direct secrets, one person withholds information from another and that other claims the right to know. To figure out what the optimal rules would be in cases like these, we should note that sometimes A will want to withhold information from B and that sometimes B will want to withhold information from A. Both A and B, then, will have some interest in choosing rules that would not work to their detriment in either situation.

In order to choose these rules, individual decision makers must first have some sense of who they would be and what they would want. But in order to minimize the overt play of narrow self-interest, a motivation unlikely to lead to the choice of fair rules, we need to restrict the ability of these individuals to foresee their own particular fortunes. As a first matter, they cannot know whether they are going to be secret-keepers or targets in any individual case or even in the aggregate. This is a minimum condition designed to keep individual decision makers from rigging the rules for their own individual benefit. They cannot know how they personally would fare under any particular regime of rules and so they cannot produce completely self-serving rules. They must make some attempt to produce rules that incorporate more impartial standards.

But what can they be expected to know about themselves and how they will act in the face of uncertainty in this ideal world? First, we will assume, like Rawls, that the individuals deciding in advance on a system of rules will be rational.[23] Rational actors will generally consider only their own self-interest in a particular decision. The fact that these individuals cannot know what will benefit them personally (because they do not know what position they will be in when the time comes) will lead them to set out to construct a set of ground rules for improving their collective lot. A set of ground rules would be agreed on in advance only if they improved the chances that each individual would be able to better her condition more reliably by following the rules than by living under a regime where odds of a good outcome were determined by chance. These rational individuals, deciding in advance of knowing their particular fates, would act not simply to promote narrow self-interest in the individual case (because they could not if they tried) but rather to promote self-interest in a broader perspective.

One may think that such rational individuals would choose rules that would make the outcome under the rules the same for all, but this is only true if these individuals are extremely risk averse[24] or willing to

23. For Rawls, this means that "[i]n choosing between principles each tries as best as he can to advance his interests" (Rawls, p. 142).

24. Extremely risk-averse individuals would probably agree on a regime that allowed for the highest possible floor. This would press the final distribution toward equality. But though Rawls is widely credited with making this point, he does not *argue* the point that individuals will choose a maximin strategy (leading to the difference principle) on grounds of risk aversion. Instead, Rawls argues for maximin on grounds that people would be unable to follow through on a commitment to live in a position that was intolerable—and that this would prevent them from making the commitment to a regime that included intolerable positions in the first place. As a result, Rawls's argument ought to commit him not to the complete equality that the risk-aversion argument suggests—nor to his own favored difference principle—but to having a social minimum below which people cannot fall. A social minimum would make each social position tolerable and would allow each person who agreed to live in such a society to have a life worth living. See Jeremy Waldron, "John Rawls and the Social Minimum," *Journal of Applied Philosophy* 3: 21–33 (1986) for the development of this argument.

live with a particular vision of equality *on average*.[25] It seems unrealistic to assume that individuals at our hypothetical decision point are completely risk averse because here, under the piecemeal approach, the only thing at stake is the particular rule about secrecy. Individuals are not choosing once and for all the complete regime of institutions that will control their entire lives, a situation in which it would make more sense to be extremely risk averse. Much of the fear of bad consequences in these sorts of contractarian choices comes from not considering what sorts of *other* institutional arrangements the society has for protecting people harmed by particular decisions or rules. If a society has a generous welfare system, for example, a group of people deciding on what sort of tort-law system to adopt may reasonably agree on rules that fail to compensate people for particular kinds of losses because they know that injured persons will be able to get aid elsewhere.[26] There is no reason to expect the sort of extreme risk aversion in piecemeal contractarianism that we find in more holistic forms if the background institutions are basically just.

There is also no reason to expect that people choosing rules will, as the utilitarians argue, opt to maximize utility *on average,* for the reasons we examined above. People do not live life as persons on average; and, if one receives a bad lot in an allocation of scarce resources, one can hardly be expected to be comforted by the knowledge that, on average, things worked out to be the best they could be. It is no justification for someone standing with one hand in a pot of scalding water and the other in a pan of ice to know that, on average, her hands are a comfortable temperature. Experience is not felt on average; the variance matters a great deal. Being a person means living a particular life. And so we might expect that persons designing a system of rules will want to make sure that the variance in outcomes does not demand more than people, living particular lives, can reasonably be expected to tolerate.

This is, in fact, what we find when real people, faced with decisions about allocation when their self-interest is not engaged, make these sorts of choices. Experiments conducted by Norman Frolich, Joe

25. John C. Harsanyi ("Morality and the Theory of Rational Behaviour," in Amartya Sen and Bernard Williams, eds., *Utilitarianism and Beyond* [Cambridge: Cambridge University Press, 1982], pp. 39–62) has argued that, in a circumstance like the original position, utility maximizers would maximize the average expected utility. Although individuals would vary in their actual allocations, their expected values would all be equal.

26. I am indebted to Jeremy Waldron for pointing this out.

Oppenheimer, and Cheryl Eavey[27] show that real individuals, confronted with a choice of regimes under circumstances that approximate Rawls's original position choose neither the maximin strategy of raising the floor as high as possible nor the expected-value strategy of maximizing the average. Instead, groups of individuals overwhelmingly agree to maximize the average with a floor constraint, a strategy that favors utilitarianism only after the system provides contractarian guarantees against losing badly.[28] Real individuals, it seems, are willing to trade off some of their average benefits in order to get a guarantee that they will not fall below a certain level. But they are not so risk averse that they would sacrifice any possibility of gain to be guaranteed the maximum possible floor.

Other evidence about how people view the variance in outcome that they are willing to tolerate can be gleaned from studies of fear of crime. These studies are likely to approximate more closely the sort of high-stakes gamble that we ask people to imagine when designing the rules they live under. Often those who are most afraid are those who have the lowest probabilities of being victimized; in particular, women and the elderly are more afraid than men and the young, even though the latter groups are much more likely to be the victims of crime. One possible interpretation is that the fear evidenced by women and the elderly keeps them out of situations in which they are likely to be victimized and that this fear therefore causes the lower victimization. But, on the basis of 130 interviews with Manhattan residents that I conducted in 1975, another explanation seems more plausible. People adjust their fear not to the *probability* that they will be attacked (since they either do not often know what these probabilities are or can not figure out what to make of small probabilities in the first place) but estimate their fear as if they were answering the question, *If* I were attacked, what would be my chances of fighting off an attacker?[29]

27. Norman Frolich, Joe A. Oppenheimer, and Cheryl L. Eavey, "Laboratory Results on Rawls's Distributive Justice," *British Journal of Political Science* 17: 1–22 (1987) and "Choice of Principles of Distributive Justice in Experimental Groups," *American Journal of Political Science* 31: 606–636 (1987).

28. Whether the experiments really approximate the conditions of Rawls's original position is clearly questionable, given that it is difficult within the bounds of ethical experimentation to force people to consider having everything in their lives be at stake at once, as the holistic approach requires. It is more realistic to imagine that an experiment like this can approximate a piecemeal contractarian strategy, in which one chooses a particular legal rule given a backdrop of knowledge about how the society is organized.

29. Evidence for this view comes from Kim Lane Scheppele, "Patterns in Fear of Crime on Manhattan's West Side" (unpublished senior thesis, Barnard College, 1975);

People are more afraid when they compare their strength against the strength of likely attackers and see that they are likely to lose a lot. The fact that being attacked is a small-probability event matters less to people than the fact that, given an attack, they are likely to suffer a great deal.

Together with the other experimental evidence, the way people decide how afraid to be of crime may serve as a model for considering the sort of variance people are willing to tolerate in the distribution of goods and bads. It is not the probability of finding oneself in a disastrous state that makes people want some guarantees against catastrophe. Instead, the probability that, *given a dreadful situation,* one would lose a *lot* seems to motivate concern for a guarantee of a floor beneath which one cannot fall. But, as the experimental evidence indicates, where there is a possibility of coming out ahead, people want to be able to take their chances, as long as they are buffered from catastrophe. People are willing to tolerate some variance as long as they are protected from losing so much that their situations would be untenable.

In the absence of strong reasons to assume otherwise, we should assume that our hypothetical decision makers, faced with a choice of rules while not knowing how they themselves would fare under them, should be similarly motivated. The empirical evidence indicates that real people demonstrate that they want guarantees against falling far when things go wrong. But they will also want to be able to have the chance to win or lose, within the limits associated with having a reasonable floor. If the individual turns out to be lucky or clever, she should like to take advantage of this fact. If she is not so lucky or clever, she should like to be protected against catastrophic failure.

The rational individual with this motivational structure will be led to distinguish, in the specific case of secrecy, between those secrets that cause a great deal of harm and those secrets that cause only minor damage. On this view, secrets that would create a catastrophe should be disclosed and secrets that have small effects should not be. This tells us what the rules should be in the extreme cases. Under *negative* contractarianism, the law ought to guarantee that people will not fall below a tolerable level as a result of harm caused by secrets. Any rule that failed to incorporate that condition would not generate the consent required for contractarian justification. But the empirical evidence also gives us reason to make a negative contractarian case for limits in

---

and Arthur L. Stinchcombe, Rebecca Adams, Carol A. Heimer, Kim Lane Scheppele, Tom W. Smith, and D. Garth Taylor, *Crime and Punishment: Changing Attitudes in America* (San Francisco: Jossey-Bass, 1980), particularly chap. 3.

the cases that are *not* so extreme. In that vast middle range of harm, where individuals may want to take their chances, legal rules should guarantee that, at a minimum, the gambles that people take are fair ones or else they will not want to take their chances. Let us develop this argument.

What chances will people be willing to take, once they are protected from catastrophic losses? Individuals, deciding before they know which position they are going to be in when disputing over disclosure of a secret, would be willing to tolerate some uncertainty—but only if they know that they have *some* nontrivial chance to win. They have to have some sense of what the odds are and how those odds are stacked in order to fit their calculations about what to do into a rational framework; without this, they are helpless in the face of hidden knowledge. But more importantly, since the individuals whom we are describing are people who want to make lives for themselves by using their powers and talents, they will want to be able to *do* something to improve their chances of coming out ahead. With the exception of small-stakes lotteries (which are blind gambles), people do not generally like being at the mercy of forces out of their control, especially when the stakes are large (as they would be in the secrecy cases). If there is nothing that a person can do to better her lot while there may be something that a secret-keeper can do to make the situation quite dreadful for her, then potential targets of secrets will want protection. When targets are at the mercy of secret-keepers and do not have the information that they would need to be able to protect themselves against the secret-keeper's wiles, they have lost critical control over the things that matter to them. And in such situations, knowing that something is a gamble and that people often take gambles is no comfort. It is the *choice* in taking a gamble that people want, not simply the gambles themselves; and any legal rule that would force people into such gambles would be objectionable. Secrets to which people would consent must be secrets that are open to efforts at discovery.

This would lead rational decision makers to distinguish, as we .
did in chapter 1, between deep and shallow secrets. Deep secrets, those secrets that those kept in the dark do not know about at all, are unresponsive to effort.[30] One can be clever and still not learn about deep secrets because one does not even know that there might be informa-

---

30. Although deep secrets may be discovered by luck, rational individuals would want to be protected against them anyway because one does not know, if the luck does not come along, how to go about making the expected value calculations necessary for making *any* rational decision under uncertainty.

tion out there that matters. One cannot rationally choose to search for information that, from the searcher's perspective, does not exist.[31] Shallow secrets, on the other hand, are secrets about which the target has at least some shadowy sense. One knows enough of their existence to be able to decide whether a search will be worth the effort.[32] Shallow secrets will be responsive to effort, in the sense that rational individuals can make decisions to search or not search for information. There is still risk involved (one may miss the information in a search or underestimate how valuable the knowledge actually is), but at least the decision problem is not completely intractable. As long as the secret is shallow, one has some chance of being able to triumph.

With this conceptual framework, then, we can analyze the situation that rationally choosing individuals would face in selecting rules about secret-keeping. For simplicity, we will talk about the two-person case, but in a situation where there are unlikely to be emergent properties in the game from coalition formation or different interests, we should be able to determine what the structure of rules should be. Two individuals, A and B, can choose one of the following four rules: (a) A and B must both disclose their secrets, (b) A must disclose while B does not have to do so, (c) B must disclose while A does not have to do so, or (d) A and B both may keep their secrets.[33] This choice is represented in the game structure shown in figure 4.1.

Regardless of whether the secret is shallow or deep, A will always prefer alternative II to all others and will prefer alternative IV the least. A would rather be able to keep all of her secrets while making B disclose all of his. Since the problem is symmetric, B, of course, would

31. We can see this problem by thinking about the structure of rational choice as seen in Bayesian decision theory. For people to learn in successive Bayesian trials, they must at least have some prior probability that can be updated with new information. If the prior probability is zero, then learning can never take place because the mathematical operation that performs the updating is multiplication. Multiplying zero by anything produces zero. A deep secret can be defined as information for which the prior probability of its existence is zero; the target of the secret does not know that the secret exists. I am indebted to John Chamberlin for pointing out the relevance of Bayesian statistics in this connection.

32. In Bayesian language, shallow secrets are those pieces of information for which one can estimate a prior probability. One may, of course, be wrong when deciding in probabilistic contexts (after all, there is still some probability that the least likely conceivable event will actually be the one that happens)—but at least one knows enough to set up the problems.

33. Note that what A and B are choosing are not cells in the figure but regimes of rules represented by each cell. A and B are each choosing from a list of four options, and the option that they are most likely to agree on will determine the regime of rules that they will face.

Figure 4.1   The Structure of Direct Secrets.

		A	
		Disclose	Not Disclose
B:			
	Disclose	I	II
	Not disclose	IV	III

Note: I–IV are regimes of rules rather than outcomes in particular plays of the game.

prefer alternative IV to all others, with alternative II being the worst. If A and B have to agree on a regime of rules, however, neither of these solutions is likely to emerge as the answer, because the problem is symmetric while alternatives II and IV are not. There would be no reason for A to agree to B's first choice; nor would there be any reason for B to agree to A's first choice. The symmetry of the game forces the mutually agreed-on solution to take the form of either I (both disclosing) or III (both hiding).[34]

In the choice between alternative I and alternative III, both A and B would want alternative I if the stakes are very high and alternative III if the stakes are very low.[35] But when the stakes are in-between, the distinction between deep and shallow secrets becomes critical. If A and B anticipate that the secret will be deep—and hence will not be open to their efforts—then they would both prefer alternative I to alternative III; that is, whenever the secret is unlikely to be one that they can rationally calculate to seek on their own, they would both want to be protected. By definition, deep secrets present circumstances in which individuals would not be able to defend themselves against strategic behavior on the part of others, and so there is no possibility of the targets *ever* winning in such a case when they are on the wrong side of such secrets. Consequently, rational individuals would prefer that others disclose, even if it means that they themselves have to disclose similar information in turn. Forbidding deep secrets prevents one party from taking advantage of another who cannot defend herself.

34. One major source of theoretical bite in the Rawlsian framework is precisely that it rules out asymmetric choices. If symmetry is an important element of fairness, then this is a large step.

35. If the stakes are very low, then it would make sense to say that these cases should not be subject to legal judgment at all, because the time and effort and expense that it would take to resolve these cases would delay resolution in cases in which the stakes were much higher and the need for relief more immediate. People who want protection against catastrophe would also want institutions to respond quickly to serious losses.

With shallow secrets, however, rational individuals of the sort described above would want to take their chances on winning, as long as they were buffered from failing too badly if losses incurred in trying to win got too big. When people indicate that they are willing to tolerate variance in outcomes, they are saying that they are willing to take a fair gamble. In the case of shallow secrets, rational deciders would prefer alternative III to alternative I because they would know enough in these situations to be able to make expected-value calculations to determine whether their interests would be served by searching for the information. With the possibility of winning open to effort, they might be able to gain. If they had to disclose all their information, they would never be able to win. With a system of rules providing incentives for searching in those cases where the ignorant parties are capable of doing so, we might expect that more information would be discovered than would be the case under a regime where all information had to be immediately disclosed. Allowing shallow secrets enables the presence of enough incentives to encourage rational searches and to promote the discovery of information.

Not all shallow secrets ought to be acceptable, however. If A and B begin their search for information at radically different starting lines, then the person beginning with the disadvantage would be taking a much bigger risk of losing—and rational individuals choosing rules would wish to ensure against being at such a disadvantage. That would make the gamble they are taking seem not fair. People facing this situation would want a rule permitting shallow secrets only under those circumstances where neither A nor B started with a large advantage. Moreover, A and B would want to be protected if either one of them turned out to be incompetent and unable to make a rational choice. Shallow secrets allow the search for information to be open to effort, thus permitting individuals to make gains at least some of the time; but individuals who start off hobbled at a disadvantageous starting point would want to be able to recover when they fail. Having a floor constraint here means that such individuals should be allowed to recover in law not only when the stakes are high but also where the probabilities of suffering medium-sized losses are very high.

If the law reflected this sort of rational decision making in a strategic structure, then one would expect the law to always require disclosure of secrets that would seriously injure someone. And one would expect the law to always require disclosure of deep secrets, except when the stakes were very small. The law should *not* generally require disclosure of shallow secrets, unless the two parties in the transaction had started under such different circumstances that the information was not equally open to their efforts. Finally, in all these transactions, the law should protect from their own bad judgment those individuals unable to make rational decisions at all.

Serial and Shared Secrets

As we saw in chapter 1, serial secrets occur when A confides in B who then has a choice about telling C. Shared secrets occur when A and B jointly create a secret as against C, and A or B then have a choice about telling C. Both of these problems present three sets of interests, instead of the two we considered in the case of direct secrets. Moreover, the three sets of interests are not symmetrical, as were the interests of A and B in the direct-secret case. In the case of serial secrets C does not necessarily benefit from the flip side of the same rules that help A; nor does B necessarily stand to gain from the inverse of the rules that work to the advantage of either A or C.

As before, we can make some progress in resolving this problem by asking which rules would be chosen by rational A's, B's, and C's if they did not know in advance either which role they would play in any given case or how often they would play each role in the aggregate. Again, people want to be buffered against serious losses but want to be able to take their chances as long as they have some chance of winning.

The structure of the game tree for serial secrets is outlined in figure 4.2. We need to think about this problem in sequential form, because first A must decide whether to disclose to B, and only then can B decide whether to disclose to C. The symmetrical 2×2 matrix used for analyzing direct secrets unfortunately does not capture the structure of three-party secrets.

We can start by assuming that C wants to find out A's secret from whatever source is available. For C to want the information, the information must be *relevant* to some concern of C. Let us assume that A has an initial monopoly on the information, that A is the only one who knows the secret.[36] If A decides not to disclose the secret to B at all (option III in the first step of the decision tree), then the serial secret collapses back into a direct secret. If C wants to find out the secret, C has to go directly to A; and the rules that applied in the direct-secret case therefore would apply here.

---

36. As was noted in the last chapter, the more widely dispersed the information initially the less likely it is to remain secret. If A is not in sole possession of the information, C may be able to acquire it from another source unconnected with A and for whom any restrictions on the disclosure of information that result from loyalty to A would be diminished.

Figure 4.2   The Structure of Serial Secrets.

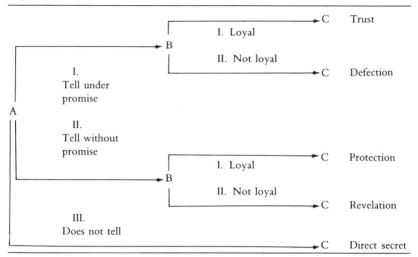

Note: Assume (*a*) that C wants to get A's secret from B and that C can establish that the information is relevant; (*b*) that the information is confidential (where, other things equal, A prefers III to II); and (*c*) that when B is loyal, C sues B—and that when B is not loyal, A sues B.

If A decides to tell B, C has another option: C can find out A's secret from B. Let us assume that when A decides to tell B, A can do so in two ways. First, A can tell B without any conditions on the further disclosure of the information (option II). A simply discloses to B without making B promise not to disclose. Second, A can tell B, but only if B promises not to reveal the information to C (option I). In this situation, A exchanges information for a promise of loyalty. The promise can be explicitly negotiated or can be implicit in the structure of the relationship between A and B.[37] We can define confidential information as information that A would prefer to tell to B only if B

---

37. A's decision to extract explicitly a promise of loyalty may be costly for two reasons: (1) the transaction costs of the negotiation (both in making the deal at the outset and in policing it thereafter) may not be negligible, and (2) extracting the promise first lets B know that there is a secret to be had. A deep secret can be converted to a shallow secret through this move, making the secret more vulnerable and perhaps requiring additional protection of the secret. A more complete representation of the problem in a game tree might include, as a separate move in the game, the decision about whether to extract a promise. For now, we can assume that such promises are costless to negotiate and police and do not affect the value of the secret itself. Relaxing these assumptions would certainly affect the calculations by A in individual cases, but it does not influence the sorts of rules that A, B, and C would agree on in advance. When the promise is implicit in the relationship, this problem would not arise because, from the ongoing routine of the relationship, B would not necessarily know that a particular secret existed to be shared.

would promise not to reveal it. In the game tree, confidential information can be described as that information for which A generally prefers option III to option II. Even with this preference structure, A may still tell B confidential information without extracting a promise if A thinks that B does not know any relevant C's (which may account for why airplane passengers tell their seat-mates so many confidential stories); if the information does not seem very sensitive to A at the time of disclosure, but later becomes so (leading the A's to want to retract what they have said after the fact); or if A slips and inadvertently reveals the information to B. Sometimes, too, there may be disagreements about the nature of the relationship between A and B, leading A to think that a specific promise is not necessary to ensure secrecy while B does not share the same view. Even though A may prefer not telling B at all to telling without a promise, then, confidential information may still be disclosed in one of these ways. Option II is still a real possibility.

If B has been told the information by A, then B has two choices. Either B can be loyal to A and not reveal the information to C or B can be disloyal and tell A's secret to C. If B is loyal after promising A not to tell, then we have a case of trust in keeping a secondhand secret. If B is loyal even though B did not promise to keep the secret, then we have a case of protection (B is protecting A by keeping A's secrets). If B is disloyal after promising not to tell, this is a defection. And if B discloses after making no promise, this is a simple case of revelation.

Obviously, A prefers trust and protection to defection and revelation. C prefers just the reverse. B may side with either A or C, depending on B's sense of loyalty and the incentives present in the situation, and may consequently adopt the preferences of either A or C.[38] B also may have preferences of her own that follow from another agenda.

But which legal rules would A, B, and C choose in advance to

38. We can think of a promise of loyalty as creating an agency relationship, if the promise is unilateral. If B has promised A not to tell C, whether gratuitously or in exchange for something other than a reciprocal promise to maintain secrets, then B can be seen as an agent of A with regard to C. But suppose that B and C were in league before A revealed the secret to B and that B has a previously established agency relationship with C. B may have an obligation to tell C after A reveals the secret. Under such circumstances, B cannot in good faith promise to A that B will keep A's secrets. If promises are reciprocal—that is, A promises not to disclose B's secrets and B promises not to disclose A's secrets—then bonds of friendship, mutual respect, or love may be strengthened. This may help to explain why one cannot buy lovers or friends but can buy agents; reciprocal promises about secrets in friendship and love must be qualitatively similar while promises in agency may exchange one good—such as the preservation of secrets—for another qualitatively different good—such as money.

deal with circumstances such as these if they did not know what their circumstances and consequent preferences would be—and if they did not even know whether they would be A, B, or C? We should first consider what rational individuals who were not able to rig the rules in their own narrow self-interest would do with the promises of loyalty that the A's would extract from the B's. If it is assumed that the promises are voluntarily made by B's,[39] rational deciders would want these promises to be enforced unless they would produce catastrophic consequences.

Because nonsimultaneous transactions of any kind are unlikely to be carried out by rational individuals in the absence of some enforcing mechanism and because nonsimultaneous transactions are essential in any moderately complex economy, the enforcement of promises is likely to emerge as a critical feature of any system of rules governing transactions. Without the ability to make transactions where one party performs and then must wait for the other party to reciprocate, much valuable exchange would be impossible. The institution of promising, then, would generate agreement among rational individuals deciding in advance.

But this institution would not be without limits. Since rational individuals desire to be protected against catastrophe, they would want to be protected if promising caused them harm, regardless of whether they turned out to be A or B or C. It would make sense, then, to say that if a particular promise caused a great deal of harm either to one of the parties to the promise or to some third party or parties, then the promise should not be enforceable. B would then have to keep promises to A, unless harm to C or others was very large. C should not be allowed to get B to break a promise of loyalty unless C or others had been badly injured as a result of such a promise (trust case), and A should be able to recover damages against B for violating confidences absent some special injury to C or others (defection case).

What would rational individuals deciding in advance choose as the rules governing situations in which B has not promised to keep A's

---

39. People who think that they someday might be in the position of B would not voluntarily agree to be forced into making such promises because involuntariness interferes with people's ability to look out for their own interests. Force and fraud would prevent such voluntary choice. (On the condition of voluntariness as it applies to promising, see Rawls, p. 345.) Note that this does not, by itself, prevent an individual from, for example, voluntarily deciding to sell herself into slavery; that situation may be prevented by providing people with a floor constraint to save them when they fall too far. Conditions of desperation may so interfere with voluntary choice that we should want to provide a social minimum to keep people from finding themselves in such a circumstance. For a similar argument, see Waldron's "John Rawls and the Social Minimum."

secrets? Generally, B would not be bound to silence and so would be free to tell C without any restriction on the part of A (revelation). In such circumstances B should be allowed to reveal A's secrets to C. But suppose that A guessed wrongly in advance in this particular case and disclosed to B, without restriction, important information, information that would now greatly harm A if revealed. With rational individuals who are deciding in advance wanting protection against catastrophe, we would expect such rational individuals to want A to recover if the situation had radically changed since the disclosure and the information would now seriously harm A.

When A and B do not have a special relationship of confidence generated by a promise of loyalty, the relationship between B and C would be just like the relationship between A and B in the direct-secret case, and the rules for direct secrets should apply. If B did not want to reveal A's secrets to C (protection), C might have some legitimate claim that would require B to disclose. In keeping with the rules for direct secrets, B should have to disclose deep secrets to C but should not have to disclose shallow secrets to C. And in either event, B would have to disclose all secrets that would cause large losses for C.

Shared secrets turn out to be very much like serial secrets. If A and B have jointly created a secret by agreeing that knowledge they have gained together is to remain hidden from others, their relationship is the same as the relationship between A and B in serial secrets when A extracts a promise of loyalty from B. A and B have established a confidential relationship because they share secret information. Confidential relationships embody agreements that prevent one of the parties from using the information gained in such a relationship to the detriment of the other party, and this is true regardless of whether the secrets are one sided (A discloses to B) or reciprocal (A and B either disclose to each other or together share secrets). Following the logic used in the case of serial secrets, we would expect that rational individuals deciding in advance would want any knowledge that had been jointly created or discovered under an agreement of secrecy to be protected from unilateral disclosure, unless the secret would cause great harm, on the theory that promises should be enforced (absent dire consequences for one of the parties to it or for a third party).

Contractarianism and Utilitarianism

Both the contractarian theory of law advanced here and the economic theory of law presented in chapter 2 may be seen, at least provisionally, as positive theories.

The economic analysis of law predicts that judges in common-law cases will use rules that maximize efficiency. In the case of secrecy, this means that judges will (*a*) provide property rights for information that, in the absence of such protection, would not be produced and (*b*) require that secrets be disclosed when the information would be produced in any event. Apart from the constraints imposed by the logic that information needs to be discovered in the first place, all information relevant to decision makers should be disclosed, even (and perhaps especially) when it harms the subject of the secret.

The contractarian theory predicts that judges in common-law cases will use rules that would have been chosen by rational individuals who do not know their own narrow self-interest in the particular case but who are deciding in advance the rules under which they would consent to be governed. All parties will be protected against catastrophic losses caused by secrets. Courts will require disclosure of deep secrets, but not of shallow ones, unless the two parties to the transaction have such different starting points in acquiring the information that they cannot be said to have equal chances of discovering it. Confidential relationships will be protected, as will individuals who are not capable of assessing what knowledge a situation requires.

Aside from the differences between a contractarian account and the economic analysis of law considered as positive theories, the two theories have radically different normative implications. The economic analysis of law, despite a dissent from Posner,[40] has a deeply utilitarian logic. Legal alternatives are disfavored when they fail to maximize some unitary end—whether that end be efficiency, happiness, or wealth—as measured in a single metric. Distributive consequences are ignored; only the totals or averages matter. The contractarian viewpoint is more Kantian. Apart from allowing more different things to be independently valued and not requiring the collapse of all potential goods into a single scale of desire, the contractarian theory of law more straightforwardly embodies those ideals that law should embody in a democracy where consent is the basis of legal and political obligation—namely, to be impartial (through the concern with symmetry), compassionate (through the provision of hedges against catastrophic loss), and just (through the triumph of principles that transcend narrow self-interest, whether of individuals or of classes). In the contractarian view, the fairness of distributive outcomes again becomes an important question for law;

40. Posner, part I.

and individuals are not trampled, or averaged out, for the common good.

The general principles that the law should embody, in the contractarian view, are liberty, equality, and community. The value of liberty is revealed in the concern that individuals should be in a position where they can meaningfully consent to the rules by which they shall be governed. When individuals cannot even frame the decision problem (as seen, for example, when deep secrets are withheld), the law should intervene to ensure that individuals have all the prerequisites of meaningful rational choice. Equality can be seen in the concern for equal starting places from which to discover information (for example, when shallow secrets are not equally open to effort). Where equality of opportunity is severely abridged, the law should intervene to ensure that individuals are not handicapped at the outset. Community can be seen in the concern for the protection of confidential relationships. Where "associative obligations" [41] have been undertaken among free and equal individuals, the law should protect these relationships unless great harm is produced by them. The triple ideals of liberty, equality, and community should, if the normative theory has positive force, be revealed when judges decide cases involving secrets. [42]

41. The phrase is Ronald Dworkin's in *Law's Empire* (Cambridge, MA: Harvard University Press, 1986), pp. 195–202.

42. This brief discussion of liberty, equality, and community disguises the fact that they are enormously complex concepts and that there are many conceptions of each. Exactly which conceptions the law embodies will be discussed in later chapters.

CHAPTER FIVE

A Theory of Legal Interpretation: The Mutual Construction of Facts and Rules

HOW DOES ONE KNOW WHETHER one theory works better than another? Ultimately, any answer to this question must rest on a theory of interpretation, however implicit or unselfconscious. A theory of interpretation is a coherent scheme for finding and organizing meaning in the world. Any particular theory of interpretation provides both a theoretical stance (in the sense that it organizes how we think about the problem of meaning) and a methodological commitment (in the sense that it gives us an answer to the question of how we know what our data tell us). In this chapter, I propose a theory of interpretation, show how it enables us to make sense of what judges do when they decide cases, and argue that it provides a reasonable method for legal analysts to use in interpreting legal texts. I use this method in the rest of this book.

On the Question of Texts

Law is an interpretive activity. The paradigmatic legal act, the framing and deciding of a legal dispute, is accomplished through the interpretation of *two* texts, a legal text and a social text. The legal text may be a prior case or set of cases. It may be a statute, an administrative regulation, or a constitution. The social text may be a social event, such as the selling of a particular house,[1] or a social practice, such as the convention that psychiatrists not reveal the secrets of their patients.[2] When judges make decisions, they decide what a specific legal text means for a specific social text, which itself is constructed to make sense in light of the legal text that is being called on as authority in the case.

1. As in *Simmons v. Evans,* 185 Tenn. 282, 206 S.W.2d 295 (1947).
2. As in *Tarasoff v. Regents of the University of California,* 17 C.3d 425, 131 Cal. Rptr. 14, 551 P.2d 334 (1976).

A text is constituted by any meaningful action, of which writing is only one example.[3] Throughout this chapter, I will use the term "text" to include written texts (such as statutes or poems) as well as unwritten texts (such as social practices or common-law rules), often called "text analogues" in the interpretive-theory literature.[4] Although there are some[5] who believe that this expansion of the commonsense meaning of text to include unwritten social forms so dilutes the term that it fails to do any interesting theoretical work, interpretive social scientists have long believed that any bounded activity that raises questions of meaning can be considered a text. What is theoretically interesting about texts is that they raise the question of multiple meanings, and it is in how one chooses among these multiple meanings that hermeneutic theories of different sorts reveal their theoretical edge. And social practice presents this dilemma just as written texts do.

Legal texts, then, are not the only things that judges interpret when they make decisions. Legal texts are generally interpreted to determine their implications for a specific empirical instance. The question that judges routinely ask is not, What does this (legal) text *mean*? but rather, What does this (legal) text mean *for this case*? And that question introduces the social text to be interpreted with the legal text.

The introduction of social texts into law does not pose as many theoretical difficulties in sorting out what a text is as does the analysis of social texts in daily life. For one thing, it is an interesting feature of Western legal practice that, in the courtroom, social events and practices exist primarily in language. The convention of taking testimony, verbal descriptions from witnesses and others, requires that those who have had some connection with the disputed event frame their perceptions in words, create texts of social practices, and present these texts to judges and juries. Although some evidence is of a nonverbal variety,

3. See Paul Ricoeur, "The Model of the Text: Meaningful Action Considered as a Text," in Paul Rabinow and William Sullivan, eds., *Interpretive Social Science: A Reader* (Berkeley: University of California Press, 1979), pp. 73–102; and Clifford Geertz, "Thick Description," in *The Interpretation of Cultures* (New York: Basic Books, 1973), pp. 3–30 for accounts of the interpretability of social practice.

4. See, for example, Charles Taylor, "Interpretation and the Sciences of Man," *Review of Metaphysics* 25: 3–51 (1971).

5. See Michael Moore, "A Natural Law Theory of Interpretation," *Southern California Law Review* 58: 277–398 (1985). Moore's position that only texts are interpretable is right, but his limitation of the notion of text to written documents such as statutes forces him, among other things, to declare that the common law is not an interpretive enterprise. It certainly is not, if interpretion only takes the form of deductive reasoning. Interpretation of social practice is both deductive and inductive—but that, I will demonstrate in this chapter, does not make it any less interpretive.

the vast majority of facts presented to courts come in the form of stories already enclosed in language. Interpretation of these stories is one of the things that judges and juries must do in the course of reaching a legal decision.

The Need for a Theory of Interpretation

This discussion may appear to beg an important question. Why do we need a theory of interpretation at all? What work can a theory of interpretation do in assessing whether the common law better fits the economic theory or the contractarian theory of law?

There is an easy answer to these questions. Determining whether one theory or another is supported by the data can only be an un-selfconscious activity when there is substantial agreement within an interpretive community[6] both about what are to count as relevant data and about what those data mean. In the more positivist portions of the social sciences, where there are substantially shared conventions about coding of data for quantitative analysis,[7] the question of what something means is rarely asked. Survey respondents, for example, are generally assumed to mean the same thing when they answer "strongly agree" to a survey question.[8] This does not mean that there are not tricky problems of meaning; it does mean that the practitioners of such research have agreed to bracket those problems—to make an assumption that the question of meaning has a fixed and unproblematic answer.

That is simply not possible in law, as a practical matter. Much of the practice of law, as well as the study of law, takes the meaning of legal opinions to be the subject of debate.[9] Opposing sides in a particu-

---

6. The notion of interpretive community is developed in Stanley Fish, *Is There a Text in This Class?* (Cambridge, MA: Harvard University Press, 1980). See also Owen Fiss, "Objectivity and Interpretation," *Stanford Law Review* 34: 739–763 (1982).

7. Although see Arthur L. Stinchcombe, *Theoretical Methods in Social History* (New York: Academic Press, 1982), chap. 1, for a discussion of coding as a theoretical activity. For one thing, one must have theories about which sorts of different things are to count as the same for the purposes of coding. These theories turn out to be very important (if generally implicit) in interpreting the results of quantitative analysis.

8. Although sometimes survey respondents' answers are "normalized" for their own particular distribution of responses. A respondent who answers "strongly agree" only once to a string of questions with a similar list of response options may mean something very different by it than does a respondent who answers "strongly agree" to every question. Normalizing the answers means taking the distance from the respondent's own mean as the measure of meaning—and not assuming that "strongly agree" meansjuthe same thing to everyone.

9. The more widely shared conventions about what laws mean are rarely litigated,

lar dispute can frequently rely on the same critical case and assert that it supports their line of argument, even when the competing lines of argument cannot be true simultaneously in any logical sense. Does *Fuller*, for example, stand for the proposition that teachers have a higher duty to be honest than others?[10] Surely the quote excerpted in chapter 1 would support that argument. Or does *Fuller* require *all* applicants for jobs to disclose anything that might be relevant to their employment? That is the way the case has generally been read. Does *Doe* support the argument that psychiatrists can never do case histories?[11] Again, the quote excerpted would seem to indicate this. Or does the case better support the line of argument that says psychiatrists cannot do case histories unless the identities of their patients are sufficiently protected? Again, this is the way the case has generally been read. The text in each instance can support both readings; the question is which argument has captured the better reading of the text.[12]

Both the legal theorist and the judge face the same dilemma in figuring out what the law implies for a particular case or whether a particular instance should be covered by a particular hypothesis or rule. The legal theorist must have a theory of what to look for in reading legal and social texts. The judge must similarly have a theory of how to read legal texts against social texts to produce a legal result in a case. For both, knowing what these legal and social texts mean is a matter of judgment, a question of interpretation within a community of discourse. There may be no single right answer to the question, What does a text mean?,[13] but the conventions within a particular

---

so one is likely to see cases and debates over meaning arise at precisely those points where the law is least clear.

10. *Fuller v. DePaul University*, 293 Ill. App. 261, 12 N.E.2d 213 (1938).

11. *Doe v. Roe*, 93 Misc. 2d 201, 400 N.Y.S.2d 668 (1977).

12. This problem exists whenever one must determine how to fit a complex piece of information into a set of fixed categories. Quantitative social science has the same dilemma, captured by legal realist Herman Oliphant ("Facts, Opinions and Value Judgments," *Texas Law Review* 10: 127–139 [1930], p. 133), writing about another profession: "The census enumerator has to struggle with the problem of what to call someone who grows and digs clams for a living—is he engaged in fishing, mining or agriculture?"

13. Some have argued that the existence of multiple answers means that legal texts are infinitely interpretable, that any reading is as valid as any other. See, for example, Mark Tushnet, "Following the Rules Laid Down: A Critique of Interpretivism and Neutral Principles," *Harvard Law Review* 96: 781–827 (1983). If texts mean nothing in particular, then the Constitution is indistinguishable from a recipe for key lime pie. This dilemma does not seem to be the one that judges face in daily practice, for their universe of interpretive possibilities is in fact a constrained one and no judge to my knowledge has ever confused the Constitution with cooking instructions. Nor has any cook to my

interpretive community may rule out some interpretations as being wrong answers. Being socialized into a community of interpretation means knowing which readings of particular texts are legitimate professional accomplishments.

Any theory about what the law "really is" must contain within it, whether implicitly or explicitly, a theory of interpretation. Arguing that a case means something *in particular* requires not just evidence from the text but also a defense against competing readings, a defense that demonstrates to the relevant audience that competing readings are not as persuasive.[14] The competition among interpretations may happen within a theory of interpretation at the level of the text, as when two interpreters who share a similar interpretive approach (for example, that the text means whatever the author intended it to mean) disagree over what a particular poem or legal opinion means. It may also happen between theories of interpretation, as when two interpreters disagree over how one interprets in the first place (when, for example, one interpreter wants to use the author's intention and another wants to use the ordinary meaning a particular interpretive community would find in the work).

A theory of interpretation, then, should help us to understand two things: (1) it should provide guidance for analysts in interpreting the texts under investigation, and (2) it should, if possible, help analysts to understand the interpretive enterprise in which the practitioners themselves engage.

In this book, I am challenging the economic analysis of law not just as a positive and a normative theory but also as an interpretive theory. Although the practitioners of the economic analysis of law have not written explicitly about *their* theory of interpretation,[15] it is implicit in the way they understand the law. In the next section, I

---

knowledge asserted that recipes reveal rights or the separation of governmental powers. The empirical fact that this does not happen should give pause to those who argue that texts can mean anything. See Frederick Schauer, "Easy Cases," *Southern California Law Review* 58: 399–440 (1985), pp. 426–430 for a similar argument.

14. E. D. Hirsch, in *Validity in Interpretation* (New Haven, CT: Yale University Press, 1967), makes the argument that persuasiveness is to interpretation what validation is to scientific method. If one can persuade one's audience with evidence, then one has validated one's interpretation. Others can challenge one's interpretation by presenting alternative interpretations and their supporting evidence. The process is rarely settled since there are generally competing interpretations that might be made, and the dominant interpretation must always fend off challengers if it is to remain successful. Of course, in many ways, scientific theories are no different.

15. Richard A. Posner has written about the way that *judges* should interpret statutes, the Constitution, and the common law. See his *The Federal Courts* (Cambridge, MA: Harvard University Press, 1985), pp. 261–315. Although Posner is himself a judge,

describe the interpretive theory implicity used in the Chicago-school economic analysis of law. I shall take Richard Posner's writings as evidence of this theory. I will then describe an alternative theory, one that focuses on the mutual construction of facts and rules and that, I argue, better captures both the interpretive nature of law and the on-going practice of judges.

The Interpretive Theory of
The Economic Analysis of Law

Following Milton Friedman, economic analysts of law of the Chicago school believe judges decide "as if" they were maximizing efficiency.[16] If judges operate as if they were deciding to accomplish a particular goal, then what they *say* they are doing is irrelevant to the analysts' interpretation of their behavior. A methodology of "as if" is free to ignore the reasoning of judicial opinions because the reasoning does not represent what is really going on in the decision. As Richard Posner writes, "[O]ften the true grounds of legal decision are concealed rather than illuminated by the characteristic rhetoric of opinions.[17]

What are these "true grounds of legal decision"? In the economic view, the true ground of legal decisions is the underlying economic logic implicit in the judgments. This economic logic is not expressed in the words of the opinion because "the language of economics is a language designed for scholars and students, not for the people whose behavior the economist studies. Poets do not use the vocabulary of literary critics, and judges do not use the vocabulary of economists.[18]

Moreover, this true ground is usually sought in the economic analyses of legal rules rather than in the economic analysis of the reasoning in particular legal decisions. The question asked in the economic analysis of law is *not* generally, Does this decision embody an economic logic? Instead, the economist asks, Does a *particular legal rule* maximize efficiency?[19] The behavior of judges as revealed in the rules they purportedly use is what the economic analyst strives to under-

the theory that he forwards is not the theory that he uses when he is being an economic analyst.

16. Milton Friedman, "The Methodology of Positive Economics," in *Essays in Positive Economics* (Chicago: University of Chicago Press, 1953), pp. 3–34.

17. Richard A. Posner, *The Economic Analysis of Law,* 3d ed. (Boston: Little, Brown, 1986), p. 21.

18. Ibid., p. 233.

19. A good quantitative measure of this concern with rules rather than with decisions can be obtained by counting the number of references to specific cases in

stand. The economists' mode of understanding is prediction—being able to guess correctly what rule the judge will use in the next case. Economics is seen as a coherent system of general covering laws allowing the analyst to deduce the rule-choosing *behavior* of judges, if not the rhetoric they use.

One problem with this view is that it misses the essentially interpretive character of the law. Certainly, there is a relationship between the outcomes of legal decisions (the behavior of judges) and the existence of a legal, particularly a common-law, rule. The former may be said to constitute the latter; a legal rule is an interpretation of what the varied legal decisions add up to. But how this interpretation is accomplished is not the subject of explicit attention in the economic analysis of law. Legal rules are, for the economist, unproblematic data; they exist as objective facts rather than as interpretive products that themselves might be modified after critical debate. How one knows, for example, that people are responsible for foreseeable consequences of negligent acts, as that rule is derived from a set of judicial opinions, is outside the frame of economic analysis, at least as it has been practiced thus far.

In addition, it is not clear how any judge, even an economically sophisticated judge, knows what a particular legal rule means for a particular case that must be decided. Although Posner urges that judges use more economics in their thinking about the common law,[20] this approach relies on judges being able to know which facts would be relevant to an economic interpretation as well as how one can achieve an economic interpretation of legal texts.[21] To do this, the judge needs to become an economist, with all the implicit interpretive conventions that come with that territory. If doing law necessarily involves work-

Posner's textbook. The 642-page third edition has references to only 146 cases, even though Posner is surveying a large fraction of American law. Most of the legal topics that he discusses are presented only as a rule; no cases are cited to support the interpretation that this is, in fact, the legal rule as used by the courts. So the theory's "predictions" of what judges do are usually presumed to be accurate if a story can be told that makes economic sense of the legal rules that judges purportedly use. (Whether the judges actually use these rules is another matter.)

20. Posner, *Federal Courts,* chap. 10.

21. Ironically, Posner's theory of "imaginative reconstruction" for interpreting statutes gives judges more guidance in knowing what to do in specific cases than his general admonition to use economic analysis in legal cases does. See his "Statutory Interpretation in the Classroom and in the Courtroom," *University of Chicago Law Review* 50: 800–822 (1983), and *The Federal Courts,* chap. 9. See Bruce Ackerman, *Reconstructing American Law* (Cambridge, MA: Harvard University Press, 1983), for a good discussion of the way in which law and economics change our sense of which facts are relevant for deciding cases.

ing within a particular set of conventions of interpretation, then it is not clear that the judge who is using the set of interpretive conventions of economics is still being a judge.

For example, suppose an economic analysis of laws forbidding baby selling (to use one of Posner's more well-known examples) produces the conclusion that it is inefficient to forbid the sale of babies (because, since there are both many couples who would like to raise children but cannot have them and many other couples who might have children but cannot or would not want to raise them, there is the potential for many advantageous trades).[22] A black market develops, but such a market is more costly to operate than an aboveboard market for babies. It would clearly be more efficient to permit a free market in babies. While such an economic analysis may be persuasive to legislators (who are free to draft wholly new laws, within the boundaries of constitutionality), such an economic analysis should not be persuasive to a judge trying to figure out what a statute means. The judge who is faced with a baby-sale case[23] arising under the purview of a state statute forbidding it cannot fail to enforce the statute on grounds of inefficiency and still be "interpreting" the law. To say a statute means whatever efficiency requires simply does not meet the requirement that an interpretation in law must be an interpretation of *that* text and not some other.[24]

The common law may be more slippery in its susceptibility to economic interpretation, since the legal texts of common law are more fluid and the interpreter is less constrained by the specific words that are used in prior cases than by the specific words of a statute. The economic analysis of law has claimed that it should have its greatest predictive strength in common-law cases, and Posner's recommendation that judges use more economic analysis in their decisions is aimed primarily at cases in which it is possible to use common-law reasoning.[25] Still, even in this situation, the use of economic analysis may

22. Posner, *Economic Analysis of Law,* pp. 137–143.

23. This construction assumes that the category of "a baby-sale case" is clear and not itself the object of interpretation. This assumption permeates conventional interpretive theories of law on the question of facts. Later in the chapter, we will take on this assumption explicitly.

24. Of course, knowing when an interpretation is an interpretation of this text and not of some other is itself an interpretive question. Ronald Dworkin wrestles with this problem in "How Law Is Like Literature," in *A Matter of Principle* (Cambridge, MA: Harvard University Press, 1985), pp. 146–166, and comes a bit closer to answering it in *Law's Empire* (Cambridge, MA: Harvard University Press, 1986).

25. Although Posner claims that many areas of law are *really* common-law areas in the sense that the law is determined as much by prior judicial opinions as by any canonical

take the judge outside the boundaries of interpretive convention, as those conventions are developed, practiced, and enforced by professional standards.

As an interpretive theory, whether directed toward economists or toward judges, then, the economic analysis of law faces difficulties. Directed toward economists, the economic analysis of law takes legal data to be legal rules—seen as unproblematic, objective facts—when legal practice would indicate that this is a peculiar view. Directed toward judges, the economic analysis of law clashes with the interpretive conventions of the judicial role. While it may be true that those whose behavior is being examined by a theory do not have to speak in the theory's terms,[26] theories whose interpretive premises are so radically different from the interpretive premises of the institution under consideration have a heavy burden of justification to bear. The concepts of coherence and predictive accuracy carry this load for the economic analyst; only because the theory gets its predictions right within a coherent framework should we take it seriously by its own standards.[27] The difficulty is that the theory does not explain how one would *know* when the theory got its predictions right.

These standards do not completely solve the problem of how we know what something means, however. In the next section, I examine the ways in which the interpretive problem has been conceived by those who have self-consciously examined the interpretive enterprise and propose a way of reading the law that enables us to distinguish whether an economic or a contractarian theory is the better description of the way judges decide cases.

A Theory of Legal Interpretation

Generally in the literature on interpretation the question being posed is, What does a particular text (or social practice) *mean*? Posed this way,

---

text. Posner claims that there are many areas of "quasi common law," including constitutional law, antitrust, choice of law, procedure and remedies, and intellectual property, among others. See Posner, *Federal Courts,* chap. 10.

26. One of my colleagues at the National Opinion Research Center once distributed a draft of a questionnaire directed to dental hygienists. The first question was, "Please estimate your job substitutability function using the following parameters . . ." The humorist who drafted the questionnaire justified it by saying that the economists would be better off if the respondents could do the estimations for them, since, after all, who knew better than dental hygienists what their job substitutability function really was?

27. As Posner writes (*Economic Analysis of Law,* p. 16), "An important test of a theory is its ability to explain reality."

the interpretive question gives rise to an embarassing multitude of possible answers, a cacophony of theories of interpretation. In this section, I ask a slightly different question about meaning, a question that (in practice) is the one actually asked in the course of lawyering and judging: what, the judge asks, does a particular text mean *for the specific case at hand*?

This apparently simple move, from asking what the text means *in general* to asking what it means *in a particular case,* has radical implications for a theory of interpretation. I will argue in this section that the "facts"[28] of a particular case constrain possible interpretations of legal texts. I will also argue that the interpretation of legal texts constrains the interpretation of facts. Interpretation in legal contexts proceeds through the mutual construction of facts and rules. We can discover the values implicit in the law, whether economic or contractarian, through studying the facts emphasized in judicial decisions.

The mutual construction of facts and rules is an iterative process in which the facts of the case determine the legal categories that will be invoked, which in turn determine how the facts will be sorted into those that are relevant and those that are irrelevant, which in turn determines which rules are to be invoked. More iterations refine these relationships, until an interpretation is constructed. The interpretation takes the form of a positive story with a normative ending, much like a story with a moral. This iterative process goes on at two stages in each legal dispute: once as each side's lawyer constructs an interpretation of the law to meet both the facts and the desired outcome as seen by that side and then again when these competing interpretations come before a court to be reinterpreted by a judge.

The best way to see this rather complicated process clearly is through an example. I will use a simple, hypothetical example from the common law. I will focus on the common law because my theory was developed in the course of analyzing common-law cases. In these cases, there is generally no single authoritative legal text that lays down a general, interpretable rule or principle. Instead, there is generally a plethora of precedent, a set of prior cases that provide support for multiple legal arguments on a particular point. Unlike constitutional or statutory interpretation, where frequently both sides agree on the provision to be construed but disagree on the meaning of it, common-

lawyers & judges

---

28. My use of the term "facts" does not imply that there is any single, unquestionable, empirical truth. Instead, as will become obvious, my approach presumes that empirical facts are like any other sort of text—interpretable, capable of multiple meanings, and indeterminate with respect to the intentions of their creators.

law litigants more typically choose *different* cases as embodying the relevant law and argue that their framing of the issue requires that case X rather than case Y serve as the binding precedent. There is often no ultimate written text to invoke to determine *which* precedent is the better reading of the law. Common-law interpretation presents a somewhat different complex of questions than does statutory or constitutional interpretation, but the basic insight that courts must interpret accounts of social practice as well as legal texts remains intact.

An Account of Lawyering

Let us assume that Jane Jones sells her house to Jim Smith. The house has termites. Jones knows this at the time of the sale and Smith does not. Smith buys the house, discovers the damage wrought by the pests, and decides to take legal action against Jones.

Smith seeks out a lawyer and describes what has happened. Smith is particularly outraged because Jones had appeared to be so nice during the whole transaction while in fact she was keeping a dark secret about the house. The secret would not have been so bad, Smith says, if only Jones had not been so cheerful about it all. Jones's false niceness is not the real issue here, says the lawyer, steering Smith back onto the path of legally relevant facts.

The lawyer ascertains that there is enough evidence to believe that Jones knew of the termite damage. Until that point, the lawyer had thought that this was probably a case of implied warranty; but now it becomes evident that there might be enough evidence to prove fraud. In addition, the lawyer knows that the local building code requires property owners to take steps to detect and control termite infestation. If he can demonstrate that Jones negligently violated the local building code and that this negligence was the cause of Smith's injury, he might have a case of negligence per se. But to demonstrate negligence per se, he must be able to show that Smith, as a buyer of real estate, is a member of the class intended to be protected by the building code. He thinks this might be difficult to argue. Okay, he says, implied warranty is a distinct possibility, but it would be even better if we could go for fraud, too.[29]

---

29. What is going on in the lawyer's mind is not just finding a legal category or set of legal categories that fit the case but also trying to get the case to fit a legal category that will allow his client to recover the maximum damages. From such a point of view, fraud, which admits the possibility of collecting punitive damages in addition to actual and consequential damages, looks much better than implied warranty, which admits only the latter two. I am grateful to Mark Brandon, who pointed out the possibility of raising

What we have seen so far might be called the process of typifica-
tion.[30] The initial naive description[31] by the potential litigant has
activated a set of legal categories in the lawyer's mind. The legal categories are tested against the raw description to find plausible fits. At
this stage, the lawyer wants to rule in as many legal avenues as possible;
each one may lead somewhere useful as the analysis proceeds. The
categories are derived from doctrine, and the facts are derived, at least
at first, from the litigant's description of the social event giving rise to
the lawsuit. The combination of the two is the first stage of the mutual
construction of facts and rules. A set of legal categories is activated by
the description, a set that in turn shapes the facts that will be taken to be
relevant. The mutual construction of rules and facts generally begins
during the first meeting of the lawyer and client.[32]

The interpretation of facts—that is, coming up with a description
of "what happened" that "makes legal sense"—is accomplished as a
dialogue between a person with the raw experience and a person with
training in professional storytelling. The description of the facts of the
case is constrained by the lawyer's view of the available courses of legal
action. The first approximation of the rules of law and their limits
constrains the first approximation of the description of the "facts."[33]

---

negligence per se in this case and who walked me through lawyers' thinking on cases such
as these.

30. The term is Gaye Tuchman's; the context is describing how journalists decide
which sort of story they are covering. Is something a fire story, a protest story, or a
political corruption story? the journalist asks. Depending on the answer, different facts are
sought, different narrative accounts are appropriate. See Gaye Tuchman, *Making News*
(New York: Free Press, 1979). Although the profession cited is different, the process is
the same.

31. The description is naive because the client generally does not know the
relevant legal categories and so the description follows narrative conventions of an
unspecialized sort. Lawyers' conventional terms for describing events are very different
from layfolks' descriptions. This is an important theme in fictional accounts of the law, as
Katherine Anne Porter's story "Noon Wine" and Susan Glaspell's story "A Jury of Her
Peers" reveal.

32. See Austin Sarat and William L. Festinger, "Law and Strategy in the Divorce
Lawyer's Office," *Law and Society Review* 20: 93–134 (1986). This article shows in some
detail how these conferences proceed and how legal categories as well as accounts of the
legal system's operation are constructed.

33. Karl Llewellyn (*The Bramble Bush* [New York: Oceana, 1930], p. 48), taking
first-year law students through this process says: "Is it not obvious that as soon as you
pick up this statement of the facts to find its legal bearings, you must discard some as of
no interest whatsoever, discard others as dramatic but as legal nothings? And is it not
clear, further, that when you pick up the facts which are left and which do seem relevant, you suddenly cease to deal with them in the concrete and deal with them instead
in *categories* which you, for one reason or another, deem significant? It is not the road

From this point on, the legal analysis in which the lawyer engages becomes more complicated. The lawyer researches the legal doctrine pertaining to those categories that have been shown to be relevant in the first iteration. Finding cases, statutes, and other relevant legal materials, the lawyer engages in the process of matching the doctrinal materials and the facts they have spotlighted with the facts at hand. The process of matching potentially relevant legal materials against the facts as described by the litigant results in highlighting certain facts, downplaying others, and omitting the irrelevant ones. This sculpting of facts[34] against the background of the legal materials produced during the research process enables the lawyer to develop theories to cover the case, theories that connect the facts with the potentially "right" legal results.

The case is then ready for its final preparation. The narrative is polished, made into a coherent story following the conventions of legal narrative.[35] The statement of the law that should apply is made into an extension of the story itself, so that the "what happened" blends imperceptibly into the "what should happen next." The result of this process, in which the facts and the rules are blended together to constitute a coherent story with a normative ending, is an *interpretation*.

An Account of Judging

In court, the interpretations of each side's lawyer come before the judge.[36] Each side presents a version of the facts along with an account of what the law requires the ending of the story to be. For simplicity's

---

between Pottsville and Arlington; it is 'a highway.' It is not a pale magenta Buick eight, by number 732507, but 'a motor car,' and perhaps even 'a vehicle'. . . . Each concrete fact of the case arranges itself, I say, as the *representative* of a much wider abstract *category* of facts, and it is not in itself but as a member of the category that you attribute significance to it."

34. It should be mentioned that this sculpting of "what happened" does not imply that the final description is false. All descriptions are partial, and the question in narrative construction is which facts to leave in and which to omit to get a "better" picture of what happened.

35. Because cases are often heard by juries, these conventions of legal narrative cannot be too different from nonspecialized conventions of narrative. In fact, it seems that the more a story "hangs together" in the minds of jurors the more likely these jurors are to believe that the whole story actually happened. See Lance Bennett and Martha Feldman, *Reconstructing Reality in the Courtroom* (New Brunswick, NJ: Rutgers University Press, 1981).

36. The process described here captures bench trials and appellate court decisions. Juries may operate similarly, although since they are technically only deciding on the facts and are not deciding on the rules at the same time, the interpretation may be primarily an

sake, let us assume that the only question the court must decide is whether fraud was involved in the sale of this house with termites.

After the arguments have been made by counsel, the judge must first decompose the facts and the rules as they have been constructed by counsel and begin the process of interpreting the facts against the rules again. As has counsel before her, the judge creates from the diverse facts presented a sculpted description. This description is sculpted in light of the legal texts that the judge, generally following the lead of the lawyers, feels are relevant. Facts in the sculpted description are matched against the facts in the legal materials to determine, within the confines of the fraud action raised by the case, to which general class of cases the termite case is similar.

To see how this is done, let us assume for the moment that no other termite cases have presented themselves in this jurisdiction. The case is a case of first impression.[37] Let us further assume that Jones argues that this case is similar to one in which a seller sold a house with a rusted staircase to a naive buyer. The buyer tried to recover money to fix the rusted staircase, but the court ruled that the buyer should have been more careful making the purchase. No recovery was allowed.[38] Smith, on the other hand, argues that the present case is like a case in which a naive buyer bought a house with a defective septic tank. The sellers of that house knew about the defect in the septic tank but did not tell the buyer. When that case came to court, the judge ruled that the buyer *could* recover the money needed to fix the septic tank.[39] Smith, of course, claims that the septic tank is like the termites, and Jones

---

interpretation of facts, not an interpretation of the intersection of the facts and the rules. But the instructions about the law that each jury hears from the judge set up the rule against which the facts are to be interpreted, so there is always a conversation back and forth between the rules and the facts. The rules are presented as uninterpretable, although whether they are treated as such is another matter.

37. This judgment requires an interpretation of facts, an interpretation that reveals that no other fact patterns are sufficiency close to count as head-on precedent in this case. But what is sufficiently close? Is a carpenter-ant case sufficiently like the termite case? What about a case with an infestation of mice? The statement that no other cases are close enough itself embodies an interpretive judgment. I am indebted to Fred Schauer for pointing out the interpretive quality of judging when a case is a case of first impression.

At the trial court level, this sifting of facts will be a much more onerous operation than it will be at the appellate court level, where the facts are assumed to be fixed and where those facts that appear unclear are resolved in favor of the winning party at trial. But see John Noonan, "The Passengers of Palsgraf," in *Persons and Masks of the Law* (New York: Farrar, Strauss and Giroux, 1976) for an example of rather dramatic changes in the facts found by an appellate court.

38. See *Riley v. White,* 231 S.W.2d 291 (Mo. App. 1950).

39. See *Rich v. Rankl,* 6 Conn. Cir. 185, 269 A.2d 84 (1969).

claims that the rusty staircase is the better comparison. How does the judge proceed?

To decide this case, the judge must examine what makes rusty staircases different from septic tanks. To do this, she looks at the other cases that have been judged to be similar to rusty staircases and septic tanks. In the rusty-staircase category, she finds that sellers did *not* have to inform buyers about recurring spring flooding,[40] about a railroad track being constructed adjacent to the house,[41] or about the high probability of a snowslide.[42] In the septic-tank category, she finds that sellers *did* have to disclose a concrete swimming pool buried in the back yard,[43] a letter from the National Forest Service indicating that the house would be demolished in two years,[44] or a judgment by a contractor hired by the original owners that, within five years, their house would probably fall off its bluff into the lake below.[45]

In the first set of cases, the rule is that disclosure is *not* required. In the second set of cases, the rule is that disclosure *is* required. Obviously, both of these rules cannot be applied at the same time. Some situations must call for the first, some for the second. Moreover, one has to be able to tell what makes situations fall under one or the other category.

The first set of cases, into which the rusty-staircase situation falls, shares a common feature that distinguishes these cases from those in the second category. In the rusty-staircase set, the defect in the property was easily visible to anyone who made a reasonably careful inspection. In the septic-tank set, the defect of the property was not obvious and in fact could not have been discerned very easily by someone not living in the house. The two general classes of situations are, then, (1) cases involving a patent defect and (2) cases involving a latent defect. In cases in category 1, disclosure is not required. In cases in category 2, disclosure is required.[46]

This interpretation of the rules and what they require is very fact

40. See *Farrar v. Churchhill*, 135 U.S. 609, 10 S. Ct. 771, 34 L. Ed. 246 (1890).

41. See *Jones v. Herring*, 16 S.W.2d 325 (Tex. Civ. App. 1929).

42. See *Doyle v. Union Pacific Railway Co.*, 147 U.S. 413, 13 S. Ct. 333, 37 L. Ed. 223 (1893).

43. See *Highland Motor Transfer Co. v. Heyburn Bldg. Co.*, 237 Ky. 337, 35 S.W.2d 521 (1931).

44. See *Kallgren v. Steele*, 131 Cal. App. 2d 43, 279 P.2d 1027 (2d Dist. 1955).

45. See *Groening v. Opsata*, 323 Mich. 73, 34 N.W.2d 560 (1948).

46. This method borrows heavily from the "moving classification system" described by Edward Levi, *An Introduction to Legal Reasoning* (Chicago: University of Chicago Press, 1949).

centered.[47] What a case, such as the septic-tank or rusty-staircase case, is taken to mean is discovered by seeing which facts are shared by cases decided the same way. The facts the similar outcomes share are immediately relevant in the next case and constrain how the rule is interpreted in the next particular instance. But since the facts mentioned in the first place were shaped by the available legal categories, we see a mutual construction of facts and rules.

Once the judge in the termite case has identified the relevant alternatives, she must still determine whether termites constitute a latent or patent defect and whether Jones knew about the damage. All other evidence is, at this point, irrelevant.[48] Jones's niceness, which so offended Smith, matters only insofar as it bears on the question of whether Jones deceived Smith knowingly. But whether Jones sold the house for cash or credit, whether the transaction took place on a weekday or a weekend, whether Smith was rich or poor, whether Jones had lived in the house or rented it out—all these things do not matter in the determination of the case. The only relevant evidence is the evidence that bears on the question of the obviousness of the termite damage and on whether Jones knew. As I have framed the case here, it is the obviousness of the termite damage that links the rules of law to the situation at hand.

Suppose the judge finds that the damage was hidden, that it would have been hard for Smith to ascertain that termites were at work on the house. In that case, the rule to be applied requires that Jones either disclose or pay subsequent damages. The judgment has been made. Termite damage in this case constituted a latent defect that, under the rule developed in previous cases, had to be disclosed or the secret-keeper could not prevail.[49]

Once the judge has decided, opinions often are written. To do

47. In this way, this method looks like that outlined by Arthur J. Goodhart, "On Finding the *Ratio Decidendi* of a Case," *Yale Law Journal* 40: 161–183 (1930). See the critical response to this influential article in J. L. Montrose, "*Ratio Decidendi* and the House of Lords," *Modern Law Review* 20: 124–130 (1957); A. W. B. Simpson, "The *Ratio Decidendi* of a Case," *Modern Law Review* 20: 413–415 (1957); J. L. Montrose, "The *Ratio Decidendi* of a Case," *Modern Law Review* 20: 587–595 (1957); A. W. B. Simpson, "The *Ratio Decidendi* of a Case," *Modern Law Review* 21: 155–160 (1958); A. L. Goodhart, "The *Ratio Decidendi* of a Case," *Modern Law Review* 22: 117–124 (1959); and Julius Stone, "The *Ratio* of the *Ratio Decidendi*," *Modern Law Review* 22: 597–620 (1959).

48. Although I did not present the cases here, proving fraud requires demonstrating that the seller knew about the defect that the buyer later discovered.

49. The question about damages will not be addressed here, although a real judge would still have this to consider.

this, the description of the facts must be polished, and the law is applied as a normative ending to a positive story. The written record that results is the judge's *interpretation* of the law for this case.

Discussion

This rather lengthy example illustrates several more abstract points. Judgments in common-law cases are justified by showing how the particular case is an example of a general class[50] to which a particular rule applies. Invoking a rule involves also invoking the set of circumstances under which the rule applies, circumstances that must be defined as abstractions from the particular facts of the particular cases to which the rule might be applied. One must explain the rule that leads to the conclusion that Y wins. And to demonstrate that the rule in fact applies in a given instance, one must express the rule in terms of the features of the dispute that make it relevant. So one says that, in situations defined by the legally relevant facts a, b, and c, this rule Q will apply. X and Y are in a situation that presents conditions a, b, and c. Therefore, since the rule Q states that when there are parties of type X and Y and conditions a, b, and c parties of type Y will win, so Y should win here. The interpretation requires a constant conversation between the facts and the rules.

Returning to the issue raised at the beginning of this section, we now can see the importance of asking the interpretive question in terms of particular instances rather than in general. If we ask what a particular legal text means *in this case,* rather than what it means *in general,* the interpretive problem is not nearly so indeterminate as it seems to be when framed in general terms. The more information there is on the way in which rules and facts have been linked before, the less indeterminate the problem of legal interpretation is.

In the sorts of common-law contexts described here, we really have two sets of texts: one is the set of legal texts, here a set of precedents; the other is the set of texts of social practice, circumstances that might count as legally relevant facts. The facts initially taken to be part of a coherent legal account of an event are selected with reference to the available set of legal rules. These legal rules are then interpreted with reference to both the set of facts that have arisen under them before and

---

50. Saying that a case is a member of a general class only invokes legal categories here. There is still the additional question, which I do not address here, of what the relation is between these legal categories and categories of fact in the world.

the way in which the present set of facts has been framed. The rules and the facts construct and constrain each other.

Implications for the Study of Law

As it has been described here, the process of legal interpretation as accomplished by legal professionals takes facts seriously, interpreting rules in light of facts and facts in light of rules. How should legal analysts then interpret what legal interpreters have done?

The first thing legal analysts should do is to also take facts seriously, carefully unraveling what the legal interpreters have woven together to see how the patterns are formed. The study of legal interpretation is the study of the way in which the general and particular find a common home in narrative. Judicial decisions are not merely statements of law; they are statements of the way in which law and fact are joined, and each cannot be made sensible without the other.

We should ask, in examining the legally relevant facts that emerge from the study of judicial decisions, Why these facts and not some others? What is it that makes these facts the normatively relevant ones? Why do these facts emerge, through all the sculpting and polishing, as the truth in this instance?

The study of facts reveals what the law values. In order for the positive account of what happened to blend into the normative account of what should happen next, the facts in the positive part must be selected to make certain normative answers follow without difficulty. The choice of which facts to emphasize determines how the story line will pull. In the example of the termite-ridden house, the emphasis on the hidden quality of the damage and Smith's difficulty in discovering it leads effortlessly to the conclusion that the information should have been disclosed. If the emphasis had been instead on the commonness of termites in that geographic area or on the fact that Jones did not prevent Smith from inspecting the house, the story line would pull a different way. The process of matching legal texts against social texts, matching by demonstrating the similarity of one set of facts with another, determines which pull is stronger in any particular case.

This observation should help us to understand the gap between the result reached in formal law and the particular legal dispute as perceived by the litigants. The process of sculpting and polishing facts creates a particular version that the litigants may not have seen, even if, in retrospect, all the elements of the formal legal version were clearly there. To the extent that this process of the legal construction of facts moves the account of what happened away from the accounts of the litigants, they may perceive the legal decision as being far removed from their lives. The perceived gap between law on the books and law in action may simply reflect the difference between facts in their raw form and facts in their judicially polished form.

TO RETURN TO THE QUESTION raised at the beginning of this chapter— that is, How can we know whether one theory fits the data of the law better than another?—an answer can now be seen. We can tell that one theory of law (for example, the contractarian one) is a better positive theory than another (for example, the economic theory of law) when it can account for the facts that are selected to be sculpted and polished by judges.

The economic and contractarian theories have already been framed in terms of the facts that each would take to be relevant in secrecy cases. The economic theory would take the distinction be- tween casually and deliberately acquired information as central: When information is deliberately acquired, no disclosure should be required; when information is casually acquired, efficiency requires that it be passed along regardless of the objections of the subject or the potential discloser, unless the disclosure would make transaction costs too high. The contractarian theory takes as central a distinction between deep and shallow secrets, a concern for equal opportunities to acquire infor- mation, and the preservation of relationships of trust and confidence: When information is the subject of a deep secret or is more easily acquired by one party than another, then it should be disclosed; when secrets are shallow or when the information can be equally easily acquired or is intimately connected with a relationship of trust, then it should not be disclosed. In the contractarian theory, these rules are modifed when great harm would be the result of applying them strictly.

The test of the economic analysis of law against the contractarian theory should depend on which set of facts is relevant in court deci- sions. Judges do not have to speak the language of economists, or even that of contractarians, but in the cases that come before them they at least have to notice the facts that the economist or the contractarian would have them see. Without a mechanism linking theory with evi- dence, an explanation hovers above the phenomena that are its object like horoscopes over the lives of Virgos. We believe theories not just when they enable us to guess correctly at least some of the time but when we can see what would make them work.

In the chapters that follow, I examine the legally relevant facts in the areas of fraud, privacy, trade secrets, and implied-warranty cases, arguing that the values of the law are revealed in the facts that courts select to highlight.

Coda: How Law Is Not Like Literature

Interpretive theorists of the law have recently looked to the varieties of literary interpretation to get their bearings on method.[51] In this chapter, I have used against the economists some of the arguments familiar to literary critics; but I also want to suggest that, in some of their own endeavors at legal interpretation, literary critics may have misread the character of the law. Despite the popular view that law is like literature, there are several critical ways in which it is *not*.

Literary texts are not "applied" in the way that legal texts are. The paradigmatic legal question is not, for example, What does the requirement that latent defects must be disclosed *mean*? (in the way that we might ask, What does *To the Lighthouse* mean?) but rather, Is this a case covered by the requirement that latent defects must be disclosed (a rule that itself is a generalization from the interpretable facts of other cases), and what does this requirement mean for the specific issues raised in this case? This is not the sort of exercise literary critics generally engage in, although both literary and legal interpretation are clearly concerned with finding meaning in texts. Interpreting legal texts against social texts so constrains the enterprise that it is quite fundamentally different from interpreting literary texts by themselves. Although *applying* the law is an interpretive matter, not all interpretation is application.

In addition, legal texts are not written by individuals acting as literary authors—that is, authors writing in their own voices. Literary texts are generally (although not always) written by specific, proper-name, identifiable authors (or, in the case of anonymous texts, are presumed to be so). Legal texts, whether written by legislators or judges, are written by individuals acting within specific roles in specif-

---

51. The extraordinarily rapid rise of literary criticism as a force in legal theory has been marked by a *Texas Law Review* symposium on "Law and Literature" (1984), by the works of James Boyd White (*The Legal Imagination* [Chicago: University of Chicago Press, 1973], *When Words Lose Their Meaning* [Chicago: University of Chicago Press, 1984], and, most recently, *Heracles' Bow* [Chicago: University of Chicago Press, 1986]; and by the movement of Stanley Fish to the Duke Law School. Dworkin's "How Law Is Like Literature" and his theory of interpretation presented in *Law's Empire* show the influence of literary theory on jurisprudence. Talk of "discourse" is everywhere in the law these days. Although not all of it was imported into legal language by literary critics, they have had a significant influence.

ic institutions. Their proper names are subordinated to their offices, as it were.[52] Although literary interpretation might reasonably take the author's intention as central,[53] legal interpretation does not need to take the author's intention so seriously. Not only are the authors of legal texts generally numerous and not perfectly agreed on what the text means (in fact, the text may be vague and more open in places precisely because the authors could not agree), but the authors of legal texts are acting within roles that infuse their work with meaning. The meaning of a legal text is in part a function of the institutional traditions of interpretation.

Writing *as a judge* means that one is writing not just on behalf of oneself but also on behalf of an institution. The intention of an independent writer and the intention of an institutionally constrained writer are not equally determinative of the meaning of the texts they create.[54] Texts written by institutionally constrained writers must be read against the backdrop of the institution's conventions of meaning. One of these conventions might be that the intent of the author matters; but the structure of legal institutions should reveal that this is not the case in law. Courts are organized so that as decisions become more important for doctrinal purposes, there are more and more judges who hear each case, to check the tendencies of judges with unusual viewpoints. The rotation of judges in panels and across types of cases indicates that judges are *supposed* to be interchangeable, that the outcome one gets should not depend on which judge heard one's case.[55] The structure of courts should give us a clue that, in the case of judicial

52. Of course, some judges become so famous that their opinions are read as statements of the judge's own legal theory. Still, even these judges (and sometimes especially these judges) have a vision of judicial role that makes what they write as judges often different from what they would write if they were composing unconstrained texts on social policy.

53. This is a topic of heated debate in literary circles these days. See W. J. T. Mitchell, ed., *Against Theory: Literary Studies and the New Pragmatism* (Chicago: University of Chicago Press, 1985) for the critical article by Michael Knapp and Walter Benn Michaels that gives the collection its title and for a collection of other articles in this controversy.

54. To be a bit flip, if authors' intentions matter then surely their intent to write on behalf of an institution should tell us that we need to look at more than what was in *their* minds!

55. Of course, we know as an empirical matter that judges to differ in the opinions that they hold and in the decisions that they make. But if one is looking to develop a theory of interpretation that reflects institutional structure and captures the best meaning of the institution of judging, then a reading of an opinion that deemphasizes its author is more in accordance with the structural framework within which judges decide.

decisions, the author's intention should matter less than the institutional framework and legal culture within which the decision is made.

The interpretations of legal texts have consequences in the world, so the relation between the text and the context must be central to any consideration of the meaning of the text. While this relationship *may* be explored in some literary analyses, it *necessarily must* be explored in legal analyses. How the categories and concepts of the text map into the world, how they are informed and shaped by ongoing patterns of social practice *may* be part of a literary analysis; but courts *must* confront such issues.

Literary interpretations are not enforced;[56] legal interpretations are. Knowing that interpretations have real consequences for real people (who, because of such interpretations, have to pay fines, go to jail, or whatever) means that legal interpretations must be concerned with legitimacy. This is the point of the contractarian theory developed in this book. Having an interpretation that incorporates the views of those against whom legal rules are enforced increases the legitimacy of the institution. Literary critics do not have quite the same worries— and, as a result, having unusual interpretations may be a sign of particular talent. In law, unusual interpretations are often suspect. They must be mapped against the values of the culture, however conflicting and conflicted. The fact that a legal dispute has reached a court at all often reveals a lack of consensus about what the law is, so talk about interpretive communities needs to include the possibility of the great gulfs of understanding both within and between them. The idea, fashionable in literary circles these days, that communities of interpreters should talk until they have agreed on an interpretation and that agreement will always happen if they talk long enough simply cannot be presumed in legal contexts. Someone always gets someone else's interpretation enforced against them. Examining the rules of law against the facts of particular cases requires judges to come face to face with the conflicting claims, with the basis of these claims in the social community and in the law and with the implications of ruling against a particular claim.

How we interpret law as opposed to literature must be influenced by these real differences. Reading legal texts against social texts, seeing interpretation as the mutual construction of rules and facts, maintains the connection between law and life. Law is, after all, an empirical

---

56. One might argue that they certainly are in departments of English and in standards of review for professional journals and judgments.

discipline that draws its cases not from imagination but from the real pain and sorrow of daily life. If legal interpretation does not stay close to this reality also, it runs the risk of becoming unintelligible, irrelevant, and, in the long run, illegitimate. And there are far worse dangers in abandoning the correspondence between legal interpretation and the social practice that grounds the rule of law than there are in abandoning favored interpretations of literary texts.

THREE
Understanding Fraud

CHAPTER SIX
The Nondisclosure Puzzle and Equal Access to Information

THERE IS AN OLD SAYING: "What you don't know won't hurt you." Clearly, this maxim is wrong in many cases. People often withhold information from others to manipulate the attitudes or actions of those who do not know. When withholding information results in innocents believing or behaving differently than they would have with full information, harm is often the result. The knowledgeable and crafty can benefit at the expense of those who do not know. In any investigation of the legal norms regarding secrecy, the legitimacy of these strategic secrets must occupy center stage.

The area of common law that is concerned with the legitimacy of strategic secrets is fraud, located at the boundary of contract and tort. Within the broader area of fraud, a smaller group of cases examine, under the general heading of actionable nondisclosure, when keeping secrets becomes fraudulent.

Not all strategic secrets create a legal cause of action. One cannot sue another person simply for withholding information.[1] One must demonstrate that one suffered an identifiable loss as a result of the secret. Courts then determine whether the loss will stay where it fell or whether the costs of that loss will be shifted back to the secret-keeper. In this section, I will describe the rules that guide this process of shifting or not shifting the costs of loss when strategic secrets cause harm.

At first, the cases in this area present a puzzle: sometimes nondisclosure is permitted (that is, the secret-keeper is not liable for the

---

1. Sissela Bok (*Secrets: On the Ethics of Concealment and Revelation* [New York: Pantheon, 1982]) observes that no one could have sued the *New York Times* for *not* publishing the Pentagon Papers. The requirement that strategic secrets be material acts as a threshold rule in the law, screening out those cases that do not present an identifiable harm. I will discuss materiality in the next chapter.

harm that befell the target) and sometimes it is not (that is, the secret-keeper bears the loss). Cases that share certain strong similarities are decided in opposing ways.

George Spencer Bower, writing a substantial treatise on the subject of actionable nondisclosure in 1915, concluded after his detailed investigation that the cases stood on no coherent set of principles: "The present work contains no . . . code. I made an attempt in this direction; but the result was not at all satisfactory, and I was soon convinced that the subject does not lend itself to this mode of treatment. The concepts and principles involved are too fluid and delicate to justify the Procrustean extension or compression which would be necessary to fit them into the rigid framework of a code."[2]

The best way to illustrate the nature of this puzzle—and why the patterns in these cases have escaped identification—is with descriptions of real cases. To simplify matters at the outset, I will present two pairs of cases. Within each pair, the cases show strong similarities; but the courts decided each differently. To further simplify, each pair of cases that will be presented has been decided in the same jurisdiction. Two are U.S. Supreme Court opinions and the other two were decided under the state law of California. Because, in each pair, the law under which the cases are decided is the same, one would not expect a divergence based on the invocation of different rules.[3] Still, the cases have been found to be hard to reconcile.

When the Buyer Knows More than the Seller: Cases from the United States Supreme Court

In chapter 1, we encountered *Laidlaw v. Organ*. Hector Organ, hearing before most others of the signing of the Treaty of Ghent, purchased a large quantity of tobacco from the Peter Laidlaw Company without disclosing his special information. The Supreme Court ruled that Organ did not have to disclose the information, as long as he did not "impose upon the other."[4] This strategic secret was acceptable in law.

In *Strong v. Repide*[5] the secret also involved speculation on the

2. George Spencer Bower, *The Law Relating to Actionable Nondisclosure and Other Breaches of Duty in Relations of Confidence and Influence* (London: Butterworth, 1915), pp. v–vi.

3. Cases involving fraud and nondisclosure generally arise under state law because they implicate contract or tort rules. Occasionally, these cases are found in federal courts in diversity actions.

4. 15 U.S. (2 Wheat.) 178, 195 (1817).

5. 213 U.S. 419, 29 S. Ct. 521, 53 L. Ed. 853 (1909).

actions of the U.S. government, this time in the Philippines. Repide was the chief shareholder, director, and general administrator of the Philippine Sugar Estates Development Company. The U.S. government decided that it wanted to buy the "friar lands" of the Philippines and began negotiating with the owners of this land for purchase. The lands owned by the Philippine Sugar Estates Development Company were among the properties to be bought by the U.S. government. In his capacity as general administrator of the company, Repide was also the chief negotiator in talks concerning the purchase of the land.

Strong and others were the owners of shares of stock in the company. Although the intentions of the United States to buy this property were well known, the negotiations were conducted in secret. Several offers made by the governor of the Philippines were accepted by the other shareholders, but Repide, owning 30,400 of the 42,030 outstanding shares, was always able to block the sale.

Repide knew from the tenor of the negotiations that the United States was willing to pay much more than the price that had been offered. He wanted to hold out for the maximum, but he knew that the other shareholders were willing to sell at the current offering price. Unbeknownst to the shareholders, Repide sent out agents to buy the other shareholders' shares for him. The shareholders sold out to Repide's agents, although they later claimed that, had they known these buyers were in league with Repide, they would never have made the deal; they claimed that they would have understood, from the mere fact that Repide was interested in buying their shares, that the value of the stock was about the rise substantially.

Strong, in particular, owned 800 shares, which he sold to Repide's agents for $16,000. A little more than two months later, these same shares were worth $76,256 when Repide finally sold the property to the U.S. government. Strong sued Repide to recover the gains that Repide had made at Strong's expense.

Unlike *Laidlaw,* in which the Court had ruled that a strategic secret was permitted, the Court here decided that a similar secret was *not* acceptable. Even though, in both cases, someone was engaging in speculation resulting from actions of the U.S. government and even though, in both cases, the buyer in the transaction withheld critical information about the impending change in value of the good exchanged from the seller, the Court reached a different conclusion.

In *Strong* the Court made much of the fact that Repide was the negotiator: "No one knew as well as he the exact condition of such negotiations. No one knew as well as he the probability of the sale of lands to the Government. No one knew as well as he the probable price that might be obtained on such sale."[6] The Court reasoned that the shareholders never would have sold to Repide had they known what he knew—or even if they had known that they were selling to Repide. As a result, the Court indicated that Repide should have disclosed his information and should not have been able to benefit at their expense.

The outcomes of *Laidlaw* and *Strong,* taken together, are puzzling. There are strong elements of similarity:

1. In both cases, the buyer was withholding information from the seller.
2. In both cases, the information withheld pertained to the impending increase in value of the thing exchanged.
3. In both cases, the increase in value was dependent on actions of the U.S. government, which was not a party in either case.
4. In both cases, the goods were bought by agents whose connection to the information was disguised from the seller. (The tobacco seller did not know that Organ knew the merchants who had been with the fleet; Strong did not know that the person who bought his shares knew Repide.)
5. In both cases, the parties who sold in ignorance knew that there was a possibility of a change in the situation. The tobacco seller knew that a treaty would probably be signed at some point, raising the price of the tobacco; Strong knew that the United States was still negotiating for the land.

The differences between the cases are not terribly illuminating at first glance either:

1. In *Strong* the transaction took place between director and shareholder, while in *Laidlaw* the transaction was between two tobacco merchants. This difference fails as a sufficient reason because the Court, in *Strong,* specifically denied that directors have any duty of disclosure to shareholders per se that is greater than their duty to anyone else.
2. In *Laidlaw* Organ's knowledge of the change in value was definite, while in *Strong* the shares were purchased before the deal had been closed and Repide did not know for certain what the final value would be. If anything, one

6. 213 U.S. 419, 432.

would think that this difference would lead to the opposite result; that is, when one has sure knowledge that one is taking advantage of another's ignorance, one should have to disclose relevant information, but when one has only speculative knowledge, one should be allowed to take one's chances. The Court's decisions went in precisely the opposite direction.

3. In *Laidlaw* Organ appeared to have acquired the information quite accidently, however fortuitously, while in *Strong* the knowledge that the United States was willing to pay more than already had been offered was clearly the result of Repide's hard work bargaining in the negotiations. Again, one would think, especially given the analysis of Kronman's article,[7] that this would lead to the opposite result; that is, when people have worked hard to acquire their knowledge, they should be allowed to use it to their advantage, but when people happen on fortunate information, they should not be rewarded for mere luck. There is certainly no evidence that Organ sent on their mission those who traveled with the British fleet and subsequently acquired the critical information, an action that would have demonstrated Organ's diligence in getting the information first. And yet the Court allowed him to profit while punishing Repide for his successful efforts at bargaining. There is clear evidence that Repide was driving a hard bargain and expected a large return as a result.

The similarities seem to speak louder than the differences. And yet the Court heard the differences.

When the Seller Knows More than the Buyer: Cases from the California District Courts

In *Dyke v. Zaiser*[8] City Councilman Albert Zaiser owned a storeroom in Oceanside, California, and he decided to convert this storeroom into an amusement center. He rented space to a number of different concessions, and the amusement center eventually housed an ice-cream stand, a hamburger stand, and a group of Digger and Lite-a-

---

7. Anthony Kronman, "Mistake, Disclosure, Information and the Law of Contracts," *Journal of Legal Studies* 7: 1–34 (1978). See extended discussion of this article in chap. 2.

8. 80 Cal. App. 2d 639, 182 P.2d 344 (4th Dist. 1947).

Line machines. The Lite-a-Line machines had been invented by John Dyke, who operated several of the concessions.

Zaiser decided that he wanted to rent out the concession business, and he approached Dyke about signing a lease. Dyke, who lived in Pasadena, came to Oceanside to look over the amusement center, and he and Zaiser negotiated a lease. The deal was closed on 18 December 1944.

On 19 December 1944, the chief of police of Oceanside, along with a deputy sheriff, appeared at the amusement center and ordered the closing of twenty-two of the thirty-two concessions in the building. The result was that most of the concessions moved out, leaving Dyke with an average monthly income of only $410.87. His rent to Zaiser was to be $2,000 per month.

Dyke discovered that Zaiser knew that the police were getting ready to crack down on concessions of this type. Zaiser had done his own investigation, checking with the police chief to determine whether anything was going to happen to his business. Because Zaiser was a town official, the police chief apparently felt free to confide in him that the concessions were to be raided. This information was not available to others who asked. Dyke sued Zaiser, seeking recission of the lease.

The District Court of Appeals of the Fourth District of California held that Dyke could be released from his lease with Zaiser. But the court's opinion relied on the way in which the negotiations proceeded. The court took note of the fact that Zaiser both had told Dyke what he himself had been making on the concessions and had given Dyke every reason to believe that this income would continue (and maybe even increase) in the future. The court noted that there was no general obligation for sellers to tell buyers about the subject of the sale (or lease in this case) but that once Zaiser undertook to express an opinion on the future income to be derived from the business he was obligated to tell all that he knew.

The court also argued that Zaiser's position as a city councilman gave him a better chance of acquiring the information:

> Zaiser, as a city councilman, it seems to us, was, by virtue of his position, in a much better position to know that those concessions might be closed by the Chief of Police of Oceanside, and that in fact they were going to be closed. It is not likely that if respondent [Dyke] had inquired of the District Attorney or the Sheriff or the Grand Jury, they would have informed him that on a day certain he was to be raided and closed,

and if his operations were legal, respondent would not be expected to make such inquiries.[9]

Thus, although Dyke was an expert in the concessions business, he could not have know that the police were about to raid the amusement center, since there were no local ordinances forbidding such concessions. Zaiser, on the other hand, could more easily inquire and find out about the impending raid.[10]

In *Jappe v. Mandt*[11] Mandt owned and operated a rubbish collection service, which he decided to sell in 1952. Part of the business, the part that served Imperial Village, was bought by two men who owned a welding shop, leaving the largest route, that which served the city of Hawthorne, to be bought by Jappe. Before Mandt and Jappe concluded the deal, Mandt allowed Jappe to inspect the customer files, to audit the accounts, and to conduct a full investigation of the business.

The city of Hawthorne, as matters turned out, was contemplating letting a contract for the disposal of combustible rubbish, a move that would have made Mandt's Hawthorne rubbish route worthless. Jappe contended that Mandt knew this and should have informed him, given that this development changed radically the value of the business.

The District Court of Appeals for the Second District in California decided the case by questioning a finding of fact by the superior court (the trial court). Although the superior court found that Jappe knew about the letting of the contract, the district court argued that the evidence indicated that Jappe did *not* know about the possibility that the route might be up for bid before the deal with Mandt was closed.

What is interesting for our purposes, however, is the dictum that accompanied this opinion. It is clear that the court wanted to make a statement about what the outcome of the case would have been had Jappe been able to demonstrate that Mandt knew, before the deal was closed, about the possible actions of the City Council of Hawthorne.

The court pointed out that the city council had not yet decided whether to put the rubbish route out to bid. "The idea," wrote the court, "was still at the conversation and rumor stage."[12] Most of the

---

9. 182 P.2d 344, 351.

10. Just why the police raided the establishment and under what authority they did so is left a mystery in the opinion written in this case.

11. 130 Cal. App. 2d 426, 278 P.2d 940 (2d Dist. 1955).

12. 278 P.2d 940, 942.

members of the city council had not committed themselves publicly one way or the other as of the time of the sale. In addition, the court noted, the parties to the sale were dealing at "arm's length" [13] and there was no fiduciary relationship between them. Jappe had every opportunity to make a full investigation of the business. The court wrote: "Under such circumstances defendant was not legally bound to tell the prospective buyer of any rumors or reports that were 'in the wind,' that the City might 'possibly' enter this field." [14] Clearly, even if it could have been demonstrated that Mandt knew what little there was to know at the time, Jappe would not have been able to recover damages on the basis of Mandt's failure to disclose.

As do the first pair, these cases show strong similarities:

1. In both cases, the seller was withholding information from the buyer.
2. In both cases, the information pertained to a pending action of a local government, an action that would radically reduce the value of the business.
3. In both cases, the actions of the city were not written into ordinances that could have been consulted.
4. In both cases, the party who bought the business knew quite a lot about the business itself. (Dyke invented machines and had operated several of them at the concession. Jappe had gone through all of the accounts of Mandt's buiness and had conducted an audit of the operation.)
5. In both cases, the buyer was taking over an ongoing business whose operation could be affected at any time by actions of the local government.

The differences deserve attention as well. The *Jappe* court explicitly distinguished *Dyke* by noting the following facts:

1. In *Dyke* Zaiser knew that the action to close the concessions was definitely going to happen, while in *Jappe* the information that the city was going to put the route out for bid was merely a rumor the credibility of which no one could have known for certain. If certain knowledge has to

13. 278 P.2d 940, 943.
14. 278 P.2d 940, 943.

be disclosed while rumors do not, then this might account for the difference.[15]

2. In *Dyke,* Zaiser knew of the impending raid on the amusement center because he was a city councilman. The ordinary citizen could not be expected to know and also could not be expected to be told about this, even if the explicit question were asked. In *Jappe,* if it is assumed that Mandt had the knowledge, then Mandt would have heard about the council's potential action by virtue of living in the city and being privy to those rumors which were "in the wind"[16] and therefore available to all who paid attention. Zaiser had information limited to a very few; Mandt would have had information available to all.

This second difference between the cases—the difference between those who have inside information not readily available to others and those who have information available to anyone who cares to find out—turns out to be the key to the contractarian theory that will be developed in the next section, a theory that, I will argue, gives us a more persuasive account of the doctrine than the economic view does.

Equal Access as a Theory of the Doctrine of Nondisclosure

The contractarian analysis in chapter 4 explained what legal rules might look like if they followed a contractarian logic. Contractarians would expect that judges would (1) provide a buffer from catastrophe when losses are large, (2) require disclosure of deep secrets and (3) ensure that, when secrets are shallow, both parties to a transaction have equal access to information. The first two expectations are straightforward, but the idea of equal access to information needs more clarification.

Contractarianism focuses our attention on the importance of equal access to information because in those cases where the two par-

---

15. Interestingly enough, when this reasoning is compared with the reasoning in the first pair of cases, we find that it is inconsistent with what we found there. In *Strong* and *Laidlaw* vague knowledge had to be disclosed although certain knowledge can be hidden. In *Dyke* and *Jappe* the vague knowledge did not have to be disclosed but certain knowledge did.

16. 278 P.2d 940, 942.

ties to a dispute are not taking the same fair gamble, the disadvantaged party will have good reason to object. If the law embodies such a concern, then, if we follow the argument in chapter 5, we should find that judges will emphasize facts that highlight inequalities in such access when they find shallow secrets unacceptable. Saying that the law guarantees that all parties will have equal *access* to information is *not* equivalent to saying that all the parties will have the same information in every case. Equality of access is not equality of information. But just what equal access *does* mean requires some explanation.

Two actors will be said to have equal access to information if they (1) have equal probabilities of finding the information if they put in the same level of effort and (2) are capable of making this equivalent level of effort. To take one example, two people would be said to have equal access to today's headlines because each could buy a newspaper, turn on the radio, watch the television, or listen to conversation on the street. Given equal levels of effort, the two people could probably discover the news. Also, most people would be capable of making this effort. This does not mean that the two people will have the same information (one may prefer to listen to a baseball game; another may have too many other obligations to pay much attention to the news). But should each actor want to know the news, each would have to put in roughly the same effort to acquire it; and the existing distribution of the news is such that most people would be capable of doing so. Equal access does not require that effort will always be successful; it only requires that equal effort is rewarded with equal *probabilities* of success. One person's lucky break does not interfere with equal access as long as the other person with whom she deals has faced the same chance of a fortuitous fate. This, of course, will be often hard to determine in individual cases because the determination will rely on some tricky counterfactual thinking, but that does not mean that the problem is always—or even usually—intractable.

Equal access may fail for these same two reasons. Two people may not have equal probabilities of finding the information. The main systematic reason why people may not have equal probabilities is that they may be differently situated with respect to the social distribution of knowledge. They may have *structurally* unequal access to knowledge. Structurally unequal access to information occurs when one actor can obtain information more easily than another actor can—and can do so because she holds some special position that provides a shortcut, as it were, to finding out the information. Two people would be said to have structurally unequal access to knowledge if, for example, one had a top-level security clearance at the Defense Department and the other did not. The person with the security clearance would find it much easier to find out about planned movements of aircraft carriers in the vicinity of Central America than would the outsider without the security clearance. When two actors would have to invest quite different levels of effort to acquire the same information, then they have unequal access to the information. If this difference in the level of effort that would have to be expended to acquire information is due to differences in the two actors' structural positions, then they would be said to have structurally unequal access to information.

In addition, the two actors may not be equally capable of making the effort required to find the information. This unequal capacity can occur because one actor (1) does not even know that the knowledge exists to be sought out while the other does (the problem of deep secrets),[17] (2) has fewer resources—and so cannot invest what it takes to acquire the information while the other can (the problem of economic inequality), or (3) has less intellectual ability or social experience to begin with and so is unequally matched with more savvy partners (the problem of unequal facility). Two actors may have very different preferences, with one preferring to acquire news about Great Britain and the other preferring to concentrate on American football, but this does not influence *capacity* to find information. Preferences, of course, influence each person's likelihood of searching for the information in the first place, but they do not generally affect the probability of finding the information once a search is begun. Only those factors which influence the probability of success, once the desire to find out is present, count as influencing capacity.[18]

The contractarian theory says that the law will not require disclosure of information in those cases where the two actors involved have equal access to information. The law *will* require disclosure in those situations where the two actors, whether because of some structural inequality or because of some lack of capacity on the part of one of

---

17. In this way, the problem of deep secrets also can be seen as a special case of structurally unequal access to information.

18. The relation between access to knowledge and preferences is actually more complicated than this if one's preferences are dependent on elements of capacity, such as what one already knows, one's economic welfare, or one's intellectual or social facility. Some of the time, at least, preferences are almost surely dependent on these things. See Jon Elster, "Sour Grapes," in *Sour Grapes: Studies in the Subversion of Rationality* (Cambridge: Cambridge University Press, 1983). Also, capacity may depend on preferences, as revealed in the evidence demonstrating that people see what they expect to see. See Elizabeth Loftus, *Eyewitness Testimony* (Cambridge, MA: Harvard University Press, 1979). Again, in any individual case, one must do the best that one can at untangling the sometimes circular effects of these elements.

the actors, have unequal access to information. The actor with superior access will have to disclose to the actor with inferior access. These concepts—and the theory itself—will be clarified as we consider the situations in which secrets are and are not permitted.

Returning to the four cases outlined in some detail at the beginning of this chapter, we can start to see how this theory would fare. None of the four cases involves a deep secret; nor do they involve catastrophic loss. We would, then, expect the cases to turn on issues of equality of access to information. In *Laidlaw* and *Strong* the situations presented to the Court were very similar; but in *Laidlaw* the Court permitted a secret, and in *Strong* the secret was not allowed. The critical difference in these two cases was the two parties' relative access to the information in question. In *Laidlaw* both Organ and Laidlaw's agent were tobacco merchants. Each could have been equally alert for news from the British fleet; each could have equally cultivated contacts among the merchants who were with the fleet when the news was reported. It seems that Organ got his information through a friend who had a brother in the know. Laidlaw's agent, if he had had the same fortune, also could have got the information in this way. The Court itself seemed to recognize this, for in its exceedingly short opinion it explicitly stated that disclosure should not be required in cases of this sort because it would be difficult to draw appropriate boundaries around this duty in situations "where the means of intelligence are equally accessible to both parties." [19] Although the facts of *Laidlaw* are rather sketchy, and although any interpretation necessarily relies on some speculation, the theory forwarded here gains some support from the fact that the Court explicitly noted that equality of access to information was a key issue.

Strong differs from *Laidlaw* primarily in the superior access of Repide to the information that he used as a strategic secret. It will be recalled that Repide was the chief shareholder, a director, and the general administrator of the company that was negotiating to sell land to the U.S. government. He was also the chief negotiator. His secret consisted in his knowing that the price that the United States would be willing to pay was higher than the offers that had been made so far. Those whose interests he bought did not have this knowledge—and, moreover, it would have been very difficult for them to find out, since the negotiations were conducted secretly. Repide clearly had structurally superior access to information; he was in a better position to

19. 15 U.S. (2 Wheat.) 178, 195.

acquire this knowledge because of the position he held as negotiator for the firm. Again, the court explicitly recognized that this was important in the determination of this case, for its opinion made special note that "no one knew as well as he" [20] the information that he used as his strategic secret. The distinction between *Strong* and *Laidlaw,* then, is precisely the distinction between structurally superior and equal access to that information that is the subject of the secret.

We can find the same distinction at work in *Dyke* and *Jappe.* Despite the fact that in both cases the seller did not disclose impending actions of a local government that would radically change the value of the business being sold, the California district court ruled that Zaiser should have disclosed information about the impending police raid while Mandt did not have to disclose the possible change in Hawthorne's rubbish-disposal situation. [21] The difference lies in the relation of each pair of parties to the information. Zaiser was a city councilman and knew of the police raid because he checked around and asked the police chief. Even if Dyke had done identical research, it was very unlikely that the police chief would have told him about the raid. The court explicitly said, "It is not likely that if respondent [Dyke] had inquired . . . they would have informed him." [22] On the other hand, "Zaiser, as City Councilman . . . was *by virtue of his position,* in a much better position to know." [23] The court obviously wanted the case to turn on this question of structurally unequal access to knowledge.

In *Jappe* the same principle is carried through. The information in question—that the city of Hawthorne was contemplating letting contracts for rubbish disposal, was "in the wind." [24] It was a topic of general discussion that all the residents of the community were likely to hear. It will be recalled that the court found not only that Mandt had not, in fact, been aware of the information and was therefore not obliged to tell Jappe but also that, even if Mandt had known, there still would have been no obligation. As the court noted, Jappe had full opportunity to find out all the facts. The court in *Jappe* explicitly

20. 213 U.S. 419, 432.
21. It may be possible to see this as a deep-secret case, depending on the legal basis for the police raid on the place. If there were no clear grounds in law for the police to conduct the raid, then we would not expect someone buying the business to know to include such a possibility in their calculations; if there were such grounds, then the relative ease of acquiring information would matter.
22. 182 P.2d 344, 351.
23. 182 P.2d 344, 351; emphasis added.
24. 278 P.2d 940, 942.

distinguished *Dyke* on the grounds that Zaiser had special knowledge by virtue of his position.

We can see from these pairs of cases, then, that cases which seem to present very similar fact patterns can be distinguished on the ground that the parties in question did or did not have equal access to information. When the two parties have equal access, the courts do not require disclosure if one of the parties took advantage of the opportunity to acquire information and the other did not. Actors are allowed to use their strategic secrets only if the secrets could be rediscovered with the same effort that it took to create them. If the parties have unequal access to information, and if one actor finds out more easily than another actor could have, the courts require that the knowledgeable actor disclose this information. If the parties cannot be on equal footing with respect to access to information, the court requires that they be put on equal footing with respect to actual information possessed.

Comparing Contractarian and Economic Theories

The equal access theory, with its contractarian roots, can already be seen to provide a better account of the case law presented thus far than does the economic theory of law, with its utilitarian logic.

Kronman, in his economic theory, argues that the distinction between deliberately acquired information and casually acquired information makes sense of the outcome of most of the cases. When the information is the product of a deliberate search, disclosure will not be required; otherwise, incentives to search for valuable information will be destroyed. When the information is casually acquired and no special incentives are needed to produce the information in the first place, disclosure will be required. This does not seem, from what we have seen thus far, to be what is going on in the case law.

The case that Kronman uses in the greatest detail to illustrate his point, as we saw in chapter 2, is *Laidlaw*. To deal with the fact that Organ apparently did not conduct a deliberate search to find out the information, Kronman argued that courts only require disclosure in cases where most information of *the type at issue* is casually acquired. Disclosure is not required in those situations that, *in general,* tend to involve information that is the product of a deliberate search.

The result in *Laidlaw* is explained, then, by a reliance on the empirical claim that most knowledge of changes in market conditions is the product of a deliberate search. Aside from the fact that it is not clear that the empirical claim is correct (for example, a great deal of market information comes from experience working in markets or from casual conversation, something that people would presumably continue to do even if there were not this additional benefit), it is also not clear why courts would be reluctant to ask whether someone searched for or stumbled on the information. This is a fact that seems no more difficult to ascertain than the other factual questions that the courts routinely determine anew for each dispute presented to them. It does seem peculiar the courts would, on the one hand, consider this distinction between casually and deliberately acquired information to be so important in the determination of these cases and yet, on the other hand, find it inconvenient to ask how the information was actually acquired. It should be remembered that *Laidlaw* was remanded to the trial court to determine whether Organ had, in fact, lied to Laidlaw's agent. The Supreme Court could have easily asked, while the lower court was at it, for a clearer statement of the way in which Organ came by his information, if that were considered relevant. Administrative costs—the main reason that likely would be used by the economic theory of law to explain why courts would not search for such information—did not appear to be much of an issue in this case.

Kronman's theory fares little better with *Strong v. Repide*. While it could be argued that Repide gained his special information as an incidental by-product of his being the negotiator, it must also be mentioned that, because he owned a majority interest in the land under negotiation, Repide had every incentive to become the negotiator and to gather information about the reservation price offered by the United States. It could very well be that this motivation—to do research and to gain as much control over the eventual selling price as possible—led to his hard work in the negotiations. Doubtless, he did things during the negotiations purely for informational purposes. He knew that the United States had not made its final offer, and he acquired this knowledge as the result of hard work. Repide found out all he could in the negotiations in order to assess the value of his interest, but he also found that the same knowledge came in handy in evaluating the value of others' interests as well. Why was Repide's secret disallowed? Deliberate acquisition alone cannot make sense of this result.

The case of *Dyke v. Zaiser* presents another problem for Kronman's theory. Apparently, Zaiser had to do some detective work, so to speak, to find out that the place would be raided; the information did not just fall into his lap because he was a city councilman. Doubtless, as the court noted, if he had not been a city councilman, he probably would have not been able to find out the information at all. Still, the court refused to let him benefit from his secret, even though this secret was the result of deliberate acquisition. *Jappe v. Mandt,* in which the seller would have heard about the information "in the wind," involved casually acquired information, did not require disclosure, and is the only case of the four that we have examined that would fit Kronman's theory with no difficulty. Kronman's theory, at first pass, does not seem to handle easily the case law in this area.

But theories should not rise or fall on the basis of four cases specially selected to illustrate the dilemma. In the next chapter, I explore a wide range of cases in this area and identify the general pattern of legally relevant facts. In the chapter that follows, I argue that the contractarian theory gives a better account of the law on this subject than the economic theory does.

CHAPTER SEVEN

Legally Relevant Facts in Fraud Cases

WHAT FACTS ARE RELEVANT IN the resolution of legal disputes over secrecy? From an analysis of a sample of cases in this area[1] and from an examination of the secondary literature on nondisclosure and fraud, I have discovered seven major categories of fact that judges highlight in their descriptions of disputes.

The Importance of Material Information

Not every secret can be the subject of a lawsuit. Inequalities in access to information are everywhere, and courts would encounter a sort of legal gridlock if all unequal information could be the subject of litigation. To prevent this, focusing litigation on just those cases where identifiable harm has occurred, courts limit the sorts of secrets that are actionable to those where the information is material to a particular transaction. The requirement of material information serves as a threshold that must be crossed before the law takes notice.

Just what is meant by "material" is a subject of some debate. The *Restatement (Second) of Torts* indicates that when a person is under an obligation to disclose information, that person must disclose

> only those matters that he has reason to know will be regarded by the
> other as important in determining his course of action in the transaction
> at hand. He is therefore under no duty to disclose matters that the
> ordinary man would regard as unimportant unless he knows of some
> peculiarity of the other that is likely to lead him to attach importance to
> matters that are usually regarded as of no moment. [2]

1. For the sampling design, see the Appendix.
2. American Law Institute, *Restatement (Second) of Torts* (3 vols.) (St. Paul: American Law Institute Publishers, 1977), vol. 1, p. 2.

The *Restatement (Second) of Contracts* takes a slightly different approach, explaining that

> The materiality of a representation is determined from the viewpoint of the maker [of the contract and] may be met in one of two ways. First, a misrepresentation is material if it would be likely to induce a reasonable person to manifest his assent. Second, it is material if the maker knows that for some special reason it is likely to induce the particular recipient to manifest his assent. [3]

Both of these restatements seem to be agreed that materiality has to do with the probability that the fact, if known, would alter the transaction in question. If the ignorant party might have behaved differently had the fact been known, then the fact can be said to be material.

Where the problem enters is that some authorities claim that the fact omitted must be material, while others indicate that the fact must be basic.[4] Basic facts are more material than material facts, it would seem. Whether the standard to be used in "basic" or "material" depends on whether the case sounds in contract or tort. Complicating this is the older and now apparently superceded distinction that some authorities have been made between intrinsic and extrinsic facts.[5] As Story explains it,

> Intrinsic circumstances are properly those, which belong to the nature, character, title, safety, use or enjoyment of the subject-matter of the contract; such as natural or artificial defects in the subject-matter. Extrinsic circumstances are properly those, which are accidently connected with it, rather bear upon it, at the time of the contract, and may enhance or diminish its value or price, or operate as a motive to make or decline the contract; such as facts respecting the occurrence of peace or war, the rise or fall of the markets, the character of the neighborhood, the increase or diminution of duties, or the like circumstances.[6]

Intrinsic circumstances generally are considered material and therefore

3. The *Restatement (Second) of Contracts* (3 vols.) (St. Paul: American Law Institute Publishers, 1979), vol. 2, p. 442.

4. See Eric M. Holmes, "A Contextual Study of Commercial Good Faith: Good-Faith Disclosure in Contract Formation," *University of Pittsburgh Law Review* 39: 381–452 (1978) for a review of this debate.

5. See W. Page Keeton, "Fraud—Concealment and Nondisclosure," *Texas Law Review* 15: 1–40 (1936), especially pp. 20–21, and Joseph Story, *Commentaries on Equity Jurisprudence as Administered in England and America,* 12th ed., rev. by Jairus W. Perry (Boston: Little, Brown, 1877), pp. 208–210.

6. Story, p. 210.

have to be disclosed while extrinsic circumstances are not considered material and as a result do not have to be disclosed. This distinction was important in the *Laidlaw* tobacco case[7] since the treaty to end the war was considered an extrinsic circumstance, less likely to be associated with a duty to disclose. But aside from *Laidlaw* and the cases that have cited it, there is little use in the current case law of the distinction between intrinsic and extrinsic facts.

The subject of materiality appears frequently in the cases, if only to establish that the case in question is properly before the court. The confusion between material and basic facts seems to be one of the problems with locating the area of nondisclosure at the intersection of contract and tort. Each standard uses slightly different criteria, but the basic point is the same: materiality places a limit on the duty to disclose, a limit that confines disclosure to those facts which bear directly on the transaction in question.

This is not much of a limitation, as the cases show. In *Kaas v. Privette*[8] Privette sold Kaas some stock in a company that Privette once had owned privately, withholding from Kaas, an employe, that the financial situation of the company was not as sound as it appeared to be. This was held to be a material fact, and Privette's conduct was found to be fraudulent. In *Musgrave v. Lucas*[9] a letter from the U.S. War Department threatening litigation against Lucas's company was held to be a material fact when Lucas sold the company to Musgrave without telling Musgrave of the letter.

Those cases which do find a fact at issue to have been not material seem to rely on the existence of narrowly drawn contracts as evidence that particular information did not matter. In *Bellwood Discount Corp. v. Empire Steel Building Co.*[10] Bellwood sued Empire for failing to disclose that the building that Empire was constructing for Bellwood failed to meet the city building code. Because it was found that the part of the building that did not meet the code was not covered in the contract between Bellwood and Empire, Judge Fox ruled that these facts were not material to their agreement.

In another case involving an explicit contract, *Smith v. Onyx Oil and Chemical Co.*,[11] Smith contracted for Onyx to sell Revitex, a product that he had invented to be used in the dry-cleaning and chemical

7. *Laidlaw v. Organ*, 15 U.S. (2 Wheat.) 178 (1817).
8. 12 Wash. App. 142, 529 P.2d 23, 80 A.L.R. 3d. 1 (1974).
9. 193 Or. 401, 238 P.2d 780 (1951).
10. 175 Cal. App. 432, 346 P.2d 467 (2d Dist. 1959).
11. 218 F.2d 104 (3rd Cir. 1955).

business. The initial meeting between Smith and Onyx had been arranged by one Harris, who also set up the demonstration of the
product at his plant. At the last minute, Onyx tried to pull out of the
deal, claiming that Smith had withheld from them the fact that Harris
would share in the profits paid to Smith under the contract. The court
noted that Onyx should not have been surprised that Harris was "a
character in this drama" [12] and that whatever Smith chose to do with
his profits was "no concern of Onyx." [13] This side agreement was not
a material fact because the contract between Smith and Onyx did not
cover what Smith was allowed to do with the profits.

It should not be surprising that courts care about whether secrets
are material, even apart from the concern to prevent a flood of litigation. For a strategic secret to be possible, the knowledgeable actor
must know some fact that would be relevant to the ignorant actor's
choices and that the knowledgeable actor knows would be relevant to
those decisions. This is almost the very definition of materiality. Unless the secret influenced or was likely to influence the ignorant actor's
attitudes or actions, it could not be a strategic secret. And only those
secrets which do so are considered the proper subject for lawsuits.
Clearly, the courts here want to single out strategic secrets for special
attention.

The Status of the Parties: Buyer and Seller

Most of the authorities who have written about these cases over the
years have noted that whether the party keeping the secret is the buyer
or seller in a commercial transaction seems to make a difference in the
outcome of cases. Buyers do not have to disclose special information
that sellers sometimes have to divulge.

W. Page Keeton discussed this problem at some length. In the
absence of a confidential or fiduciary relation with the buyer, sellers, he
pointed out, have no general duty to disclose. In a few areas, however,
sellers must disclose information, although these areas still constitute
the exceptions rather than the rule. Sellers generally have to disclose
information about latent defects likely to produce harm, about conditions likely to constitute a breach of warranty, or about the defective
condition or title of real property. [14] Buyers have to disclose much less.
As Keeton wrote, "In general, the buyer has not been held for fraud in

12. 218 F.2d 104, 109.
13. 218 F.2d 104, 110.
14. Keeton, p. 14–20.

failing to disclose circumstances which make the property much more valuable than the vendor thinks, and this is true regardless of whether the fact concealed is intrinsic or extrinsic, whether it is open to observation or concealed, and whether the vendor is negligent or not negligent in failing to know of its existence." [15]

One reason for this disparity was elucidated in the early part of the century by John Norton Pomeroy: "The law assumes that the owner has better opportunities than any one else to know all the material facts concerning his own property, and is thus able under all ordinary circumstances to protect his own interests." [16] Pomeroy noticed that the law seems to have different standards for buyers than for sellers, and he attributed this to the fact that ownership generally gives someone a better chance of finding out information about the things that they own.

Writing more recently, Eric M. Holmes also noted that "a buyer . . . is generally held to a lower standard of disclosure than is a seller," [17] although he attributed this difference to differences in what counts as good faith for people in those positions. William B. Goldfarb, too, considered the differences in the duty to disclose imposed on the buyer and seller: "I concluded that he [the vendor] is 'hardly ever' under such a duty [to disclose information]. When we turn to the other side of the vendor-purchaser relation and inquire as to the duty of the purchaser to make such disclosures we find that he is 'almost never' under an obligation to do so. The distinction between 'hardly ever' and 'almost never' is a real one." [18] Goldfarb argued that the reason why there might be such a difference in obligation is that the seller is more likely to have information about the good than is the buyer. If the tables are turned and the buyer has information that the seller could not obtain, then the buyer might have to disclose. This rarely happens, however.

We have already seen, in the last chapter, that both buyers and sellers are sometimes required to reveal their information and sometimes allowed to keep their secrets. There are more cases in which sellers are forced to disclose than cases in which buyers are forced to disclose, however. Most of the cases involving buyers are similar to *Laidlaw,* in which the buyer both knows that a good is worth more

15. Ibid., p. 21.

16. John Norton Pomeroy, *A Treatise on Equity Jurisprudence as Administered in the United States of America* (3 vols.) (San Francisco: Bancroft-Whitney, 1901), p. 1274.

17. Holmes, p. 448.

18. William B. Goldfarb, "Fraud and Nondisclosure in the Vendor-Purchaser Relation," *Western Reserve Law Review* 8: 5–44 (1956), p. 26.

than it appears to be worth and fails to disclose this information to the seller.

Holly Hill Lumber Co. Inc. v. McCoy[19] presents a good example of this class. McCoy owned some land near the Atlantic Lime Company mining area, although he claimed he had never noticed the existence of the extensive mining operation located near his property. He contracted with Holly Hill to sell his land and later found out that he could have gotten a lot more for his land if he had known that it was likely to have lime deposits also. He wanted to rescind the contract, over Holly Hill's objections.

Holly Hill, as the buyer of the property, was found to have no obligation to disclose information about the mine. Both parties were experienced businessmen, the court noted, and each should have been aware that the other would bargain to maximum advantage. The court wrote, in particular, that buyers cannot be forced to disclose their reasons for believing the property to be valuable. McCoy could not recover his property under these circumstances. Other cases with similar fact patterns—that is, cases in which the buyer knows some hidden fact about the property—tend to be decided similarly. Rarely is the buyer obligated to disclose information. *Strong v. Repide*[20] is unusual in this regard.

If a duty to disclose is found in a sales transaction, it is generally the seller who has to reveal his secrets. In *Dyke v. Zaiser*[21] Zaiser had a legal obligation to reveal that the police were about to raid the amusement center that he sold to Dyke. Similarly, in *Kallgren v. Steele*[22] Steele had a legal obligation to reveal that the National Forest Service was about to close down the Bear Creek Lodge that Steele sold to Kallgren.

In *Groening v. Opsata,*[23] the case of the disappearing house, Groening bought from Opsata a house on a bluff overlooking Lake Michigan. One year after the house was purchased, the bluff on which the house sat fell into the lake, taking the house with it. Opsata had said that the house was perfectly safe, and since there was ice and snow on the ground when Groening bought it, Groening could not check Opsata's claim. Clearly, this is a case that involved an intentional misrep-

19. 201 S.C. 427, 23 S.E.2d 372 (1942).

20. 213 U.S. 419, 29 S. Ct. 521, 53 L.Ed. 853 (1909), discussed in the previous chapter.

21. 80 Cal. App. 2d 639, 182 P.2d 344 (4th Dist. 1947), discussed in the previous chapter.

22. 131 Cal. App. 2d 43, 279 P.2d 1027 (2d Dist. 1955).

23. 323 Mich. 73, 34 N.W.2d 560 (1948).

resentation, and the court ruled against Opsata as a result. Even if Opsata had not lied, however, the court indicated that it would not have allowed this secret, because this was information that Opsata should have disclosed, according to the decision. Reasons *why* Opsata was bound to disclose this information were not given, however. It should be clear that sellers are often in a better position to make false representations than are buyers because sellers are likely to know more in the first place. Consequently, courts are often in the position of finding that sellers should have disclosed their true information.

It should be remembered, however, that Goldfarb said sellers "hardly ever" had to disclose their knowledge. In a great many cases, buyers are left to fend for themselves. In *Balogh v. Sacks*[24] Balogh bought a lot from Sacks with the intention of building a house on it. Soon after Balogh took possession of the lot, he discovered that there was an eighteen-inch gas line concealed under the ground at a depth of about three feet and running the entire way across his land. He could not build the house that he wanted to build on the land, and so he sued Sacks.

The court ruled against Balogh, pointing out that there was no special relation of trust between the parties. Besides, the court argued, notice of the easement for the gas line had been recorded in the county public records, which anyone could have seen. Balogh's failure to look at the public records indicated that he was proceeding blindly, and he could not expect the seller under such circumstances to volunteer information.

The Balogh case should recall *Jappe v. Mandt*,[25] the rubbish-route case. In both cases, the burden was placed on the buyer to discover the information that later caused the damage. Similarly, in *Kamuchey v. Trzesniewski*[26] the lessee was not allowed to get out of a lease after he discovered that the furnace, which he paid to have operated, heated the whole building and not just his portion. The court in this case said that he should have noticed that there was only one furnace in the building.

In sales transactions, in the absence of special agreements, a requirement of disclosure is the exception rather than the rule, for both buyer and seller. When there is a requirement, however, it is more likely to fall on the seller than on the buyer because the seller is presumed to have easier access to knowledge of the good being exchanged.

24. 55 Ohio Ops. 185, 97 Ohio App. 17, 123 N.E.2d 37 (1954).
25. 130 Cal. App. 2d. 426, 278 P.2d 940 (2d Dist. 1955), discussed in the previous chapter.
26. 8 Wis. 2d 94, 98 N.W.2d 403 (1959).

Equal or Superior Means of Knowledge

Although it is usually true that no obligation to disclose information exists in the general case when the parties are dealing at arms's length, the courts on occasion do manage to find a duty to disclose. One of the persistent themes running through the cases and commentaries is that when one party to a transaction has superior means of knowledge and the other party does not have the knowledge so readily available, the knowledgeable party must disclose the information. The legal encyclopedia, *American Jurisprudence* 2d, outlines this criterion as follows:

> There is abundant authority to the effect that if one party to a contract or transaction has superior knowledge, or knowledge which is not within the fair and reasonable reach of the other party and which he could not discover by the exercise of reasonable diligence, or means of knowledge which are not open to both parties alike, he is under a *legal* obligation to speak, and his silence constitutes fraud, especially when the other party relies upon him to judge the expediency of the bargain or transaction. [27]

Goldfarb also noticed the importance, in courts' judgments, of unequal means of knowledge: "If the facts are *exclusively* in the possession of one party and absolutely inaccessible to the other, the same result [a duty of disclosure] will occur." [28] Thus, a duty to disclose seems to be created in those circumstances in which one party has information that the other party would be hard-pressed to acquire.

Surprisingly, this criterion for disclosure has received more support from the cases than from the commentators. Over and over again in the cases, judges indicate that a duty to disclose exists in those cases where the ignorant party could not easily have found out the information and where the knowledgeable party had the information more readily available.

Simmons v. Evans[29] is a classic case of this sort. The buyers of the waterless house could not have known to ask whether they would have water all the time. The sellers, on the other hand, had the water situation ever present in their minds, having learned about it easily through the experience of living in the house. Clearly, the buyers and the sellers in this case had vastly different access to the information about the water stoppage; and the court pointed this out in the opinion, noting that the water situation, from the point of view of the buyers, was so

---

27. *American Jurisprudence 2d,* 1968, s.v. "Fraud."
28. Goldfarb, p. 43.
29. 185 Tenn. 282, 206 S.W.2d 295 (1947), discussed in chapter 1.

unusual that it would have been "more or less ridiculous" [30] for them to have inquired about it. Not knowing to ask reflects the presence of a deep secret and, necessarily, unequal access to the information.

A duty to disclose has been found in a variety of circumstances that fit this general pattern. In *Highland Motor Transfer Co. v. Heyburn Bldg. Co.*[31] Heyburn was found to have concealed the existence of a swimming pool buried underground from Highland, a company that had bid for and won a contract to construct a building on that site. The court noted that the existence of the swimming pool was not something that Highland reasonably could have anticipated. Since the swimming pool was there because it had been covered over by Heyburn when a parking lot was built on top of it, the court found that Heyburn had an obligation to disclose this condition that Highland could not easily have discovered for itself. A similar point was made in *Clauser v. Taylor*,[32] where the land in question had been filled with debris and then covered over. A duty to disclose this nonobvious condition was also based on the argument that such facts were outside the "diligent attention and observation"[33] of the buyer and that, since they had been created by the seller, were more easily known to the seller.

Courts have found a duty to disclose that a house is built on unstable soil (in a case where the house later cracked and sank),[34] that assumption of a mortgage also involves assumption of the obligation of the unpaid interest,[35] that a septic tank is defective,[36] and that the water in a well that provides the water supply for a home is contaminated with harmful bacteria.[37] In each of these cases, the condition that had to be disclosed would not have been easy to uncover unless one knew specifically what to look for—and, in the absence of knowing the problem, one would not know where to look. All of these circumstances made the acquisition of the fact more difficult for the ignorant actor. What these cases share is that the information was not readily available without a significant effort on the part of the ignorant actor. Moreover, the ignorant actor would have to know exactly what he was looking for.

30. 206 S.W.2d 295, 297.
31. 237 Ky. 337, 35 S.W.2d 521 (1931).
32. 44 Cal. App. 2d 453, 112 P.2d 661 (1941).
33. 112 P.2d 661, 662.
34. *Cohen v. Vivian*, 141 Colo. 443, 349 P.2d 366, 80 A.L.R.2d 1448 (1960).
35. *Everett v. Gilliland*, 47 N.M. 269, 141 P.2d 326 (1943).
36. *Rich v. Rankl*, 6 Conn. Cir. 185, 269 A.2d 84 (1969).
37. *Janinda v. Lanning*, 87 Idaho 91, 390 P.2d 826 (1964).

When there are equal means of knowledge, the courts generally argue that there is *no* obligation to disclose information. In *Gibson v. Mendenhall*[38] Gibson purchased from Mendenhall a beer parlor in Commerce, Oklahoma. During the course of negotiations to sell the place, the town of Commerce was engaged in passing an ordinance outlawing all beer parlors. Mendenhall neglected to tell Gibson of this development; and after Gibson bought the beer parlor, he learned that he could not get a license. The court in this case ruled that Mendenhall did not have to tell Gibson, since the pending ordinance was public knowledge.[39] The court noted that it was "pertinent" that "the very information the plaintiff alleged to have been concealed from him undoubtedly, by its very nature, was the subject of general knowledge and discussion in the locality."[40] The procedures for getting a license were laid out in statutes to which everyone had access, and Gibson could not require that Mendenhall disclose this information.

Doyle v. Union Pacific Railway Co.[41] presented the sad case of a woman whose six children had been crushed to death in a snowslide. Marcella Doyle lived as a boardinghouse keeper in a section house owned by the Union Pacific Railway. The section house was in the Colorado Rockies in a place susceptible to snowslides. When the massive snowslide hit, injuring Doyle and killing her six children, she sued the company, claiming that they had known about the snowslide danger but had failed to tell her. The Court said: "The plaintiff's evidence fails to show that there was any special and secret danger from snowslides which was known only to the railway company and which could not have been ascertained by the plaintiff."[42] The danger, argued the Court, came from the climate, which was well known to both parties. In the absence of superior means of knowledge on the part of one of the parties, the Court could not require disclosure and hence could not find liability of the company.

Other, less dramatic, cases present the same sort of argument. Courts have found that a city does not have to disclose information about subsurface rock to a construction company bidding on a job to build a sewer, when the presence of rock can be determined from a

---

38. 203 Okla. 558, 224 P.2d 251 (1950).
39. Note how the public ordinance makes this case different from the *Jappe* rubbish-route case and from the *Dyke* concessions-raid case.
40. 224 P.2d 251, 254.
41. 147 U.S. 413, 13 S. Ct. 333, 37 L. Ed. 223 (1893).
42. 147 U.S. 413, 429.

careful examination of the blueprints.[43] Neither have they found a duty to disclose information about a major flood that had happened in the area a year before.[44] There has been no disclosure required when a buyer first has the contents of a store appraised by someone who bungles the job and later claims that the seller should have revealed the value of the contents.[45] No disclosure has been required when the information in question could have been acquired if the plaintiff had done some simple arithmetic,[46] when the signs that a company was having financial trouble should have been obvious to the experienced businessman who continued to sink money into a project beyond what the contract called for,[47] or when the defect was patent, as in the case of a rusty staircase,[48] a railroad track running alongside the property,[49] or a drainage vent installed below water level.[50]

What this latter set of cases demonstrates is a reluctance on the part of the courts to hold anyone liable for failing to disclose information that the ignorant party easily might have found out. In a case involving a boundary dispute between Massachusetts and Rhode Island in 1840, in which one of the many points of contention was that one side had failed to disclose to the other the distance between certain markers and a river, the Supreme Court wrote: "Equity will not relieve where the means of information are open to both parties; and where each is presumed to exercise his own judgment."[51] If one party knows something that the other could easily find out, then there is no duty to disclose the information.

The general rule seems to be, then, that when two parties have an inequality in their "means of knowledge,"—that is, when one party can come by the information more easily than another—the law requires the one for whom the information is more readily available to disclose this knowledge. When strategic secrets are permitted (in other words, when there is no obligation to disclose information), the igno-

43. *Commissioners of Sewerage of the City of Louisville, Ky. v. Davis*, 88 F.2d 797 (6th Cir. 1937).

44. *Farrar v. Churchhill*, 135 U.S. 609, 10 S. Ct. 771, 34 L. Ed. 246 (1890).

45. *Rothermel v. Phillips*, 292 Pa. 371, 141 A. 241, 61 A.L.R. 489 (1928).

46. *Berman v. New Hampshire Jockey Club, Inc.*, 324 F. Supp. 1156 (D.C.N.H. 1971).

47. *Oates v. Taylor*, 31 Wash. 2d 898, 199 P.2d 924 (1948).

48. *Riley v. White*, 231 S.W.2d 291 (Mo. App. 1950).

49. *Jones v. Herring*, 16 S.W.2d 325 (Tex. Civ. App. 1929).

50. *Gutelius v. Sisemore*, 365 P.2d 732 (Okla. 1961).

51. *State of Rhode Island and Providence Plantations v. State of Massachusetts*, 39 U.S. 210, 274; 10 L. Ed. 423 (1840).

rant party has to have the knowledge within reasonable reach. When these two elements of the rule are taken together, then, it is clear that the law allows strategic secrets only in those situations where they are most likely to be uncovered.

The Relation of the Parties to Each Other

Probably the most widely noted and pervasive distinction used by the courts in the cases involving nondisclosure and fraud is the distinction made between those parties who are involved in a confidential or fiduciary relationship and those parties who are not. Generally, those who are involved in a confidential or fiduciary relationship owe a greater duty of disclosure to each other than do those who are not so involved. Although the determination of a confidential relationship is generally considered to depend on the facts of each case (since the extent to which confidentiality is expected is not necessarily delineated in the description of the relationship),[52] certain associations almost always give rise to a finding of a confidential relationship and a concomitant obligation to disclose. The relations of principal and agent, trustee and cestui que trust, partners, part-owners, guardian and ward, parents and children, and attorney and client generally give rise to a duty to disclose all facts relevant to transactions that occur in the context of these relationships.

The existence of this rule is supported by a number of commentators on the subject. Story noted about relations of confidence: "In these, and the like cases, the law, in order to prevent undue advantage, from the unlimited confidence, affection or sense of duty, which the relation naturally creates, requires the utmost degree of good faith . . . in all transactions between the parties. If there is any misrepresentation, or any concealment of a material fact, or any just suspicion of artifice or undue influence, courts of equity will interpose and pronounce the transaction void and, as far as possible, will restore the parties to their original rights."[53] Clearly, withholding information in relationships of this kind would be a cause for legal action.

Pomeroy observed the same phenomenon. When there is a confidential or fiduciary relationship, Pomeroy noted, "the obligation of perfect good faith and of complete disclosure always arises from the existing relations of trust and confidence, and is necessarily imposed

52. Bower, p. 306–313.
53. Story, p. 217.

upon any transaction which takes place between such persons." [54] This duty to disclose does not exist in ordinary transactions between buyers and sellers, who are presumed in the general case not to have a confidential relationship.

More recent writers, including Keeton,[55] Goldfarb,[56] and Prosser,[57] have also elaborated on this distinction. Confidential relationships give rise to special duties, but, in the absence of a prior confidential relationship, nondisclosure is more likely to be the rule. This distinction is supported by a long line of cases, only a few of which will be discussed here.

In *Sellers v. Sellers*[58] James Sellers asked his brother, William Sellers, if he could buy his brother's shares of stock in the bank in which they jointly exercised a controlling interest. Although William did not particularly want to hold onto the stock himself, he was adamant that the stock remain in the family. After William sold James the stock, James then sold the combined shares to two men named Eyestone and Fowler. William sued James, contending both that James knew when he bought the stock that he would sell the shares outside the family and that James intentionally withheld this information from him.

The court's opinion rested heavily on the obligation to one other of parties in a confidential relationship. Although the court indicated that the determination of a confidential relationship was properly a question for the jury, it went on to note that in this case the two men were both brothers and business partners who had agreed to work together. It was clear from the facts that William would not have sold the shares to anyone other than James, that William allowed James to determine the value of William's shares, and that James knew that he was going to sell the combined shares to someone outside the family. When there is a confidential relationship, the court wrote, there must be the "fullest and fairest explanation and communication of every particular."[59] The court ruled for William.

In *Popejoy v. Eastburn*[60] the Popejoys found themselves in a difficult situation. They had bought a farm near Fairfield, Iowa, but they

54. Pomeroy, p. 1272.
55. Keeton, pp. 11–12.
56. Goldfarb, p. 7.
57. Prosser, p. 697.
58. 428 P.2d 230 (Okla. 1967).
59. 428 P.2d 230, 237.
60. 241 Iowa 747, 41 N.W.2d 764 (1950).

had not yet sold their house in the city. The Popejoys had got the down payment for the farm from a bank in Fairfield, a bank that had Eastburn as its president. Eastburn had, in fact, negotiated the loan for them. Several days before the repayment of the loan was due at the bank, Eastburn indicated to the Popejoys that he knew someone who wanted to buy the house. Although the house was listed at a value of $4,500 with local real estate brokers, Eastburn said that the Smiths, the interested parties, would be willing to pay only $3,300 for it. With time running out, the Popejoys reluctantly agreed to sell the house for that amount, and they signed a contract of sale with Eastburn. Later, the Popejoys found out that Eastburn had subsequently sold the house to the Smiths for $4,500.

The Supreme Court of Iowa focused attention on the relationship between the Popejoys and Eastburn. The Popejoys thought Eastburn was acting in their interest by giving them advice. Again, the court indicated that the determination of a confidential relationship was really a question for a jury but, in giving guidance for a jury to answer such a question, noted that Eastburn had purported to act in the Popejoys' interest. The Popejoys trusted him. Eastburn, because he knew that their down-payment repayment was due in short order at the bank, was able to take advantage of their awkward position when they thought he could be trusted. The case was remanded, but the point seems clear. One cannot undertake to advise others with their interests apparently in mind and then take advantage of special knowledge to hurt them.

A similar question was posed in the case of *Griffing v. Atkins (Sims, Intervenor)*.[61] Willie Sims found a ring under the stadium seats after a Louisiana State University football game. He gave it to his wife. A friend of Sims who worked for a jewelry store told him that he really should have the ring appraised. Sims took the ring to the jewelry store where his friend worked. Griffing, an employee at the store, inspected the ring and offered Sims $130 for it. Sims agreed to sell it. Several days after Griffing bought the ring, the police appeared at his doorstep and seized the ring, claiming that it had been stolen and was worth $1,250. Chief of Police Atkins later discovered that he could provide no evidence that the ring had been stolen. Griffing sued to get the ring back, and Sims intervened in the suit, claiming that the ring was his own.

The majority opinion pointed out that Sims had gone to the jewelry store seeking advice. The employees of the store were therefore in a fiduciary or quasi-fiduciary relationship with him. Rather

61. 1 So. 2d 445 (La. App. 1941).

than receiving advice, Sims got an offer of sale, an offer that he assumed to be a reasonable one since he had come there to get an appraisal. He thought that the statement of an offer of sale represented the value of the ring. The court ruled that the store employees, Griffing included, owed Sims a duty of disclosure and that they should have informed him of the value of the ring. The dissent, by Judge Ott, cited *Laidlaw v. Organ* and argued that Sims could have taken the ring elsewhere for evaluation before he sold it. Since Griffing did not give an opinion as to the ring's value and since it was clear from the facts of the case that Griffing was buying the ring personally and not on behalf of the jewelry store, Sims should have known to get a proper appraisal before he sold it. Ott reckoned that Sims should have been able to tell the difference between an offer of sale and an appraisal.

These three cases, taken together, point to the importance of the specific facts of the disputes in determining the existence of a confidential relationship. It seems clear that when one party purports to act in the interest of another and when, on the basis of the nature of the relationship between the parties, this behavior seems reasonable, the courts will not look favorably on one who takes advantage of the resulting trust and confidence.

Two other cases show how sensitive the courts can be on this topic and how narrowly confidential relationships are construed. In *Plews v. Burrage*[62] Plews and Burrage had an agreement to jointly develop a copper mine in Chuchicamata. Ross, a friend of Burrage, negotiated an option contract with Plews on the copper-mine deal without telling Burrage. When Burrage found out Ross had done this, Burrage got very angry and convinced Ross to agree to turn the option contract over to him. Burrage then exercised his option, much to the surprise of Plews. Apparently, the copper-mine project was going very well at that point and Burrage knew just when to exercise his option to maximum advantage. Plews sued Burrage, claiming that Burrage should not be able to exercise the option.

Despite the fact that Plews and Burrage were arguably in a confidential relationship by virtue of having this joint project, the court noted that Burrage had not used Ross as his agent to obtain the option contract from Plews on the sly. Burrage had no idea that Ross was trying to do this at the time. Plews was not in a confidential relationship with Ross, so anything that Ross cared to do with the option contract once it was signed was out of Plews's control. The court in this case was clearly announcing that a confidential relationship was to

---

62. 19 F.2d. 412 (D.C. Mass. 1927).

be very narrowly construed. The presence of a third party in transactions where that third party was not an agent for either party in the confidential relationship could radically change the outcome of the case.

Another case, *Peckham v. Johnson*,[63] illustrates how fragile confidential relations can be under the harsh scrutiny of the law. Peckham and Johnson were partners in a business that involved oil leases. Johnson had moved to another county, leaving Peckham to operate the business alone. The property that they jointly owned increased in value as new oil discoveries were made on adjacent properties. Peckham went to Johnson and told him that the land had *decreased* in value and that he (Peckham) wanted to buy Johnson's interests in the property so that he could regroup the leases for sale. Johnson sold his interests to Peckham for much less than they were worth, given the oil discoveries. When he discovered his loss, he sued Johnson to recover the difference.

The court immediately looked for the existence of a confidential relationship, noting that when one exists there must be a full disclosure. The evidence indicated, however, that despite the fact that Johnson and Peckham were business partners, they recently had had a falling out. Johnson had failed to pay Peckham his portion of the drilling costs on their property, and Peckham had a suit pending against Johnson at the time of the property sale. Surely, the court reasoned, Johnson could not expect Peckham to act in Johnson's interests under the circumstances.

The court wrote: "If the confidential relation fixed by law between the parties be shown by evidence to have been shattered, then neither party can rely upon the relation and duties of his copartner imputed by law, and close his eyes to the fact that he had ceased to repose confidence in his associate in business the law presumes to exist."[64] Johnson and Peckham showed many signs that their relationship had been strained. If a confidential relationship no longer existed in fact, a question that is properly determined by a jury, then full disclosure could not be required.

Plews and *Peckham* show that a mere label, partner, will not suffice to demonstrate that a confidential relationship exists. The circumstances surrounding each transaction are to be examined to see whether the parties' assumption of confidentiality was warranted in a given instance. If a confidential relationship exists, then disclosure is re-

63. 98 S.W.2d 408 (Tex. Civ. App. 1936).
64. 98 S.W.2d 408, 413.

quired; if it does not, then strategic secrets may be employed, within the limits set by the other legally relevant facts.

One reason why existence of a confidential relationship might matter so much can be found in the requirements for strategic secrets. For strategic secrets to be possible, the interests of the parties must diverge. In confidential relationships, as in coordination games with identical preference orderings, the actors are presumed to have identical interests over the range of the confidential relationship. If it is presumed by one party that the other is acting with their joint interests in mind, then the first party has every reason to expect that asymmetric information will be shared, not exploited. Strategic secrets in the context of an allegedly confidential relationship violate this basic expectation. For the party who is being fooled, the game is represented as being something other than what it really is. As Story indicated, "the party who sees that a confidence is created, that the other party has fallen into a delusion in consequence, is bound, in morals and in law, either to destroy the confidence or else remove the delusion." [65] The expectation of common interest gives rise to an expectation of full disclosure.

The Nature of the Agreement

Another fact that is consistently recognized as being important in determining the legitimacy of strategic secrets involves the nature of the agreement itself. Certain sorts of agreements are considered to be "intrinsically fiduciary" [66] or "*uberrimae fidei*" [67] and to require full disclosure. Insurance contracts and contracts of suretyship are most frequently mentioned as examples in this area, [68] but agreements of agency, [69] marriage, [70] and partnership [71] sometimes also are included. Although Keeton has suggested that this designation is unnecessary— that the agreements under this heading belong to a more general class

65. Story, p. 213.
66. Pomeroy, p. 1272.
67. Bower, p. 58; and Keeton, p. 12.
68. Pomeroy, p. 1280; Gulian Verplanck, *An Essay on the Doctrine of Contracts: Being an Inquiry How Contracts Are Affected in Law and Morals by Concealment, Error or Inadequate Price* (New York: G. C. Cariull, 1825), pp. 40–48; Keeton, p. 13; and Edward H. Wilson, "Concealment or Silence as a Form of Fraud and the Relief or Redress Afforded Therefor, Both in Law and in Equity," *Counsellor* 5: 230–238 (1895), p. 237.
69. Keeton, p. 14.
70. Bower, p. 40.
71. Bower, p. 40; and Wilson, p. 237.

involving the "special confidence"[72] of one party in another (a consideration that we will discuss shortly)—there does seem to be substantial support in the case law for special treatment of certain categories of agreements purely because the agreements pertain to special subjects.

There is a surprising lack of discussion in the secondary literature about why this should be so. In one of the very few discussions of the basis for this rule, Bower explains that the requirement of disclosure arises in these inherently fiduciary situations because they involve "contracts in the negotiation for which one of the parties must, from the very nature of the transaction, have either actual or presumptive knowledge of circumstances which ordinarily are not within the actual or presumptive knowledge of the other party, and the knowledge of which is, or may be, of importance to that other party to enable him to judge of the expediency of entering into the particular contract proposed."[73] In other words, what makes disclosure of information required in these cases is the fact that one party generally has information that cannot easily be discovered by the other party. These agreements are, necessarily, ones into which the parties enter on unequal terms. To ensure that one party, by virtue of superior knowledge, does not take advantage of the less well-informed party, the law requires disclosure. Of course, one could argue that this inequality in information is what gives rise to *all* nondisclosure cases, and it is unclear exactly why these situations have been singled out for special treatment.

Two writers on the subject, in fact, argue that these situations do not require different rules. Verplanck[74] suggested that rules requiring disclosure in insurance and suretyship should be extended to the whole of contract law. All agreements, Verplanck proposed, should be made with full disclosure of relevant facts on both sides. Much later, faced with the preservation of the double standard though having just the reverse sentiment about how the gap should be closed, Harnett[75] claimed that the special rules of disclosure in insurance contracts ought to be abandoned in favor of the existing rules of contract law, which require disclosure in a much smaller range of situations. Harnett noted that the duty to disclose originated when the most common form of insurance was marine insurance and when the common practice was to

---

72. Keeton, p. 12.
73. Bower, p. 58.
74. Verplanck, *An Essay on the Doctrine of Contracts*.
75. Bertram Harnett, "The Doctrine of Concealment: A Remnant in the Law of Insurance," *Law and Contemporary Problems* 15: 391–414 (1950).

insure vessels when they were already out to sea, out of reach of the insurer's inspection. But, Harnett explained, most modern insurance is negotiated in a context where the insurer can get quite a lot of information about the nature of the things which are to be insured (including people—for example, by requiring medical examinations before the insurance contract is signed). In some cases, the insurer may actually know more about the risks involved and the variables that affect the risk than does the insured, making the old disclosure rules no longer applicable.

Despite the recommendations of Verplanck and Harnett, the cases seem to resolutely support the view that certain sorts of agreements give rise to a duty to disclose because of the nature of the agreement itself. The most cited early case on this subject is *Carter v. Boehm*.[76] Although the case is generally cited as evidence that there *is* a duty to disclose all relevant facts in insurance contracts, the case, interestingly enough, actually failed to require that Carter disclose to insurer Boehm the information that he had.

Governor George Carter was stationed on the island of Sumatra in the East Indies, and Fort Marlborough served as his headquarters. Despite its title, Fort Marlborough was not properly a fort at all, in the sense that it had been built to resist attacks by European forces, but rather was a trading center, built with just enough strength to keep the residents of the island from getting in. Fearful that the fort would be attacked by a European power against which the fort would be powerless to resist, Carter decided to insure at least some of the contents of the fort, and he sent a letter back to England with instructions to insure half of his effects against European attack during the period of October 1759 to October 1760. Although Carter wrote the letter in September 1759, Charles Boehm, the insurer, did not receive it until May 1760. When Boehm received the letter, he immediately wrote out the insurance policy.

On 1 April 1760, the fort was in fact attacked by the French, using Dutch pilots to navigate the river on which the fort was located. Faced with a French man-of-war with sixty-four guns and a French frigate with twenty guns, the fort was surrendered. All of the goods in the fort were taken, and prisoners were sent to Batavia.

Although this was clearly the risk against which Carter had sought to be insured, Boehm sought to avoid payment on the policy on the grounds that Carter had failed to disclose certain critical facts about his situation. For one thing, Boehm claimed, Carter did not tell

76. 3 Burr. 1095, 97 Eng. Rep. 1162 (K.B. 1766).

him the condition of the fort, that it was not at all equipped to resist attacks by any European power; for another, Boehm claimed, Carter knew that there was a substantial chance that the fort would be attacked by either the French or the Dutch—or else he would not have wanted the insurance. Boehm claimed that since Carter had not told him everything that he knew about the risk, Carter should not be able to collect on the policy.

Lord Mansfield's opinion is perhaps most well known for its general statement on the obligation to disclose in insurance contracts:

> Insurance is a contract upon speculation. The special facts, upon which the contingent chance is to be computed, lie most commonly in the knowledge of the insured only; the underwriter trusts to his representations and proceeds upon the confidence that he does not keep back any circumstances in his knowledge. . . . The keeping back of such circumstance is a fraud, and therefore the policy is void . . . because the risque run is really different from the risque understood and intended to be run at the time of the agreement. . . . Good faith forbids either party by concealing what he privately knows, to draw the other into a bargain, from his ignorance of that fact, and his believing the contrary.[77]

With this sort of statement, one might expect that poor Carter was out of luck in collecting on his insurance policy. But the court found a way to rule for Carter in this matter, anyway.

Lord Mansfield went on to write: "But either party may be innocently silent, as to grounds open to both, to exercise their judgment upon."[78] In other words, there are certain secrets that do *not* have to be disclosed. These are pieces of information that either party could derive from available knowledge and that therefore are not included in the general category of facts that are the province of the insured only. Mansfield elaborated: "There are many matters as to which the insured may be innocently silent—he need not mention what the underwriter knows. . . . The insured need not mention what the underwriter ought to know. . . . Men argue differently, from natural phenomena, and political appearances: they have different capacities, different degrees of knowledge, and different intelligence. But the means of information and judging are open to both: each professes to act from his own skill and sagacity; and therefore neither needs to communicate to the other."[79] Thus, when there is information within the reach of

---

77. 97 Eng. Rep. 1162, 1164.
78. 97 Eng. Rep. 1162, 1164.
79. 97 Eng. Rep. 1162, 1165.

both parties or when the information available to both must be evaluated, there is no obligation for the knowledgeable party to disclose what he knows to the ignorant party.

Lord Mansfield found in this case that the condition of Fort Marlborough "was, in general, well known, by most persons conversant or acquainted with Indian affairs . . . and could not be kept secret or concealed from persons who should endeavor by proper inquiry, to inform themselves." [80] Because the condition of the fort was generally known, Carter did not have to disclose this fact. Boehm easily could have found out this information with a minimum of effort.

As to Carter's knowledge of the possibility that the fort might be overtaken by the French or the Dutch, Lord Mansfield took note of the fact that Carter had written his letter asking for insurance in September 1759 and that Boehm had received the letter in May 1760, at which time he wrote out the policy:

> The under-writer at London, in May 1760, could judge much better of the probability of the contingency, than Governor Carter could at Fort Marlborough, in September 1759. He knew the success of the operations of the war in Europe. He knew what naval forces the English and the French had sent to the East Indies. He knew, from a comparison of that force, whether the sea was open to any such attempt by the French. He knew, or might know every thing which was known at Fort Marlborough in September 1759, of the general state of affairs in the East Indies. . . . He knew what probability there was of the Dutch committing or having committed hostilities. [81]

Mansfield argued that Boehm was in a much *better* position than Carter to judge the probability that an attack would take place and yet he issued the policy. The court said that the proper thing for Boehm to have done if he thought that the risk was too high was not to issue the policy, rather than issuing it and then claiming, when the loss occurred, that Carter had failed to reveal important information.

The importance of this case, for our purposes, lies in the fact that the opinion simultaneously recognized both a broad duty to disclose all information that was uniquely in the possession of one of the parties and that was not readily available to the other *and* a lack of such duty when the information was either within easy reach of the ignorant party or the result of a considered judgment that each person could make on the basis of the same facts. Many commentators[82] have noted

80. 97 Eng. Rep. 1162, 1166.
81. 97 Eng. Rep. 1162, 1167.
82. See, for example, Verplanck, pp. 37–39; and Holmes, pp. 427–428.

only that Mansfield's opinion imposes a general obligation to disclose and have not mentioned the grounds on which the court enabled Carter to collect on his insurance policy. But the simultaneous statement of these two aspects of disclosure gives a strong clue as to why the disclosure requirement is there in the first place. Disclosure is not required simply because certain contracts require good faith (a notion that would imply that other contracts do not do so!), but because certain kinds of contracts have a higher probability than others that one of the parties will come to the agreement with knowledge that is out of reasonable reach of the other party. In these circumstances, where the ignorant party is unlikely to find out the facts unless the knowledgeable party reveals them, disclosure is required.

This observation gives support to Bower's argument that transactions requiring full disclosure are those in which the parties are likely to have unequal access to information in the first place, information that would be difficult for the ignorant party to acquire. Other insurance cases bear this out. In *Equitable Life Assurance Society v. McElroy*[83] McElroy got his secretary to sign him up for a life insurance policy two days before he died from appendicitis and the effects of the resulting surgery. Although McElroy had considered taking out the life insurance policy before he was taken ill, he speeded up the process considerably once he discovered that an operation was imminent. Equitable's doctors had given him a checkup about a month before he died and had pronounced him to be in good health. Obviously, they were wrong.

The court ruled that the McElroy family could not collect on the policy, writing:

> Fraud vitiates all contracts. But misrepresentations or concealments of the facts relative to the health of those whose lives are insured are peculiarly fatal to contracts of life insurance, because the companies necessarily rely upon the statements and acts of the assured in making their contracts. Companies cannot know and surgeons cannot discover by the appearance and examination of subjects many insidious and often fatal diseases, the symptoms of which are felt by their victims. Hence the companies require them to answer many questions as to their habits, their health, their symptoms, the longevity of their ancestors, and the causes of their disease. . . . In other words, the honesty, good faith, and truthfulness of the person whose life is insured form the actual foundation of the agreement of life insurance.[84]

83. 83 F. 631 (8th Cir. 1897).
84. 83 F. 631, 636.

This excerpt clearly demonstrates that it is the fact that the information is peculiarly within reach of the insured and not easily obtainable by anyone else that makes insurance contracts require disclosure of these sorts of facts.

Special Confidence

When two parties stand in a relation of "special confidence," the knowledgeable party may not take advantage of the ignorant party's lack of information. This notion of special confidence has been used by commentators to include all those relations that are not covered under the umbrella of confidential relationships but that involve the ignorant party placing some sort of justifiable trust in the knowledgeable actor.

About these relationships, Story has written: "And the rule [requiring disclosure] is the same, in morals and in law, where there is a special confidence, in fact, between the parties, whether it arises from peculiar relation or not. And one who takes advantage of such special confidence, to deceive and damage another, although he is able to effect it by mere silence, is none the less liable to an action." [85]

Just what constitutes a relation of special confidence is quite vague, even in the description by the usually clear Pomeroy: "The second class [of cases that require disclosure] embraces those instances in which there is no existing fiduciary relation between the parties, and the transaction is not in its essential nature fiduciary, but it appears that either one or each of the parties, in entering into the contract or other transaction, *expressly* reposes a trust and confidence in the other; or else from the circumstances of the case the nature of their dealings, or their position towards each other, such a trust and confidence in the particular case is *necessarily* implied." [86] In other words, when a person places justifiable trust in another, a relation of special confidence will be found; but what counts as justifiable trust is hard to define. As Pomeroy states, "each case must depend upon its own circumstances." [87]

In examining the cases that involve this legally relevant fact, it becomes clear that special confidence is generally called into play when someone takes advantage of another who is particularly vulnerable. Such a case is *Barry v. Orahood*.[88] Barry was an agent of the Pure Oil

---

85. Story, p. 212.
86. Pomeroy, p. 1272.
87. Pomeroy, p. 1272.
88. 191 Okla. 618, 132 P.2d 645 (1942).

Company, a company trying to buy a block of land that was strongly suspected of containing large deposits of oil and gas. Barry had searched at some length for Orahood, who owned some of the land in the area that Pure Oil wanted to buy. Barry finally found Orahood, hospitalized in rather dire condition. On the day that Barry appeared, Orahood had been treated with a variety of drugs (including morphine), had received a transfusion, and was recovering from surgery. Doctors thought that it was doubtful that Orahood would recover. Under these circumstances, Barry appeared at Orahood's hospital bed and told him that he wanted to buy Orahood's land. Barry neglected to mention the possibility of valuable mineral deposits under the land, and Orahood agreed to the sale.

The court allowed Orahood to cancel the deed to the 320 acres of land, even though it found no confidential relationship between Barry and Orahood. Noting that a duty to speak depended on "the situations of the parties, the matters with which they are dealing, and the subject matter in hand,"[89] the court argued that Barry knew that Orahood was in a weakened condition and should not have taken advantage of this.

Vokes v. Arthur Murray, Inc.[90] presents a less dire but similarly vulnerable circumstance. Audrey Vokes, a fifty-one-year-old widow from Clearwater, decided to learn to dance. She started with a mere eight hours of dancing lessons at the local Arthur Murray dance studio and was soon embarked on "an almost endless pursuit of the terpsichorean art."[91] Eventually, she found herself committed to 2,302 hours of dancing lessons, costing her $31,090.45. She was convinced to take these lessons through a "constant and continuous barrage of flattery, false praise, excessive compliments and panegyric encomiums,"[92] although "she did not develop in her dancing ability, she had no 'dance aptitude,' and in fact had difficulty in 'hearing the musical beat.'"[93] As Judge Pierce wrote, "while she first exulted that she was entering the 'spring of life,' she finally was awakened to the fact that there was 'spring' in neither her life nor her feet."[94]

The case presented the question of whether the dance studio had an obligation to tell Vokes that she was making no progress. The opinion argued that the dance-studio personnel were in a much better

89. 132 P.2d 645, 647.
90. 212 So. 2d 906, 28 A.L.R.3d 1405 (Fla. 1968).
91. 212 So. 2d 906, 907.
92. 212 So. 2d 906, 907.
93. 212 So. 2d 906, 908.
94. 212 So. 2d 906, 908.

position than Vokes to know what her potential would be (that is, they had superior knowledge) and that the studio, since it undertook to comment on her dancing abilities at all, was obligated to tell her the whole truth. But the opinion also took note of the fact that there was something between an arm's-length transaction and a fiduciary relationship here and that this relationship presented opportunities for undue influence.

Vague phrases such as "undue influence" and "fair dealing" provide the justificatory scheme for cases in which one party is vulnerable to another. A duty to disclose has been found in cases where a man bought stock considerably below market value from a seventy-nine-year-old doctor who did not know how to read stock tables. The court noted that even though a buyer generally does not have to disclose information, a duty to disclose does arise when "the vendor is in such a position that he cannot well find out such facts for himself." [95] Similarly, a duty to disclose was found in a case where an oil man wanted to buy property from a man who did not live near the land in question. The buyer concealed that he wanted it for oil development, despite the fact that the seller said that he would not sell it for that purpose. The buyer withheld the information that adjacent lands were being developed, and the court found that this secret was impermissible. [96]

In all of these cases, the court found that the ignorant parties were not in a reasonable position to find out the facts for themselves, and so the court required disclosure. When the ignorant party counts on the knowledgeable party to reveal information because the ignorant party is in a vulnerable condition (by being sick, by not being near the property being sold, or by being particularly unaware of the nature of the situation) and the knowledgeable party knows of this vulnerability, the knowledgeable party cannot take advantage of this through the use of strategic secrets.

The Conduct of the Knowledgeable Party

The courts, in deciding whether secrets constitute fraud, examine quite closely the conduct of the knowledgeable party. While there are a number of circumstances in which secrets are acceptable, one false move by the knowledgeable actor may result in action considered actively fraudulent. If the knowledgeable actor actually lies, intentionally misrepresenting some critical facts, then a charge of fraud is

95. *Chandler v. Butler*, 284 S.W.2d 388, 394 (Tex. Civ. App. 1955).
96. *Feist v. Roesler*, 86 S.W.2d 787 (Tex. Civ. App. 1935).

more likely to stick. Similarly, if the knowledgeable actor actively conceals information from the ignorant party, reveals misleading half-truths, or fails to update previously revealed true information that is now false, the law is much less forgiving than it may be in cases involving simple secrets. We will consider each of these types of situations in turn.

1. *Intentional Misrepresentation.*—While the law hedges and qualifies where secrets are concerned, the law surrounding outright lies is unequivocal, according to the *Restatement (Second) of Torts*: "One who fraudulently makes a misrepresentation of fact, opinion, intention or law for the purpose of inducing another to act or to refrain from action in reliance upon it, is subject to liability to the other in deceit for pecuniary loss caused him by his justifiable reliance upon the misrepresentation." [97]

In other words, if one actor causes harm or loss to another through a lie, then the lying actor is responsible for this harm or loss. It is generally agreed that fraud consists of five elements: (1) a false representation that (2) the person making it knew was false, which (3) was made with the intention that another act on the basis of this representation, (4) when the other person actually acted in reliance on this representation and (5) was hurt as a result. [98] Intentional misrepresentations present a much clearer legal picture than do secrets because all of the qualifications that accompany the legitimacy of strategic secrets are absent when the conduct in question becomes a lie. As Prosser has pointed out, [99] however, there are still some legal troubles, because the issue of misrepresentation runs throughout the law of torts, making a clear definition of it evasive. In addition, misrepresentation can be the basis for an action in tort or in contract, which also makes the standards surrounding it difficult to discern. The basic principle is clear, however: "Fraud vitiates everything." [100]

Because the principle is so straightforward, a couple of examples will suffice. In *Crompton v. Beedle*[101] Cora Crompton owned a farm at

97. American Law Institute, *Restatement (Second) of Torts*, vol. 2, p. 55.
98. See statements by William L. Prosser, *Torts*, 4th ed. (St. Paul: West Publishing, 1971), pp. 685–686; and Oliver Wendell Holmes, *The Common Law* (Boston: Little, Brown, 1881), pp. 132–138. See also *Hart v. McLucas*, 535 F.2d 516 (9th Cir. 1975) and *Venture Investment Co. Inc. v. Schaefer*, 478 F.2d 156 (10th Cir., 1973), among many others.
99. Prosser, p. 684–685.
100. W. W. Kerr, *W. W. Kerr on the Law of Fraud and Mistake*, 7th ed., rev. by Denis Lane McDonnell and John George Monroe (London: Sweet and Maxwell, 1952), p. 8.
101. 83 Vt. 287, 75 A. 331 (1910).

some distance from her home. She had never been to the farm, having bought it for the use of a relative. One day, Albert Beedle came to her house and said that he would like to buy a particular pasture from her so that he could get better access to his own adjoining land. She sold him the pasture for $400 and later learned that Beedle knew of a valuable granite quarry on the land that made it worth $15,000.

Although the outcome of the case would have been a matter of dispute if Beedle had merely concealed his knowledge of the quarry,[102] his active misrepresentation of his intention made the court decide for Crompton. Citing *Laidlaw,* the court argued that it is generally not the case that a buyer must disclose his special knowledge before purchasing from an ignorant seller. But in this case Beedle did more than keep a secret; he lied about the use to which he expected to put the land. And that lie made all the difference.

In *Thorwegan v. King*[103] Thorwegan was the owner of a steamboat called the "Grand Republic," a boat that was encumbered with liens, claims, and debts in the sum of $75,000. Thorwegan went to King, told him that he had a steamboat free of debts, and proposed that he (Thorwegan) start a corporation, with the boat as a major asset. King gave him $12,000 and received 125 shares in the new corporation in return. When Thorwegan went bankrupt, King lost everything.

The Supreme Court said that, although Thorwegan did not have a duty to tell King of all the encumbrances on the ship, he was under an obligation to tell the truth because he had said *something* about the financial condition of the ship. Because Thorwegan falsely represented the ship's financial shape, he could be held liable, even though he did not have a duty to speak in the first place.

As these two cases demonstrate, secrets may be acceptable when lies are not. If the knowledgeable parties misrepresent any of the facts within their knowledge, then they might be held liable for the damage that results, even if a secret would not have given rise to the same liability. Earlier, we saw the same dilemma in *Laidlaw,* where the Supreme Court clearly wanted an answer to the question of whether Organ had lied about his knowledge when he bought the tobacco. The Court remanded that case for further fact-finding.

Although a lie is often merely a secret with a story on top, the courts treat the story as the basis for liability even when the simple

102. I believe that the court would have ruled for Crompton even in the absence of intentional misrepresentation, because this case would have been very similar to those in which "special confidence" is invoked.

103. 111 U.S. 549, 28 L. Ed. 514, 4 S. Ct. 529 (1884).

secret is not actionable. If the knowledgeable party lies in saying that there are no secrets or says anything that constitutes a false statement, courts will pounce on that fact and find liability for another's harm.

2. *Active concealment.*—Courts also make a distinction between merely remaining silent about one's knowledge and actively doing something to conceal that knowledge from someone else. If one takes steps to prevent another from finding information, the courts generally treat that as though it were an intentional misrepresentation and therefore wrong. Wilson summarized the difference between silence and active concealment this way: "Concealment is always fraudulent, and, if the other elements of fraud as given above are present, will always entitle to relief. . . . Silence is fraudulent when, and only when, there is a duty to speak." [104] And Goldfarb described the matter similarly: "If there is, in addition to silence, any statement which tends *affirmatively* to a suppression of the truth, or to the withdrawal or distraction of the other party's attention from the real facts, the concealment becomes fraudulent." [105] Just as with intentional misrepresentation, then, the courts treat intentional concealment as objectionable even when the underlying secret might not be.

In *City of Salinas v. Souza and McCue Construction Co.* [106] the city's chief engineer and other officials knew that there were "highly unstable" soil conditions at the site where the Souza Company was supposed to construct a sewer. The city engineer employed an independent testing firm to take borings of the earth at preselected spaces to make the area look its best. Souza submitted a bid on the basis of this information, and when it was discovered that he could not perform according to the specifications, he attempted to rescind the contract. The city sued for specific performance.

The court took particular note of the fact that the city had had the borings taken so that the true condition of the soil would be concealed. It was this active concealment that gave the court its basis for arguing that Souza should not have to perform under the agreement as specified. Interestingly enough, there is other authority to the effect that parties do not have to disclose what they know about subsoil conditions that are none of their making [107] But in this case, where the concealment was active and deliberate, the courts intervened to relieve the misled party.

104. Wilson, p. 234.
105. Goldfarb, p. 24.
106. 66 Cal. 2d 217, 424 P.2d 921, 57 Cal. Rptr. 337 (1967).
107. *Simpson Timber Co. v. Palmberg Construction Co.,* 377 F.2d 380 (9th Cir. 1967).

In *Stewart v. Wyoming Cattle Ranche Co.*[108] Stewart offered to sell Wyoming Cattle Ranche Company (a British corporation) a herd of cattle. The British company sent an agent to look the cattle over. Steward told Clay, the agent, that he expected to have four thousand cattle in 1882 when the herd would be sold. Apparently, despite the fact that Clay wanted to look around, Stewart requested that he not do so. When the corporation bought the herd, it found it had substantially fewer cattle than Stewart had said were there.

The Supreme Court noted that this case presented both intentional misrepresentation and active concealment, either one of which would have been sufficient to cause Stewart to lose his case. The court wrote specifically that silence is a different sort of thing than concealment. In this case, where Stewart prevented Clay from seeing for himself, active concealment was involved.

These cases demonstrate that when silence spills over into action designed to prevent another party from finding out the truth, the law treats active concealment as though it were an active lie. Again, in this situation as with intentional misrepresentation, a secret may be acceptable when active concealment is not. The line walked by a knowledgeable person who wishes to keep a secret is a fine one indeed.

3. *Half-truths.*—Another way in which the conduct of the knowledgeable party can influence the outcome of a case is through telling half-truths. Even in situations where there is no obligation to disclose information, once one begins to say anything, one must tell the whole truth. Goldfarb explains the matter this way: "While silence alone may not be actionable, if the vendor undertakes to speak, he must not conceal anything which would tend to qualify or contradict the facts which he had stated. In other words, to tell half of the truth is to make a half-false representation." [109] Half-truths differ from intentional misrepresentations and active concealments in that all of the information that is stated or otherwise represented is, as it stands, true. The problem is that the information, while true, conveys a misleading impression. What is left out—that is, kept secret—is essential for understanding the matter. This sort of secrecy is generally not tolerated in the law.

The *Restatement (Second) of Contracts* indicates [110] that one of the few situations in which the law requires disclosure occurs when the knowledgeable party knows that "a disclosure of the fact is necessary

108. 128 U.S. 383, 9 S. Ct. 101, 32 L. Ed. 439 (1888).
109. Goldfarb, p. 24.
110. American Law Institute, *Restatement (Second) of Contracts*, vol. 2, p. 431.

to prevent some previous assertion from being a misrepresentation."
And the *Restatement (Second) of Torts* requires disclosure in those situations where there are "matters known to him [the knowledgeable party] that he knows to be necessary [to disclose] to prevent
his partial or ambiguous statement of the facts from being misleading."[111]

Bower's statement about the obligation to reveal the complete
truth—and not just a part of the truth—is particularly forceful: "The
party on whom the obligation lies must not leave the other party to put
two and two together. He must put them together himself and call
them four."[112] The commentators make it clear that once one undertakes to speak, nothing less than the full truth will suffice. Even though
one might have kept a secret with impunity, one does not have this
luxury once one says anything at all about the matter. This is yet
another way in which the courts watch closely the conduct of the
knowledgeable party. Two cases will illustrate how this principle
works.

In *Tyler v. Savage*[113] Sarah Savage wanted to find a job for her son
with the Virginia Oil Company. John Tyler was the president of this
company, and he told her that if she invested $10,000 in the purchase of
the company's capital stock her son could get a job. In his letter to her,
Tyler indicated that the company paid semiannual dividends and that
the last dividend payment had been 7 percent on 1 June. Savage relied
on Tyler's statement and bought the stock. Savage later learned that
the company had in fact paid a 7 percent dividend on 1 June and
that that was the company's most recent dividend. The problem was
that the dividend had been paid on 1 June 1882 rather than on 1 June
1883 as Savage had assumed (since the latter date was the most recent 1
June as of Tyler's letter). Since the earlier date the company had been in
such bad financial shape that it had been unable to pay dividends at all.
The company was actually insolvent at the time that Tyler wrote the
letter to Savage.

The Supreme Court found that there indeed had been fraud in
this transaction. Savage would never have brought the stock had she
known the whole truth. The fact that Tyler had withheld certain critical portions of the truth from her while saying nothing that was
technically false made the resulting secret unacceptable to the Court.
Combined with this half-truth was the fact that Tyler's salary came

111. American Law Institute, *Restatement (Second) of Torts,* vol. 2, p. 119.
112. Bower, p. 11.
113. 143 U.S. 79, 36 L. Ed. 82, 12 S. Ct. 340 (1892).

directly from Savage's money. The Court said that the effect of the fraud was to directly increase Tyler's personal advantage and that he had accomplished this through the use of forbidden half-truths.

Berry v. Stevens[114] presented a case of a half-truth in an oil deal. Berry owned interests in land that had been his father's. Berry moved and, after a while, decided to sell his interests in the land. He called Stevens, an old family friend, and asked him to find a buyer for the land. Stevens cooperated and found two men, Pruett and Wamsley, who were willing to purchase the property from Berry. The property looked particularly attractive at that time, because a huge new oil discovery had been made on an adjacent property. Stevens told Berry that there had been a new discovery, but he neglected to mention how large the discovery was. He also kept secret that he himself was a partner of Pruett and Wamsley, a fact that would have tipped Berry off right away. Without this full knowledge, Berry sold the property for substantially less than it was worth.

The court noted the issue of a confidential relationship between Berry and Stevens, since Stevens had purported to act as Berry's agent. But the court, in remanding the case to determine the extent of the confidential relationship between Berry and Stevens, also noted another feature of the case that would make a great deal of difference as well. Even if no confidential relationship were found, the court indicated, a duty to disclose was created because Stevens undertook to tell Berry *something* about the oil discoveries. A duty to speak could be created by a half-truth. A person disclosing anything was obligated to disclose everything.

These cases indicate that although a secret may be acceptable a half-truth in the secret's place is not. Once the knowledgeable party undertakes to say anything, everything must be revealed. A secret hidden by a half-truth is as unacceptable as a secret hidden by a lie or by some active concealment on the part of the knowledgeable actor.

4. *Failure to update information.*—The final way in which courts consider the behavior of the knowledgeable actor is through examining whether the knowledgeable actor made an agreement revealing all genuinely believed information but later learned critical facts that changed the nature of the bargain before the agreement was finalized. If the knowledgeable party said something that was genuinely believed to be true at one point and later learns that the statement either was false at the outset or had become false, the knowledgeable party's initial statement creates an obligation to disclose later information that turns

114. 168 Okla. 124, 31 P.2d 950 (1934).

out to be more accurate. In short, once an actor says something, all updates of that information must be disclosed to the person who received the initial information, until the information can no longer influence the ignorant actor in making an agreement with the knowledgeable actor.

This requirement is very much like the rule mentioned above with regard to half-truths. In the situation involving half-truths, starting to say something means that one is obligated to finish. In the case of updating, saying something at one time creates an obligation to disclose new information at a later time. In both cases, the same basic principle applies: partial information is misleading and creates for the knowledgeable actor an obligation to disclose.

Wilson states this obligation as follows: "Where one party had made a material representation which is true at the time, but which subsequently to his knowledge, but not to the knowledge of the other, becomes, through the alteration of circumstances, untrue, it is his imperative duty to communicate to the other information of the change in affairs; and silence under these circumstances is fraudulent."[115]

The *Restatement (Second) of Contracts* makes a similar point in claiming that the obligation to disclose arises when one must prevent some previously stated fact from becoming a misrepresentation.[116] Keeton refers to this fact pattern as a "continuing misrepresentation"[117] and makes the important point that there is a difference between the duty to correct a generally held false impression and the duty to correct a false impression that one's own prior conduct has caused. The case for liability is much stronger in the second case than in the first.[118]

In *Guastella v. Wardell*[119] Guastella owned a subdivision that contained thirty lots. Wardell and others were purchasers of the lots. Guastella had represented that the subdivision was limited to residential construction and that, although there were no zoning regulations covering the area, there were restrictive covenants. Wardell's attorney checked but could find no restrictive covenants on file with the city, so Guastella's attorney supplied Wardell's attorney with copies. Later,

---

115. Wilson, p. 236.
116. American Law Institute, *Restatement (Second) of Contracts,* vol. 2, p. 431.
117. Keeton, p. 9.
118. Keeton, pp. 9–10.
119. 198 So. 2d 227 (Miss. 1967).

Guastella filed restrictive convenants only on the lot that Wardell bought and one other. Guastella failed to tell Wardell about the change.

The court made a point of the fact that Guastella and his attorney had made one representation but had failed to inform Wardell when the situation changed. Because Wardell believed that the first representation was still true, he bought the lot when he would not have done so otherwise. Guastella's previous representation gave rise to a duty to disclose all future changes until the contract was signed. In this case there was considerably more than mere silence, according to the court.

A similar problem can be seen in the *McElroy* insurance case mentioned above.[120] It will be recalled that in that case McElroy sent his secretary to sign an insurance policy for him. Although the case was decided on the grounds that insurance contracts require disclosure of all relevant facts, the point about updating is also important. In that case, McElroy had submitted to a physical exam that showed him to be in good health. During the time between the checkup and his secretary's signing of the insurance policy, however, McElroy had taken ill with a serious case of appendicitis that soon would prove fatal. Even if the insurance setting did not in itself require disclosure, this failure to update information would have made McElroy's claim invalid.

As in the case of half-truths, failing to provide a current and complete picture when one reveals information leads to liability when that incomplete picture results in loss to the person misled. This liability results not from keeping a secret—a practice that would have been perfectly acceptable in many of these cases if it had not been accompanied by these other considerations—but from the active participation in misleading another actor. If one tells someone something and then remains silent when the situation changes, one has participated in the harm caused; and liability flows from this.

WHAT ALL OF THESE CASES show is that, for a secret to be acceptable, the conduct of the knowledgeable actor must be beyond reproach. Secrets may only be kept in those circumstances where silence alone is the means of maintaining the secret. If the knowledgeable actor fortifies the secret with a lie, actively attempts to conceal the information from those who do not know, tells only part of the secret in such a way that the true information is disguised, or fails to inform the ignorant actor when previous statements become false, the law's permission to keep a

---

120. *Equitable Life Assurance Society v. McElroy*, 83 F. 631 (8th Cir. 1897).

secret is revoked. All of these actions actively create or help to maintain false impressions; and this the law does not allow. It is quite difficult to keep a "pure" secret—that is, one into which one of these forbidden activities does not creep. But the law allows only pure secrets, guarded simply by silence.

Cases concerning legal secrets turn on this set of legally relevant facts. In the next chapter we will explore which theory best accounts for why this set of facts, rather than some other, matters in law.

CHAPTER EIGHT

Comparing Economic and Contractarian Theories of Nondisclosure and Fraud

WHY SHOULD THESE LEGALLY RELEVANT facts matter and not some others? What picture of the world would take these sorts of considerations as important while relegating other features to the sidelines? In this chapter, we will explore the different accounts of the economic and the contractarian analyses of law to see which best accounts for the facts that are taken to be relevant in legal decisions.

The Economic Analysis of Nondisclosure

Anthony Kronman's analysis starts by simplifying the task a great deal; he leaves out quite a few of the cases. In particular, he removes from consideration all of those cases that present confidential relations, inherently fiduciary transactions, or active concealment or intentional misrepresentation. He implicitly excludes other issues—such as half-truths and failure to update—that might be considered in a discussion of disallowed means of keeping a secret. In addition, cases presenting relations of special confidence are nowhere to be found in the analysis. Cases whose outcomes depend on superior means of knowledge and the miscellaneous cases that present differing obligations for buyers and sellers are the only ones that Kronman's analysis covers. In short, Kronman has selected only a rather small subset of all the cases dealing with a duty to disclose. He writes of his decision to omit some of these cases: "I have chosen not to discuss these two problems [special obligations and active fraud] because they are centered on difficult questions of fact (when does a fiduciary relationship exist? where do we draw in the line between nondisclosure and fraud?) about which it is difficult to generalize in a way that is theoretically interesting." [1] While I believe

1. Anthony Kronman, "Mistake, Disclosure, Information and the Law of Contracts," *Journal of Legal Studies* 7: 1–34 (1978), p. 19.

that it would be very difficult for Kronman to extend the theory that he proposes into these areas, this is not a reason for discarding his theory at the outset. But it might be argued that a theory that explains both the cases that he has selected for study *and* those cases that he leaves out will be considered to be a better theory that one that simply explains a subset of the cases.

Kronman's theory relies heavily on the distinction between deliberately acquired information and casually acquired information. When the information is the product of a deliberate search, disclosure will not be required; when the information is casually acquired, disclosure will be asked. He argues that courts do not look in detail at whether the information in the particular case was deliberately or casually acquired, that they instead tend to require disclosure in cases where most information of the type at issue is casually acquired. Disclosure is not required in those situations that, *in general,* tend to involve information that is the product of a deliberate search.

Courts, as the previous chapter demonstrates, do not distinguish between casually and deliberately acquired information. Nor do they routinely and deliberately collect information about whether information was casually or deliberately collected, although, as we have seen, they do collect information about a number of other facts that are no easier to locate. But the success of a theory is not to be measured, necessarily, by whether the actors whose behavior one wishes to understand use the same conceptual framework. One could claim that if the theory works to predict behavior, attitudes, or even legal decisions, then the correspondence between the conceptual framework of the analyst and that of the subject is irrelevant.[2] But if a theory *both* explains the phenomena *and* corresponds to the way in which the subjects of the theory view the world, then it might be claimed that, as between two theories that explain equally well, the one that also corresponds to the view of the subjects is better, on the view that theories that explain more are better than theories that explain less. It does work against the theory, however, if, when one is studying decision making, it is discovered that the distinction that is posited to be at the center of the decision-making process is something about which information is routinely *not* collected by the decision makers whose behavior one is studying. They may not have to be conscious of the fact or of its influence on their actions, but it is hard to imagine how a fact could be

2. Milton Friedman, "The Methodology of Positive Economics," in *Essays in Positive Economics* (Chicago: University of Chicago Press, 1953), pp. 3–34; and Richard A. Posner, *The Economic Analysis of Law,* 3d ed. (Boston: Little, Brown, 1986), p. 15–17.

decisive if the actors do not know it at all and if there is no other mechanism through which the alleged cause could be shown to work its effect.

Let us examine the cases that Kronman cites as supporting his theory that the courts are really trying to encourage the production of socially valuable information that is the product of a deliberate search. Among cases that involve a buyer knowing the value of a subsurface oil or mineral deposit when the seller is ignorant of it, Kronman presents the case of *Neill v. Shamburg,*[3] in which Shamburg bought from his cotenant, Neill, her interest in the tract on which they jointly held an oil lease. Unbeknowst to Neill, Shamburg's adjacent properties were producing large quantities of oil. In the absence of this information, Neill sold her interest for less than it was worth. The court ruled that Shamburg did not have to disclose his information, making a special point of noting how much he had invested in developing that area (although some of the language of the court is quite ambiguous as to whether Neill had a legitimate expectation of being told these facts, as Kronman notes).

Information about oil deposits presents a clear case of deliberately acquired knowledge, in Kronman's view. The court, as Kronman noted, allowed the secret in this case (although the court could have argued that information about oil deposits under the tract jointly owned with Neill could have been acquired as a by-product of developing his own adjacent land). But not all cases involving information about oil deposits are decided in this way. The case of *Barry v. Orahood,* in which Barry bought Orahood's property when Orahood was on his deathbed, came out differently.[4] Even though Barry undoubtedly did a great deal of research to learn about the deposits under Orahood's land, he was not allowed to keep his secret in a situation where Orahood was in a weakened condition. If the courts are really trying to encourage the production of socially valuable information, then the condition of the ignorant actor should have little to do with the result.[5] The same research that would be protected if Barry were dealing with a healthy person is not protected against disclosure if the ignorant actor is sick.

3. 158 Pa. 263, 27 A. 992 (1893).
4. 191 Okla. 618, 132 P.2d 645 (1942).
5. Posner has argued that in fact this rule does make economic sense, for it prevents the largely wasteful search for information that one can use against the mentally or physically infirm. To prevent this socially wasteful searching, it makes economic sense to forbid profiting from this sort of information (personal communication, 14 December 1985, during my dissertation defense.) Still, this seems to be exactly the sort of case that

In the *Neill* and *Laidlaw* cases,[6] another consideration mars the simple elegance of Kronman's theory. If the ignorant actor in either case had asked the simple question, Do you know something about this deal that makes it more valuable for you than it appears to be? and if the knowledgeable actor had answered no, then neither Organ nor Shamburg would have been able to profit from his knowledge. The answer no would have constituted an intentional misrepresentation, and the courts would have disallowed the secret. In fact, in *Laidlaw* the outcome was ordered to turn on that fact when the case was remanded.

If the courts were really trying to protect investments in the production of socially valuable information, then the protection accorded should not turn so completely on whether the knowledgeable party is completely honest. It is very hard to maintain silence in the face of persistent questioning, and yet silence is the only method that the law allows for protecting a secret. From an economic point of view, as Darby and Karni point out in their article on fraud, the optimal amount of fraud in a system is not zero but rather varies with the conditions of the market.[7] Why should all fraud be disallowed when secrets pertaining to deliberately acquired information are permitted? Although Kronman explicitly excludes cases involving intentional misrepresentation, it is difficult to consider the rules in this area without noticing the complete reversal of result that happens in many cases when a lie creeps in. Why should someone invest in the production of expensive information when the investment can be wiped out with a single inappropriate word? Kronman's theory does not answer this question.

Kronman does grapple with the apparent inconsistency between his theory and the patent- and latent-defect cases. We have seen patent-defect cases under the heading of "equal means of knowledge," where the courts indicate that the ignorant party should have found out information that was easily within the reach of a simple investigation. Latent-defect cases were discussed, in part, under the heading of "superior means of knowledge," where courts note that the ignorant party would be hard-pressed to find out what the knowledgeable party

---

Coase had in mind when he argued that efficiency was increased by transferring goods from lower- to higher-valuing uses. See Ronald Coase, "The Problem of Social Cost," *Journal of Law and Economics* 3: 1–44 (1960). Clearly, the land in the hands of the oil company is worth more in economic terms than the same land in the hands of a very sick man who is not capable of exploiting the resources.

6. Kronman's analysis of *Laidlaw v. Organ,* 15 U.S. (2 Wheat.) 178 (1817) was discussed in chapter 6.

7. Michael Darby and Edi Karny, "Free Competition and the Optimal Amount of Fraud," *Journal of Law and Economics* 13: 67–88 (1973).

knows. Kronman argues that latent-defect cases overwhelmingly involve casually acquired information. He uses the example of termite infestation; and we have seen examples of defective septic tanks, contaminated wells, and unstable soil conditions. One learns about termites (or, presumably, about a defective septic tank) as a by-product of living in a house. One does not do things that one would not otherwise do just to find out the information. In these cases, Kronman argues, the law requires disclosure because the incentives to acquire this information will not be adversely affected by a requirement of disclosure.

But his theory does not explain why patent defects do not have to be disclosed. Patent defects, such as the placement of drainage vents so that they cannot possibly drain,[8] are also discovered by simple observation rather than by deliberate search. This is why the courts claim that ignorant parties should be aware of them. To explain these cases, which in the original version of Kronman's theory would have required disclosure, Kronman shifts ground. Instead of arguing that casually acquired information should be disclosed, he argues that requiring disclosure of things that should be obvious greatly increases transaction costs. In other words, if people were required to disclose all their casually acquired information before finalizing an agreement, they would take a long time, an inefficiently long time, in reaching these agreements. Requiring disclosure of obvious things would be inefficient because it would hinder transactions that would promote the transfer of goods to their most valued uses. Since the law is striving for this sort of allocative efficiency, no disclosure is required in these special cases.

Of course, the problem here is that what is required by efficiency shifts also. Originally, efficiency was promoted by getting information to the markets as quickly as possible so that goods could more rapidly reach their most valued uses. This required incentives—for example, property rights in information—and so secrets were permitted when those incentives were necessary to get the information produced and used. In the patent-defect cases, efficiency is promoted by making agreements without undue burden on the negotiating parties. Efficiency here requires *lowering* unbearable transaction costs, while in the first instance efficiency required *increasing* transaction costs. If people know that other people will be allowed to keep secret any deliberately acquired information, then ignorant people will adjust

---

8. *Gutelius v. Sisemore,* 365 P.2d 732 (Okla. 1961).

their behavior accordingly, if they are rational. Either ignorant parties will engage in duplicate research (which might be considered to be socially wasteful because there is an overinvestment of resources in producing knowledge) or they will spend much effort trying to screen transaction partners for honesty and openness. Either way, transaction costs in a system that permits secrecy are bound to increase. Getting around the patent-defect exception to Kronman's theory involves constructing a transaction-costs argument that is hard to square with the thrust of his main argument. Transaction-costs explanations seem quite malleable.

Aside from the potential problem mentioned at the outset—that is, that Kronman excludes from consideration many of the cases that fall under the heading of a duty to disclose (for example, the cases involving special obligations and active fraud)—Kronman's theory also faces the difficulty that, even within the narrow range of cases that he has chosen to explain, there are quite a few that simply contradict his theory. *Strong v. Repide*[9] and *Dyke v. Zaiser*[10] are two obvious counter-examples.

Still another case that contradicts Kronman's expectations is *Feist v. Roesler*.[11] In this case Feist failed to tell Roesler of the oil development proceeding adjacent to Roesler's land. Feist bought Roesler's property at less than it was worth because Roestler did not know of the new oil well. Although the opinion is not closely reasoned, the court seems to indicate that Feist was not allowed to keep his information secret because Roesler was living at some distance from the property and relied on Feist to tell him the truth. Similarly, in *Crompton v. Beedle*[12] Beedle was not allowed to profit from his knowledge about a valuable granite quarry on Crompton's property because he told her that he wanted to buy the land to get better access to his own property, a statement that the court later indicated was a lie. Crompton also lived at some distance from the property that she owned and was therefore relying on Beedle's statements about the value of the land.

Clearly, deliberate acquisition alone is not sufficient to explain why some cases require disclosure and others do not. Similarly, casual acquisition does not work perfectly either. The cases present a more complicated puzzle than Kronman's theory would admit, despite the fact that he has already confined his analysis to those cases that present a

9. 213 U.S. 419, 29 S. Ct. 521, 53 L. Ed. 853 (1909).
10. 80 Cal. App. 2d 639, 182 P.2d 344 (4th Dist. 1947).
11. 86 S.W.2d 787 (Tex. Civ. App. 1935).
12. 83 Vt. 287, 75 A. 331 (1910).

narrow sort of fact pattern. We have already seen that this theory would not work well with intentional misrepresentation cases or with special confidence cases. The theory also fails to explain why deliberately acquired information must be disclosed in confidential relationships.

Legitimate Nondisclosure and Equal Access to Information

The contractarian approach emphasizes equal access to information, with special attention being given to buffering the parties from catastrophic loss and to requiring the disclosure of deep secrets. To show in some detail how this theory works, I will review each of the legally relevant facts and show how each can be understood in light of the equal access view.

Materiality

The rule that a fact must be material if it is to be the subject of a disclosure requirement is a way of limiting the equal access principle to those situations in which one party might withhold information to control another's attitudes or actions. If the information that one actor possesses is not material to a transaction between that actor and another, then the information cannot be used as a strategic secret. The threshold rule of materiality, which limits the sorts of cases that can be litigated, serves to confine the equal access principle to only those cases in which one actor may control another through the selective revelation of information. In short, only strategic secrets are of concern to the law. And this makes contractarian sense. If a secret does not have an impact on someone else, then there is no reason to interfere with the person holding it.

Buyer and Seller

This set of cases is probably the most confusing to legal analysts. Buyers are generally held to a lower duty of disclosure than are sellers. The confusion can be remedied as soon as it is realized that buyers are not generally in a position of superior access to information, although occasionally they may have superior information. *Laidlaw* presents one of those unusual situations where the buyer has more information about a good than does the seller, although the buyer does not have superior *access* to information. This principle applies as well to the other cases that we have considered.

In *Holly Hill Lumber Co. v. McCoy,* where the buyer did not have to disclose the existence of lime quarries in the vicinity of the owner's land, it is clear that either party could have come by this information by making a simple drive around the area.[13] If anything, the seller had superior access to the information, since he lived in the area and easily could have found out what most people knew, that a large lime-mining company was operating there. The buyer did not have to reveal what the seller easily could have discovered. In *Kallgren v. Steele,*[14] however, Steele did have to disclose to Kallgren that the National Forest Service was about to close down the lodge that Steele was selling to Kallgren. Steele, being the owner, had been explicitly informed. Kallgren, not being in a position to be informed until after the sale, would have had to go to greater lengths to find out the information (especially since, in this case, the court noted that although Kallgren had gone to the Forest Service for information the Forest Service would not release it to him). Clearly, Steele had superior access, and disclosure was required.

Most of the buyer-seller cases hinge on whether the information at issue pertains to a latent or a patent defect of the thing being sold. Generally, sellers have to disclose latent defects (such as the unstable condition of a bluff on which a house that is for sale sits).[15] Latent defects are discovered through owning the house or the good in question, and it is generally more expensive for someone who does not own the house or the good to find out its hidden properties. Testing water supplies for bacteria,[16] checking round-the-clock to determine variations in the water supply,[17] or taking samples of the soil on the lot[18] involve much more effort when the person does not own the property than when she can learn about these things as a by-product of ownership.

Of course, this explanation is now sounding quite similar to the one forwarded by Kronman in these cases. It is true that deliberately acquired information generally takes more effort to obtain than casually acquired information. The main difference between the economic and contractarian theories is that Kronman would have the cases turn only on the level of investment of the knowledgeable actor, while the

13. 201 S.C. 427, 23 S.E.2d 372 (1942).
14. 131 Cal. App. 2d 43, 279 P.2d 1027 (2d Dist. 1955).
15. *Groening v. Opsata,* 323 Mich. 73, 34 N.W.2d 560 (1948).
16. *Janinda v. Lanning,* 87 Idaho 91, 390 P.2d 826 (1964).
17. *Simmons v. Evans,* 185 Tenn. 282, 206 S.W.2d 295 (1947).
18. *Cohen v. Vivian,* 141 Colo. 443, 349 P.2d 366, 80 A.L.R.2d 1448 (1960).

equal access principle requires that the cases turn on the *relative* levels of investment by both parties.

Some information is available to people only if they engage in significant research. If everyone would have to engage in a similar research effort, then whoever finds the information first can withhold it from others and use it as a strategic secret. The oil-discovery cases provide good examples of this. But if some actors can acquire the information through casual means while others would have to search for it, then those who can acquire the information casually must disclose to those who cannot do so. The structural position of being the owner of a house provides special access to information that would have to be disclosed to those who are not in this position of special access. It would follow from this, however, that if two people jointly owned something and one wanted to buy out the other's share, then there would be no obligation to disclose, absent a confidential relationship (which we will discuss shortly). This was, in fact, the case with Kronman's example in *Neill,* where one cotenant bought out the other's interest in an oil lease. Ownership gave both cotenants access to information about oil deposits; each only had to put forth the effort to discover it. Shamburg invested in the production of this information; Neill could have but did not. And the court ruled, as we would expect, that there was no duty to disclose.

The reason why there seems to be a difference between casually acquired and deliberately acquired information is because casually acquired information can generally only be casually acquired by *one* of the parties while the other party would have to engage in a deliberate search. Casually acquired information that can be casually acquired by *both* parties does not have to be disclosed. On this point, the patent-defect cases provide excellent examples. If either party can determine equally well the danger of a snowslide,[19] the existence of a major flood,[20] or the presence of a rusty staircase,[21] then there should be no obligation for either to tell the other about it. One need not rely on the highly flexible rationale of high transaction costs to explain these cases; they provide simple examples of equal access to information.

Deliberately acquired information, in Kronman's scheme, often does not have to be disclosed because the nature of the information is

19. *Doyle v. Union Pacific Railway Co.,* 147 U.S. 413, 13 S. Ct. 333, 37 L. Ed. 223 (1893).

20. *Farrar v. Churchhill,* 135 U.S. 609, 10 S. Ct. 771, 34 L. Ed. 246 (1890).

21. *Riley v. White,* 231 S.W.2d 291 (Mo. App. 1950).

such that all parties would have to do equal amounts of searching. Thus, the city of Louisville did not have to disclose subsurface rock to a construction company because it would have taken the same effort by the contractors to discover the condition.[22] But when one party has special access to the information, disclosure is required, as is evidenced by the requirement to disclose a hidden concrete swimming pool[23] or a special kind of landfill.[24] In both of these cases, the defendant's own action had provided special knowledge of the hidden conditions that others would have been hard-pressed to discover. Most of the court decisions that have allowed secrets about deliberately acquired information to be kept do so because the other party would have had to put in the same effort to find out the information. Hence the result is nondisclosure in *Laidlaw* and *Neill,* both of which Kronman cites as supporting his theory.

It is clear, then, that the cases that pose different obligations to disclose for buyers and for sellers do so because buyers and sellers have different probabilities of having structurally superior access to information. Sellers are more frequently in that advantaged condition than are buyers, hence the apparent difference in the outcomes when buyers and sellers are involved. Where sellers are not in such a position, we find previously puzzling exceptions to the rule that sellers disclose special knowledge. Kronman's theory to explain these buyer-seller cases can, in fact, be seen as a special instance of the equal access theory. Information that is deliberately acquired does not have to be disclosed only if others would have to put in the same effort to deliberately acquire it also. Casually acquired information only has to be disclosed when others would have to invest substantially more effort to find it than the knowledgeable party already has invested. It is the inequality in access to information that gives rise to the duty to disclose.

Equal Means of Knowledge

It should be clear that what the courts mean by "superior means of knowledge" is nothing other than our "superior access to knowledge." Over and over again in these cases, courts decide explicitly on the grounds that one party has information that is not within the "fair and reasonable reach of the other party and which he could not dis-

22. *Commissioners of Sewerage of the City of Louisville, Ky. v. Davis,* 88 F.2d 797 (6th Cir. 1937).
23. *Highland Motor Transfer Co. v. Heyburn Bldg. Co.,* 237 Ky. 337, 35 S.W.2d 521 (1931).
24. *Clauser v. Taylor,* 44 Cal. App. 2d 453, 112 P.2d 661 (1941).

cover by exercise of reasonable diligence, or means of knowledge which are not open to both parties alike." [25] This is obviously the same as the equal access principle.

Confidential Relationships

Many confidential relationships present situations in which one of the parties is much more likely than the other to have information within easy reach. Attorney-client, guardian-ward, and trustee-cestui are generally relationships in which one party has superior access to information.

One of the important bits of information that actors should know when they enter a transaction is in whose interests the other party is acting. The interest structure of the relationship is one of those factors that directly influences the interpretation given to the other person's actions. Just as knowing the state of war or peace mattered in *Laidlaw* because it affected the going price of tobacco, knowing whether someone else is acting in your interests matters because it affects directly the evaluation of the advice that you get from the other.

When Eastburn advised the Popejoys to sell their house while they had an offer from the Smiths, the Popejoys, believing Eastburn was acting in their interests, took his advice. [26] When Griffing bought the ring from Sims, the court argued that Sims believed that Griffing was advising him as to the true value of the ring. [27] And when William Sellers sold his stock in the bank to his brother James, he assumed that he and James had the same interests in keeping the bank in the family. [28] What these ignorant actors were ignorant of was not just the information about the true value that others would be willing to pay but also information about the context in which a transaction was taking place. Just as Laidlaw's agent would have evaluated the price of the tobacco differently if he had known about the treaty being signed, so Sellers would have evaluated the value of his stock differently if he had known that his brother did not share his intentions. If the Popejoys had known Eastburn was not acting in their interests and if Sims had known about Griffing's intentions, each would have behaved differently. The point here is that information about whether someone else is acting in one's interests is important information to have in evaluating a particular

---

25. *American Jurisprudence 2d*, 1968, s.v. "Fraud."
26. *Popejoy v. Eastburn*, 241 Iowa 747, 41 N.W.2d 764 (1950).
27. *Griffing v. Atkins (Sims, Intervenor)*, 1 So. 2d 445 (La. App. 1941).
28. *Sellers v. Sellers*, 428 P.2d 230 (Okla. 1967).

transaction. If the other actor withholds this information, it influences the transaction as much as if information about the good itself were withheld.

But this approach does not explain why this obligation exists only in cases where judges have found confidential relationships but not in all cases where someone is being misled about another's intentions. Something makes confidential relationships different from other sorts of relationships, different enough to require a different sort of rule.

The equal access theory does not work comfortably in this area. The cases indicate that the mere existence of a confidential relationship makes necessary more disclosure, especially about one's intentions, than is required in situations where the parties are dealing at arm's length. Cases involving partners or some other roughly equal relationship do not usually present unequal costs of acquiring information. Thus, while some of the confidential relationship cases can be explained by the equal access theory, others cannot.

Many confidential relationship cases can be better understood as expressing a principle of promissory obligation. The principle of promissory obligation simply says that when the parties have explicitly agreed that they share common interests over the range of their relationship, they should disclose relevant information and, in addition, should not use information gained in the context of the relationship to the detriment of their partners. The initial agreement gives rise to the later obligation. Thus, in the case involving Peckham and Johnson,[29] when their initial agreement was apparently broken by Peckham's earlier lawsuit, no current agreement was found to exist and no obligation of disclosure was found either. When these confidential relationships exist, strict rules of equal access are bent, and parties are obligated to disclose information relevant to their common interests regardless of the acquisition costs. We saw this part of the rule in effect in *Griffing,* where Sims easily could have taken the ring to another appraiser to find out its worth. The second part of the rule, that information gained in the context of the relationship cannot be used against the other party, was evident in *Popejoy.* Clearly, Eastburn knew of the Popejoys' vulnerability by virtue of his close relationship with them; and he was prevented from taking advantage of this special information. In cases presenting confidential relationships, the equal access rule seems to be trumped by the principle of promissory obligation.

29. *Peckham v. Johnson,* 98 S.W.2d 408 (Tex. Civ. App. 1936).

Given the contractarian analysis that we have been developing, this should not be surprising. A clear contractarian story can be told about why people would want a regime of promise-keeping, as long as they were buffered from catastrophe. Without the ability to count on promises, much of what is important and valuable in social life would be impossible to obtain. Only when the promise has not been voluntarily made or when someone stands to suffer a catastrophe as a result of the promise should such promises be unenforceable. On this view, we would expect confidential relationships to be accompanied by obligations to disclose, unless the secret would be expected to damage someone severely.[30]

Inherently Fiduciary Agreements

The courts in nondisclosure cases recognize that certain sorts of relationships and agreements lead to a special obligation to disclose all relevant information. This, too, may at first glance seem to have little to do with the principle of equal access as it has been discussed here. But the cases that present transactions considered to be inherently fiduciary also present problems of unequal access to information. If one thinks of the typical case in this category, insurance, one can see that there is frequently unequal access to information about the thing to be insured. In fact, this has often been explicitly forwarded as a rationale for the requirement of disclosure in insurance cases, as we have seen. One would expect, from the theory that has been forwarded here, that information to which one party had superior access would have to be disclosed while other information, equally within the reach of both parties, would not have to be disclosed.

Clearly, in *Carter v. Boehm,*[31] the leading case on the subject of disclosure in insurance law, this is precisely what Lord Mansfield wrote in his opinion. He indicated that "the special facts, upon which the contingent chance is to be computed, lie most commonly in the knowledge of the insured only"[32] and that therefore they have to be disclosed. But Lord Mansfield also wrote that "either party may be innocently silent, as to grounds open to both, to exercise their judgment upon."[33] In the case that Lord Mansfield was called on to decide, he ruled that Governor Carter did not have to disclose information that

---

30. When we discuss serial secrets and privacy, we will see more cases of this sort.
31. 3 Burr. 1095, 97 Eng. Rep. 1162 (K.B. 1766).
32. 97 Eng. Rep. 1162, 1164.
33. Ibid.

Boehm, the insurer, would have easily been able to find out. Neither did Carter have to disclose information to which Boehm had superior access (such as the movement of European fleets) but which Boehm did not bother to discover. It is clear that Mansfield intended by his decision to require disclosure only in those cases where the parties could not come by the information with roughly equal effort. He did not intend (as he is sometimes misunderstood to have meant) that the parties in these transactions should disclose everything that they know, no matter what the other party might discover. Mansfield in 1766 outlined the very principle that is being forwarded here as a basis for all nondisclosure decisions: when there is equal access to information, there is no obligation to disclose.

These "inherently fiduciary" transactions generally require disclosure because the usual case is one where the parties face very different levels of effort if they hope to acquire the same information. If the insured must disclose information to the insurer, it is because the insured is likely to have acquired the information much more easily than the insurer could. Thus, in the *McElroy* insurance case,[34] McElroy got sick after he had passed the physical exam required for the life insurance policy. He could find out about his state of health following the exam much more easily than the insurance company could. He therefore had to disclose this information. Only when the information is within equal reach of the insurer is there no obligation to disclose.

Special Confidence

The "special confidence" cases require a bit more explanation. It was argued earlier that the special confidence cases overwhelmingly involved situations where the ignorant party had some special conditions that created vulnerability. This observation can be stated differently in terms of the equal access theory. When an actor is in a position where the search for information would be difficult, the law still requires equal access. But equal access requires in these situations that the knowledgeable actor disclose information because the condition of the ignorant actor creates an inequality that would not exist for most other actors. For equal access to be found, it will be recalled, both actors must be capable of making equivalent efforts. Obviously, Orahood on his deathbed was in no condition to search for the information about the oil discoveries that might be made on his land.[35] Even though

---

34. *Equitable Life Assurance Society v. McElroy,* 83 F. 631 (8th Cir. 1897).
35. *Barry v. Orahood,* 191 Okla. 618, 132 P.2d 645 (1942).

Barry (or Barry's company) had invested quite a lot in the search for oil in that area, he was not allowed to use this information against someone who was not in any position to engage in an equal effort. Similarly, in the oil case involving Feist and Roesler, disclosure was required because Roesler, living at a distance from his property, could not make the observation (or at least could not make the observation as easily) that wells were springing up all around the adjacent properties.[36] The seventy-nine-year-old doctor who could not read stock tables[37] and the fifty-one-year-old widow who took endless dancing lessons[38] were obviously unable to evaluate their own assets, and those with superior access to information were not allowed to take advantage of this inability. One may quibble with the notion of access to information in these cases, but the courts seem to take cases of extreme ignorance as evidence that the ignorant party was incapable of the effort. In this case, those who do discover information that could be used against these disadvantaged folk are obligated to reveal their knowledge. Inequality in access caused by the ignorant party's disability still creates an obligation to disclose.

Methods of Secret-Keeping

It will be recalled that the law requires those who keep secrets to do so only with silence. Any other, more active means of guarding the secret is not allowed. At first glance, this rule may seem to have little to do with the question of equal access, but, as we will see, this rule is perfectly consistent with the theory that in nondisclosure cases the courts are trying to ensure equal access to knowledge.

Active concealment presents the clearest case. When one party actively conceals information from another party, the first party is trying to make the information harder for the other party to find; that is, the first party is increasing the effort that the other party would have to take to uncover the secret. If the law is concerned primarily with ensuring equal access to information, this sort of activity will clearly be found inappropriate. In the *Stewart* cattle case, for example, Stewart actually prevented the agent of Wyoming Cattle Ranche Company from coming onto the property and counting the cattle.[39] Clearly, if the agent still had wanted to get this information, he would have had to

36. *Feist v. Roesler,* 86 S.W.2d 787 (Tex. Civ. App. 1935).
37. *Chandler v. Butler,* 284 S.W.2d 388 (Tex. Civ. App. 1955).
38. *Vokes v. Arthur Murray Inc.,* 212 So. 2d 906, 28 A.L.R.3d 1405 (Fla. 1968).
39. *Stewart v. Wyoming Cattle Ranche Co.,* 128 U.S. 383, 9 S. Ct. 101, 32 L. Ed. 439 (1888).

engage in considerably more effort than he would have originally to make his count. One can imagine that disclosure of the number of cattle would not necessarily be required (after all, most everyone can count), but it was Stewart's act of making the information harder to acquire that served to create unequal access to the information.

The cases involving intentional misrepresentation, half-truths, and failures to update information all require a bit more sophisticated understanding of what equal access entails. For two actors to have equal access to information, they need to be able to put in the same effort with the same probability of success. One important determinant of this ability is that they need also to know that the information is there to be got. Deep secrets present enormous inequalities in access to information. The courts clearly recognize that if one actor has absolutely no idea that the information might exist, then equal access to that information means more than just putting in the effort. In *Simmons,* where the Evanses failed to tell the Simmonses that the water in their house was shut off twelve hours per day, the court noted that even though the Simmonses easily could have asked the neighbors, this condition was so bizarre that they could not be expected to know that it was necessary to ask.[40]

A similar principle is at work in the intentional misrepresentation, half-truth, and updating cases. In all of these cases, the knowledgeable party's actions led the ignorant actor to believe that the information was actually obtained and that therefore there was no need to search for the information because the effort would be wasted. Just as the old adage reminds us that things are always in the last place that we look, these cases should remind us that we stop looking for information if we think that we already have it. We do not know that we still need to look for it. When Beedle told Crompton that he wanted to buy her property because he needed better access to his own adjacent land, Crompton felt that she needed to look no further into his motivation.[41] When Thorwegan told King that the boat that Thorwegan owned was free of debt, King thought that he (King) knew all that he needed to know.[42] In the half-truth cases, the same effect can be seen. Savage thought Tyler told her the current financial condition of the company, when he in fact failed to tell her that the report was from the preceding year.[43] Berry thought that Stevens had told him the whole truth when Stevens

40. *Simmons v. Evans,* 185 Tenn. 282, 206 S.W.2d 295 (1947).
41. *Crompton v. Beedle,* 83 Vt. 287, 75 A. 331 (1910).
42. *Thorwegan v. King,* 111 U.S. 549, 28 L. Ed. 514, 4 S. Ct. 529 (1884).
43. *Tyler v. Savage,* 143 U.S. 79, 36 L. Ed. 82, 12 S. Ct. 340 (1892).

reported some oil development near Berry's property, when the oil development was in fact actually quite massive.[44] In the updating cases, Wardell assumed that the situation was as he had been told, and he saw no need to check things again. The insurance company also, no doubt, thought the same about McElroy.[45]

These cases raise the problem of justifiable reliance: should the ignorant actors be allowed to take the word of the knowledgeable actors without questioning? Certainly, the critic might say, we should not be able to get out of deals that we have made because we were simply gullible or did not do our own homework on the issue. The cases that we have seen here do not present such easy puzzles. In each of the cases, the ignorant actor faced substantial search costs if the claim at issue were to be checked. Moreover, in each instance the knowledge in question (whether Crompton's property could be used as access to Beedle's, whether Thorwegan's boat was free of liens, whether Tyler's company was solvent, whether Berry's or McElroy's stories were true) was clearly more easily accessible to the secret-keeper than to the ignorant person. In other words, in each case the information was easier for the knowledgeable person to acquire than it would have been for the ignorant person to locate. If the knowledgeable actors were deceiving the ignorant actors about things that should have been obvious (if, for example, A sold B a car with no engine), then I suspect that the law would have a difficult time finding for the ignorant parties. Fraud seems to be an acceptable justification for ignorant parties to get out of agreements only when the information about which they were deceived is difficult to check.

All of these cases demonstrate that the effect of lies, half-truths, and failure to update information is to make the ignorant party think that she has the information and stop looking any further. Because she stops looking, the true information is effectively out of reach. Intentional distortions of information thus have the same effect as active concealment; they make finding the real information less likely to occur. If the law is really concerned about equality of access to information, then all fraud, half-truths, and failures to inform someone when conditions change should not be permitted. Even if the information were initially equally accessible to both parties, fraud has the same effect as if the information had suddenly become more difficult to acquire, more inaccessible.

44. *Berry v. Stevens,* 168 Okla. 124, 31 P.2d 950 (1934).
45. *Equitable Life Assurance Society v. McElroy,* 83 F. 631 (8th Cir. 1897).

WE HAVE SEEN FROM OUR review of the contractarian and economic approaches to law that the contractarian theory is able to make sense of a number of features of the common law that the economic theory is not. Requiring disclosure of deep secrets and of information to which both parties do not have equal access makes good sense within a contractarian framework. The economic theory stumbles on these requirements, among others, making it less of a contender as a positive theory of the common law. Moreover, the contractarian approach has the advantage that it sees as important the same facts that judges highlight in their opinions, winning it an advantage not just in predictive power but also in its ability to represent with less distortion what the judges claim to be doing.

FOUR
Understanding Privacy

CHAPTER NINE

Secrecy and Privacy

Secrets in the Shadow of Privacy

AT FIRST GLANCE, ANY CLAIM of a right to privacy would seem inconsistent with the rules about withholding information that are found in the fraud cases. In those cases the guiding principle was that social actors should have equal access to information. But when the subject turns to personal information, we can see the tension between claims of equal access to information and claims of a right to privacy. If one has privileged access to information about oneself (that is, if one can acquire information about oneself more easily than others can), then how can one claim that there can ever be a right to privacy doctrinally consistent with the common law of nondisclosure and fraud?

One way around this dilemma is to claim that nondisclosure cases in fraud do not need to be doctrinally consistent with cases involving privacy. A number of authors have claimed that personal information about individuals is a fundamentally different kind of information than information about goods or transactions. This fundamental difference, many authors suggest, demands a different treatment in law. The arguments supporting this position have been quite varied:

1. *The autonomy defense.*—Edward Bloustein[1] and others[2] view personal control over personal information as critically important in preserving the autonomy of the individual from other actors in the social environment. Without the ability to withhold some thoughts and inclinations from the scrutiny of others, Bloustein argues, a person

---

1. Edward Bloustein, "Privacy as an Aspect of Human Dignity: An Answer to Dean Prosser," *New York University Law Review* 39: 962–1007 (1964) and *Individual and Group Privacy* (New Brunswick, NJ: Transaction Books, 1978).
2. See particularly Joseph Bensman and Robert Lilienfeld, *Between Public and Private: Lost Boundaries of the Self* (New York: Free Press, 1978).

would "merge with the mass. . . . [H]e is not an individual."[3] It is implied in Bloustein's work that the costs of sacrificing this individuality would be too great a burden for the society to bear; the right to privacy is necessary for the autonomy of individuals, even at the cost of some flawed decisions on the part of ignorant others.

2. *The sanity argument.*—Sidney Jourard, while agreeing that privacy is necessary for individuality to develop, adds another wrinkle to this argument. Without individual control over disclosure and non-disclosure of personal information, Jourard argues, mental health is threatened. Noting that a "society that would endure must draw a sharp distinction between public and private, if for no other reason than to make it a fit society in which people will gladly live,"[4] Jourard argues that there is a need for privacy, to encourage people to be open with themselves, thereby enabling them to adjust to the demands of modern society.

3. *The exchange argument.*—Charles Fried takes a different stance in defending the need for privacy. Arguing that control over information about oneself is a necessary precondition for entering into intimate relations with others, Fried observes that relations of love, friendship, and trust require "the voluntary and spontaneous relinquishment of *something* between friend and friend, lover and lover."[5] This "something," Fried notes, is the "title to information about oneself."[6] Privacy enables people to share information at the discretion of the subject of that information and, perhaps more importantly, provides the necessary resource to be exchanged in these intimate relationships. As Fried puts it, "privacy creates the moral capital which we spend in friendship and love."[7]

4. *The role-strain defense.*—A number of authors[8] have noted the close correspondence between the ability to hide information (often by withdrawing from interaction or observability) and the ability to carry

---

3. Bloustein, "Privacy as an Aspect of Human Dignity," p. 1003.

4. Sidney M. Jourard, "Some Psychological Aspects of Privacy," *Law and Contemporary Problems* 31: 307–318 (1966), p. 311.

5. Charles Fried, "Privacy," *Yale Law Journal* 77: 475–493 (1968), p. 482.

6. Ibid., p. 482.

7. Ibid.

8. See particularly Robert K. Merton, *Social Theory and Social Structure* (New York: Free Press, 1968); Robert K. Merton and Elinor Barber, "Sociological Ambivalence," in *Sociological Ambivalence* (New York: Free Press, 1975), pp. 3–31; Erving Goffman, *The Presentation of Self in Everyday Life* (Garden City, NY: Anchor Books, 1959); Rose Laub Coser, "Insulation from Observability and Types of Social Conformity," *American Sociological Review* 26: 28–39 (1961); and Barry Schwartz, "The Social Psychology of Privacy," *American Journal of Sociology* 73: 741–752 (1967).

on normal interaction or successful role performances. Often, credibility in a role requires conduct that an actor would find difficult to
maintain continually. In addition, because these roles often demand
contradictory behavior, it is important to the smooth functioning of
the society that individuals be allowed to withhold information about
themselves that is inconsistent with particular role demands. Only
when individuals have control over information about themselves can
credible role performances be maintained.

    5. *The corporate-actors problem.*—One of the most persistent
themes in the privacy literature has been the concern expressed by a
number of authors about the required disclosure of information about
individuals to large corporate actors. Authors such as Shils,[9] Westin,[10]
Westin and Baker,[11] Rule,[12] Rule et al.,[13] Miller,[14] and Coleman[15]
have noted the special problems that arise when massive quantities of
information are forwarded to the government or to large corporations.
The greater resources and power of corporate actors as compared with
that of individuals—and their ability to use the information to the
detriment of the individual—have been causes for alarm. Noting the
voracious appetite of organizations for information about the people
with whom they come in contact, many of these authors have argued
for a particularly strong right to privacy in contexts involving disclosures to these large corporate actors.

    As the variety of these arguments suggests, there is a widespread
feeling that personal information should not be subject to the same
rules and standards that the law of fraud and nondisclosure requires for
other information. Most of the authors mentioned above would probably be willing to argue that there are at least some circumstances in
which personal information should not be revealed. This would seem

    9. Edward A. Shils, *The Torment of Secrecy* (Carbondale, IL: Southern Illinois
University Press, 1956), "Privacy: Its Constitution and Vicissitudes," *Law and Contem-
porary Problems* 31: 281–306 (1966), and "Privacy and Power," in *The Intellectuals and the
Powers* (Chicago: University of Chicago Press, 1972), pp. 317–344.
    10. Alan F. Westin, *Privacy and Freedom* (New York: Atheneum, 1967).
    11. Alan F. Westin and Michael A. Baker, *Databanks in a Free Society: Computers,
Record-Keeping and Privacy* (New York: Quadrangle, 1972).
    12. James B. Rule, *Private Lives and Public Surveillance* (New York: Schocken,
1974).
    13. James B. Rule, Douglas McAdam, Linda Stearns, and David Uglow, *The
Politics of Privacy* (New York: New American Library, 1980).
    14. Arthur R. Miller, *The Assault on Privacy: Computers, Data Banks, and Dossiers*
(Ann Arbor: University of Michigan Press, 1971).
    15. James S. Coleman, *Power and the Structure of Society* (New York: Norton, 1974)
and *The Asymmetric Society* (Syracuse, NY: Syracuse University Press, 1982).

to put the law of fraud on a collision course with those who argue for a right to privacy.

On the other side of this debate, Richard Posner has argued forcefully against a right to personal privacy being granted in law,[16] precisely on the grounds that personal information is essentially no different than other information:

> We think it wrong (and inefficient) that the law should permit a seller in hawking his wares to make false or incomplete representations as to their quality. But people "sell" themselves as well as their goods. They profess high standards of behavior in order to induce others to engage in social or business dealings with them from which they derive an advantage, but at the same time they conceal some of the facts that these acquaintances would find useful in forming an accurate picture of their character. . . . [E]veryone should be allowed to protect himself from disadvantageous transactions by ferreting out concealed facts about individuals which are material to the representations (implicit or explicit) that those individuals make concerning their moral qualities.[17]

Posner argues that those from whom information might be withheld must also be considered, since they may be harmed by someone else's failure to disclose information about herself. There is no difference, Posner would claim, between being misled when an unscrupulous homeowner sells a house full of hidden termites and being misled by a prospective friend who hides his self-serving intentions; in both cases we lose, and in both cases we would be better off if we knew the information that the other person tries to conceal.

Privacy in Posner's discussion and in the discussion of legal secrets in this book does not include all the various things that one might mean by that term. Here we are only interested in that part of privacy that is concerned with the maintenance of secrets. Others have claimed that privacy is at its core the right of people to control information about themselves,[18] but in law generally, privacy suffers from an em-

16. Richard A. Posner, "The Right of Privacy," *Georgia Law Review* 12: 393–422 (1978), "Privacy, Secrecy and Reputation," *Buffalo Law Review* 28: 1–55 (1979), "The Uncertain Protection of Privacy by the Supreme Court," *Supreme Court Review* 1979: 173–216 (1980), and *The Economics of Justice* (Cambridge, MA: Harvard University Press, 1981). Although he argues *against* a right of personal privacy, he argues *for* a more extensive right to corporate privacy, as well as for a right to the privacy of conversations.

17. Posner, "The Right of Privacy," p. 400.

18. See, for example, Westin, p. 7; Fried; and Elizabeth L. Beardsley, "Privacy: Autonomy and Selective Disclosure," in J. Roland Pennock and John W. Chapman, eds., *NOMOS XIII: Privacy* (New York: Atherton, 1971), pp. 56–70.

barrassment of meanings, going well beyond the right to control information about oneself. The right to privacy has been invoked to enable married couples' use of birth control without restrictions imposed by the state[19]—and to extend this principle to unmarried people as well.[20] It has been used to enable people, particularly famous people, to prevent their name or likeness from being used for commercial purposes—at least not without requiring permission and, if desired, payment.[21] Privacy has been called on to prevent unrelated and uninvited men from observing women during childbirth[22] and to prevent police from including in a rogue's gallery of convicted criminals the photographs and fingerprints of a man who had not been convicted previously of a crime.[23] Formulations much like privacy have been used to forbid courts from ordering plaintiffs suing to recover for injuries from undergoing compulsory physical examinations[24] and used to enable Queen Victoria and Prince Albert to stop a private printer from continuing to publish reproductions of sketches that they had had made for each other and to show to friends.[25] Landlords have been punished for "bugging" the bedrooms of tenants,[26] and a veterinarian has been allowed to sue a garage owner for putting a five-by-eight-foot sign in his window advertising the veterinarian's debt.[27]

Clearly, in law privacy has come to mean something much more than simply the ability to control information about oneself.[28] It is no

19. *Griswold v. Connecticut,* 381 U.S. 479, 85 S. Ct. 1678 (1965).

20. *Eisenstadt v. Baird,* 405 U.S. 438 (1972).

21. See, for example, *Pavesich v. New England Mutual Life Insurance Co.,* 122 Ga. 190, 50 S.E. 68 (1905).

22. *Demay v. Roberts,* 46 Mich. 160, 9 N.W. 146 (1881).

23. *Itzkovitch v. Whitaker,* 115 La. 479, 39 So. 449 (1950).

24. *Union Pacific Railway Co. v. Botsford,* 141 U.S. 250 (1891).

25. *Prince Albert v. Strange,* 2 DeGex & Sm 652 (Q.B. 1849).

26. *Hamburger v. Eastman,* 106 N.H. 107, 206 A.2d 239, 11 A.L.R.3d 1288 (1964).

27. *Brents v. Morgan,* 221 Ky. 765, 299 S.W. 967 (1927).

28. The tort claim for invasion of privacy did not exist in American law until the late nineteenth century, and there is still no common-law action for invasion of privacy in Britain. See Walter F. Pratt, *Privacy in Britain* (Lewisburg, PA: Bucknell University Press, 1979). An article in the *Harvard Law Review* written by Samuel Warren and his former law partner Louis Brandeis ("The Right of Privacy," *Harvard Law Review* 4: 193–220 [1890]) is widely credited with giving rather sudden birth to an action in tort based explicitly in privacy. Although the article was primarily concerned with the excesses of the yellow press and its coverage of "blue blood" society events (like the wedding of Warren's daughter), it has been read as a justification for a great many other legal claims loosely organized around the many meanings of the central term, privacy. Probably the most influential—and certainly the most cited—attempt to organize into a single coherent scheme this vast and confusing array of cases that resulted from the recognition of a new cause of action was William L. Prosser's contribution in 1960 ("Privacy," *California Law*

wonder that judges and scholars, in a hurry to get on with a substantive problem at hand and confused about what else privacy might entail, do little more than quote Cooley's influential textbook on torts that what is behind all this is the right "to be let alone." [29]

All of the cases that will be analyzed in this section involve one social actor consciously withholding (or claiming the right to withhold) information from another social actor. This information pertains either to the social actor who is doing the withholding or to someone else who would rather that the information not be revealed.

The claim that one should be allowed to withhold information is not the same as the claim that others should be allowed to pry. Secret-keeping describes the act of withholding information from someone else, while prying describes actions designed to uncover information possessed by others. The two are clearly related. One may make a stronger argument for a right to pry (within limits) if the information that one is searching for is not legitimately a secret. These sorts of arguments are most common in Fourth-Amendment and in some trade-secret cases, where limitations on prying are at center stage. Presumably courts would not allow prying at all if the information to be uncovered were something that the possessor of the secret were entitled to keep secret. But there are other limits on prying as well. In both Fourth-Amendment and trade-secret cases, careful attention is often given to the precise means used as well as to the nature of the

---

Review 48: 383–423 [1960], p. 389). Prosser's article dealt only with the tort claim of a right to privacy and argued that there was not a single underlying interest that was represented but, rather, four separate torts under that heading. They were (1) intrusion on the plaintiff's seclusion or solitude or into his private affairs, (2) public disclosure of embarrassing private facts about the plaintiff, (3) publicity that places the plaintiff in a false light in the public eye, and (4) appropriation, for the defendant's advantage, of the plaintiff's name or likeness. As happens with particularly influential articles, Prosser's discussion of privacy became not only an attempt to find order in the cases but a standard against which other cases came to be judged. Many courts have cited Prosser as authority for their decisions, listing the four separate torts, placing the case at hand into one of the categories, and using Prosser's suggested standards to decide the case. With the publication of the *Restatement (Second) of Torts*, Prosser's categories have become the American Law Institute's statement of what constitutes the tort of invasion of privacy. Edward Bloustein's effort to argue that these four torts were merely an expression of the law's interest in human dignity ("Privacy as an Aspect of Human Dignity") was to little avail; Prosser's description stands as the definitive statement of the law's recognition of privacy as a tort.

29. Thomas McIntyre Cooley, *A Treatise on the Law of Torts or the Wrongs Which Arise Independent of Contract* (Chicago: Callahan, 1888), p. 29. As Posner points out (*Economics of Justice*, p. 315.), Cooley's phrase was meant to apply not to privacy but to assault and battery!

information sought. This should alert us to the fact that there is more involved in these cases than merely an interest in secrecy of the information. An illegitimate secret is a necessary though not a sufficient condition for allowing someone to pry into that secret. The means that the prying actors use are also subjected to scrutiny.[30]

An illegitimate secret may serve as one justification for prying, but it cannot be the only standard. Even if an illegitimate secret is present, not all means of prying are allowed by courts. The permission to pry is probably a relatively good indicator of the presence of an illegitimate secret, but the failure of a court to grant permission to pry does not necessarily imply that the secret is legitimate. Because prying and secret-keeping are conceptually distinct, this chapter will not address the legitimacy of prying per se. Only cases where the legitimacy of withholding information arises *in itself* will be considered here.

This section, which discusses the legally relevant facts in common-law cases that address whether personal secrets are legitimate, parallels the preceding section on fraud and nondisclosure. But there are a couple of peculiarities of the law about privacy that make it different from the law of fraud. It is to these differences that we now turn.

Privacy Claims and Standing to Sue

Privacy is a purely personal right. The only person allowed to sue for invasion of privacy is the person whose privacy was allegedly invaded. This means that another party cannot sue on behalf of someone who has suffered, even if the other party is a close relative of, as in one case, a diplomat endeavoring to sue on behalf of his emperor.[31] Occasionally, a person is allowed to sue on behalf of a dead relative—but only when there is an argument that the claimant's privacy was invaded also or when statutes explicitly provide for such an action. Most of the authority suggests that only the person who is the subject of the disclosure can bring a suit for invasion of privacy.

---

30. This concern with the appropriate means probably reflects a concern with intrusion rather than just a concern with public disclosure of private facts. Since privacy is a complicated notion, it is not surprising that individual cases present a number of different legal claims under the heading of privacy. Intrusive prying not only damages legitimate secrets but also seclusion. Insofar as secrecy and seclusion are separable interests (see Posner, *Economics of Justice*, pp. 268–272), one might expect somewhat different legal logics to apply to each.

31. *Von Thodorovich v. Franz Josef Beneficial Association*, 154 F. 911 (E.D. Pa. 1907).

When someone is allowed to press a charge of invasion of someone else's privacy, it is generally because some statute permits it. For
example, *Cox Broadcasting v. Cohn*[32] presented a father suing for invasion of privacy on behalf of his murdered daughter because her name
had been broadcast on television. He brought his case under a Georgia
statute that forbid disclosure of rape victims' names. Without this
statute, it is unclear that he would have had standing. More typical are
cases such as *Mettier v. Los Angeles Examiner*[33] and *Abernathy v. Thorn-
ton*,[34] in which relatives were not allowed to claim an invasion of
privacy on behalf of others. In *Mettier* the husband of a woman who
had committed suicide by jumping from a tall downtown building in
Los Angeles sued a newspaper for printing a photograph of his dead
wife. The court found that the right to privacy is purely personal and
cannot be claimed by a husband on behalf of his late wife. In addition,
the court indicated, the woman had waived any right to privacy that
she might have had by killing herself in such a dramatic and public
way.

Abernathy also involved a relative's death. Lucy Abernathy's son,
Curtis, had been shot and killed. She sued the local newspaper that had
published a picture showing the boy's body at the funeral home, with a
metal object protruding from the head. The reporter had written
a story indicating that the boy was on parole for having committed a
federal offense. Again, the court ruled that the shooting made the boy
a public figure not entitled to the degree of privacy accorded those who
were living outside the public spotlight. Besides, the court indicated,
the boy's mother could not press a privacy claim on behalf of her son,
since the claim had died with the boy.

Rules about standing raise two points that are relevant to our
discussion here. First, the person from whom information is withheld
cannot, by definition, sue under a privacy claim. If B wants to know
A's secret, B cannot sue A by claiming that A is taking too much
advantage of a right to privacy. Instead, if B wants to enforce a claim of
a right to know, then B would have to argue from some theory other
than privacy.

Probably what happens to most of these sorts of claims is that B's
in these positions forward a charge of fraud. We have already seen in
the fraud cases that information can be about one of the individuals

32. 420 U.S. 469, 95 S. Ct. 1029, 43 L. Ed. 2d 328 (1975).
33. 35 Cal. App. 2d 304, 95 P.2d 491 (1939).
34. 263 Ala. 496, 83 So. 2d 235 (1955).

who is a party to the transaction. In the case of *Fuller v. DePaul University*,[35] for example, DePaul was successful in claiming that Fuller's application for a job with DePaul was fraudulent because Fuller had failed to tell the university that he was a former priest who had abandoned his calling to get married and have children. DePaul was able to successfully argue that Fuller had an obligation to disclose his hidden past. In a similar case, the Jewish Center of Sussex County, New Jersey, was able to fire its rabbi, Chaim Whale, after it discovered that he had failed to reveal that he had been disbarred and convicted of bribery.[36] Both of these cases involved disputes over disclosure of information pertaining to an individual, but both cases were raised as fraud rather than as privacy claims. Because fraud cases may be brought by the person who is not the subject of the information and because privacy cases may only be brought by the person who is, it should not be surprising that some of the fraud and privacy cases present mirror images of the same disputes. The distinction between fraud and privacy cases does not necessarily reflect a difference between personal and nonpersonal information; rather, the distinction lies in who is allowed to press the legal claim.[37]

Because privacy claims must be brought by actors who want the information to be kept secret, a catch-22 problem arises. To defend one's right to keep certain information secret, one must sue someone else in a public courtroom. Almost inevitably, the information that the plaintiff wants to keep secret becomes part of the public record. To protect one's secrets, then, one must publicize them. One might expect that this sort of irony would lead particularly secretive or reclusive potential plaintiffs to turn away from the courts. Although it is impossible to tell just how many potential privacy claims are never made, one thing is clear: fraud and privacy cases may present symmetrical sorts of claims, but they do not present symmetrical sorts of incentives for filing lawsuits.

The second reason why questions of standing are relevant to our discussion involves corporate actors. Corporations are held to have no

35. 293 Ill. App. 261, 12 N.E.2d 213 (1938).

36. *Jewish Center of Sussex County v. Whale,* 165 N.J. Super. 84 (1978).

37. Not all cases in the common law that present claims of a right to know are fraud cases. In an interesting case in 1917, *State v. Lankford,* 6 Boyce 594, 102 A. 63 (Del. 1917), a jury in Delaware found a man guilty of assault and battery for failing to tell his fiancée that he was suffering from syphilis. By accepting her uninformed consent and communicating the disease to her, he was held to be inflicting an injury on her.

right to privacy.[38] Generally, courts assert this without providing further explanation. Only natural persons can bring a charge of invasion of privacy; either natural persons or corporate actors can be defendants in these actions, but only natural persons can be plaintiffs.

What happens in cases where "private" information about a corporation is revealed to someone else? If one takes the cases involving privacy and corporations literally, then one might think that the corporate actor has no recourse. But this, of course, is not true. Just as in privacy cases, where those who claim that they should know the information can possibly bring an action in fraud, so corporations whose secrets have been divulged can sometimes bring an action for trade-secret violation.

Trade secrets, I would argue, are the corporate version of a right to privacy. In trade-secret cases, the subject of the secret, the corporation, initiates the suit, just as in privacy cases. The situations that arise in trade-secret cases are formally identical to the cases that arise under a claim of privacy. The only difference is in who has standing to sue. Privacy claims are brought by individuals; trade-secret claims are generally, though not always, brought by corporations.

In this section, I will show not only that the formal situations raised in privacy and trade-secret cases are identical but also that the sorts of legally relevant facts that judges emphasize are also identical. The logic that can be seen in the privacy cases applies equally well to trade-secret cases. Although it is generally more common in the legal literature to deal with one area of legal doctrine at a time, we will take on two at once to show that the legal categories really differ only in their rules of standing, not in their rules about which sorts of secrets count as legitimate ones.

38. *Maysville Transit Co v. Ort*, 296 Ky. 524, 177 S.W.2d 369 (1943); *U.S. v. Morton Salt Co.*, 338 U.S. 632 (1950); and *Tomlin v. Taylor*, 290 Ky. 619, 162 S.W.2d 210 (1942).

CHAPTER TEN

Threshold Rules and Direct Secrets

WHICH LEGALLY RELEVANT FACTS MATTER in the determination of privacy-as-secrecy cases? In this chapter and the next, I will review the case law, focusing on the sorts of facts that judges take to be most relevant in these cases. In this chapter, I will first examine the threshold rules that hold across the whole area. Then, I will focus on two-party or direct secrets. The next chapter explores what happens when a third party is added, creating the possibility of serial secrets.

Threshold Rules

Threshold rules are those rules of a legal system that screen out cases failing to present justiciable issues. They ensure that cases reach some minimal level of seriousness, and they eliminate cases that fail to present a legally recognized claim. In the area of privacy-as-secrecy, two threshold rules can be located.

Secrecy

To be able to successfully claim that one's privacy has been invaded, one must first demonstrate that the information in question is actually secret. If the information has been publicly revealed before, either by being demonstrated in a public place or by appearing in public records, then one has no legal right to claim invasion of privacy when someone uses or further publicizes that information.[1]

---

1. We will see later, however, that occasionally someone can claim that previously public information that has not been public for some time should be kept secret now. Also, information public in some contexts may not be considered public in other contexts. Generally, however, a plaintiff needs to show that the information was not, at the time of the alleged invasion of privacy, public in that context.

In *McLain v. Boise Cascade Corp*[2] McLain applied for workmen's compensation after he had injured his back carrying a one-hundred-pound bag of flour. His employer, Boise Cascade, had his injury investigated by the firm that they used to check workmen's-compensation claims. The investigating firm told Boise Cascade that they could discover nothing wrong with McLain and that they had had reports that McLain had worked for a mortuary while he allegedly was disabled. Boise then terminated McLain's payments, and he petitioned to reinstate his claim. At this point, Boise hired a detective agency to spy on McLain, and detectives took eighteen rolls of movie film showing McLain working around his house and mowing his lawn. When McLain showed up at the hearing that was called to discuss his claim, he learned of the movies for the first time and was outraged. He sued Boise Cascade for invasion of privacy.

The Oregon court acknowledged that a right to privacy exists in the state, but also noted that "one who seeks to recover damages for alleged injuries must expect that his claim will be investigated and he waives his right of privacy to the extent of a reasonable investigation."[3] In this case, the court continued, the investigation was reasonable because the information turned up could have been seen by any passerby near McLain's house. Because McLain's actions were visible to anyone watching and because he made no effort to keep them secret, the investigation ordered by Boise was not an invasion of privacy. In short, McLain did not appear to be keeping his health a secret and public information was fair game for investigators.

In a similar case, *Schwartz v. Thiele*,[4] Judith Schwartz was walking across a parking lot with her sister after they had had breakfast in a local restaurant. David Thiele, a physician and surgeon who happened to be in the same parking lot, came up to her and purported to do a quick examination of her for signs of mental illness. Following this incident, Schwartz called her attorney immediately, complaining about Thiele's behavior. Thiele, for his part, wrote a letter to the Psychiatric Department of Superior Court, claiming that Schwartz was mentally ill and that she was likely to injure herself and others if she were not hospitalized or detained immediately. A judge appointed a doctor to examine Schwartz, and Schwartz got an opinion from her own doctor. Both doctors agreed that she suffered from no mental

---

2. 271 Or. 549, 533 P.2d 343 (1975).
3. 533 P.2d 343, 346.
4. 242 Cal. App. 2d 799, 51 Cal. Rptr. 767 (1966).

illness, and the proceedings were dismissed. Schwartz sued Thiele for invasion of her privacy.

Noting that Thiele had observed Schwartz's behavior in a public place, the court went on to indicate: "If a person in good faith and probable cause makes a written statement to an agency charged with the enforcement of law, designed to give such agency information upon which it can conduct an investigation, such communication is not an invasion of the right of privacy of the person who is the subject of the communication."[5] This sort of reasoning implies that any publicly observable behavior can be reported to authorities without liability attaching to the person who forwards the information. Any right to privacy that one may claim cannot stand if the information was revealed in a public place.[6]

Information is considered public when it is revealed in a public place, but it is also considered public if it is part of public records. In *Hendry v. Conner*[7] Judy Hendry took her child to the hospital for treatment. While she was waiting, an employee of the credit department told her that her child could not be admitted because Hendry had filed for bankruptcy and had not paid her previous bills. Apparently, this information was revealed in a voice loud enough that the whole waiting room could hear. Embarrassed, Hendry filed charges against the employee for invasion of privacy.

The court wrote that Minnesota did not recognize a common-law action for invasion of privacy but that even if it did, this would not be an instance of one. The fact of Hendry's bankruptcy had appeared in public records, and, as a result, she could not claim that revealing this information constituted an invasion of privacy; the information was already public.[8]

5. 51 Cal. Rptr. 767, 771.

6. It should be noted that some privacy opinions are written by judges who seem to take the spirit of an invasion-of-privacy claim seriously. In *Schwartz* the judge did not describe the behavior that apparently gave rise to Thiele's investigation, since that would have given further publicity to the incident that Schwartz claimed was private. Schwartz claimed in her charge that she had been stopped without probable cause and that Thiele had been malicious. Thiele claimed that he had had good reason to believe that Schwartz was ill. Without a description of Schwartz's behavior, though, it is hard to tell just what sort of actions provide a legitimate basis for complaint to authorities. Apparently the court did not think that Thiele was being malicious.

7. 303 Minn. 317, 226 N.W.2d 921 (1975).

8. The fact that the information was in the public record did not mean that the information was public in the hospital setting, however. Clearly, Hendry believed that others in the waiting room were told something that they did not previously know.

In *Baker v. Burlington Northern*[9] Baker's complaint of invasion of privacy was dismissed for the same reason. In this case, Baker's criminal record came to the attention of his employer, Burlington Northern, and he was fired as a result. A letter detailing Baker's record was circulated to a variety of officials around the company, sent to his union, and mailed to the Idaho Department of Employment. Baker sued for invasion of privacy and lost because his criminal record was on public file. Even though the letter revealed information that the recipients did not otherwise know, the fact that they could have found out from publicly available files made the information not secret.

In a more publicized case, *Cox Broadcasting v. Cohn,*[10] the Supreme Court reiterated this point. Georgia's statute forbids news media from publicizing the names of rape victims; yet the names of these rape victims appeared in the public records of the trials. Justice White's opinion noted that by allowing the victim's name to appear in the record "the state must be presumed to have concluded that the public interest was thereby being served. . . . If there are privacy interests to be protected in judicial proceedings, the States must respond by means which avoid public documentation or other exposure of private information."[11] Rather than bend the rule that information in public files cannot be considered private, the Court suggested the possibility that the states not include this information in the files to begin with, since anything that appears in the public files could be considered appropriate information for the press.

What all of these cases show is that information that is already available to the public cannot be considered to be private, even if the person charged with invasion of privacy brought this information to the attention of people who did not already know. In short, it is not whether a person already knows that matters; rather, what is important for a privacy claim is that a person could not have found out from publicly available sources. What is not secret cannot be considered private.

Serious Harm

Although in torts it goes almost without saying that there is no liability without loss, privacy cases seem to present the courts with a number of

9. 99 Idaho 688, 587 P.2d 829 (1978).
10. 420 U.S. 469, 95 S. Ct. 1029, 43 L. Ed. 2d 328 (1975).
11. 420 U.S. 469, 495–496.

complaints where the loss is not sufficient for the courts to conclude that a serious invasion of privacy has occurred. Kalven argued that actions for invasion of privacy in tort would tend to be trivial, because serious invasions were already covered under other torts (trespass, defamation, or intentional infliction of emotional distress, for example).[12] Incidents argued simply in privacy, then, were bound to present relatively trivial issues, Kalven predicted. A number of cases seem to bear out his fear. Obviously the incidents bothered the plaintiffs, but it is not always so clear that the incidents caused enough harm to present a legal claim. Law generally does not enforce good manners; it tries to struggle with who should bear serious losses.

Three sorts of cases illustrate attempts by courts to screen out complaints that do not allege significant enough harm. In the first sort of case, information is revealed about the plaintiff that may be considered to be private, but it does not reflect badly on the plaintiff. Such a situation was presented in *Hamilton v. Crown Life Insurance Co.*[13] Betty Hamilton's husband killed himself. When Crown Life Insurance paid her the insurance claim, an agent for Crown Life went around Hamilton's neighborhood attempting to sell insurance and telling the neighbors the amount that she had received. When Hamilton sued for invasion of privacy, the Supreme Court of Oregon indicated that not every disclosure of personal information created a right of action. The court distinguished between bad manners and action giving rise to legal liability: "It must be conceded that the defendant's conduct was offensive and boorish. It was in complete disregard of the plaintiff's wishes and feelings, and was no doubt well outside the ethical norms of the insurance industry."[14] But, the court continued, even though the information disclosed was private, it was not shocking to an ordinary, reasonable person and, as such, was not actionable.

In *Wheeler v. P. Sorensen Manufacturing Co.*[15] P. Sorensen, Wheeler's employer, distributed a large printed sheet with a photocopy of Wheeler's paycheck printed on it. Also included was information about the recent raise that Wheeler had received. The poster was part of an antiunion campaign being run by P. Sorensen, and the information on the poster was intended to convey how well P. Sorensen treated workers who worked hard. Following the release of the poster,

12. Harry Kalven, Jr., "Privacy in Tort Law—Were Warren and Brandeis Wrong?" *Law and Contemporary Problems* 31: 326–341 (1966).

13. 246 Or. 1, 423 P.2d 771 (1967).

14. 423 P.2d 771, 773.

15. 415 S.W.2d 582 (Ky. 1967).

Wheeler was shunned by her fellow employes, was later fired[16] and then blacklisted by other employers. Despite these apparently dire consequences, the court ruled that the information on the poster showed Wheeler to be a competent, commendable, and praiseworthy employee and that publishing such information was not unreasonable. Because the private information published about Wheeler was not discreditable, she could claim no invasion of privacy. As both of these cases demonstrate, then, information that the court believes does not show the plaintiff in a bad light is outside the bounds of a right of privacy, even if the information was not previously publicly available.

The second sort of case that presents insufficient harm involves oral declarations. It is the rule in some states, but not in others, that one's privacy cannot be invaded by "merely oral declarations."[17]

What seems to be going on in these cases is not some distinction between oral and written communication per se (although the distinction persists in defamation); rather, the courts seem to use this distinction whenever they wish to throw out a case that does not present a significant enough harm. *Hendry,* where those present in a hospital waiting room were able to hear about the woman's financial affairs, provides one example. In *Pangallo v. Murphy*[18] a woman sued her landlord for announcing in front of some friends that he had thrown her out of his apartment and that she was dirty and unfit to live there. The court indicated that merely oral declarations were insufficient to justify an invasion-of-privacy claim; but, clearly, in this case there was no special harm alleged. Most of the cases thrown out for presenting merely oral declarations involve approximately this level of harm. In cases presenting oral declarations alleging greater harm, the courts do not generally seem to have trouble finding some way to reach them. In *Biderman's of Springfield v. Wright*[19] a debt collector came frequently to Wright's cafe and announced that Wright was a deadbeat. The harrassment forced Wright to move and get a new job. The court noted that "the oral publication of a private matter with which the public has no proper concern may be just as devastating and damaging as a written

16. The opinion does not make clear whether the firing had anything to do with this incident, but the reaction of fellow employees both there and in other, similar establishments indicated that they believed that Wheeler was part of the employer's anti-union crusade.

17. See *Grimes v. Carter,* 241 Cal. App. 2d 694, 50 Cal. Rptr. 808, 19 A.L.R.3d 1310 (1966), particularly the annotation that sets out the differences among states in adhering to this rule.

18. 243 S.W.2d 496 (Ky. 1951).

19. 322 S.W.2d 892 (Mo. 1959).

communication." [20] Clearly, the intention here is not to make an arbitrary distinction between the written and the spoken but to distinguish between complaints that present serious harm and those that present trivial harm. In this case, Wright won her suit for invasion of privacy. The distinction between oral and written statements as a basis for invasion of privacy seems to be at its core a measure of severity of harm. When the harm is serious, the distinction melts and oral declarations are found to be invasions of privacy.

The third sort of case that demonstrates the severity of harm and its importance in privacy disputes involves collection but no use of information. Merely demonstrating that someone has private information that one would rather this person not have is not sufficient. One must be able to demonstrate that this possession results in some harm.

In *Benjamin v. Ribicoff*[21] Winifred Benjamin was admitted to the hospital. When she left, the hospital forwarded her medical records to the local social security office that processed Benjamin's checks. She sued the Social Security Administration for accepting this personal information about her, but her claim failed. Since the social security office had apparently not used or disclosed the information, Benjamin had no cause of action. The social security office's mere possession of the information did not create an invasion of privacy.

Similarly, in *Wilson v. Colonial Penn Life Insurance Co.*[22] Wilson charged her insurance company with disclosing information from her insurance records to other insurance companies. In the absence of any evidence of harm to Wilson, she was found to have no justifiable claim that an invasion of privacy had been created by the dissemination of the information. As these cases demonstrate, to justify a claim of invasion of privacy one needs to show that some specific harm results from the disclosure of personal information; not liking the disclosure is not enough.

A CASE THAT SHOWS ALL of the elements we have discussed thus far is *Nader v. General Motors*.[23] Just before the publication of *Unsafe at Any Speed*,[24] Ralph Nader's book critical of the automobile industry, General Motors began an investigation of him. Agents of General Motors

20. 322 S.W. 892, 897.
21. 205 F. Supp. 532 (D. Mass. 1962).
22. 454 F. Supp. 1208 (D. Minn. 1978).
23. 25 N.Y.2d 560, 255 N.E.2d 765 (1970).
24. Ralph Nader, *Unsafe at Any Speed* (New York: Grossman, 1970).

asked friends of Nader about his views of current social issues and about his sexual proclivities, followed him around in public places, watched him, and tapped his telephone, among other things. The Court of Appeals of New York, applying District of Columbia law, indicated that there was no basis for a public-disclosure-of-private-facts privacy claim here.[25] Watching Nader in a public place was no violation of privacy, because the information was not private. Asking questions of Nader's acquaintances was not an invasion of privacy because nothing discreditable was turned up (or at least nothing discreditable was alleged to have been discovered). Besides, there was no harm alleged, since it was not clear that the information ever had been used. Although the court did not rely on the oral declarations argument, it could have done so, since the disclosures that Nader's friends made to the General Motors agents were merely oral. The general point, however, is that the court found Nader's complaint wanting both because the information discovered was not kept secret and because the harm alleged was not sufficient. This illustration should demonstrate that threshold rules are not innocuous; they screen out a substantial number of cases, cases that might strike some readers as deserving of more serious legal attention.

Clearly, limiting privacy complaints to those cases that present material not previously made public or to those that present substantial harm radically truncates the range of complaints that are actionable. As we have seen, there are disclosures that cause harm but involve public information and there are disclosures that involve private information but do not cause sufficient harm. Only in situations where private information is disclosed and causes substantial harm is a claim of invasion of privacy likely to stick. But, as we will see, there are still a number of hurdles to jump, even when one has crossed the threshold into actionable claims.

Direct Secrets

When A has a secret and B wants to know it, the situation presents a direct secret. Disclosure occurs when A volunteers the information to B, and a simple secret can be found when A hides the information from B. Not surprisingly, both of these situations can be found in common-law cases, and each has a somewhat different logic. In disclosure the

---

25. Although the court did remand the case on the basis that wiretapping and particularly intrusive surveillance might have stated a cause of action for invasion of privacy under intrusion rather than under public disclosure of private facts.

cases turn on the issue of consent, while in simple secrets the cases turn
on the issue of relevance.

Consent

Although such cases are not very common, occasionally A volunteers
information to B and then wishes to take it back. Knowledge being
what is it, repossession is not a real possibility. A's only recourse is to
ask for damages from B for invasion of privacy.

Just such a case arose in *Vespa v. Safety Federal Savings and Loan*.[26]
Marianne Vespa was two years behind in her house payments, and
Safety Federal began foreclosure proceedings. Just before the formal
proceedings began, John Wiggins, a vice-president of Safety Federal,
called on Vespa to inquire whether she were going to pay and, if she
were not, whether the house needed repairs before being sold. Apparently, Vespa invited him in, made him feel welcome, and talked with
him for three hours. She had even invited him back, and when he took
her up on her offer, she again was friendly. Sometime later, however,
as foreclosure became inevitable, Vespa sued Safety Federal for send-
ing Wiggins out to invade her privacy. Ruling that there was no
invasion of privacy because Vespa had not objected to Wiggins's presence at the time, the court appeared to rely on the notion that she had
volunteered the information. Her earlier consent ruled out the later
claim.

A similar case is presented in *Shorter v. Retail Credit Co*.[27] Drop-
ping by the Shorter residence, Wimberly, an agent of the Retail Credit
Company, asked Sarah Shorter her age, number of children, her husband's occupation and salary, the age of their house, and whether they
had fire and theft insurance on their house. Sarah Shorter answered
these questions with no sign that they were troublesome. Apparently,
however, when her husband got home he became outraged on hearing
of the matter. Sarah Shorter sued Retail Credit for invasion of privacy
and lost. The court indicated that there was "neither rudeness nor
coercion."[28] Besides the fact that most of the information was public
anyway (Sarah Shorter did not know her husband's salary and so did
not answer that question), the inquiry was polite and limited, and
Sarah Shorter volunteered the information easily. Here again, consent
seems quite important.

26. 219 Kan. 578, 549 P.2d 878 (1976).
27. 251 F. Supp. 329 (D.S.C. 1966).
28. 251 F. Supp. 329, 332.

In *Solis v. Southern California Rapid Transit District*[29] Solis was hit by a bus and taken to the hospital. While she was still in the emergency room, investigators from the bus company came and asked her questions about the accident. Both a nurse and a doctor had told the investigator that she could answer questions, and the woman had volunteered the answers without complaint at the time. After satisfying itself that there had been no deception and no coercion, the court ruled that Solis could get no solace from the court. There was no invasion of privacy because she had volunteered information without objection. She had consented.

What this indicates is that disclosure cases are bound to lose, unless the plaintiff can demonstrate that the consent was not real. In the absence of fraud or coercion, a voluntary disclosure can never be grounds for a claim of invasion of privacy.

Relevance

If A does not voluntarily disclose information to B and B wants that information, B may ask A about it. But what if A refuses to answer? Can A ever claim that B's questions were unreasonable and that A does not have to answer them? In these cases, A sues B for invasion of privacy because B asks the questions in the first place. The question for the courts is whether A should recover from B either for the annoyance that the asking caused or, more likely, because B took some action against A when A refused to answer.

Cases that involve a question of this type turn on the notion of relevance. If the information that B seeks is relevant to a legitimate purpose of B, then B can either demand that A turn the information over or B can act against A's interests because A has refused. The burden of proof appears to be on B in these cases; B has to explain why the information is necessary.

In *Cangelosi v. Schwegmann Brothers Giant Super Markets*[30] a shopper wrote a check for her purchase and gave it to checkout clerk Cangelosi. When the shopper's check was returned with her bank statement, she discovered that the check had been altered to read $57 instead of $37. In investigating this incident, the manager of the supermarket called Cangelosi in for questioning. Cangelosi refused to answer any questions (although she asked to be given a lie detector

29. 105 Cal. App. 3d 382, 164 Cal. Rptr. 343 (1980).
30. 379 So. 2d 836 (La. App. 1980).

test), and she ran out of the room, sobbing. Even though her lie detector test results showed no evidence of deception, she was fired from her job. She sued for invasion of privacy.

The court ruled that the employer was entitled to investigate, as long as the investigation was reasonable and conducted in good faith. In this instance, the court noted, the questioning was brief, took place at a reasonable time and place, and was appropriately limited. There was found to be no invasion of privacy. Attention in this opinion was focused on whether the questions were reasonably related to some-thing that the defendant was entitled to ask; in short, the court exam-ined relevance.

We can see this emphasis on relevance in *Pitcher v. Iberia Parish School Board*.[31] The plaintiff in this case was a teacher who had refused to supply to the school board the results of an annual physical. She was fired and she sued for invasion of privacy. Despite the precedent of *Union Pacific Railway Company v. Botsford*,[32] in which a woman was permitted to refuse to undergo a compulsory physical exam, the court in *Pitcher* found that the teacher had to submit to such an exam. The court noted that all of the items that were to be included in the physical were reasonably related to the job and that therefore there was a good reason for requiring it; this was not, so the court wrote, an invasion of privacy.

But "relevance" is not so clear a notion. To judge from the court opinions given along these lines, it seems as if almost any argument that the defendant can make to show that the information might be relevant is accepted by the courts. In *Hines v. Columbus Bank and Trust Co.*[33] J. T. Hines, then ambassador to Costa Rica, was sent a letter by the Columbus bank. The letter asked him whether he was planning to apply for Costa Rican citizenship, what his salary was, whether Hines had any stock in a particular company doing business in Costa Rica, and what his connections with any businesses there might be. His staff received the letter and began their customarily efficient routine of answering all the ambassador's mail, even though the ambassador had no account with the bank, did not owe the bank money, and had no business with them at all. The letter from the bank touched off an investigation of Hines in which he very nearly lost his job owing to the suspicion that surrounded him as a result. In the opinion there is one

31. 280 So. 2d 603 (La. App. 1973).
32. 141 U.S. 250 (1891).
33. 137 Ga. App. 268, 223 S.E.2d 468 (1976).

brief mention of a lawsuit in which the Columbus bank was engaged for which the information might be related, but this is not explained in any detail.

The court concluded that this did not constitute an invasion of privacy. The majority opinion reasoned: "In making our decision, we balance the precious 'right to be let alone' which is desired by everyone against the necessities of commerce. When put on the scales, it is apparent that the courts should not interfere with the established business practice whereby inquiries are made concerning activities, reputations, and financial responsibility—provided it is sought legitimately and not for a malevolent purpose. Everyone in our workaday world recognizes the importance of this kind of information."[34] Apparently everyone recognizes the importance of this kind of information except the three dissenting judges, for the dissenting opinion argued that "There is nothing in the complaint to show the defendants had any reason whatever to make inquiries regarding the plaintiff."[35]

Although the majority and dissenting opinions disagreed about whether the information was legitimately sought, both opinions were couched in the language of relevance. The majority opinion insisted that the disclosure was required because it was so important to established business practices. The dissent argued that the information was not relevant. Both opinions acknowledged that what one has to demonstrate is a reasonable relation between the questions and the defendant's legitimate purpose. What they disagreed about was whether the queries directed at Hines represented a fishing expedition or a set of questions that provided necessary information.

Throughout the cases decided on relevance grounds, courts often seem uncomfortable with having to decide whether information is reasonably related to the inquirer's interests. Over the vast majority of situations, there is no clear answer to this question, and the courts generally take the inquirer's arguments at face value. It should not be surprising that much of the legislative initiative in this area takes the form of pronouncements on the issue of relevance. Some statutes indicate that arrest records (as distinguished from conviction records) are not to be considered in employment decisions.[36] Still others pre-

---

34. 223 S.E.2d 468, 470.

35. 223 S.E.2d 468, 472 (Gullian, J., dissenting).

36. See, generally, Robert Ellis Smith, *Compilation of State and Federal Privacy Laws* (Washington, DC: Privacy Journal, 1981), pp. 3–4, for a convenient summary of state statutes on this point.

vent employers from asking about an applicant's birthplace, religion, bank accounts, marital status, maiden name, names and addresses of relatives other than spouses, and number of dependent children.[37] There is a clear thrust in much privacy legislation to specify which sorts of information should be considered relevant for specific sorts of decisions. Again, since these statutes generally prohibit use of a particular piece of information in a particular decision, this area of statutory law has a fairly ad hoc character.

Although courts may differ about what counts as relevant information and although decisions in specific cases provoke dissents more frequently than do the fraud cases discussed in the last chapter, relevance is clearly the central organizing notion in both majority and dissenting opinions. Majority and dissenting opinions may differ over whether some particular information needs to be disclosed, but both sides generally agree that the standard that should be used is the standard of relevance. That, at least, should tell us something.

DIRECT SECRETS SEEM TO PRESENT a simple logic. If a person voluntarily discloses personal information to someone else, that person cannot recover when the tide shifts and she feels awash in publicity or second thoughts. Initial consent cannot be transformed into later damages. If instead of disclosure, we have a simple secret and B is trying to get information from A, then, for A's suit against B to be blocked, B merely needs to demonstrate that the information is relevant for a decision that B is entitled to make.

Just a bit of reflection on these rules should make it clear that privacy is a very fragile thing indeed. In fact, it is hardly ever the case that a right to privacy is upheld in direct-secret cases, unless the person complaining was tricked into revealing information through force or fraud or unless the actor seeking the information is clearly looking for information beyond the bounds of relevance. Privacy in these cases sounds very much like the old line, Heads I Win; Tails You Lose. If A can make it over the threshold rules, A gets tripped up on the twin issues of consent and relevance, particularly the latter. Almost no matter what the fact pattern is, cases involving direct secrets are very unlikely to succeed, given these legal odds.

---

37. A summary of restrictions on preemployment inquiries can be found in the Labor Relations Reporter (BNA), Fair Employment Practices Manual, §8A.

CHAPTER ELEVEN
Serial Secrets

HOW ARE SERIAL SECRETS DIFFERENT from direct secrets? As Georg Simmel was perceptive to notice, the enlargement of a group from two to three actors presents enormously more complicated social arrangements. Alliances are possible; new tensions arise that were not present with a smaller number. The major difference in formal relations in small groups arises when a third member is added to a group of two. As Simmel wrote, "(T)he triad is a structure completely different from the dyad but not, on the other hand, specifically distinguished from groups of four or more members."[1] Claims surrounding disclosure of secrets can be formally reduced to either direct or serial claims. For example, if C tries to get a secret from A, it becomes formally identical to a direct secret (in which A tries to hide information from B), while if some actor D tries to get the information about A from C, the situation is formally identical to a serial secret (in which A tells B, who may or may not tell C). In this chapter, we will explore the legally relevant facts in privacy-as-secrecy cases involving three actors.

When A and B share a secret, two new sorts of threats are posed to the existence of a secret. B can decide to reveal A's secret to C (a betrayal) or C can try to pry the secret loose from B (a secondhand secret).[2] In betrayals, A sues B for invasion of privacy, claiming that B

---

1. Georg Simmel, "Quantitative Aspects of the Group," in Kurt Wolff, ed., *The Sociology of Georg Simmel* (New York: Free Press, 1950), pp. 87–177, (quote from p. 141).
2. It is interesting to note that although Simmel wrote perceptively both about numbers and group structure and about secrecy, he never explored the connection between the two. In his discussion of secrets, where he considered the effect of secrets on social relations ("The Secret and the Secret Society," in Wolff, p. 330), he wrote: "Whether there is secrecy between two individuals or groups, and if so how much, is a question that characterizes every relation between them." But when, in his discussion of secret societies, he talked about secrets shared among more than two actors, he did not

should not be able to distribute A's secrets without A's approval. In short, A is claiming that A should be able to restrict B's actions because the information that B is distributing pertains to A. When betrayal cases arise in tort, the cases turn on one or more of three legally relevant facts:

1. *Overdisclosure.*—In a number of the cases, judges allow B to disclose A's secret—but only if the scope of the disclosure is narrowly consistent with legitimate objectives of B. If B overdiscloses (that is, if B's revelations are unrelated to a legitimate purpose, if B tells more people than B needs to, or if B tells a few people too many times), then B may be found to have violated A's privacy.

2. *Identification.*—For some B's (particularly the press), publicity of all information in B's possession is consistent with B's legitimate objectives. Overdisclosure cannot act as a limiting force. If overdisclosure fails to provide any limits on the disclosure of A's secrets, courts look to something that might be called identification. Identification links A's personal secret with A. For example, suppose Mary flunked a chemistry test in college and would like to keep this fact a secret. Bob knows about the failed exam. If he revealed to a third party that a friend of his had flunked a test but did not name the friend (that is, did not link Mary's secret with Mary), then he would not, in our terms, have "identified" the secret. Courts, as we will see, allow people to keep their secrets from being identified if identification is not necessary for understanding the information that is the content of the secret, if the subject's deliberate actions did not call attention to the secret, and if the information is not already public.

3. *Confidential relations.*—If A and B are in a confidential relationship, then courts often find that B cannot disclose A's secrets over A's objections.

In cases of betrayal, then, there are three legally relevant facts that courts consider, all going to the question of whether A is entitled to restrict B's actions. To reach the situation of the secondhand secrets, no new legally relevant facts need be presented, since, instead of B claiming the right to reveal A's secrets to C, C is claiming that B should have to reveal A's secrets, whether B wants to or not. Secondhand secrets contain elements of a simple secret and of a betrayal. As with the simple secret, C is trying to get B to reveal the secret, but as with

---

apply his insights about triads to his understanding of secret societies. What I am doing in this section can be thought of in Simmelian terms as applying the notion of *tertius gaudens,* the third party who derives advantage from a quarrel between two others (Simmel, "Quantitative Aspects of the Group," pp. 154–162), to the study of secrets.

the betrayal, whether B can reveal the secret depends on the sort of claims that A can make on B. As we will see, in secondhand secret cases this adds up to a concern with both consent and relevance (the legally relevant facts in simple-secret cases) and confidential relations (one legally relevant fact in betrayal cases). Since both overdisclosure and identification deal with limits on publicity of A's secrets, neither enters in when C is only trying to get B to tell A's secrets to C.

Overdisclosure

When B shares A's secret and B decides to disclose it, courts ask why B is disclosing the information, to whom the information is being disclosed, and how the information is being disclosed. If B's reason for disclosing has little or nothing to do with some legitimate purpose of B, if the information is disclosed to more people than it needs to be, or if the information is disclosed repeatedly enough to constitute harrassment, then courts will generally find that B has invaded A's privacy.

The vast majority of cases that present this sort of situation are debt-collection cases. A is indebted to B. B wants to collect. To pressure A into paying or to insure that some payments are forthcoming, B's in these cases start to publicize the secret of A's debts.

The most common sort of case (probably the most common of all common-law privacy cases) involves a creditor who contacts the debtor's employer. Such were the facts in *Patton v. Jacobs,*[3] *Lucas v. Moskins Stores,*[4] *Gouldman-Taber Pontiac v. Zerbst,*[5] and *Yoder v. Smith.*[6] In each of these cases, the plaintiffs complained that their employers had been told a secret that the defendants should have kept quiet. But in each of these cases, the courts held that the creditors had the right to take reasonable actions to collect debts. Decisions for the defendants in these cases rested on the reasoning that the creditors were pursuing something that they were entitled to pursue and that the revelation of the secret was narrowly directed at helping the creditors accomplish their purposes; in short, the courts held that the secrets had not been overdisclosed.

This sort of logic applied even if the creditor had called the employer of a debtor's spouse.[7] As long as the revelation of the secret had

3. 118 Ind. App. 358, 78 N.E.2d 789 (1948).

4. 262 S.W.2d 679 (Ky. 1953).

5. 213 Ga. 682, 100 S.E.2d 881 (1957).

6. 253 Iowa 505, 112 N.W.2d 862 (1962).

7. *Lewis v. Physicians and Dentists Credit Bureau,* 27 Wash. 2d 267, 177 P.2d 896 (1947); *Zimmerman v. Associates Discount Corp.,* 444 S.W.2d 396 (Mo. 1969).

been narrowly directed toward collecting the debt, courts would not call this an invasion of privacy. In *Davis v. General Finance and Thrift Corp.*[8] no claim for invasion of privacy was recognized when a man complained that a debt collector had sent a telegram through Western Union telling him to pay. Publicity to the employees of Western Union and to the plaintiff's wife did not make the debt collector's behavior an invasion of the plaintiff's privacy. In all these cases, the disclosure was seen as the minimum necessary for the defendant to accomplish something that the defendant was entitled to accomplish.

Beaumont v. Brown[9] reveals when focused disclosure can turn into overdisclosure. Barry Brown was the boss of Robert Beaumont. Beaumont missed a month of work, claiming that his obligations to the National Guard prevented him from showing up at his job. Eventually, Brown directed the personnel director, Arthur Zink, to write a letter to the National Guard inquiring about Beaumont's status, telling the National Guard that Beaumont had not been at work and inquiring how Beaumont could be fit to serve in the National Guard given all of the doctor's excuses that Beaumont had presented at work. Apparently, Beaumont had been playing each off the other, but he claimed that his employer's disclosure of his work absences and medical records constituted an invasion of privacy.

The court held that Beaumont's absences were clearly subjects into which the employer was entitled to inquire. But the court also noted that the letter had been publicized and put in a public record so that many others could learn of the derogatory (and occasionally irrelevant) accusations. This *could* be overdisclosure—and so a claim of invasion of privacy could go to a jury.

Generally, there are three ways in which a defendant can overdisclose. The first is when the disclosure of someone's personal secrets bears no reasonable relation to the discloser's legitimate concerns. *Carr v. Watkins*[10] was such a case. Carr previously had been employed at the Naval Ordnance Laboratory. While he was so employed, he was charged with molesting children and being drunk on the job. These charges were investigated, found to be groundless, and dropped. Carr had since gone to work at a new place when a former co-worker, out of the blue, called his current employer to tell him of the old charges. When Carr's new employer heard about the charges that had been

8. 80 Ga. App. 708, 57 S.E.2d 225 (1950).
9. 401 Mich. 80, 257 N.W.2d 522 (1977).
10. 227 Md. 578, 177 A.2d 841 (1962).

made against Carr, he fired Carr. Carr then sued the former co-worker for invasion of privacy.

The court focused on whether the co-worker's disclosure was in any way related to a duty that he had to carry out: Was the disclosure related to a legitimate concern of the discloser? In this case, the court found that it was not. The court wrote that "it is difficult to perceive, or indeed to conceive, how [the co-worker's] duties as an officer of the security division of the Naval Ordnance Laboratory required or permitted him appropriately to volunteer, directly or indirectly, to the employer of a former coworker."[11] In other words, there seemed to be no particular reason why the guard should have disclosed this information to anyone else. This being the case, the court found that there could be a cause of action for invasion of privacy, although none had been recognized in Maryland until that time. The case was remanded.

It should be noted that part of the court's concern in this case stemmed from the problem of federal agents' liability for harm, given a qualified privilege. But what is interesting in this decision is that any immunity for liability evaporates when the person is acting outside the scope of the person's office (in other words, when the disclosure has nothing to do with the legitimate concerns of the person doing the disclosing). It may be that severely drawing the boundaries of legitimate interests is more likely to occur in cases involving agency than in cases that do not present such a relationship, but that disparity may just testify to the difficulty of determining what counts as a legitimate purpose. In the absence of some definition of legitimate purpose (which is more likely to be defined in a case involving agency), courts probably give the defendant the benefit of the doubt, as they also do in cases involving relevance.[12]

The second sort of case in which overdisclosure is found is characterized by disclosure to too many people. Prosser argues that sufficient publicity is one of the requirements if a claim of invasion of privacy is to be upheld under the rubric of public disclosure of private facts.[13] But publicity alone cannot explain the cases; it is publicity to

11. 177 A.2d 841, 844.

12. If I am right that disclosure unrelated to a legitimate purpose is the basis for privacy claims, then perhaps this would also explain some cases involving blackmail. Although a detailed examination of the cases cannot be done here, it would seem that when private personal information is revealed by someone else who should have been disinterested but obviously is not, an actionable claim is created, if the harm is large enough.

13. William L. Prosser, "Privacy," *California Law Review* 48: 383–423 (1960), p. 393.

C's who would not help B to accomplish B's purposes that seems to matter. Prosser's article takes publicity very literally; for him, without publicity, there can be no invasion of privacy. I am suggesting that another formulation is more consistent with existing decisions. It is not publicity in itself that creates the invasion of privacy; it is publicity of a certain sort. When B's publicize A's' secrets and tell more people than are necessary to accomplish B's legitimate objectives, then this is over-disclosure. Telling a debtor's employer about the debtor's debts may actually aid the creditor in accomplishing the goal of collecting the debt. But telling every third stranger on the street is not likely to help the creditor. It is this latter sort of publicity that the law seems to look at suspiciously. Prosser's notion that publicity in itself is sufficient to state a cause of action for invasion of privacy does not go quite far enough. It is not how many people have been told that matters but how many of them it was *necessary* to tell for the discloser to keep increasing her chances of succeeding at her legitimate goals. A few cases should illustrate the point.

In *Brents v. Morgan*,[14] the leading case on this point, W. R. Morgan was a veterinarian who had had his car fixed by George Brents, owner of a garage. Apparently, Morgan did not pay his bill and Brents, determined to make him pay, put a five-by-eight-foot sign in his window announcing the veterinarian's debt. Morgan sued Brents for invasion of privacy. The court ruled that Morgan did in fact present an actionable claim of invasion of privacy. The law only allowed publication of information that was of general or public interest, and the court left the suggestion that the information on the sign was not one of those things.

A clearer case is presented by *Santiesteban v. Goodyear Tire and Rubber Co.*[15] Jose Santiesteban bought a set of tires from Goodyear on credit and had remained current in his payments. Without warning, Goodyear agents swooped down on Santiesteban's car while he was at work, removing all the tires and leaving the car sitting on its rims in the parking lot. Employed as a waiter at a country club, Santiesteban was very embarrassed to have his car so displayed in front of co-workers and employers. Using Florida law, the Court of Appeals found that this would count as sufficient publicity for cause of action in privacy.

In *Trammell v. Citizen's News Co.*[16] Reverend P. L. Trammell

---

14. 221 Ky. 765, 299 S.W. 967 (1927).
15. 306 F.2d 9 (5th Cir. 1962).
16. 285 Ky. 529, 148 S.W.2d 708 (1941).

owed some money to the Service Cafe store. He had fallen on hard times and had not been able to pay. The owner of the store warned Trammell that she would publish a notice in the newspaper advertising his debt if he did not pay by a certain date. Desperate to stop the notice, Trammell went to the newspaper and asked it not to print the notice. The paper did so anyway. Trammell sued the paper. The court ruled that Trammell should be able to recover for invasion of privacy. This was not, the court argued, a matter of public interest. Even though the owner of the store had the right to demand payment, she did not have the right to expose the reverend to ridicule. Moreover, the paper knew in advance of publication that Trammell was worried about the notice's appearance.[17]

What these three cases share is the creditor's attempt to use indiscriminate publicity as a way of getting the presumed debtor to pay. But in each case the court ruled that the publicity was excessive; in each case, the courts noted that these were not matters of public interest— meaning, I would argue, that there was no particular reason why the discloser should have told those particular people. Disclosure of identifiable personal information is not allowed if it is addressed to people who are not directly involved with either party. Overdisclosure occurs when disclosure of personal information spills over into the lives of a number of people unconnected with the event.

Finally, the third way in which overdisclosure can occur is if the discloser discloses to the same few people too often. In *Housh v. Peth*[18] the plaintiff was called by a debt collector every day for three weeks. Peth, the debt collector, also called the plaintiff's employer and the plaintiff's landlord. In addition, Peth called the plaintiff's place of employment three times in fifteen minutes, getting her out of the classroom in which she was teaching. The plaintiff sued for invasion of privacy and prevailed on the grounds that this was a "deliberately initiated . . . systematic campaign of harassment."[19] Under these circumstances, Peth's persistence interfered with the plaintiff's privacy.

In *Boudreaux v. Allstate Finance Corp.*[20] Allstate was attempting to collect on an outstanding obligation. Adam Boudreaux was unemployed and had told Allstate that he would resume payments when he

---

17. On the basis of this sort of rationale, one would think that Trammell would have a stronger case against the store owner than against the newspaper.

18. 99 Ohio App. 485, 59 Ohio Ops. 330, 135 N.E.2d 440 (1955), *affd.* 165 Ohio St. 35, 59 Ohio Ops. 60, 133 N.E.2d 340 (1956).

19. 135 N.E.2d 440, 449.

20. 217 So. 2d 439 (La. App. 1968).

again found work. But Allstate insisted on calling Boudreaux's neighbors repeatedly, since Boudreaux did not have a telephone. At all hours of the day and night and in terribly inclement weather, Allstate went on calling and Boudreaux's neighbors were repeatedly disturbed, being asked to go and get Boudreaux to the phone. The court ruled that this, too, was beyond the bounds of decency. This calculated disclosure to his neighbors of Boudreaux's debts counted as an invasion of privacy.

When someone discloses information to the same few people too often, as in the two cases just mentioned, the case spills over into intrusion. What seems to be at work here is the view that people should, within limits, be left alone. But the three sorts of cases that I have just discussed (disclosure beyond legitimate purpose, unselective disclosure, and harassing disclosure), taken together, support another argument as well. What courts seem to be trying to encourage in all of these overdisclosure cases is limit the revelation of personal information by someone who is not the subject of that information. Only when the information is (a) related to a legitimate purpose of the actor disclosing, (b) not revealed unselectively, and (c) not used to harass the subject is it allowed to be revealed. The law strikes the balance between the claims of A and B in these cases such that A is entitled to the minimum disclosure of personal information consistent with B being able to realize B's legitimate interests.

Identification

The concept of legitimate purpose is fuzzy at the boundaries, but it does give clear results for most actors most of the time. A problem arises, though, when one tries to apply the logic of overdisclosure to the press, which arguably has as its central legitimate purpose publication of matters of public concern. How can a right to privacy ever coexist with such a legitimate purpose? Clearly, the principle of overdisclosure developed above will have little bite in these cases, as long as the press can successfully argue that publication of private facts about an individual serves a legitimate purpose.

The special case posed by the press has been the subject of a great deal of scholarly concern.[21] The general view, now enshrined in the

21. Some of the commentaries in this area include Linda Woito and Patrick McNulty, "The Privacy Disclosure Tort and the First Amendment: Should the Community Decide Newsworthiness?" *Iowa Law Review* 64: 185–232 (1979); Edward Bloustein, "Privacy as an Aspect of Human Dignity: An Answer to Dean Prosser," *New*

Restatement (Second) of Torts, is that the press may publish anything, so long as what is published is a matter of legitimate public concern or does not include private facts that would be highly offensive to the ordinary reasonable man.[22] Needless to say, these standards are highly flexible and, as a result, of relatively little help in either guiding the press or understanding the outcome of specific cases. Both public concern and offensiveness are standards that have been thought to be highly dependent on community mores, and as a result this area has been characterized by delegating to juries the tough questions.[23]

What makes the press a special case of the more general class of betrayal is that the special constitutional status of the press gives it a distinct claim of legitimate purpose. Since the function of the press is to publicize, it is hard to see what publication can be inconsistent with its legitimate purpose. Therefore, the overdisclosure rules outlined in the previous section fail to apply to the press.

Although the cases here are not nearly so tidy as those in the other areas being discussed, there is still a definable center of gravity in them. I will argue that these cases have the same logic as the overdisclosure cases. In both sets of cases, the principle is that A is entitled to the minimum disclosure of information consistent with B being able to realize B's legitimate interests.

The way in which this principle is upheld in both the personal invasion-of-privacy and the press cases is through the concept of identification. Identification refers to the connection of a secret with the subject of the secret. In *Sidis v. F-R Publishing Co.,*[24] for example, former child prodigy William James Sidis was featured in a *New Yorker* magazine profile. His current life, which he was attempting to keep as private as possible, was connected with his formerly public identity. This connecting of the secret (in this case, Sidis's fascination with streetcar transfers, Okamakammessett Indians, and obscurity) with

---

York University Law Review 39: 962–1007 (1974); Marc A. Franklin, "Constitutional Problems in Privacy Protection: Legal Inhibitions on Reporting of Fact," *Stanford Law Review* 16: 107–148 (1963); and a relatively recent rash of law review notes.

22. American Law Institute, *Restatement (Second) of Torts* (St. Paul: American Law Institute Press, 1977), vol. 2, pp. 383–394.

23. Woito and McNulty examine the role of community standards in a variety of First-Amendment contexts, focusing particularly on the evolving notion of community standards in public-disclosure-of-private-facts privacy cases. Judge Peters, in his opinion in *Briscoe v. Reader's Digest Assn.,* 4 Cal. 3d 529, 483 P.2d 34, 93 Cal. Rptr. 866 (1971), provided an extensive list of questions that juries might consider in privacy cases.

24. 113 F.2d 806 (2d Cir. 1940), *cert. den.* 311 U.S. 711 (1940).

the individual (in this case, Sidis) creates identification. Identification consists in revealing not only a personal secret but also the identity of the person to whom the secret pertains.[25]

In cases involving press disclosure of personal secrets, the courts often focus on this matter of identification. If a person's name is not necessary for understanding the meaning of a news story, courts will often consider identification of the secret with the person to be an invasion of privacy. This statement is subject to three important qualifications: (1) the information must be private, (2) the revelation must have caused harm, and (3) the subject's deliberate actions must not be responsible for the press attention in the first place. The first two points recall our earlier discussion of the threshold rules and need not be repeated here; the third point is related to our earlier discussion of consent. The press will almost always be allowed to write about whichever subject it chooses; the only limitation is that the subject's identity not be revealed if it is not strictly necessary for understanding the meaning of the news story. To understand this logic, we will start with what consent means in this context and work our way back to identification.

If press attention has been gained by the subject's deliberate actions, then identification of the alleged secret with the subject is permissible. In *Smith v. Doss*[26] James Doss's radio program, "Tuscaloosa Town Talks," featured the story of John Lindgren. Lindgren had been thought murdered twenty-five years before, but he had staged the apparent murder to get away to California. When he died twenty-five years later, his will revealed his identity as well as the identity of his daughters (one of whom had married a Smith). When Doss's show laid out the story, daughter Smith and another of Lindgren's daughters sued for invasion of privacy. The court ruled that John Lindgren's own acts had made him a public character and that his story had therefore

25. A similar formulation has been suggested by Edward Bloustein in *Individual and Group Privacy* (New Brunswick, NJ: Transaction Books, 1978). Taking his cue from Alexander Meikeljohn, *Political Freedom* (New York: Harper, 1960), Bloustein argues that it is reasonable to limit the press when it publishes information that is not relevant to governing purposes (that is, information that enables a democratic state to function). Particularly when the press caters to the appetite of the public for gossip, Bloustein argues that personal identification is generally not necessary. His argument is based heavily on the notion that the press serves an essential function in a democratic society. He does not seem to realize that the press feels itself to have an obligation to publish a good deal that does not bear directly on governance. As we will see, courts do give the press a great deal more latitude than Bloustein would be willing to offer.

26. 251 Ala. 250, 37 So. 2d 118 (1948).

become part of the history of the community. No invasion of privacy could be found because his actions implied that he had consented to public attention.[27]

This logic of implied consent leads public figures to have a lesser right of privacy than do people living their lives outside the spotlight. Beginning with the now-famous libel case, *New York Times v. Sullivan*,[28] the Supreme Court announced a distinction between public and private persons, the former being permitted to prevail in libel cases only if they could demonstrate actual malice or reckless disregard of the truth on the part of the press. The same sort of distinction can be found in the invasion-of-privacy cases, and public figures are generally considered to have waived most of their right to privacy. This can be seen in *Estill v. Hearst Publishing Co.*,[29] where Estill was a public official who had once had his picture taken with the infamous John Dillinger. When the photograph was published years later, Estill sued the *Chicago Herald-American,* a Hearst paper, for invasion of privacy. The court ruled that Estill's status as a public figure made him ineligible for such a claim of privacy. Similarly, in *Cohen v. Marx*[30] Groucho Marx was sued for telling a joke on his network television show, "You Bet Your Life." The butt of the joke, and the plaintiff in the suit, was a professional boxer who fought under the name Canvasback Cohen. The court argued that by becoming a prizefighter, Cohen had waived his right to privacy and that "he could not at his will and whim draw himself like a snail into his shell and hold others liable for commenting upon the acts which had taken place when he had voluntarily exposed himself to the public eye."[31] This is a clear statement of the general principle that pertains to public figures. It also illuminates the reason why public figures are treated differently than those who keep to themselves. Consent is the underlying notion here. The reasoning in this case and others indicates that by becoming a public figure a person

27. As this case demonstrates, the deliberate actions of a person who has a secret may be sufficient to remove a claim of privacy from those whose lives are intertwined with the subject of the secret. No one else can claim invasion of privacy if the person to whom the secret pertains has deliberately called attention to the secret. This is similar to the situation in *Mettier v. Los Angeles Examiner,* 35 Cal. App. 2d 304, 95 P.2d 491 (1939), where a husband was unable to claim invasion of privacy after his wife jumped from a tall building in downtown Los Angeles. In both *Smith* and *Mettier* the subjects would have had no personal claim of privacy if they had lived, because their actions called public attention to the information that they later might have wanted to conceal.

28. 376 U.S. 254 (1964).

29. 186 F.2d 1017 (7th Cir. 1951).

30. 94 Cal. App. 2d 704, 211 P.2d 320 (1949).

31. 211 P.2d 320, 321.

implicitly consents to publication of personal facts. In this way, the cases are identical to disclosure cases discussed in the previous chapter, cases in which consent made a later claim of invasion of privacy untenable. Although it may certainly be the case that people who place themselves in the public eye for one purpose may not intend to consent to publication of every detail of their private lives, courts act as though consent to publication of certain facts necessarily entails consent to publication of other facts.

This is illustrated in *Kapellas v. Kofman*.[32] Inez Kapellas was a candidate for city council. Abraham Kofman was the owner and publisher of the *Alameda Times Star* and the *Times Star Advertiser*. An editorial appearing in both papers said that Kapellas had been married twice and that several of her six children had been picked up by the police for shoplifting, burglary, loitering, and truancy. The editorial concluded that Kapellas had enough on her hands without adding the burden of the city council. When Kapellas sued for invasion of privacy, the court ruled that her claim could not stand. The court wrote: "Generally, courts will be most reluctant to impede the free flow of any truthful information that may be relevant to a candidate's qualifications for office."[33] Even though the court acknowledged that facts about Kapellas's children probably were not very important, the court declined to find for her because she had placed herself in the public eye by running for office.

Thus, when people's actions call attention to them, the press is allowed to pursue and publish almost anything about them. Although this is apparently based on a logic of consent, in some of the cases consent is a convenient fiction. Still, courts use the language of consent because it represents an important way of justifying decisions for the defendant.

The press has clear sailing with no privacy waves to worry about if the person is a public figure and if the information with which the press is dealing is not private. But when the person is not a public figure (or used to be but is arguably no longer a public figure) and when the information is private, things are not so simple. This is when we can see the principle of identification at work.

The notion of identification as a principle that limits the press can be seen most clearly by contrasting two well-known privacy cases, *Barber v. Time, Inc.*[34] and *Sidis*. Dorothy Barber, a woman suffering

32. 1 Cal. 3d 20, 459 P.2d 912, 81 Cal. Rptr. 360 (1969).
33. 459 P.2d 912, 923.
34. 348 Mo. 1199, 159 S.W.2d 291 (1942).

from a rare disease, was admitted to a hospital in Kansas City. She ate huge quantities of food and kept losing weight. *Time* magazine published an article about Barber under the headline "Starving Glutton." The article featured a picture of Barber in her hospital bed as well as an article that detailed her condition. She sued for invasion of privacy.

Aside from the fact that the court was not pleased that the photographer had apparently taken the photograph of Barber surreptitiously and without her consent, the court noted that Dorothy Barber had not called attention to herself. Moreover, the court noted, "while the nature of the plaintiff's ailment may have been a matter of public interest, certainly the identity of the person who suffered this ailment was not."[35] The ruling in the case apparently rested on the argument that the secret might be published, as long as the subject were not identified. Presumably, someone reading the article did not need to know precisely who the sufferer was to appreciate the significance of the medical condition. The information that it was Dorothy Barber did not add much to the account of the disease itself. *Time* was found to be liable for invasion of privacy.

At age eleven Sidis had lectured to a group of prominent mathematicians on four-dimensional bodies. His precociousness was widely reported at the time, but Sidis soon afterwards vanished from the public stage. When the *New Yorker* wondered "Where Are They Now?" (the title of its series), its investigation located an insignificant clerk who preferred to hide his substantial abilities and live in a shabby room. The story was merciless in its dissection of the details of Sidis's private life. Sidis sued.

The court ruled against Sidis. The opinion said:

> Since [his earlier achievements] Sidis has cloaked himself in obscurity, but his subsequent history, containing as it did the answer to the question of whether he had fulfilled his earlier promise, was still a matter of public concern. The article in the *New Yorker* sketched the life of an unusual personality and it possessed considerable news interest. . . . Revelations may be so intimate and so unwarranted in view of the victim's position as to outrage the community's notions of decency. But when focused upon public characters, truthful comments upon dress, speech, habits, and the ordinary aspects of personality will usually not transgress this line.[36]

35. 159 S.W.2d 291, 295.
36. 113 F.2d 806, 809.

What makes *Sidis* different from *Barber* is that the information in
Sidis would simply not have the same meaning if it did not mention his
name. A reader could not see why such an insignificant clerk would
make a fitting subject for a feature piece unless it were known that this
insignificant clerk used to be someone of extraordinary talents. The
story might have said that this person used to be an extraordinarily
gifted child prodigy, not mentioning his name, but this would presumably identify him also. His name was already linked with the child-
prodigy label. The court ruled that there was no invasion of privacy in
this case because it simply would not have made sense to print the
information without the identification. In addition, it might be noted
that in the excerpt above the court was close to arguing a rationale
consistent with the view that there could be no liability without sufficient harm, because here the information published was not judged to
be particularly discreditable. Sidis felt himself to be quite harmed,
however, because he apparently committed suicide shortly after he lost
his case.[37]

If the courts find invasion of privacy when the case meets all the
threshold rules and when identification of the subject is not necessary
to understand the meaning of the story, then we would expect decisions in other cases to follow a similar logic. Although the courts do
not always use this logic explicitly in their decisions, most decisions are
consistent with this reasoning. In *Smith v. NBC*[38] and in *Bernstein v.
NBC*[39] no invasion of privacy was found in either case. In the first,
NBC broadcast an episode of "Dragnet" featuring Smith's past in
which he reported as missing a vicious black panther to the police.
After creating a general state of panic, Smith indicated that he had
made the story up. In the second case, NBC broadcast a story about
Bernstein, who had been convicted of murder and later been pardoned
when it was discovered that he had not actually committed the crime.
In neither case did NBC use the men's current names, and in neither
case was a claim of invasion of privacy successful. In *Bernstein* the court
wrote, "the protection which time may bring to a formerly public
figure is not against repetition of the facts which are already public
property, but against unreasonable public identification of him in his

---

37. Another troubling aspect of the *Sidis* case is that Sidis apparently consented to
the *New Yorker* interview, and there were questions about whether the interviewer concealed her identity. The interview then might have been fraudulent, vitiating consent.

38. 138 Cal. App. 2d 807, 292 P.2d 600 (1956).

39. 129 F. Supp. 817 (D.C.D.C. 1955), *affd.*, 232 F.2d 369, *cert. den.*, 352 U.S. 945
(1956).

present setting with the earlier incident."[40] This makes the logic explicit. It is not the publication of the secret itself but identification of the personal secret with the person that provides the grounds for invasion of privacy.

California seems to be in the vanguard in developing this theory. The early and controversial case of *Melvin v. Reid*[41] can be seen as using identification as its main rationale. In this case, the plaintiff was a former prostitute who had been accused of murder, and was acquitted in a much publicized trial. Following the acquittal, she abandoned her prior life, got married, became a housewife, and "thereafter, at all times, lived an exemplary, virtuous, honorable and righteous life."[42] The defendants made a movie called *The Red Kimono* that used her maiden name, Gabrielle Darley, and recounted her story. When her friends found out about her past, she was abandoned and ridiculed. She sued for invasion of privacy, and, surprisingly to many, she won.

The court noted how the movie portrayal of Melvin interfered with her ability to obtain happiness, pursuit of which was guaranteed in the California Constitution. But, throughout the opinion, the subject of the use of her real name kept reappearing. The opinion specifically stated that the use of Melvin's life story was not actionable; what made it an invasion of privacy was the use of her maiden name, which identified her with her secret. The use of her true name indicated, according to the court, "a willful and wanton disregard of that charity which should actuate us in our social intercourse and which should keep us from unnecessarily holding up another to the scorn and contempt of upright members of society."[43] Moreover, the publication of her true name, the court continued, "was not justified by any standard of morals or ethics known to us."[44] The court ruled in favor of Melvin and explicitly used the rationale that the mention of her name was not necessary for telling the story. Although she undoubtedly would have lost a suit for invasion of privacy if she had tried to bring it eight years earlier during her sensational trial, when she would probably have been considered to be a public figure, she was able to argue successfully that she was no longer a public person after all that time had passed.[45]

40. 129 F. Supp. 817, 828.
41. 112 Cal. App. 285, 297 P. 91 (1931).
42. 112 Cal. App. 285, 286.
43. 112 Cal. App. 285, 291.
44. 112 Cal. App. 285, 292.
45. It may seem difficult to square *Melvin* and *Sidis* since in both of them the subject's unique and visible pasts made identification reasonable. Perhaps the difference

A similar case was presented to the California courts in *Briscoe v. Readers' Digest Assn.*[46] Marvin Briscoe had hijacked a truck eleven years earlier, and *Reader's Digest* mentioned this fact with his name in a story about hijacking. Because of the publication of this story, Briscoe's eleven-year-old daughter learned of his past for the first time, since he too had got married and abandoned his previous course.

Here, also, the court noted that nothing should stop *Reader's Digest* from publishing the fact of the hijacking. What was at issue was the publication of Briscoe's name. The court wrote that "identification of the actor . . . serves little independent public purpose. . . . Unless the individual has reattracted the public eye to himself in some independent fashion, the only public 'interest' that would be served [by publication] is that of curiosity." [47] The court, citing *Melvin,* specifically called attention to the publication of the name as constituting the invasion of privacy. The facts by themselves, without such attribution, would have presented no privacy claim.

Although identification (absent public information or a public person) as a basis of liability is fairly settled in California, the rest of the country does not necessarily follow this rule. In *Barbieri v. News-Journal Co.*[48] the court explicitly rejected the authority of *Melvin. Barbieri* involved a news story which mentioned that eleven years earlier John Barbieri had been convicted of beating a woman in her home and punished by receiving twenty lashes. The story in which this information appeared dealt with the reinstatement of whipping as a punishment for certain crimes, noting that Barbieri was the last one to be so treated. The *Barbieri* court ruled that this situation was unlike the circumstances in *Melvin* because the former case presented a news story while the latter case did not. Calling them newsworthy, the court allowed the facts to stand without liability for the newspaper. This seems flatly in contradiction with the argument that has been forwarded in the present chapter, unless one argues that former public punishment is a present public fact. Courts are clearly split over the issue of recent publicity for past crimes.

---

lies in the degree of harm caused by connection of the person's present life with the person's past deeds. Sidis was being identified with a praiseworthy past while Melvin was being identified with a discreditable past. As was mentioned earlier, in the section on sufficient harm, publicizing information that puts the subject in a good light does not seem to be actionable.

46. 4 Cal. 3d 529, 483 P.2d 34, 93 Cal. Rptr. 866 (1971).
47. 93 Cal. Rptr. 866, 873.
48. 56 Del. 67, 189 A.2d 773 (Del. Super 1963).

But there is more recent evidence that the notion of identification is gaining ground. In *Virgil v. Time, Inc.*[49] Mike Virgil claimed that his privacy was invaded when *Sports Illustrated* ran a story about him. Virgil was a well-known bodysurfer who frequented a California beach called The Wedge. His apparently reckless disregard for his own safety prompted the reporter to interview him to discover why he was willing to take such chances. Virgil disclosed that he ate spiders, that he had put out cigarettes in his mouth and burned holes in the backs of his hands, that he once had dived headfirst down a flight of stairs to impress some women, that he had bit someone's cheek in a fight, and that he never had learned how to read. Although the disclosures were apparently voluntary at the time, Virgil retracted his consent before the article was published. When the article appeared, all 7,000 words of it, Virgil sued.

The court remanded the case, but in doing so it suggested two lines of argument that the lower court might adopt. The first argued that even though Virgil might be a public person in one regard, this did not mean that all other aspects of his life were fair game after he specifically had revoked his consent to publish them.[50] The court attempted to distinguish between relevant and irrelevant facts rather along the lines outlined in the previous chapter regarding direct secrets. But the second line of argument came closer to our present concern with identification. The court seemed concerned with limiting the prying power of the press and its current privileged status: "To hold that privilege extends to all true statements would seem to deny the existence of 'private' facts, for if facts be facts—that is, if they be true—they would not, at least to the press, be private, and the press would be free to publicize them to the extent that it sees fit. The extent to which areas of privacy continue to exist, then, would appear to be based not on rights bestowed by law but on the tastes and discretion of the press. We cannot accept this result."[51] Later in the opinion, in suggesting questions that the trial court might consider, one prominent question arose: "whether the identity of Virgil as the one to

---

49. 527 F.2d 1122 (9th Cir. 1975), *cert. den.,* 425 U.S. 998 (1976), *on remand,* 424 F. Supp. 1286 (D.C. Cal. 1976).

50. Note how different the result would have been in *Sidis* if the *Virgil* court had been able to decide it. Perhaps all the attention that the *Sidis* case has received has made courts reconsider the matter of the printing of private facts without the subject's explicit consent. If this section is correct, we might see increased both attention paid to the problem of identification and increased sensitivity to the consequences of publication of identified secrets.

51. 527 F.2d 1122, 1128.

whom such facts apply is a matter in which the public has a legitimate interest." [52]

The real problem in this case is the same as the problem posed by *Sidis*. Would these outrageous stories mean what they do if they were not attached to a description of Virgil's daredevil bodysurfing? And would that not identify him? Even without the use of his name, that sort of behavior would only make sense to publish against his particular background. In this situation the name would appear to be necessary to understand the story. It is not surprising that the trial court on remand found that there was no invasion of privacy. The main rationale given by the district court, though, ignored both of the appeals court's recommended lines of argument. Instead, the court reverted to the threshold rule, in which nondiscreditable information cannot be the basis of a privacy claim. The district court wrote: "The above facts are generally unflattering and perhaps embarrassing, but they are simply not offensive to the degree of morbidity or sensationalism. In fact, they connote nearly as strong a positive image as they do a negative one." [53]

This area of law is not as coherent as the others that we have discussed, since it seems to be in a state of flux. At least California has been developing what appears to be a more unified jurisprudence. I would argue that, insofar as these cases present a clear center of gravity that can be perceived, that center of gravity is identification. The courts show a clear tendency to stay away from deciding what the press can and cannot publish. But when called on to define the boundary between an unfettered press and the rights of individuals to privacy, the courts seem most comfortable drawing the line at identification. The press can publish whatever true information it chooses, so long as the private subject of private information is left unidentified. If identification is crucial to understanding the meaning of the story (as would generally be the case with public figures or people whose exceptional accomplishments put them in a category of one), then the press may go ahead and link the secret with the subject of that secret.

The press presents a special situation because it has a different set of legitimate purposes than do other actors. But the logic of these cases is the same as the logic in the overdisclosure cases. In both sets of cases, the law seems concerned with allowing B to distribute to C any information that enables B to accomplish B's legitimate purposes. But the courts also seem at least somewhat concerned with A's claims that A

52. 527 F.2d 1122, 1129.
53. 424 F. Supp. 1286, 1289.

should be able to control the distribution of information about herself. Courts seem to reconcile these two conflicting interests by permitting disclosure by B—but only the minimum disclosure consistent with the realization of B's legitimate purposes. The minimum-disclosure principle allows A to recover for invasion of privacy if B has disclosed to actors who are not likely to help B in reaching B's goals. In the case of the press, the minimum-disclosure principle can be seen when the courts allow recovery for an A who has been identified with a personal secret. Minimizing disclosure in these instances means not disclosing names, even though the other information disclosed may be acceptable. In both cases the law attempts to keep information available to those who need it ("need" being broadly conceived) while shielding private identities from those to whom they would be incidental and largely irrelevant details.

Confidential Relations

The one exception to this overdisclosure principle can be found in courts' scrutiny of confidential relations. If A and B have shared an understanding that A was telling B personal information in confidence, then A can often prevent B from disclosing this information to C, even when B claims that some legitimate interest of B's would be served by B's doing so.

In *Doe v. Roe*[54] the psychiatrist's attempt to publish a book revealing personally identifiable information about her former client was stopped. The court found that the nature of the disclosures strongly suggested that patient Doe had trusted Dr. Roe not to disclose her secrets. Because of this relationship of trust, Roe could not reveal Doe's secrets, even though Roe argued that publication of the book advanced scientific knowledge.

In another case involving a psychiatrist, *MacDonald v. Clinger*,[55] the psychiatrist told intimate details about a patient to the patient's wife. As a result of this disclosure, the patient argued, their marriage deteriorated, the plaintiff lost his job, and he suffered great financial and emotional upset. Here again, the court relied on a theory of implied contract to reach the conclusion that "the relationship of the parties here was one of trust and confidence out of which sprang a duty

---

54. 93 Misc. 2d 201, 400 N.Y.S.2d 668 (1977), discussed in more detail in chapter 1.
55. 84 A.D.2d 482, 446 N.Y.S.2d 801 (1982).

not to disclose." [56] Again, the court held that the promise of confidentiality gave rise to a duty not to reveal the plaintiff's secrets, even to someone who arguably had considerable interest in knowing them. Although the court relied on a contract theory, the court also argued that a tort theory might reach the case as well, through breach of a duty of confidentiality. [57]

A similar case implying breach of confidence is *Horne v. Patton*. [58] In this case, Horne's doctor disclosed to Horne's employer details of Horne's medical condition. Although a more detailed description of the facts is difficult to infer from the opinion, it does seem clear that the disclosure was a rather complete account of Horne's medical condition. The court ruled that doctors have a "duty not to make extrajudicial disclosures" [59] about their patients, and also noted: "Nor can it be said that an employer is necessarily a person who has a legitimate interest in knowing each and every detail of an employee's health. Certainly, there are many ailments about which a patient might consult his private physician which have no bearing or effect on one's employment." [60] Clearly, this is an attempt to justify the decision on grounds of relevance as well as on grounds of breach of a confidential relationship.

Just as with the fraud cases, though, the courts do not assume that all relations of a certain sort (for example, doctor-patient relations) are necessarily confidential ones. Instead, the courts look to the specifics of the individual relationship. Thus, in *Bond v. Pecaut* [61] Deborah Bond was unable to sustain a charge of invasion of privacy when a court-appointed psychologist testified in court to Bond's mental fitness to keep custody of her child. The court noted that the testimony "does not recite plaintiff's revelations in the course of therapy but only what she had willingly told the defendant in a phone conversation." [62] This

56. 446 N.Y.S.2d 801, 805.
57. Whether there is really an independent tort action for breach of confidence is a matter of some debate, although Alan B. Vickrey's note on the subject ("Breach of Confidence: An Emerging Tort," *Columbia Law Review* 82: 1426–1468 [1982]) makes a convincing case for one. Despite the fact that England has no common-law action for invasion of privacy, England does have a well-established action for breach of confidence. See Law Commission, *Breach of Confidence*. Working paper no. 58. (London: Her Majesty's Stationery Office, 1974).
58. 291 Ala. 701, 287 So. 2d 824 (1973).
59. 287 So. 2d 824, 830.
60. 287 So. 2d 824, 831.
61. 561 F. Supp. 1037 (N.D. Ill. 1983).
62. 561 F. Supp. 1037, 1041.

statement calls attention to the lack of a continuing ongoing relationship that would justify the charge of a breach of confidence.

Similarly, in *Collins v. Howard*[63] the court refused to let a claim of confidential relationship stand when Collins claimed that the disclosure of a police-ordered blood test was an invasion of privacy. The court noted that the doctor had merely supervised the administration of the test and had not treated Collins in any way. In the absence of some more enduring relationship implying confidence, the court held that no invasion-of-privacy claim could succeed.[64]

Sometimes, however, the courts seem inclined to permit a person arguably in a confidential relationship with the plaintiff to disclose the plaintiff's secrets to someone who is also in a confidential relationship with the plaintiff, provided that it seems to be in the plaintiff's interest to do so. In *Tooley v. Provident Life and Accident Insurance Co.*[65] and in *Mikel v. Abrams*[66] the spouses of hospitalized patients were informed of the patients' conditions by the patients' doctors. In both cases, the medical information revealed was later presented in divorce proceedings by the nonhospitalized spouse against the hospitalized spouse. In both cases, the formerly hospitalized spouse sued the doctor for invasion of privacy. And in both cases the formerly hospitalized spouse lost.

In *Tooley* the court reasoned that a husband was entitled to know what medical procedures had been performed on his wife, since he was responsible for her debts. In *Mikel* the court reasoned that the wife's knowledge of her husband's drug, alcohol, and tension problems was necessary for her to help him get better. In both cases, the doctors had no reason to expect that this disclosed information would be used against their patients; apparently, in both cases, the disclosures were made to help the patient. This is in marked contrast with the *MacDonald* case mentioned above, in which the psychiatrist's disclosures did not seem to have such a benign purpose, even though they were

63. 156 F. Supp. 322 (S.D. Ga. 1957).

64. It should be noted that there is a difference between disclosure to a private party and disclosure as testimony in the course of a trial. In general, the standards for a confidential relationship are stricter in the latter case than in the former. Any indication that the plaintiff consented to have the alleged confidant disclose information will generally be taken by courts as a lifting of the veil of secrecy. See *Glenn v. Kerlin,* 248 So. 2d 834 (La. App. 1971). In addition, court cases often present medical evidence that was obtained at the initiation of some party other than the plaintiff in the privacy action.

65. 154 So. 2d 617 (La. App. 1963).

66. 541 F. Supp. 591 (W.D. Miss. 1982).

225

made to someone who also had a confidential relationship with the patient.

It seems that to demonstrate a confidential relationship, one must first show that the disclosures were made with the understanding that they be kept secret. Once B learns A's secret under a promise of confidentiality, B cannot tell others who might use the information to harm A's interests. But B does seem to be justified in telling a C who apparently has A's best interests at heart and who is apparently expected to share with A the same sense of A's interests. Thus, what is at issue is not whether B's interests would be served by the disclosure (as is the case with overdisclosure and identification) but whether A's interests would be served by the disclosure. The presence of a confidential relationship changes the rules for disclosure rather radically in both fraud and invasion-of-privacy cases.

Sometimes, however, other considerations outweigh the protection normally accorded confidential relationships. Probably the most famous exception to the doctrine that B is only allowed to disclose information about A that is obtained in a confidential relationship when it serves A's interests is *Tarasoff v. Regents of the University of California.*[67] In that case the threat of murder had to be disclosed by a psychiatrist to the former girlfriend of the patient, even though the psychiatrist and patient had a confidential relationship. When the consequences to third parties are grave and people would want to be buffered against these extraordinarily disastrous consequences, the law requires disclosure despite the existence of a confidential relationship.

This common-law area of confidential relations has been subject to statutory alterations. At one time a common-law rule was developing that banks and their depositors were in a confidential relationship. In *Milohnich v. First National Bank of Miami Springs*[68] Milohnich sued his bank for telling third parties about the status of his bank account. Reviewing a long line of cases that had held that a bank owes a duty to its depositors not to disclose information about them to others who ask, the court held that such a duty does exist. The leading case in this area, *Peterson v. Idaho First National Bank,*[69] did not use a privacy theory in its reasoning but instead used a theory of agency. Other cases that followed on this point similarly tended to shy away from deciding on

67. 17 C.3d. 425, 131 Cal. Rptr. 14, 551 P.2d. 334 (1976), discussed in more detail in chapter 1.

68. 224 So. 2d 759 (Fla. 1969).

69. 83 Idaho 578, 367 P.2d 284, 92 A.L.R. 891 (1961).

grounds of invasion of privacy. But the agency theory is remarkably similar to the theory found in other privacy cases: "Unless otherwise agreed, an agent is subject to a duty to the principal not to use or to communicate information given him by principal or acquired by him during the course of or on account of his agency." [70] This view—that information acquired in the course of certain sorts of relationships cannot be disclosed or used against the subject of that information— seems to be present throughout discussions of privacy, although it is justified variously under agency, general contract or tort theories. In the case of banks, the common-law rule is clearly that banks should not be allowed to disclose information about their depositors to anyone else. All that changed, however, with the Bank Secrecy Act [71] and with the Supreme Court decision, in *California Bankers' Assn. v. Shultz,* [72] upholding the act. The Bank Secrecy Act is rather inappropriately named, since its main effect is to open up bank records to investigators. Requiring that checks of a certain magnitude or above be photocopied and kept for five years and that such records be made available to law enforcement officials, the Bank Secrecy Act does not seem to increase the secrecy of bank records. Instead, if anything, it undermines the common-law rule that would provide more privacy with regard to bank records.

All of this discussion indicates that confidential relations generally do have a powerful influence in common-law cases, although there is a growing number of exceptions. Implied contract and agency are often called on to decide privacy cases that present confidential relationships. Generally, the rule seems to be that when A and B are in a confidential relationship, B cannot use against A's interests information acquired from A. But some rulings are chipping away at this rule, for example, in circumstances where others are endangered by it or where legislative purpose overrides the common-law rule. These developments should not obscure the fact that confidential relations still matter a great deal in privacy cases.

A Note on Secondhand Secrets

Most of the cases that have been discussed in this section on serial secrets present betrayals, cases where A sues B because B has claimed the right to reveal A's secrets to whomever B chooses. Overdisclosure

---

70. 367 P.2d 284, 287.
71. 12 U.S.C. §1829b (1972).
72. 416 U.S. 21 (1974).

and identification generally appear as factors in betrayals because both address issues of the proper scope of disclosure. Generally this issue is relevant only when B wants to distribute the information, rather than when A is claiming that an inquiry on the part of C should be blocked. The C's generally already know the identity of the subject and generally claim that only they should be let in on the secret (thus making the principle of overdisclosure inapplicable).

What, then, *does* matter in secondhand-secret cases? The legal claims presented by secondhand secrets are really a composite of claims present in other sorts of secrets. They share with disclosures the claim that A revealed the information to B voluntarily, with simple secrets the claim that someone else should not be allowed to pry into A's secrets, and with betrayals the claim that A should be able to restrict B's disclosures. It should not be surprising that the logic of secondhand-secret cases presents the legally relevant facts used in each of these claims. Both consent and relevance, from direct-secret cases matter; and confidential relationships, from betrayal cases, matter.

The importance of consent can be seen in *Bloomfield v. Retail Credit Co.*[73] Bloomfield had applied for a job with the Puritan Life Insurance Company. As part of his application, he listed his former employers. Puritan then asked Retail Credit to undertake an investigation of Bloomfield, and Retail Credit turned up some damaging information about Bloomfield.[74] Bloomfield sued for invasion of privacy, but his listing of employers on the job application was held to be evidence that he had consented to his former employers' release of information about him.

Another credit dispute demonstrates the importance of relevance in these cases. In *Tureen v. Equifax*[75] Tureen applied for insurance, and the insurance company requested information from Equifax. Equifax reported to the insurance company that Tureen apparently already had taken out twenty-three policies, which made the insurance company suspicious of Tureen's intentions. When Tureen sued Equifax, the court made a classic statement of the importance of relevance: "In order to make informed judgments in these matters [extending credit and detecting fraudulent insurance claims], it may be necessary for the decision maker to have information which would normally be consid-

73. 14 Ill. App. 3d 158, 302 N.E.2d 88 (1973).

74. This was not a pure privacy case, since there was evidence that the information dredged up was inaccurate and possibly defamatory. The court did rule on a privacy issue, however.

75. 571 F.2d 411 (8th Cir. 1978).

ered private, provided the information is legitimately related to a legitimate purpose of the decision maker."[76]

In this case, then, the information was judged to be relevant to the decision, and, as in the simple-secret cases, it was allowed to be revealed. This case, however, provoked a dissent, again partly on the issue of relevance. Judge Heaney argued that some of the information involved in the case was twenty-five years old and therefore should no longer be considered relevant. In addition, he argued, the fact that Equifax offered information of this sort to anyone who asked for it made the case rather like the overdisclosure cases. Although the first argument still accords importance to the issue of relevance, the second argument makes less sense. Clearly, the distinction between betrayals and secondhand secrets makes a doctrinal difference, so it seems wrong to equate the voluntary disclosure by B to C with C requiring disclosure by B. This does not disturb the conclusion, however, that secondhand-secret cases use the same standard of relevance as do simple-secret cases.

With consent and relevance at center stage in secondhand secrets, things look bad for privacy. The notion of relevance is sufficiently powerful to justify almost any request to B on the part of C. And whenever relevance appears as the standard of judgment, all the defendant has to do is give some plausible reason why the information is relevant to something that the defendant is entitled to do. There is one additional constraint in secondhand secrets, however. That constraint is the constraint of confidential relations.

Berry v. Moench[77] demonstrates the importance of confidential relations in warding off nosy requests. Robert Berry was dating Mary Boothe. Boothe's parents did not like Berry much, and so they decided to investigate his background. They asked their family doctor to contact Berry's doctor to get the doctor's opinion of the young man's stability. Dr. Hellewell contacted Dr. Moench, asking about Berry. Moench responded by saying that Berry had been diagnosed as a psychopath and added: "My suggestion to the infatuated girl would be to run as fast and as far as she possibly could in any direction away from him. Of course, if he doesn't marry her, he will marry someone else and make life hell for that person. The usual story is repeated unsuccessful marriages and a trail of tragedy behind."[78] Needless to say, this did not reflect well on Berry. Boothe's parents urged her not to marry

76. 571 F.2d 411, 416.
77. 8 Utah 2d 191, 331 P.2d 814 (1958).
78. 331 P.2d 814, 816.

him, but she went ahead and did so anyway. Berry sued his doctor for invasion of privacy.

The court argued that a confidential relationship existed in that situation: "If the doctor could with impunity publish anything that is true, the patient would be without protection from disclosure of intimacies which might be both embarrassing and harmful to him. This would make him reluctant to tell some things even though they might be important in the treatment of his ills. For this reason, it is obligatory upon the doctor not to reveal information obtained in confidence in connection with the diagnosis or treatment of his patient." [79] Even though the information was arguably relevant to Boothe's parents in their attempt to dissuade their daughter, the court ruled that, because of the circumstances giving rise to a relation of confidence, the information should not be disclosed. Clearly, in situations such as these, a claim of confidential relationship is sufficient to block an inquiry, absent extraordinary circumstances.

The simultaneous operation of all three of these factors—consent, relevance, and confidential relations—can be seen in *Earp v. The City of Detroit*.[80] Richard Earp was a telephone installer for Michigan Bell. As part of an investigation of illegal wiretapping operations, Michigan Bell asked its employees to agree to be interviewed by the Detroit police. Earp consented and was told by the police that all information would be confidential. Earp told them what he knew about wiretapping, which was not much, and he also volunteered that he had altered records and taken tips, acts not illegal but contrary to Michigan Bell policy. Several days after the interview, Earp was fired. It seemed that the police had turned over the records of their interviews to Michigan Bell, including records that showed Earp's actions to be in violation of company policy. Earp sued both the police and Michigan Bell for invasion of privacy.

The court noted that there was a duty for the defendants not to pry into Earp's private life but that here Earp had volunteered the information. Moreover, the information was relevant to Michigan Bell's interests. Although the court noted that they would not determine whether the police owed something to Earp because they promised him confidentiality, they decided that "here the confidential information that Earp gave to the police was not of such a nature that he was entitled by law to require all who knew of it to say nothing. . . . It would seem that it would be in their [Detroit police's] duty to inform

79. 331 P.2d 814, 817.
80. 16 Mich. App. 271, 167 N.W.2d 841 (1969).

Bell that their facilities were being used for illegal purposes." [81] The opinion emphasized that Bell had set up the interviews in the first place, a circumstance making this case much like the ones in which court-ordered tests are immune from any doctor-patient privilege. Bell's initial involvement precluded any confidential relationship, even if the police made a promise. The court not only sidestepped the issue of the police promise, but later in the opinion it also called Earp's acts illegal. Earlier in the same opinion, Earp's acts had not been called illegal, just contrary to company policy.

Earp does show, however, how these three factors of consent, relevance, and confidential relations could all work together in a secondhand-secret case. It is relatively rare when all are present simultaneously, but it is clear that any one of them could provide the backbone for an opinion. Secondhand secrets present an amalgam of claims and an amalgam of legally relevant facts.

IN SERIAL SECRETS, THEN, WE find a complex pattern. In betrayals, where B discloses A's secret to C, we find that A has redress in an invasion-of-privacy claim when B overdiscloses the secret, unnecessarily identifies A, or is in a confidential relationship with A. In secondhand secrets, where C tries to get A's secret from an unwilling B, C must demonstrate that the information is relevant or that A consented to the disclosure; but B can block these claims when A and B share a relation of confidence.

81. 167 N.W.2d 841, 844.

CHAPTER TWELVE

Trade Secrets as Corporate Privacy

WHAT HAPPENS IN THE CASE of corporate secrets? Although corporations have been held to have no right of privacy, corporate actions in trade secrecy look very much like personal actions in privacy for public disclosure of private facts. As I will argue in this chapter, the legally relevant facts are very much the same.

Trade-secret cases almost always involve serial secrets. A, a corporation or occasionally an inventor, discloses some secret to B, usually an employee but occasionally a contractor. B then either appropriates the secret, claiming to be able to use it to forward B's interests to the exclusion of A's interests, or tells C, often a competitor of A. The general similarity between privacy and trade secrets is that in both cases the information pertains to A and represents some usually important fact about A that A would rather that others not know. In addition, since A has shared the secret with B, A later claims that A should be able to restrict B's future actions as a result of this disclosure. B generally claims that B should not be so restricted in the use of this information and that B has important interests that also must be considered. The main structural difference between the two forms of legal action is that in privacy cases B generally claims the right to publicize the information about A to C, while in trade-secret cases B generally claims the right to use the information about A, not necessarily involving C. Publication is rarely an issue in trade-secret cases; a more obvious form of appropriation is present. Still, the sorts of claims presented are very similar, and it should not be surprising that courts tend to emphasize the same set of legally relevant facts.

The legally relevant facts in trade-secret cases are (*a*) the secrecy of the information in the first place (paralleling the concern in privacy cases that the information be actually private), (*b*) whether there has been investment in the creation of this secret (which I will argue is structurally similar to the threshold rules in privacy cases) and (*c*) whether a confidential relationship was present. Generally, over-disclosure and identification do not enter into trade-secret cases because the extent of publication is rarely at issue.

Secrecy

The first question that courts ask when confronted with a trade-secret case is, Is the information secret in the first place? The answer to this question comes in two parts: the court must first find that the information is neither general knowledge nor revealed in the manufacture of the product itself, and the court must then find that the corporation made efforts to keep the secret a secret.

In *Kaumagraph Co. v. Stampagraph Co.*[1] the secret at issue involved a process of making transfer stamps and embroidery patterns that could be fixed onto fabric with the application of heat. Chadwick and Scott had come to the United States from England, where the process was already in use, and they went to work for Kaumagraph. Fifteen years later, Chadwick and Scott started their own firm, Stampagraph, in competition with Kaumagraph, making the same heat-transfer stamps. Kaumagraph sued, claiming that the two Englishmen had stolen trade secrets.

The court discovered that the process that Chadwick and Scott allegedly had pilfered was in fact in wide use in England and had been the subject of two patents there. The information used by the pair was entirely disclosed by the British patents, and so, the court argued, there could be no claim that it constituted a secret. As a result, no claim of theft of trade secrets could stand.

Similarly, in *Louis Milani Foods v. Scharf*[2] a claim of a trade-secret violation failed because Milani had not shown that the seventy recipes that he claimed that his former employee had taken with him to his new employer were really secret; if the information were generally known in the trade, then it could not be protected as a trade secret. The same argument was made in *National Starch Products v. Polymer Industries Inc.*,[3] where the defendant was allowed to argue that the information claimed as a trade secret was actually general knowledge already. No secret could be claimed if the information were widely known.

1. 235 N.Y. 1, 138 N.E. 485, *affd.* 188 N.Y.S. 678, 197 App. Div. 66 (1923).
2. 335 Ill. App. 569, 82 N.E.2d 75 (1948).
3. 273 App. Div. 732, 79 N.Y.S.2d 357, 77 U.S.P.Q. 644 (1948).

Another important element of secrecy, besides the information not being generally known or disclosed in patents, is that the secret not reveal itself in the manufacture of the article to which the secret pertains. If it is possible to detect a secret through "reverse engineering" (that is, taking the thing apart and figuring out how it went together in the first place), then there is no secret.

This was the case in *Permagrain Products v. U.S. Mat and Rubber Co.*[4] Permagrain sued U.S. Mat for making a floor covering that was similar to Permagrain's design. At issue was whether a former employee of Permagrain had revealed secrets to his new employer, U.S. Mat. The court found that whether the employee had or had not made no difference. The secrets claimed by Permagrain had been disclosed by the product itself. It was a relatively easy matter to take apart the floor covering and see which layer followed upon the layer below. In addition, other information about Permagrain's alleged secret was revealed in Permagrain's patent as well as in Permagrain's advertising. There was simply no secret there.

In *Carver v. Harr*[5] the subject was blackout screens. Carver invented a blackout screen that was particularly well suited to portholes on ships. Carver filled a number of orders for the popular screens before he told Harr about their design. Harr then proceeded to make the screens himself, and Carver claimed that his trade secrets had been stolen. The court in this case disposed of the matter easily by noting that there was nothing special about the blackout screens that would not be obvious on inspection. Because they revealed their secrets in their very appearance, no claim of secrecy could be upheld. A similar fate befell Nat Wissman's versatile fishing pole, which served as a fly rod, casting rod, or general all-around fishing pole and, when disassembled, could serve both as its own container and as a walking stick. Once someone saw it, the secret was unmasked.[6]

Not only does the possessor of a potential trade secret have to show that the information is secret, but the claimant also must show that efforts were made to keep the secret a secret. What this generally means is that the plaintiff in a trade-secret action must demonstrate that there was concern and protection of the secret in advance of a trial over it. In *Kodekey Electronics v. Mechanix Corp.*[7] Kodekey was found to have a trade secret in part because everyone to whom Kodekey dis-

4. 489 F. Supp. 108 (E.D. Pa. 1980).
5. 132 N.J.Eq. 207, 27 A.2d 895 (1942).
6. *Boucher v. Wissman*, 206 S.W.2d 101 (Tex. Civ. App. 1947).
7. 486 F. 2d. 449 (C.A. Colo. 1973).

closed the secret had to sign an agreement pledging not to tell others the information. In *Crown Industries v. Kawneer Co.*,[8] however, such agreements were not present and there was found to be no trade secret. The fact that the plaintiff had placed his reverse-engineerable product where thousands of people could see it daily did not help either.

If anything less than reasonable diligence in protecting the secret is shown, courts will often find that the plaintiff has nothing to complain about. In *Sachs v. Cluett Peabody and Co.*[9] Sachs filed a trade-secret action against Cluett a number of years after it became apparent that the company was using a fabric-shrinking process similar to his. In fact, he waited long enough for Cluett to take out a patent and use the process for twenty years. The court took this as an indication that Sachs was not adequately protecting his secret.

In *Brown and Root Inc. v. Jacques*[10] inventor Jacques made a portable chain saw, which he showed to Brown and Root without asking for a pledge of confidentiality. Brown and Root liked the saw but thought that Jacques was asking too much for it. They devised their own saw, similar to Jacques's, for use in clearing a reservoir basin. The court was influenced to decide in Brown and Root's favor partly because they had made the saw for their own use and not to sell to others. But the court was also influenced by Jacques's efforts to sell the saw, which would have revealed the secrets that he claimed. By making the product available for sale and because sale would have made the secrets visible, Jacques was found to have no ground for claiming that a trade secret existed.[11]

8. 335 F. Supp. 749 (N.D. Ill. 1971).
9. 265 App. Div. 497, 39 N.Y.S.2d 853 (1943).
10. 98 S.W.2d 257 (Tex. Civ. App. 1936).
11. Occasionally, however, courts are willing to maintain trade-secret protection even when there has not been an explicit agreement of confidentiality. In *Smith v. Dravo Corp.*, 203 F.2d 369 (7th Cir. 1953), for example, the court found that Smith's disclosure, without a promise of confidentiality, of the design of his steel freight containers did not destroy the secret. Instead, the court found that Smith only disclosed the secret to representatives of Dravo because they had expressed an interest in purchasing his business. They would not have known the worth of the business without knowing something about the product that Smith claimed was worth so much. The court found that a relationship of trust and confidence was present, and that the secret therefore was maintained. Dravo lost. Just how this is different from *Brown and Root* is not immediately obvious, although there are two possible reasons: (1) In *Brown and Root* Jacques would have sold the chain saw, thereby disclosing the secret, whereas in *Smith* the business would have been sold, enabling the new possessor to keep the secret; and (2) In the former case, Brown and Root used the saw for their own personal project and did not anticipate selling it in competition with Jacques whereas in *Smith* Dravo went into direct competition manufacturing a steel freight container almost identical to the one that Smith had designed.

But diligence has its reasonable limits. In *E.I. DuPont de Nemours v. Christopher*[12] the court was presented with "a case of industrial espionage in which an airplane is the cloak and a camera the dagger."[13] While DuPont was building a plant that would use a new process to make methanol, Rolfe and Gary Christopher were spotted flying low over the plant in their airplane. An investigation disclosed that the Christophers were photographers who were busily engaged in documenting the arrangement of machines inside the plant. Since the plant's construction was incomplete, the roof had not yet been finished, leaving the machines visible to anyone who was flying over. Although the Christophers claimed that they were flying in public airspace and that DuPont had left its secrets unprotected, the court thought otherwise. Ruling that this was an improper means of discovering DuPont's secret, Judge Goldberg wrote:

> We think . . . that the Texas rule is clear. One may use his competitor's secret process if he discovers the process by reverse engineering applied to the finished product; one may use a competitor's process if he discovers it by his own independent research; but one may not avoid these labors by taking the process from the discoverer without his permission at a time when he takes reasonable precautions to maintain its secrecy. To obtain knowledge of a process without spending the time and money to discover it independently is *improper* unless the holder voluntarily discloses it or fails to take reasonable precautions to ensure its secrecy.[14]

Later in the opinion, Goldberg argued that

> our devotion to free wheeling industrial competition must not force us into accepting the law of the jungle as the standard of morality expected in our commercial relations. Our tolerance of the espionage game must cease when the protections required to prevent another's spying cost so much that the spirit of inventiveness is dampened. Commercial privacy must be protected from espionage which could not have been reasonably anticipated or prevented. . . . To require DePont to put a roof over the unfinished plant to guard its secret would impose an enormous expense to prevent nothing more than a school boy's trick. . . . We should not require a person or corporation to take unreasonable precau-

12. 431 F.2d 1012 (5th Cir. 1970), *cert. den.* 400 U.S. 1024, 92 S. Ct. 581, 27 L. Ed. 2d 637 (1970), *reh. den.* 401 U.S. 967, 91 S. Ct. 968, 28 L. Ed. 2d 250 (1971).
13. 431 F.2d 1012, 1013.
14. 431 F.2d 1012, 1015–1016. Note how the language in this portion of the opinion sounds very much like the equal-access-to-information logic of the fraud cases. We will return to this point later.

tions to prevent another from doing that which he ought not do in the first place.[15]

The court in this case is at pains to draw the boundaries between legitimate secret-keeping and illegitimate prying. Clearly, in this case the methods used were judged inappropriate because no one could expect a company to anticipate (at least in advance of this case) that aerial photography might be used to steal secrets. But whether a particular method of acquiring secrets is legitimate depends in part on whether the secrets desired to be uncovered are legitimate or not. In *DuPont* the information was not only in fact a secret and being kept secret by the company; it was also of such a nature that trade-secret protection was allowed.

What all of these cases show is that, before they will broaden the principle of trade-secret protection, the courts require that the information be truly secret. This is virtually identical to the concern in privacy cases—that the information must be private to warrant protection. Once information has been distributed at all, courts seem concerned to avoid restricting distribution in the future. Courts generally do not make narrower the scope within which knowledge is available, although they may on occasion keep the scope from broadening.

Investment

Not all information that is kept secret and not generally known can count as a trade secret. Another essential element of trade secrecy is that the information be the result of a nontrivial investment of time, money, or energy.

The principle can be most clearly seen in *Heyden Chemical Corp. v. Burrell & Neidig Inc.*[16] Heyden was a chemical company in Garfield,

---

15. 431 F.2d 1012, 1016–1017. The fact that the court referred to trade secrets as commercial privacy should give further support for the argument that the trade-secret cases are really the corporate version of a right to privacy. This language is further reinforced by the opinion of former Chief Justice Burger in *Kewanee Oil Co. v. Bicron Corp.*, 416 U.S. 470, 94 S. Ct. 1879, 40 L. Ed. 2d 315 (1974). In that opinion, concerned with the question of whether federal constitutional patent protection preempted state common-law trade-secret protection, the former Chief Justice wrote: "A most fundamental human right, that of privacy, is threatened when industrial espionage is condoned or is made profitable" (94 S. Ct. 1879, 1889). The notion of trade secrets as a version of privacy is not so farfetched as it at first may seem.

16. 2 N.J. Super. 467, 64 A.2d 465 (1949).

New Jersey, that made formaldehyde and pentaerythritol, having 45 percent of the U.S. market in the former and 50 percent in the latter. Burrell and Neidig were engineers who had worked for Heyden. After leaving Heyden's employ, they set up their own firm and began manufacturing the two chemicals. Heyden sued, claiming that the former employees were using trade secrets.

The two chemicals in question had been the subject of a great many scientific articles. During the trial, it was estimated that about 850 articles had been published about formaldehyde and that between five hundred and six hundred articles had been published about pentaerythritol. The defendants contended that they were using only material that had already been made public. But Heyden won its case because it was able to successfully argue that even though the information necessary to duplicate its processes was published, it took a great deal of time and effort as well as trial and error to figure out the precise process that Heyden used. The court agreed with this, finding that a trade secret existed whenever substantial effort would be required to rediscover the exact process used. The defendants were not allowed to shortcut this effort.

In *Fairchild Engine and Airplane Corp. v. Cox*[17] the court also indicated that the test of effort was necessary to show that the process was in fact a trade secret. In *USM Corp. v. Marson Fastener Corp.*[18] the secret at issue pertained to the design of a machine that was able "to provide a means of reliable and rapid assembly of mandrels and rivet bodies into rivets."[19] Whether the design of the machine constituted a trade secret was held to depend on whether it was "ultimately found that the development of the USM machine involved considerable time, effort and expense, that the development of the machine was relatively difficult and that its combination of features was unique and effective when devised and did not constitute a matter of public knowledge or of general knowledge in the industry."[20] Clearly, all these cases indicate that investment is an important factor in determining whether some piece of information should be considered a trade secret.

Nowhere is the distinction between investment and noninvestment clearer than in the customer-list cases. In these cases, B has been an employee of A, generally charged with customer contact of some sort. B strikes out on her own, creating her own firm by starting with

17. 50 N.Y.S.2d 643, 62 U.S.P.Q. 98 (1944).
18. 379 Mass. 90, 393 N.E.2d 895 (1979).
19. 393 N.E.2d 895, 897.
20. Ibid.

the clients of A that she knew of by virtue of working with A. A then sues B for purloining a trade secret.

The cases usually hinge on the level of investment that A made in getting the list of customers to begin with. In *Robert B. Vance and Associates v. Baronet Corp.*[21] just such a customer list was at stake. The plaintiff in this case manufactured women's purses that included a built-in checkbook. The purses were sold through banks that had been canvassed by salesmen. The defendant had worked for Vance but subsequently departed to start a competing firm. Although the product that he made was slightly different, he sold the purse through the same banks that he knew, from his employment with Vance, would be interested in such an idea. Vance sued on a number of grounds, one of which was that the customer list represented a trade secret.

In deciding this case the court had to determine whether this customer list was in fact a trade secret, and the court looked directly to the issue of investment. The court reasoned "that customer lists which are simply compilations of public information . . . would not be deemed to constitute trade secrets. However, where, as in the instant case, the party compiling the customer lists, while using public information as a source, i.e., names of banks, expends a great deal of time, effort and expense in developing the lists and treats the lists as confidential in its business, the lists may be entitled to trade secret protection." [22] Clearly, the level of investment made all the difference. No investment, no trade secret.

The case of *Abdallah v. Crandall*[23] demonstrates the effect of a lack of investment. Abdallah ran a dairy that employed Crandall as a driver. When Crandall left to open a competing business, he took with him the knowledge of Abdallah's customers. He was able to convince 150 of Abdallah's customers to change dairies, and Abdallah became angry and sued. In this case, however, Abdallah was out of luck, because there was no secret; nor was there any investment: "the delivery of milk from the very nature of the business is open and notorious. . . . A trade secret, like any other secret, is nothing more than a private matter; something known only to one or a few people and kept from the general public; and not susceptible to general knowledge. A list of milk customers in a small city like Cortland and a village like Homer hardly meets such a definition." [24] The court made the additional point that

21. 487 F. Supp. 790 (N.D. Ga. 1979).
22. 487 F. Supp. 790, 799.
23. 273 App. Div. 131, 76 N.Y.S.2d 403 (1948).
24. 76 N.Y.S.2d 403, 406.

since everyone was a potential customer, no special investment was required to figure out who the potential customers were.

The logic in these cases sounds very much like the rationales given in the privacy cases when the harm alleged is judged to be insufficient. In the privacy cases, one has to demonstrate that the information is really discreditable, that there was more than merely an oral declaration, or that the information was actually used to the plaintiff's detriment. The latter two rarely apply in trade-secret cases (although in *Permagrain* the court noted that U.S. Mat's product had been so spectacularly unsuccessful that it could not have affected sales of Permagrain much). The investment cases are very much like the discreditable-information cases. If one has not invested very much in the information at stake, then, just as when information is published that does not actually do harm to the plaintiff's reputation, the loss simply is not sufficient to warrant court action. The rule about investment, like the rule about discreditable information, requires that the cases present real harm and discourages cases where the plaintiff simply does not like the fact that the information has got around.

The rule about investment is similar to rules in privacy cases also in that, if no investment is required, then the knowledge must be obvious, in which case it is probably not secret. The decision in the milk-delivery case is consistent with the interpretation that the information was really not secret to begin with. Although the investment rule may sound different from the rules encountered in the earlier privacy cases, it is actually quite compatible with the two threshold rules uncovered there. Investment is required either as a way of demonstrating harm or as evidence against the charge that the information was not public by virtue of being obvious.

By establishing that investment is necessary to justify giving information trade-secret protection, courts may appear simply to be giving property rights to those who have created new knowledge in order to encourage investment in its production. But trade-secret protection does not protect the trade-secret owner against all others who acquire the information. Courts seem to examine investment not to establish that the knowledge is deliberately acquired, in Kronman's sense, but rather to establish that anyone similarly situated could have come up with the same information. Courts may look to the level of investment made as a way of judging whether another actor who steals the trade secret significantly reduced her costs of acquiring the information in the process. When B, by getting the information directly from A rather than engaging in the search process herself, so lowers the cost of acquiring information that she now has an advantage over A, the equal-search-costs rationale requires that A be allowed to recover.

Confidential Relations

Just as we have seen for fraud and for privacy cases, there is a concern in trade-secret cases with confidential relations. In fact, the presence of a confidential relationship can be said to be at the heart of the protection of trade secrets. A number of cases have indicated that it is breach of confidence, rather than any property theory, that underlies the decisions in these cases.[25] This indicates that it is really the relationship, rather than the information per se, that the law protects.[26] In *E. I. DuPont de Nemours Powder Co. v. Masland*[27] Justice Holmes wrote: "The property may be denied but the confidence cannot be. Therefore, the starting point for the present matter is not property or due process of law, but that the defendant stood in confidential relation with the plaintiffs or one of them."[28]

Similarly, in *Cataphote Corp. v. Hudson*[29] the court explained that "[trade secret] protection is not based on a policy of rewarding or otherwise encouraging the development of secret processes or devices. The protection is merely against breach of faith and reprehensible means of learning another's secret."[30] And in *Monolith Portland Midwest Co. v. Kaiser Aluminum and Chemical Corp.*[31] the court indicated that "California does not treat trade secrets as if they were property. It

25. Trade secrecy has been justified with a number of theories, including property, quasi-contracts, unjust enrichment, and fair dealing, as well as breach of confidence. See Ridsdale Ellis, *Trade Secrets* (New York: Baker, Voorhis, 1953). In all of the cases, whatever their theory, trade secrets are only protected when someone who knew the plaintiff—and knew the secrets as a result of knowing the plaintiff—uses the secrets for personal gain. Independent discovery of the secret and reverse engineering result in no liability for the person who obtains the secret. It is also instructive that if A tells B a trade secret and B then tells C, C is not liable for a trade-secret violation if it can be shown that C had no idea that it came from A. Only the person who is in a relation of trust and confidence with the secret-holder is liable if the secret escapes as a result.

26. The main exception to this comes when some C engages in prying. If the initiation for disclosure comes from C, as in *Atlantic Wool Combing Co. v. Norfolk Mills Inc.*, 357 F.2d 866 (1st Cir. 1966), discussed below, then A may be able to sue C. Given that we have limited our discussion to legitimate secrets and have excluded a discussion of legitimate prying, we will not encounter very many of these cases.

27. 244 U.S. 100, 37 S. Ct. 575, 61 L. Ed. 1016 (1917).

28. 244 U.S. 100, 110.

29. 422 F.2d 1290 (5th Cir. 1970).

30. 422 F.2d 1290, 1294.

31. 407 F.2d 288 (9th Cir. 1969).

is the relationship between the parties at the time the secret is disclosed that is protected."[32]

In an important Supreme Court case on the subject of trade secrets, former Chief Justice Burger indicated in *Kewanee Oil Co. v. Bicron Corp.*[33] what the core of trade-secret protection was:

> The protection accorded the trade secret holder is against the disclosure or unauthorized use of the trade secret by those to whom the secret has been confided under the express or implied restriction of nondisclosure or nonuse. The law also protects the holder of a trade secret against disclosure or use when the knowledge is gained, not by the owner's volition, but by some "improper means." . . . A trade secret law, however, does not offer protection against fair and honest means, such as by independent invention, accidental disclosure, or by so called reverse engineering, that is by starting with the known product and working backward to divine the process which aided in its development or manufacture.[34]

There is substantial authority to the effect that the element of breach of confidence is really what trade-secret cases are all about, as the above quotes show. Confidential relationships, then, are very important. In fact, the maintenance of secrecy and the presence of investment can be thought of as threshold rules underlying the more general principle that confidential relationships should not be breached.

In *Atlantic Wool Combing Co. v. Norfolk Mills Inc.*[35] an engineer with Atlantic Wool had devised a plan for a machine that would dehair cashmere more efficiently than did other machines currently in use. Atlantic Wool then contracted with Henry Lawton, the owner of a small machine shop, to construct this machine. Meanwhile, Norfolk Mills had managed to hire a mechanic who had formerly worked for Atlantic Wool. This mechanic told Norfolk Mills that Atlantic Wool had devised a new and superior machine and had contracted with Lawton to build the machine. Norfolk Mill representatives then approached Lawton and asked him to build a similar machine for them. Lawton did. When Atlantic Wool discovered this,[36] Norfolk Mills was sued for theft of trade secrets.

---

32. 407 F.2d 288, 293.
33. 416 U.S. 470, 94 S. Ct. 1879, 40 L. Ed. 2d 315 (1974).
34. 94 S. Ct. 1879, 1883.
35. 357 F.2d 866 (1st Cir. 1966).
36. It is not always the case that enterprises will discover that their secrets have been taken. One of the interesting properties of information is that many people can

The court in this case stated the principle clearly:

> In general, the essence of the wrong [trade secret theft] is the obtaining of unjust enrichment and unfair competitive advantage through inequitable conduct, usually a breach of confidence. In particular application of this doctrine, the courts rather consistently impose liability on a proprietor of a business who employs unfair means, characterized by breach of confidence, to acquire otherwise undisclosed plans and specifications for a competitor's distinctive structure or machinery and uses them to produce a similar competitive device for his own use and to his competitor's economic detriment.[37]

In this case, the court found that just such a situation was present. Finding that Lawton had specifically promised that he would not disclose the secrets that Atlantic Wool had revealed to him, the court went on to note that neither Lawton nor Norfolk Mills had done any of its own work on the machine. Norfolk Mills was using a pure copy, and this could not be allowed. The court found for Atlantic Wool and found that Norfolk Mills could not pull the wool over its competitor's eyes.

Atlantic Wool is an easy case. Lawton made an explicit promise; Norfolk Mills used a pure copy. When there is an explicitly negotiated agreement to preserve secrets and when one of the parties takes a secret that would not have been known save for this confidential disclosure and uses it for personal gain, the decision is clear. *E. L. Bruce Co. v. Bradley Lumber Co.*[38] presents just such a case. Bruce had patented a machine that completely finished and waxed floors in twelve minutes while moving continuously along a production line. The method of applying the wax so that the machine would work most effectively, however, was a trade secret. Bruce disclosed the secret to the defendant under license. After the termination of the license, Bradley continued to use the secret, claiming that it was nothing new. In this case, the court found that the information was not obvious and that Bradley and

---

simultaneously possess it without knowing who else has it. In many cases, the trade secret pertains to a process. It is generally not possible to tell from observing the final product just which process is used. See Edmund W. Kitch, "The Law and Economics of Rights in Valuable Information," *Journal of Law and Economics* 9: 683–723 (1980), pp. 689–691. In one case, for example, a firm did not learn that its trade secrets had been stolen until that firm bought out the firm that previously had got its secrets. See *Northern Petrochemicals Co. v. Tomlinson*, 484 F.2d 1057 (7th Cir. 1973).

37. 357 F.2d 866, 869.

38. 79 F. Supp. 176 (W.D. Ark. 1948).

Bruce had been in a confidential relationship, which then made any further use of Bruce's secret illegitimate.

In *L. M. Rabinowitz v. Dasher*[39] the court found that the hook-and-eye machines that Rabinowitz had developed had been kept secret and that their design had been disclosed confidentially to Dasher. Dasher then made copies of the machine. This conduct made Dasher liable for trade-secret theft.

There are two interesting knots in this otherwise smooth logic that information that is part of a confidential relationship should not be disclosed. One occurs when the defendant in the trade-secret action actually contributes a good deal to the creation of the knowledge in the first place; the other occurs when the trade-secret holder tries to claim that quite a lot of the defendant's knowledge is really a trade secret and cannot be used. The first problem is rather like negotiating a property settlement in a divorce, complicated by the fact that knowledge is not easily divisible. The second problem also results from the difficulty in dividing knowledge into pieces and presents the similarly sticky question of how one is allowed to use one's mind following exposure to trade secrets. In each case, the information that is a trade secret of the plaintiff must be separated from the intellectual abilities and general knowledge of the defendant.

When the defendant in a trade-secret action has contributed to the creation of the knowledge itself, the general rule is that the defendant's rights in the trade secret are very much dependent on the nature of the agreement between the plaintiff and defendant. In the absence of an explicit agreement, it is generally the case that the employer is allowed to keep trade secrets if the employee was specifically hired to create them. Thus, in *Ultra-Life Laboratories v. Eames*[40] L. W. Eames was hired by Ultra-Life to perfect a method of chicken culling (sorting out chickens that do not lay eggs from those that do). Although Eames had already been working on the problem when he arrived at Ultra-Life, it was also clear that he was hired to work on his discovery and to teach it exclusively in Ultra-Life's schools. In fact, Ultra-Life set up the Eames Institute of Poultry Technology and kept Eames from running afoul of debts. Each person who took Eames's course had to sign a secrecy agreement, so the method was preserved as confidential. Eames left Ultra-Life and started his own school. Ultra-Life sued.

The court noted that even though this was a method that Eames had developed, he could not have done so without Ultra-Life. Eames

39. 82 N.Y.S.2d 431, 78 U.S.P.Q. 163 (1948).
40. 240 Mo. App. 851, 221 S.W.2d 224 (1949).

had signed an agreement giving Ultra-Life the exclusive right to teach his method. Even though he had invented it, the trade secret rested with Ultra-Life and they could prevent him from using it.

In *Byrne v. Barrett*[41] Barrett was a salesman for a firm of real estate brokers. He negotiated a deal and saw that he could profit by setting up his own company to take advantage of this information that he had created. In the tangle of lawsuits that resulted, the court found that Barrett could not use in this way the information that he had acquired on this job, even though he was responsible for negotiating the deal. Because that was what Barrett had been hired to do, he could not claim that the knowledge was his alone.

These sorts of decisions make one wonder what the limits of trade secrecy are—and whether one needs to leave one's entire memory at the door as one moves from one job to the next. The courts have shown a fair amount of sensitivity to this problem (perhaps too much, according to at least one commentator[42]). The general rule is that an employer cannot use the claim of trade secrets to shackle a former employee. When the claim of trade secrets starts to interfere with former employees' abilities to remain in the same line of work, courts decide in favor of the liberty of the employees rather than in favor of the sanctity of trade secrets. In other words, one cannot use the claim of a confidential relationship to put significant limits on someone else's freedom. Confidential relationships have limits.

This can be seen most clearly in *Continental Car-Na-Var Corp. v. Moseley*.[43] Car-Na-Var was a corporation that produced and sold compounds for finishing floors. A group of former Car-Na-Var employees decided to go into business for themselves, and their former employer sued them for taking trade secrets. No evidence was presented that the defendants were using the same formulas as the plaintiff. The court, noting this fact, said that it seemed as though the defendants had used their general knowledge of chemistry rather than the specialized knowledge that they might have gained by working at Car-Na-Var. Grounding its decision in equity, the court wrote about "the right inherent in all people . . . to follow any of the common occupations of life. . . . Every individual possesses as a form of property, the right to pursue any calling, business or profession he may choose." [44] Since there was no evidence that the defendants had done anything

41. 268 N.Y. 199, 197 N.E. 217 (1935).
42. Kitch, "Law and Economics of Rights."
43. 24 Cal. 2d 104, 148 P.2d 9 (1944).
44. 148 P.2d 9, 12.

other than use their general knowledge, no violation of a trade secret was found.

Similarly, in *Ridley v. Kraut*[45] Kraut went to work for Ridley's bicycle shop and then later set up his own business. Ridley sued, claiming that Kraut had stolen his secrets. Here again, the court argued that Kraut was free to use his general knowledge of bicycles and that Ridley could not use the excuse of trade secrets to keep Kraut from peddling his services.

What these confidential relationship cases show is that the law is generally willing to enforce promises to keep information secret. More generally, they show that within certain sorts of relationships, knowledge has a special role. When A discloses to B in confidence, B is not allowed to use that information to the detriment of A. B may not use it for personal gain in the trade-secret cases. This is consistent with what we saw in the fraud and privacy cases, where B was obligated to share with A all relevant information and where B was obligated not to publicize information about A over A's objections. In short, once A and B throw in their lot together, they must share all relevant information and not use that information against each other. The one limitation on this seems to be that A cannot use the existence of shared secrets to place extreme restrictions on B's other legitimate actions. When B's sharing of A's secret becomes a barrier to B's liberty in critical ways, the law seems to emphasize liberty over loyalty.

Independent Discovery

To further emphasize the point that confidential relationships are at the heart of trade secrets, it will be useful to show that the law only protects trade secrets to the extent that they are disclosed by people formerly trusted not to reveal them. The law of trade secrets does not protect the information in question per se; it only protects against abuses of trust.[46] This can be seen most clearly in cases involving

---

45. 63 Wyo. 252, 180 P.2d 124 (1947).

46. This is the main difference between patents and trade secrets. Patents require the inventor to publicize the information, and in exchange the inventor reaps the benefits of the information for seventeen years. A patent holder can exclude all others from using the information no matter how these others have obtained it; it is no defense in a patent-infringement suit to claim that the discovery was independent. In trade-secret cases, however, the law does not exclude all others from using the information. In fact, it is entirely possible that a large group of firms could all have the same information and each use this as its own trade secret (although if the number of firms possessing the secret becomes too large, the information could be said to be common knowledge in the field).

independent discovery, where B gets the trade secret not from A but by independent effort. In short, when B recreates the information, A has no cause of action in trade secrets.

In *Radioptics v. United States*[47] Radioptics in 1963 submitted a proposal to the Atomic Energy Commission, where it was classified, reviewed, and rejected. In 1967, the AEC published a notice indicating that it had declassified all documents relating to the use of lasers in separating isotopes of uranium, the subject of the Radioptics proposal. Two years later, another company applied for a patent for a process of this sort. Radioptics sued the AEC, claiming that this agency had revealed the secrets in their proposal. There was no evidence that the AEC had ever released the proposal except to ask for outside reviews, and these reviews had apparently been done in confidence. The court could find no evidence of disclosure on the part of the AEC, and, absent evidence that a confidence had been breached, the court noted that independent discovery could not be enjoined.

In *Droeger v. Welsh Sporting Goods Corp.*[48] Droeger had sent Welsh Sporting Goods a sketch of an idea that he had for a new sort of backpack. Droeger and a representative from Welsh met frequently to discuss the design, but the representative gave him no firm sense of Welsh's interest in the idea. Welsh later came out with a backpack of almost identical design, and Droeger sued.

Welsh argued that it had got the design from someone else who had never seen Droeger's sketches. The representative from Welsh who had discussed the matter with Droeger said that he had never told anyone else within the company about the matter. The trial court held for Droeger, but the court of appeals argued that, in the absence of evidence that there was really any knowledge of Droeger's design on the part of the person who designed the similar backpack, there could be no cause of action.

WHAT THESE CASES SHOW IS that, if it is to receive protection from the courts, a secret must be a significant secret that is really, in fact, secret. In addition, evidence must be presented to demonstrate a link between the secret-holder and the person who is alleged to have taken the secret.

All trade-secret law protects the owner against both not having the secrets disclosed by someone whom the owner has entrusted and not having the secret taken by improper means. We will not be considering most of the improper-means cases here because that would take us into legitimate prying rather than into legitimate secrets.

47. 621 F.2d 1113 (Ct. Cl. 1980).
48. 541 F.2d 790 (9th Cir. 1976).

Since independent discovery is allowed, the trade-secret provision only protects against someone else procuring the secret through a breach of confidence. Trade-secret protection in the cases that we have discussed seems to be primarily a protection against breach of confidence—and a logical extension of the concern with confidential relationships that we have seen in secrecy cases considered in earlier chapters.

CHAPTER THIRTEEN

Comparing Economic and Contractarian Theories of Privacy

HOW ARE WE TO UNDERSTAND why these legally relevant facts in the privacy and trade-secret cases matter while other facts do not? In this chapter, we will compare the economic theory forwarded by Richard Posner and the contractarian theory offered in chapter 4 to see how each would make sense of the facts that courts emphasize.

The Economic Theory of Privacy

Privacy of Individuals

At the heart of Posner's discussion of personal privacy is a distinction between discreditable and nondiscreditable information. If the information is discreditable and would serve to correct misperceptions, then the law should *not* assign the property right to the individual, according to Posner. But if the information is not discreditable, then the individual *should* be given the property right in such information; that is, the property rights should be assigned in this way if the law embodies an economic logic as Posner suggests.

The set of cases Posner that uses to support his theory is thin indeed, and most of the cases that he himself cites do not neatly back him up. He calls on *Daily Times Democrat v. Graham,*[1] the "Fun House" case. Since publishing the photograph of the woman with her dress blown up around her waist did not correct any misapprehensions about her, Posner writes, there is a good case for finding an invasion of privacy—which the court did.[2] But he is puzzled by *Melvin v. Reid,*[3]

---

1. 276 Ala. 380, 162 S. 2d 474 (1964).
2. Richard A. Posner, *The Economics of Justice* (Cambridge, MA: Harvard University Press, 1981), p. 259.
3. 112 Cal. App. 285, 297 P. 91 (1931).

the case in which the former prostitute and murder suspect sued the makers of a film about her past for using her real name. Melvin's current friends knew nothing about her past, and, if one follows Posner's analysis, they should have been enlightened about it by the showing of this film. Instead, the California courts found for Melvin, indicating that the filmmakers should not have used her real name. Posner then cites approvingly *Briscoe v. Readers' Digest Assn.,*[4] the truck-hijacking case, indicating that the court ruled that only remote criminal history could not be published, but recent criminal history could be. Although it was true that the court did make that distinction, most of the opinion rests on the question of whether the former truck hijacker should have been mentioned by name. Still, Posner claims that the *Briscoe* court's decision

> moves the law in the right direction but, from an economic standpoint, not far enough. Remote past criminal activity is less relevant to a prediction of future misconduct than recent—and those who learn of it will discount it accordingly—but such information is hardly irrelevant to people considering whether to enter into or continue social or business relations with the individual; if it were irrelevant, publicizing it would not injure the individual. People conceal past criminal acts not out of bashfulness but because potential acquaintances quite sensibly regard a criminal past as negative evidence of the value of associating with a person. In light of this analysis, one is not surprised to find out that outside of California the principle of *Melvin v. Reid* is rejected.[5]

While it is true that some courts have rejected the logic of *Melvin,* it is also true that other courts have adopted the same principle of identification that *Melvin* forwards. *Barber v. Time* (the "starving glutton")[6] and *Virgil v. Time* (the daredevil bodysurfer)[7] are visible examples of case decisions that do not rely on California law.

If Posner were correct that discreditable information should generally not be a basis for a successful claim of privacy invasion, then we would expect many cases to be decided differently than they have been decided. When privacy invasion is found in press cases, it almost always involves identifying discreditable information with specific individuals. Publishing the information without the identification,

---

4. 4 Cal. 3d 529, 483 P.2d 34, 93 Cal. Rptr. 866 (1971).

5. Posner, pp. 260–261.

6. 348 Mo. 1199, 159 S.W.2d 291 (1942).

7. 527 F.2d 1122 (9th Cir. 1975), *cert. den.* 425 U.S. 998 (1976), *on remand,* 424 F. Supp. 1286 (D.C. Cal. 1976).

which the law seems to allow, defeats the whole purpose that Posner claims the law is supposed to accomplish. But in case after case (*Melvin, Briscoe, Barber,* and *Virgil,* for example), invasion of privacy is found in identifying private discreditable facts with real names of real people, ruling out precisely the salutory effect that Posner feels the law should be trying to accomplish.

Moreover, not only are cases involving discreditable information the ones that tend to allow recovery for plaintiffs, but they seem to be the *only* ones that do so. When the information distributed about the plaintiff is nondiscreditable, the courts rarely find an invasion of privacy. This is just the reverse of what Posner's theory would predict. If the information would not uncover any misperceptions that the privacy seeker is trying to exploit, then Posner argues that there is no good economic reason for not assigning the property right in that information to the individual; in other words, information that is not at variance with the impression that the individual is trying to convey should be protected by a right to privacy.

But this is precisely what the law does *not* do. If the information does not reflect badly on the plaintiff, then the plaintiff cannot recover. We saw this principle in action in the *Virgil* bodysurfer case, and we also saw it in *Hamilton* (where the plaintiff could not recover when her insurance agent told her neighbors the amount of her check)[8] and in *Wheeler* (where the plaintiff's paycheck and history of raises were published by her boss).[9] In all these cases, the court explicitly said that there was no harm when the information put the plaintiff in a positive light—and that no recovery would therefore be allowed. In fact, the only cases that seem to allow the plaintiff to recover for release of nondiscreditable personal facts are cases that involve intrusion, such as *DeMay,*[10] in which a stranger was found liable to a woman for watching her give birth. In the absence of intrusion, which even Posner argues represents a different interest than the one protected by claiming a right to withhold information about oneself,[11] courts generally find that distributing nondiscreditable information about someone results in no legal liability for the distributor. Only cases involving discreditable information are candidates for successful privacy suits.

Posner's theory encounters difficulty when he discusses the *Sidis*

8. *Hamilton v. Crown Life Insurance Co.,* 246 Or. 1, 423 P.2d 771 (1967).
9. *Wheeler v. P. Sorensen Manufacturing Co.,* 415 S.W.2d 582 (Ky. 1967).
10. *DeMay v. Roberts,* 46 Mich. 160, 9 N.W. 146 (1881).
11. Posner, pp. 268–273.

child-prodigy case,[12] which he cites in support of his interpretation. No invasion of privacy was found in *Sidis* "despite the absence of potential misrepresentation."[13] How does Posner square this with his economic theory? He relies on a transaction-costs argument, in much the same way that Kronman did. Posner argues:

> Once the *New Yorker* published the story, any other magazine or newspaper could, without compensating it, publish the facts that the *New Yorker* had gathered (perhaps by costly research), so long as the republication did not contain the actual language of the original story. Given the number of potential republishers, there was no market mechanism by which the full social value of the *New Yorker*'s information could be brought to bear in negotiations with Sidis over purchasing the right to his life story. In these circumstances, there is an argument for not giving him that right—in other words, for allowing the *New Yorker* to externalize some of the social costs (those imposed on Sidis) of its research—since it must perforce externalize some of the benefits.[14]

Given the transaction costs involved in negotiating with all potential publishers the precise value of the information, Posner argues, potentially wealth-maximizing transactions would not take place and the wealth-maximizing goal of the law would not be achieved. Therefore the law should permit an enterprise such as a newspaper to spread some of the costs of acquiring information to other parties. Just why newspapers should be able to pass these costs on to the subject of the information rather than to those who presumably benefit from learning this information is not discussed. But then again, ignoring these sorts of distributional consequences is not unique to this area of economic analysis of law.[15]

---

12. *Sidis v. F-R Publishing Co.*, 113 F.2d 806 (2d Cir. 1940), *cert. den.* 311 U.S. 711 (1940).

13. Posner, p. 261.

14. Ibid., p. 262.

15. Posner had claimed, in *The Economic Analysis of Law*, 2d ed. (Boston: Little, Brown, 1978), pp. 143–144, that the recipient of damages did not matter; what mattered was who had to pay, not who got the money. The important thing, in Posner's view, was to deter the potential tortfeasor, not to compensate the victim. But Posner has since changed his mind, in *The Economic Analysis of Law*, 3d ed. (Boston: Little, Brown, 1986), pp 176–177. He now argues that paying damages to the *victim* is essential for two reasons: (1) to give the victim incentive to sue and (2) to prevent the potential victim from taking too many precautions. The point stands, however, that the distribution of resources does not matter for its own sake; who has to pay whom matters only to get the incentives straight.

The shift to a transaction-costs argument seems to retain the integrity of the economic approach, since both the initial theory (that is, that hiding discreditable information impedes the movement of goods to higher valued uses) and the modification (that transaction costs also impede wealth maximization) share the superficial similarity of economic language. But there are two intellectual fault lines through this reasoning, one logical and the other evidentiary.

The logical problem is the same one that we encountered in Kronman's article. If the point of requiring disclosure of potentially damaging information is to reduce transaction costs by providing the market with the information that it needs to ensure that goods keep getting transferred to ever higher-valuing users, then anything that raises those transaction costs will interfere with the market's tendency to maximize wealth. Allowing newspapers to shift the costs of ferreting out information to those who are potential subjects (rather than to those who might benefit from the information and who, therefore, might be able to compensate the losers) merely encourages these subjects to invest in converting their secrets from shallower to deeper secrets, thereby increasing transaction costs even further. If potential subjects of newspaper disclosure are rational, they will invest in hiding their secrets even more than they would without such a rule. Because under Posner's proposed rule the probability of the newspaper discovering their secrets would be higher than under a rule where the newspaper had to compensate the victim, the expected cost of disclosure will be increased all around. Of course, if the newspaper had to pay these costs, the optimal amount of information would not be produced, given the external benefits. If the newspaper could recoup its costs of acquiring information from those who also stand to benefit from it,[16] then the newspaper would not overinvest in the production of private information, because at some point the potential beneficiaries would be unwilling to pay. But if the newspaper could externalize its costs to the subjects of the information, then there is effectively no economic restraint on press prying. Individuals who would prefer to be left alone by a curious press will have to invest in secret-keeping much more under Posner's rule than they would under a standard that produced the optimal amount of public knowledge. Thus, private people (those who value having control over information about them-

---

16. This possibility has been foreclosed by *Associated Press v. International News Service,* 245 F. 244 (2d Cir. 1917) *affd.* 248 U.S. 215, 39 S. Ct. 68 (1918). In that case, the court ruled that the Associated Press could not prevent other news organizations from picking up its stories without compensating it.

selves, whether it be discreditable or not) will invest valuable scarce resources in hiding information if the press can uncover this private information and shift the cost of the investigation to the subject of the information without restraint. What all this means is that a rule of the sort that Posner suggests will actually serve to increase transaction costs in the long run, by encouraging people to be less candid generally and less inclined to speak to the press in particular. And this increase in transaction costs will so affect the ability of the press to acquire information for which beneficiaries would be willing to pay that the economically optimal result cannot be achieved. In addition, Posner's rule fails to achieve his stated goal of wealth maximization, since it logically leads to investment in the unproductive activity of hiding information from public view.

The second objection to Posner's theory of the privacy cases is that it is empirically inaccurate. The only cases in which the courts have found an invasion of privacy by the press are cases where the information was discreditable and where the individual's name was used. The only cases in which Posner would have them find an invasion of privacy by the press are cases where the information is nondiscreditable. Identifying discreditable information with specific people is precisely what Posner would urge, given that this sort of information is likely to be of the most use to others judging whether to interact with this person. But those are precisely the sorts of cases in which the courts allow plaintiffs to recover.

Despite the fact that Posner claims that his theory is not prescriptive but is rather descriptive of real cases, the evidence does not bear him out. If anything, there is more support for a formulation in which all of Posner's propositions are reversed. Posner's theory has the advantage of having at its core a distinction (between discreditable and nondiscreditable information) that actually appears in the courts' reasoning (unlike Kronman's theory, which relies on a distinction that the courts do not note). But his predictions of outcomes are precisely backwards in the majority of cases, even in those that he cites in support of his own argument. This is not the only area where Posner claims to have a theory that explains the cases, however. He has a somewhat different theory for the privacy of corporations in trade-secret cases.

Privacy of Corporations

Although the common law does not allow corporations to claim a right of privacy, the rules about trade secrecy seem to cover the same ground. Both Posner and I are agreed that the trade-secrecy cases look like corporate-privacy cases.

Following the logic that without property rights in expensive-to-produce information the information will not be produced in the first place, Posner argues that corporations should be able to withhold information in which they have invested. Posner cites only two cases in support of his argument. He mentions *Smith v. Dravo,* the case in which Smith disclosed the design of its freight containers to Dravo when Dravo was negotiating to buy out Smith.[17] He also cites the *DuPont,* aerial photography case.[18] Both of these cases, Posner argues, illustrate how investment in the production of socially valuable information is protected by trade-secret law.

But once again, the case law shows Posner's emphasis to be misplaced. Certainly the courts do require that investment in the production of the knowledge be shown, as we have seen. But investment is merely a threshold that needs to be crossed to demonstrate an appropriate level of harm for the courts to act. Mere investment is hardly sufficient to demonstrate the property right. Investment must be combined with some breach of confidence if it is to result in liability for a trade secret purloiner (as was noted in the *Smith* case), or it must be found along with particularly inappropriate or intrusive means (as was noted in the *DuPont* case); in the absence of either of these factors, there is no liability even if there is investment. We saw this in our discussions of products whose secrets were revealed in manufacture. There can be no doubt that the creation of flooring,[19] blackout screens,[20] and improved fishing poles[21] required investment of time and energy. But there also can be no doubt that they cannot be kept as trade secrets when they reveal the method of their manufacture. Patent law will protect such products—but only if they are not kept secret anymore. So, there is obviously a trade-off between the ability to keep information secret and the ability to prevent all others from using the information and thereby recouping one's investment. If the secret is discovered through reverse engineering or independent means, the investment in the secret is lost. The common law does not use trade

17. *Smith v. Dravo Corp.,* 203 F.2d 369 (7th Cir. 1953).

18. *E.I. DuPont de Nemours v. Christopher,* 431 F.2d 1012 (5th Cir. 1970), *cert. den.* 400 U.S. 1024, 92 S. Ct. 581, 27 L. Ed. 2d 637 (1970), *reh.den.* 401 U.S. 967, 91 S. Ct. 968, 28 L. Ed. 2d 250 (1971).

19. *Permagrain Products v. U.S. Mat and Rubber Co.,* 489 F. Supp. 108 (E.D. Pa. 1980).

20. *Carver v. Harr,* 132 N.J.Eq. 207, 27 A.2d 895 (1942).

21. *Boucher v. Wissman,* 206 S.W.2d 101 (Tex. Civ. App. 1947).

secrecy to protect investment; it does prevent abuse of relationships of trust or particularly inappropriate prying.

While it is undoubtedly possible to create an economic argument, based in the similarity of trust and contracts, for why one should protect relationships of this kind, this is not the sort of fact pattern that seems to have an economic logic at its root. It is connected directly with neither of the two economic arguments forwarded for why secrets should be permitted. In the first argument, which we saw in personal privacy cases, secrets were permitted only when the information was not discreditable. But what if someone tells discreditable information in confidence to a friend? We have seen that the friend cannot then reveal it. It seems inconsistent that the law should require discreditable information to be revealed when entrusting the same information to a friend protects it. It should not be surprising that the law does not maintain these inconsistent positions. In the second argument, present in corporate-privacy cases, secrets are held to protect investments. But why is it that secrets are protected only when entrusted to someone who then violates that trust? It seems in this case that the investment is incidental to the offense. What the law seems to protect is relationships of trust in and of themselves.

Here again, although Posner does take note of a fact that the courts care about and look for, he seems to mistake a corner of the canvas for the big picture. Trade secrets are not given legal force merely to protect investments. The patent system does that explicitly. Trade secrets seem to accomplish something else, something that relies on protecting relations of confidence. Perhaps Posner can explain this when he turns to privacy of communications.

Privacy of Communications

Posner argues in favor of granting a right to privacy in communications because then discreditable information about individuals will be more likely to spread. This will, in Posner's view, produce more knowledgeable transacting partners who will be less likely to be defrauded. If the law has an underlying economic logic, as Posner suggests, then the law should permit privacy of conversations.

It is in fact true that the common law protects privacy of conversations, but not at all in the way that Posner suggests. Once again, the law is more nearly consistent with the reverse of Posner's theory. The conversations that the law protects are private conversations between A and B, where A is revealing secrets about A to B in confidence. This we have already seen in our discussions of confidential relationships.

What the law specifically does *not* protect (and in fact punishes) is when B then tells those things learned in confidence, discreditable or not, to C. The only circumstances under which the law allows B to tell C discreditable things about A is when C is somehow endangered by A. This was the situation in *Tarasoff*,[22] where the psychiatrist was held liable for not warning his former patient's girlfriend that the former patient intended to kill her. But this was not the situation in *Mac-Donald*,[23] where the psychiatrist was held liable for revealing to his patient's spouse details that the patient had revealed in therapy, details that apparently did not endanger her. The common law generally protects private conversations between A and B but explicitly does not allow B to then reveal those confidences to C, except under extreme and exceptional circumstances such as potential catastrophe for C.

The situation is somewhat different if B knows something about A that was not gained in confidence, as we saw in the debt-collection cases. But even in this situation B is only allowed to reveal A's secrets if it is necessary for B to accomplish B's legitimate purposes. If B volunteers information that is unrelated to B's legitimate objectives—as was the situation in *Carr*,[24] where the plaintiff's former co-worker forwarded unsolicited information about charges filed against the plaintiff to the plaintiff's current employer—then B may be held liable for damage that results to A even when the information provides valuable discreditable information about A. C may request information if it is shown to be relevant to C's activities, but B may only reveal information about A on request by C when there is no confidential relationship between A and B.

This seems a far cry from Posner's argument. The sort of privacy in communication that Posner argues for is precisely the sort that is generally disallowed. On the other hand, the sort of privacy of communication that is allowed in the common law serves no useful purpose in the economic scheme. In fact, Posner does not deal with the subject of confidential relationships in his discussion of privacy. In this way, he is similar to Kronman, who also excluded confidential relationships from consideration. Perhaps the exclusion of confidential relationships from economic discussions of legal doctrine when such relationships clearly matter occurs because the protection of confidential relationships has no straightforward economic explanation.

22. *Tarasoff v. Regents of the University of California*, 17 C.3d 425, 131 Cal. Rptr. 14, 551 P.2d 334 (1976).

23. *MacDonald v. Clinger*, 84 A.D.2d 482, 446 N.Y.S.2d 801 (1982).

24. *Carr v. Watkins*, 227 Md. 578, 177 A.2d 841 (1962).

Assessing the Economic Theory of Privacy

In all three of the areas that Posner discusses, the actual outcomes of common-law cases are different from Posner's arguments based on economic theory. In none of the three areas does Posner's theory work well as a positive theory of privacy-as-secrecy cases.

Posner himself admits that the legislative trends in privacy are not consistent with the economics of the privacy problem. But for common-law cases he claims to have a positive theory. He ended his first article on the subject with a claim that he had generally succeeded in developing a positive theory of privacy: "The analysis in . . . this Article suggests that the common law response to the problem of privacy has been broadly consistent with the economics of the problem. . . . I have not discussed all of the privacy cases nor are all those I have discussed consistent with economic theory. Nonetheless, especially given the absence of a well-developed competing positive theory of the privacy tort, the economic approach holds promise of increasing our understanding of this puzzling branch of law." [25] Posner recognizes that his economic theory of privacy is not perfect, but he maintains: "In law, as in consumer behavior and every other activity studied by economists, economics is more successful in explaining central tendencies than in accounting for individual decisions." [26]

After a review of Posner's theory and the evidence for it, it seems fair to say that, once again, just the reverse is true. The economic approach seems more successful at explaining individual cases than in accounting for the central tendencies. I have argued that there are three central tendencies in privacy-as-secrecy cases:

1. In direct secrets, individuals are allowed to withhold information from others only if this information is arguably not relevant to the others' interests.
2. In serial secrets, the law encourages minimal disclosure of personal information consistent with others being able to realize their interests as narrowly defined. B may only volunteer information to C if the information does not violate a confidence or is necessary if B is to accomplish B's legitimate goals. C may only demand information from B if

---

25. Richard A. Posner, "The Right of Privacy," *Georgia Law Review* 12: 393–422 (1978), p. 422.
26. Posner, *Economics of Justice,* p. 299.

the information does not violate a confidence and is relevant for C's goals.
3. Trade secrets protect primarily against breach of confidence.

Posner's economic theory of law does not have a ready explanation for several of the important features of these central tendencies. There is no explanation for why confidential relationships should matter so much or for why disclosures that are not narrowly relevant in specific contexts should be forbidden. There is no explanation for why the press should be found liable precisely when it publishes true and discreditable information about someone (at least sometimes) but is never held liable for publishing nondiscreditable or unidentified information. There is no explanation for why the law should protect A disclosing information in confidence to B and then find B liable for spreading A's secrets to C. In short, most of the general features that we find in the law of privacy seem to defy the economic theory. Posner manages to explain a few individual cases, but he tends not to be able to explain the central tendencies. The economic theory does not work well as a positive theory in this area. It simply does not describe accurately the way in which cases are decided or the sorts of features that tend to matter in judges' decisions.

A Contractarian Theory of Privacy

If the underlying logic of the law in this area is not efficiency, then what is it? In this section, I will argue that we usefully might view privacy cases as being very much like their sibling cases in secrecy. Privacy cases, too, can be best understood in contractarian terms as attempts to ensure that actors have equal access to information when that information is being used as a strategic secret. In practice this means that the law examines whether the secret is being kept to influence someone else—and, if this is true, the law then requires disclosure if the other party did not have the same probability of locating this information with the same level of effort. Because of the special nature of personal information, however, privacy cases are decided with special attention to the spread of information beyond the bounds necessary to ensure that social actors have equal access to relevant and necessary information. Generally, though, the equal access argument applies with equal force in the privacy and fraud cases.

Privacy of Individuals

We might start by asking what it would mean for two individuals to have equal access to personal information about someone. Clearly, if one of those individuals is also the subject of the information, then that individual will have superior access to that information. After all, we are likely to know more about ourselves than others know about us.[27] In economic parlance, we might say that this is because information about ourselves is cheaper for us to acquire than it is for others to acquire. We live with ourselves every day, and, as a result, we learn quite a lot about ourselves, particularly about what we have done and intend to do. Others get more fragmentary exposure and do not have the added advantage of being able to read our minds.

This discussion may seem both obvious and silly, until we realize its implications for any theory of equal access to information. If we follow the logic developed in the fraud cases, then our superior access to knowledge about ourselves would mean that we should not be allowed to claim any right to withhold information about ourselves from others. This would imply that there could be no right to privacy that is consistent with the principle of equal access to information.

We must remember, however, the limits within which the principle of equal access was found to apply in the fraud cases. The threshold rules in fraud cases limited the application of the equal access principle to just those situations that presented strategic secrets. Only when one actor was using a secret to influence another actor (that is, only when the information was material) did the information have to be disclosed if the secret-keeper had superior access. A similar logic is found in privacy cases, because individuals who claim invasion of privacy cannot recover when the information is material and not within reach of the ignorant party. One does not have to disclose in privacy cases, but one cannot recover for inquiry into or disclosure by others of material information that one might consider private.

The criterion of materiality in fraud cases is virtually identical to the criterion of relevance in privacy cases. In both areas, the person who wants to know the secret has to demonstrate that the information is necessary for some decision that the actor is entitled to make. We see this in direct-secret cases in privacy, where the person seeking information can provide a defense to a charge of invasion of privacy by

---

27. Of course, this is not always true, as the theory and practice of psychiatry reveals.

demonstrating that the information was relevant. Only when the information is not judged to be relevant can the privacy seeker get some relief. But if the information is relevant, either it must be disclosed or the privacy seeker must suffer the consequences. In *Pitcher* a schoolteacher was fired for refusing to reveal the report from her annual physical,[28] and in *Cangelosi* a supermarket clerk was fired for failing to answer questions about an altered check.[29] Plaintiffs in these cases were faced with the choice between revealing information judged to be relevant and having actions taken against them for maintaining the secret. Courts find no privacy interest in direct secrets when the information is being used strategically. In serial secret cases, where C is trying to get information about A from B, relevance also must be demonstrated. In the absence of a confidential relationship between A and B, B must disclose personal information about A if it is judged relevant to C.

This does not sound like much of a right to privacy, but it does represent what we saw in the cases. Disclosure is required (or, put more straightforwardly, privacy is not allowed) when the information has been judged necessary for someone else to know in order to make decisions that she is entitled to make.

Why is virtually automatic disclosure required in privacy cases involving strategic secrets? Unlike the fraud cases, where courts have developed a long laundry list of factors that must be considered, these cases are rather more straightforward. If one demonstrates relevance, then no privacy is allowed. I would argue that this is because information about individuals is almost always more accessible to those individuals than to others. The common law of privacy does not need a laundry list of factors that specify when someone will have superior access to information. The answer is generally obvious in privacy cases. The individual claiming a right to privacy will virtually always have the superior access to the information. And courts act as though this equal access principle were guiding them.

Privacy of Corporations

This principle becomes even more obvious when we consider trade secrets. In trade-secret cases, information that is the subject of the trade secret is almost by definition equally accessible to the two parties in

---

28. *Pitcher v. Iberia Parish School Board,* 280 So. 2d 603 (La. App. 1973).
29. *Cangelosi v. Schwegmann Brothers Giant Super Markets,* 379 So. 2d 836 (La. App. 1980).

dispute. Two firms in the same area will probably face roughly equal search costs (as those costs are assessed by courts) in making advances in the area. If corporation A could invest in the production of trade secrets, then presumably corporation B could, with the same level of effort, also find this information.[30] There would be equal access to the information, and no disclosure by A to B would be required. This is exactly what we found in trade-secret cases.

The equal access argument is further buttressed by consideration of the circumstances where B could find out A's secrets legally. If B independently discovers the trade secret (that is, if B puts in roughly the same level of effort that A did to find the information), A cannot claim that B improperly acquired a trade secret. Both A and B can hold as separate and independent trade secrets information so acquired, and each can maintain an action against anyone else who shortcuts this process. In addition, B can find out the secret through reverse engineering, applying effort to the product that A has produced to independently discover its secret. Information, once publicized, cannot be restricted. This is rather like the consent argument in privacy cases, where information voluntarily disclosed cannot later be withdrawn. Publicizing information at one point and later withdrawing it creates inequalities in the distribution of knowledge. Those who happened to be around when it was disclosed will then have structurally superior access to that information relative to those who were not around at the time. Publicizing and hiding information in sequence creates the sort of inequalities that the law is trying to overcome. Not surprisingly, throughout the common law on secrets it is consistently held that information once made public can generally not be made secret again.[31]

Courts frequently express this equal access logic quite explicitly in their opinions. In the *DuPont* aerial piracy case, for example, Judge Goldberg specifically wrote that obtaining someone else's trade secret

30. Just as in the fraud cases, the *ability* to make the investment might be considered. But since, for corporations, ability is generally defined by the possession of the resources to make the investment, and since, in deciding fraud cases, courts generally do not consider economic inequality a barrier to ability, we might expect, as we actually found, that there is no required disclosure of trade secrets in these cases either.

31. The main exception to this comes in those privacy and press cases where newspapers have been found to have invaded someone's privacy when they publish long-dormant facts about someone's discreditable past. We will discuss shortly how, in the case of personal information about individuals, there are certain qualifications to the general rule. But even in these cases, all that is suppressed is the person's name when it is not essential to understanding the other information.

"without spending the time and money to discover it independently is *improper.*"[32] Because trade-secret cases generally involve competitors, both parties to the dispute are often in a position to invest roughly equal amounts of time and money in acquiring the information. This being the case, courts routinely allow corporations to withhold trade secrets but do not allow individuals to withhold private information about themselves.[33]

The equal access logic helps us to understand how the privacy and trade-secret cases, superficially dissimilar, are really quite consistent with one another. In both sets of cases, as in the fraud cases, courts seem concerned with making equal the starting line from which parties to a transaction take off. Knowledge is one of the critical elements in equality of starting position, and the courts seem to require disclosure only when information is relevant and cannot be acquired by both parties with equal effort.

Privacy and Equal Access

There are two qualifications to this simple logic in the privacy and trade-secret cases, however. The first is that the courts seem to take great pains to ensure that personal information about an individual go no further than necessary to achieve this result of equal access. As a result, we find a concern throughout the privacy cases with minimal disclosure. The emphasis on overdisclosure and identification, which we earlier discussed at some length, can be seen as an attempt by judges to balance the need for equal access with concern for the individual's interest in retaining control over the information. In each case, the law allows disclosure of personal information to those who arguably find it

32. 413 F.2d 1012, 1015.
33. The equal access principle allows us to predict what would happen in cases where corporations claimed the right to withhold information from someone who is in no position to invest comparable time and energy in discovering the information. We almost saw such a case in Dow Chemical's defense in the Agent Orange matter, a case that was settled out of court, and it might be argued that the Ford Pinto case falls into the same category. In each case, the corporation knew (or allegedly knew) about the dangers of their product, dangers that were not revealed to individuals who allegedly were injured by the product. These individuals were not in a position to find out this information because only the company had access to the statistical results that indicated the danger. Reproducing the studies would not have been possible for the plaintiffs since they did not have access to the chemical or design information that would be necessary to duplicate the research. In these cases, one would think that the equal access principle would require that companies disclose information about latent dangers to consumers. The outcomes in the Pinto and Agent Orange cases seem consistent with this principle.

relevant for judgments that they must make or to those who can help secret-keepers realize their legitimate interests. But when personal information starts being spread around indiscriminately, the courts are likely to find an invasion of privacy. This makes privacy cases different from fraud cases, and it shows that judges are inclined to think of information about people as being different from information about transactions or objects. Still, equal access to information that is kept as a strategic secret is ensured first. Then courts try to minimize subsequent identifiable disclosure.

The second qualification involves confidential relationships. Throughout our discussion of legitimate secrets, we have encountered something of a double standard. In relations among relative strangers, the equal access principle applies without exception. In cases involving people who know each other very well and have established a relationship of trust and confidence, the rules are somewhat different. We saw in the fraud cases that people in a confidential relationship were both obligated to reveal all relevant information to each other and obligated not to use this information to the detriment of the other party. In privacy and trade-secret cases, we find something quite similar. In these cases, information gained in a confidential relationship cannot be used against the interests of the actor who disclosed it in confidence. Candor is encouraged in the relationship by making breaches of confidences outside the relationship actionable. Thus, we find the principle of promissory obligation, a principle present in the fraud cases, to be applicable also to privacy and trade-secret cases.

There are some cases where the equal access principle and the principle of promissory obligation clash. If B is good friends with A and A entrusts secrets to B as a result, then doesn't B have structurally superior access to information about A relative to C, who is a stranger to A? If the equal access principle were followed with secondhand secrets, then it would seem that any inquiry by C to B about A would result in B's having to disclose A's secrets to C. But the law does not require this—and in fact gives a cause of action to A against B if B does disclose. This would seem to be in direct opposition to the equal access principle.

Not only can A sue B if B discloses A's confidences on C's request, but A can also, within limits, prevent B from volunteering information about A to anyone, even someone else in a confidential relationship with A if that information would damage this second relationship. The only exceptions, as we saw in *Tarasoff*, are when the disclosures by B would be necessary to save C's life or to protect some fundamental interest of B that is in conflict with A. We saw this latter rule in action in those trade-secret cases where trade secrets were so mixed up with the employee's general knowledge that to require silence would be to prevent the employee from ever working again in that occupation. Only extreme harm to others can pry A's secrets from those in whom they are entrusted.

This complicated set of principles makes sense against a contractarian backdrop. Equality of access to strategic information and the protection of confidential relationships both have solid contractarian pedigrees. Courts try to ensure that both conditions are met, which generally means protecting confidential relationships before equal access is assured. We might think of the law as encouraging global equality but permitting local inequalities in the vicinity of confidential relationships. However, when catastrophe looms—that is, when the person who stands to lose will lose a great deal (in the *Tarasoff* case her life), then the confidential relationships give way to an obligation to disclose personal information.

The special rules that we find to be protecting personal information, rules not present in the fraud cases, are not surprising on a contractarian analysis either. It is certainly reasonable to expect that an individual deciding in advance of knowing which role she will play in a secrecy dispute will want personal information to be protected when possible. After all, the ability to retain control over personal information is linked with other important things, such as the ability to create and maintain intimate relationships, the capacity for autonomy, the resources to juggle conflicting role demands, and the ability to create and maintain a healthy mental life. Only when the demands of others are particularly pressing (as when information that one person possesses can seriously damage another) should a right to privacy be abrogated.

The major problem with the privacy cases, from a normative viewpoint, is that almost any justification that a probing actor can offer will be accepted by a court. Those who want private information to be disclosed can use arguments both great and small to compromise another's privacy. The bank that wanted information about the American ambassador to Costa Rica[34] and the psychiatrist who evaluated a woman in a parking lot without her permission, reporting her behavior to authorities,[35] seemed to have (at best) minimal interests in the information sought. General Motors had a great interest in Ralph Nader's activities, since they anticipated that his book would hurt their

---

34. *Hines v. Columbus Bank and Trust Co.*, 137 Ga. App. 268, 223 S.E.2d 468 (1976).
35. *Schwartz v. Thiele*, 242 Cal. App. 2d 799, 51 Cal. Rptr. 767 (1966).

sales,[36] but that does not mean that that interest was of the sort that would justify their intrusive probing. General Motors was looking for information to discredit Nader and prevent him from revealing secrets that General Motors had used strategically against others, and this interest is hardly one that the law should protect at the cost of another's privacy.

Some of the privacy cases seem lacking on contractarian grounds *not* because they have got wrong the *sorts* of facts that should be noticed, as was the problem with the economic theory. The central tendencies of the privacy cases clearly support a contractarian logic. In some individual instances, however, it is hard to imagine why contractarian courts would read the facts of specific cases they way in which they do. In *Hines, Schwartz,* and *Nader,* it is difficult to see how someone who thought she might be either party in those disputes would strike the balance so as to compromise privacy. The interests on the side opposed to privacy are either insufficiently weighty or of such a devious nature that one cannot imagine them trumping a legitimate desire to keep some personal information secret. While the criteria used in the privacy opinions seem appropriate to a contractarian, the application of those criteria has sometimes been faulty, leading to decisions that do little justice. Any assessment of the relative success of the economic and contractarian views as *positive* theories, however, shows that the contractarian view explains the central tendencies of the privacy cases better than the economic perspective does.

36. *Nader v. General Motors,* 25 N.Y.2d 560, 255 N.E.2d 765 (1970).

FIVE
Understanding Implied Warranties

CHAPTER FOURTEEN

The Rule and Reality of Caveat Emptor in New York State, 1804–1900

HOW DEEPLY DO CONTRACTARIAN PRINCIPLES run in American law? Thus far, we have looked at three areas of doctrine without considering the evolution of law. A case from the eighteenth century was juxtaposed with cases decided in the 1950s; cases from the early part of this century were used to illustrate the same point as was a case from this decade. In each of the sections that have gone before, the case law was located by examining contemporary sources that listed those cases as still being good law. All the cases, then, were read as if doctrine had never changed. They were yanked out of the historical context in which they arose to make points about the state of contemporary American law. The cases run from the late eighteenth century to the present, but that does not mean that they represent the. dominant thinking of earlier ages of American law. They reveal only what has survived to be cited approvingly now.

In this chapter, I try to correct the ahistorical treatment of case law in the earlier chapters to see whether the coherence that I have located in the contemporary doctrine is a new phenomenon. To do this, I examine the rise and fall of a legal rule that seems most at odds with the argument presented thus far—the rule of caveat emptor.

Caveat emptor, requiring that the buyer beware, seems to be difficult to square with rules about equal access to information; after all, buyers generally are at a disadvantage when it comes to information about a good being sold.[1] That is why the contemporary doctrine

---

1. Caveat emptor cases do not always feature secrets. While sometimes defective products are known by the sellers to have certain faults, buyers and sellers often claim equal ignorance of the products' defects. Why, then, should these cases be included in a book about secrets? The first answer is that *some* of the caveat emptor cases *do* involve secrets. But, second, even when buyer and seller both deal in the dark, courts *could* choose

generally requires more disclosure by sellers than by buyers. But the rule in the early part of the nineteenth century in the United States throws the losses of a sale gone wrong on buyers rather than on sellers. Does this mean that the equal access principle apparent now did not exist then?

I will argue in this chapter that caveat emptor was *not* stacked against ignorant buyers in favor of crafty and devious sellers. Instead, it was an effort to let losses fall on the party who had superior access to information. Although caveat emptor is thought to have faded as the century progressed, the exceptions made to this doctrine are the exceptions that prove the rule that the courts were trying to assign losses to the party with superior access to information about the good. Caveat emptor's vitality in the early nineteenth century can be traced to the presence of a certain form of sales transaction in which the merchant-seller knew less about the good than did the manufacturer-buyer. When the changing economy presented the courts with different sorts of sales transactions, caveat emptor was abandoned in favor of the increasing inference of warranty, although the underlying logic of the doctrine remained the same. Throughout the century, the ignorant won and the knowledgeable lost, a state of affairs that did little to encourage the progressive efficiency of markets or the ascendancy of the manufacturing over the agrarian classes.[2] Both the economic and the critical interpretations of this area of nineteenth-century common law seem misguided.

I argue this case by examining the development of the doctrine in New York State. The New York courts, through *Seixas v. Woods* (1804),[3] were the first to introduce caveat emptor into American law. Perhaps because it was the first, New York grasped the caveat emptor doctrine more tenaciously than did other states, making it the best place to see the rule in its most severe application. When Pennsylvania

---

to apply in such cases the principles that they articulate in the secrecy cases. Courts might assess whether both parties, given equal levels of effort, had equal probabilities of acquiring the information and then rule that the party with superior knowledge should bear the loss. This would expand contractarian principles into the area where both parties are ignorant, and that might be a sensible thing to do.

2. This alleged ascendancy of the manufacturing over the agrarian classes is, to Morton Horwitz, at the root of the changing principles of American contract law in the early nineteenth century. See Morton Horwitz, "The Triumph of Contract," chap. 6 in *The Transformation of American Law 1780–1860* (Cambridge, MA: Harvard University Press, 1977).

3. 2 Caine R. 48 (N.Y. 1804).

hemmed and hawed,[4] for example, New York never seemed to have doubts. New York's influence in this area was quite important, because New York simply had more commercial cases than other states. By 1830 New York had established itself as the state with the most manufacturing and trade, a status that it did not relinquish for the rest of the nineteenth century. The New York courts developed a density of doctrinal evidence unparalleled elsewhere in the United States and so provide the best lens through which to view the development and decline of the doctrine of caveat emptor. In this chapter, I trace the development of the doctrine of caveat emptor by examining every case[5] on implied warranty and caveat emptor that came before New York's highest courts[6] between 1796 (when the modern reporting system began) and 1900.

Caveat Emptor as Legal Puzzle

Even in its heyday in early nineteenth-century America, the common-law rule of caveat emptor was controversial and confused. That buyers should be stuck with products either defective in character (a whatchit was sold for a widget) or defective in quality (a grade B widget was sold for a grade A widget) was either morally reprehensible or eminently sensible, deeply and inevitably embedded in the common law or capable of wide variation, depending on the court and the case.

4. *Borrekins v. Bevan,* 3 Raule 23 (Pa. 1831) held that all sales implied warranties. But in *McFarland v. Newman,* 9 Watts 55 (Pa. 1839) the Pennsylvania Supreme Court changed its mind. See the discussion of these cases below.
5. I have only included cases involving sales of chattels here. Cases involving either sales of real property or sales of stock are excluded.
6. Between 1796 and 1848, the highest court in New York was the Supreme Court of Judicature, with infrequent appeals to the state senate, sitting as the Court for the Correction of Errors. In 1848, a judicial reorganization resulted in the Court of Appeals serving as the state's highest court. For a brief time in the early 1870s, a new Commission of Appeals was created as a temporary high court. This court consisted of the judges of the then-current Court of Appeals, who were to labor for three years cleaning up the backlog of cases and then retire as judges. See Karl Llewellyn, "On Warranty, Quality and Society: II," *Columbia Law Review* 37: 341–409 (1937). In the meantime, a wholly new Court of Appeals was elected. The Commission's decisions, then, represented the last gasp of a dying Court of Appeals bench. This study examines all cases on this subject that came before the Supreme Court and the Court for the Correction of Errors between 1796 and 1848 as well as all cases reported by the Court of Appeals and the Commission of Appeals between 1848 and 1900. All cases decided before 1848 are decided by the Supreme Court unless otherwise indicated. All cases after 1848 are decided by the Court of Appeals unless otherwise indicated.

Judge Gantt, for example, writing for the Constitutional Court of South Carolina, declared in an opinion that cited the Golden Rule as authority: "[T]he mind of every honest, upright man revolts at such a doctrine. . . . [I]n no case ought a contract to be enforced, where contracting parties have entered into it under a misapprehension and ignorance of such defects as would have prevented the contract, had the defect been known at the time."[7] But the New York courts, resolutely holding the line against the invasion of the civil-law notion of caveat venditor (where the seller was generally held responsible for the sale of defective goods) decided otherwise. Judge Thompson, in the first American case presenting the problem, wrote: "I see no injustice or inconvenience resulting from this doctrine, but, on the contrary, think it best calculated to excite that caution and attention which all prudent men ought to observe in making their contracts."[8]

Perhaps some of the controversy over caveat emptor arose from the rather curious pedigree of the rule. As Walton Hamilton has shown, the rule in Roman law, in civil-law countries, and even throughout medieval and early modern England was just the reverse. In medieval England, for example, if a seller sold unfit wares (particularly unsound bread or ale), he was fined or pilloried.[9]

American decisions traced their ancestry to an ambiguously reported English case, *Chandelor v. Lopus* (1603),[10] in which the sale of a false bezoar stone was challenged by the buyer. Absent an explicit warranty by the seller and absent evidence that the seller knew that the stone was not bezoar, the Exchequer ruled that the buyer could not recover. A later reference to the case, however, reports that the buyer won.[11] In any event, the subsequent history of the rule is clouded, for until the late eighteenth century there are apparently no reported cases involving the sale of defective goods. The doctrine of caveat emptor was not announced in any systematic way until *Parkinson v. Lee* (1802).[12] In some American jurisdictions this case, along with *Chandelor,* was frequently cited as evidence that the common law had always supported the rule.

American courts were deeply divided over the issue. New York

7. *Barnard v. Yates,* 1 Nott & McCord 142, 148 (S.C. 1818).

8. *Seixas v. Woods,* 2 Caine R. 48 (N.Y. 1804).

9. Walton H. Hamilton, "The Ancient Maxim *Caveat Emptor,*" *Yale Law Journal* 40: 1113–1187 (1931), pp. 1136–1144.

10. Cro. Jac. 4, 79 Eng. Rep. 3 (1603).

11. Hamilton, pp. 1167–1168.

12. 2 East 314, 102 Eng. Rep. 389 (1802). The court in this case refused to hold an obviously innocent seller liable to the buyer for the fraud of the grower of hops.

took the lead in *Seixas* by applying caveat emptor strictly. South Carolina, in *Barnard,* opted out of following the rule entirely. Pennsylvania struck out on its own in *Borrekins,* holding that in all sales there was an implied warranty that the good was what the seller said that it was. But a few years later, in *McFarland,* the Pennsylvania Supreme Court backed off from this apparently radical view. Chief Justice Gibson wrote: "The judges [in *Borrekins*], in pursuit of a phantom in the guise of a principle of impracticable policy and questionable morality, broke away from the common law. . . . [I]f the buyer, instead of extracting an explicit warranty, chooses to rely on the bare opinion of one who knows no more about the matter than he does himself, he has himself to blame for it." [13]

Karl Llewellyn, commenting on the confusion of doctrine that characterized the early nineteenth century, wrote:

> It is as good as a three-cornered hockey game, in the first half century, to watch the competition of star-cases for outside recognition. *Seixas v. Woods* stars for Primitive-Mercantile. *Borrekins v. Bevan* stars for Mature-Mercantile. *Conner v. Henderson* (15 Mass. 319 [1818]) is drafted, over and over again, into company which must have been, at least, uncomfortable. *Bradford v. Manly* (13 Mass. 139 [1816]), for all its eloquence and realism, spends much time on the bench or in the penalty-box. *Gardiner v. Gray* (4 Campb. 144 [N. P. 1815]) from across the water, and its earlier compatriot, *Parkinson v. Lee,* are not only used in every position, on every side, but meanwhile beaten often into unrecognizability. They seem too easily blocked and beaten to be reliable, though one cannot deny their power when let alone.
>
> All discussion, in the first fifty years, and on this subject, presupposes that there is "a" common law to be set against "a" civil law—*until* an issue gets close *and* a local precedent is in point to the writer's opinion. [14]

With all of this moral debate and doctrinal uncertainty, one might expect the justification and application of caveat emptor to be a difficult and controversial enterprise. Yet some states, notably New York, defended the rule vigorously. To see how this was possible, one needs to understand both the context in which the rule was applied and the way in which that application was justified. Surely, if the New York courts were using a rule that was generally thought to be outrageous or

13. 9 Watts 55, 56–57 (Pa. 1839).
14. Karl N. Llewellyn, "On Warranty, Quality and Society," *Columbia Law Review* 36: 699–744 (1936), p. 715 (repetitious citations omitted).

stacked unfairly against innocent buyers,[15] one of three things would
have happened:

1. Plaintiffs (who were most frequently buyers complaining of
their losses) would have by-passed the court system altogether if they
thought that they would not get a fair hearing. But there was a steady
stream of cases brought before the courts by precisely those buyers
who were supposed to beware. Between 1800 and 1819 twelve cases on
the issue of implied warranty were heard on appeal to New York
State's highest courts. Between 1820 and 1839 twenty-one such cases
were heard. The period 1840–1859 saw twelve such cases. Nineteen
such cases were brought up on appeal between 1860 and 1879, and
eighteen were appealed between 1880 and 1900. This relatively constant flow of cases before New York's courts indicates at least that the
dissatisfied buyers were not avoiding the courts.[16]

2. Pressures would have built up for legislation to supplant the
common law. But there was no legislation in New York on this point
until the general nationwide movement to pass a uniform sales act was
organized in the twentieth century.[17] If anything, there was legislative

15. This does not, of course, mean that public sentiment is presumed to be
unanimous or even that the general public at all knew of court decisions about caveat
emptor. A rule of this sort would probably have a particular reference group that would
pay attention to court decisions on the subject. Whether this reference group could succeed in getting the rule changed if it so desired is another question, beyond the scope of
the present chapter. The important point here is that the New York courts managed to
apply caveat emptor with great vigor, seemingly unaffected by the debates raging in the
national community over the appropriateness of the rule. The New York courts could
only have remained as committed as they did to the principle of caveat emptor if the
objections brought in other places either were not brought or were weakened as New
York doctrine was developed.

16. Three important qualifications of this statement need to be made. First, not
all the cases were brought by buyers; sometimes dissatisfied buyers refused to pay, and
the sellers brought an action to recover the price. Throughout the century, however,
buyers steadily continued to press lawsuits. Second, the constant number of cases
appealed throughout the century does not necessarily reflect a constant number of cases
filed or brought to trial. A great decline in the number of cases still could produce a
constant number of appeals, under the right circumstances. Finally, while the raw number
of sales no doubt increased over the century, the volume of appeals remained roughly
constant, indicating that the tiny fraction of sales that went up on appeal became even
smaller. For our purposes here, the important point is that the numbers indicate that
dissatisfied buyers were not completely avoiding the courts, which meant that at least
some of them believed that they could win on doctrinal grounds, that the legal deck was
not so stacked against them that bringing the case to court would be useless.

17. Alternative readings of the absence of legislation could be (*a*) that the legislature was not given to legislating or (*b*) that the affected groups either could not organize
(for the sorts of reasons identified by Mancur Olson in *The Logic of Collective Action* [New
York: Schocken, 1965]) or did not have the legislature's ear.

pressure to *prevent* the courts from abandoning caveat emptor. Senator Tracy, for example, bemoaning the tendency of some lower courts to want to move away from the rule, wrote in 1837:

> I am getting to learn that the spirit of the age, which is disposed to consider nothing settled that it imagines susceptible of improvement . . . is extending its influence to the oldest and deepest rooted principles of the common law. This even might not be so much regretted, if it were proposed to be brought about only through the open and responsible agency of legislation; but when pursued through the devious and occult processes of judicial exceptions and qualifications, it becomes a subject of some solicitude and apprehension.[18]

3. The judges invoking such a harsh rule would have been impeached or more subtly pressured to change their minds. At least, they might be expected to have disagreed with each other. But when there was a wholesale reorganization of the New York court system at midcentury, with judges being elected for the first time, there was little or no change in doctrine.[19] Moreover, the vast majority of these cases provoked no opposition from judges on the bench (only seven of the eighty-two cases heard by New York's highest courts during the entire century produced dissents). All of these observations provide evidence that the doctrine was much less controversial in application than it was in theory.

As in the preceding chapters, I examine the facts that the New York judges stress in their effort to determine whether the rule of caveat emptor should apply. In so doing, I aim first at description, asking, Which facts, in fact, matter? The next step, though, is to ask, Why do *these* facts matter and not others? I will argue in this chapter that all of the legally relevant facts in these cases identify the party that is likely to have superior access to information about the good being bought and sold.

Core Applications of the Doctrine of Caveat Emptor

Courts in caveat emptor cases are generally confronted by a buyer stuck with a defective good and a seller who claims no responsibility

---

18. *Wright v. Hart,* 18 Wend. 449 (Court for Correction of Errors, 1837), 459.

19. Until 1848, the Supreme Court of Judicature, New York's highest court, had judges that were appointed. A number of these judges sat for long periods on the bench. In 1848, the New York court system was reorganized and judges were elected to a newly created high court, called the Court of Appeals.

for the buyer's ill fortune. In deciding the case, the court must ask, Is there some reason why the seller should be responsible for the defective good? In jurisdictions using the caveat emptor rule, the buyer is found to be without remedy, absent fraud on the seller's part, explicit warranty on the sale, or one of the exceptions that will be discussed later. The buyer either should have been smarter, more observant, and more cautious or should have extracted an explicit warranty from the seller. The law, under the rule of caveat emptor, did not look out for the buyer who did not look out for herself.

In New York State, the cases where caveat emptor was actually applied present one of two clear factual patterns: (1) The seller was a merchant who had had possession of the good for sale only a short time and did not himself know much about it. The buyer, on the other hand, was often a manufacturer using this good in his business (or at least someone who knew precisely for what purpose the good would be employed). (2) The defect in the good was clearly visible, but the buyer failed to notice it. In both situations, the buyer had at least as much—and often more—knowledge about the good than did the seller; and caveat emptor was held to apply. Caveat emptor, then, was in practice a rule that required that the party who knew the most should bear the risk. When the parties were equal in access to knowledge, the courts let the loss remain where it fell.

Seixas v. Woods (1804), the first American case on this point, provides an excellent illustration of this principle. The defendant received from a home in New Providence some wood to sell. The invoice that the defendant received labeled the wood braziletto, a very valuable commodity. Not knowing the difference and advertising the wood as braziletto, the defendant caught the attention of the plaintiff, who bought it from him at a braziletto price. Later, the plaintiff discovered that the wood was peachem, a most inferior variety.

Writing for the majority, Justice Thompson cited *Chandelor* as evidence of the permanence of caveat emptor within the common law. Noting that the plaintiff's agent was present when the wood was delivered and that "the defect now complained of was within the reach of his observation and judgment, had he bestowed proper attention," [20] Thompson held that caveat emptor gave the buyer no recourse subsequently. Justice Kent agreed and further explicated the rule to be applied. The seller has no obligation to disclose what is within the

20. 2 Caine R. 48, 54.

"reach of [the buyer's] observation and judgment," Kent wrote, but the seller must communicate those defects "which cannot be supposed to be immediately within the reach of such attention." [21] Justice Lewis dissented for reasons that he did not explain. Clearly, in this situation, where the seller had just received the good without knowing much about it and where the plaintiff inspected the good but did not notice the failure of description, the court found no basis for shifting the loss back to the seller. The buyer knew at least as much as—if not more than—the seller.

Other caveat emptor cases indicate that the nineteenth-century courts were trying to allocate risk where the knowledge was. In *Swett v. Colgate* (1822),[22] for example, the defendants, soap manufacturers, bought 35 tons of barilla from the plaintiffs, who were New York merchants. The plaintiffs had received the shipment from merchants in Boston, who had ordered it through consignment merchants in England who worked for the harvester. But when Colgate received the cargo, the barilla proved to be kelp. While barilla of the sort specified in the invoice contained 50 percent alkali, perfect for making soap, the kelp that they received contained only 5 percent alkali, making it worthless for that purpose. Colgate refused to pay for the kelp.

The New York Supreme Court, with Woodworth writing, noted that there was no fraud or warranty. Here the rule was clear: "By the common law, where there is no fraud or agreement to the contrary, if the article turns out not to be that which it was supposed, the purchaser sustains the loss: the rule is *caveat emptor*." [23]

Although the rule is very broadly stated, the facts in this case make the logic apparent. The seller knew very little about the product, having bought it through a long and convoluted chain from the original producer. Kelp and barilla are physically indistinguishable except on chemical analysis. Neither buyer nor seller, therefore, could determine easily the true identity of the good. But in this case the buyer was a soap manufacturer whose main raw material was barilla; one might expect that this manufacturer would know more about the product than the seller, who was a merchant dealing in many things. The seller allowed the buyer to take a sample, which could have been but was not chemically analyzed. What the court appears to be doing in this case is,

21. 2 Caine R. 48, 53.
22. 20 Johnson 196 (N.Y. 1822).
23. 20 Johns. 196, 201.

again, letting the loss rest with the party who knew the most about the particular good being bought and sold.[24]

In *Sands & Crump v. Taylor* (1810),[25] the plaintiffs were merchants who sold a shipful of Southern wheat to the defendants, who were brewers and malsters. When the wheat arrived, it turned out to be rotten and unfit for malting. The defendants did not pay for it, claiming that they should not have to pay for unusable goods. But the court disagreed. Judge Spencer wrote that it was common knowledge that Southern cargoes would frequently become overheated and rotten and that the defendants must have known this when they made the deal. Judge Van Ness noted that every fact about the wheat was as well known to the buyers as it would have been to the sellers. Since the knowledge of the two parties was equal, the court would not remake the deal. The loss stayed where it fell.

In *Hart v. Wright* (1837)[26]—and its appeal to the Court for the Correction of Errors, *Wright v. Hart* (1837)[27]—the same principle is evident. Wright, a starch manufacturer, had bought 315 barrels of E. S. Beach's flour from Hart, a commission merchant. The flour could not be used to make starch, since it had been made from sprouted wheat. The flour was, however, made by E. S. Beach, and so it answered to the description.

Justice Cowen's opinion for the Supreme Court said that the general sale of merchandise does not imply a warranty where the goods are open to inspection by the buyer. But Cowen suggested that if the goods were impossible to inspect, then perhaps the rule ought to be relaxed. On appeal, there was some debate about whether sprouted wheat could be spotted on sight.

When the case got to the Senate sitting as the Court for the Correction of Errors, it met with a sharp dissent that insisted that the sale of food constituted an exception (of which we will hear more later) because it could potentially endanger public health. But the 15-9 majority stood behind the opinion of Chancellor Walworth that caveat emptor was the rule and that as long as the provisions were good for some use, they did not constitute an exception. Senator Tracy added:

---

24. Of course, what this means is that the court is not presuming that the owner of the good will invariably know more about it. In fact, this rule provides incentives for merchants to deliberately remain ignorant of the qualities of their wares. Who knows what is a matter of fact and not of law. Presumptions of knowledge so prevalent in later tort and even contract cases have not yet made their appearance here.

25. 5 Johnson 395 (N.Y. 1810).

26. 17 Wend. 267 (N.Y. 1837).

27. 18 Wend. 449 (Court for Correction of Errors, 1837).

"The buyer and seller both had equal means of knowing, and equal knowledge of the article sold. The defect was latent and of a character which, though it deteriorated in quality, and consequently somewhat diminished the value of the article, did not absolutely change its nature or render it utterly unfit for the ordinary purposes for which it is used." [28] What emerges from this case is a clear statement that when the buyer has the opportunity to find out and the seller does not know, the seller does not bear the loss—the buyer must beware. Throughout the nineteenth century, New York courts applied the caveat emptor rule to cases such as these. [29]

What is striking about all these cases is how similar are the basic facts to which the rule was applied. The seller was always found to be ignorant of the defect, so the choice facing the court was between making an innocent buyer or an innocent seller the bearer of the loss. Moreover, the sales transactions were generally between a merchant

28. 18 Wend. 449, 463.
29. The other cases, in chronological order, that presented this sort of fact pattern and where the New York courts applied caveat emptor are *Snell, Stagg & Co. v. Moses & Sons*, 1 Johnson 96 (N.Y. 1806) (cotton cloth imported from India was defective; merchant-seller knew no more about it than did merchant-buyer); *Holden v. Dakin*, 4 Johnson 421 (N.Y. 1809) (plaintiff-buyer bought defective paint from retailer-seller; the quantity of paint bought makes it appear as though the buyer must have been in a business that used paint; also, the retailer had not inspected the paint that was received from a distant supplier); *Davis v. Meeker*, 5 Johnson 354 (N.Y. 1810) (plaintiff bought a wagon from defendant; wagon was perfectly visible for all to see); *Thompson v. Ashton*, 14 Johnson 316 (N.Y. 1817) (plaintiff purchased crockery from defendant's store; crockery had been shipped to plaintiff from the warehouse, where it never had been inspected by defendant); *Welsh v. Carter*, 1 Wend. 185 (N.Y. 1828) (after performing chemical analysis on it, plaintiff bought barilla from defendant; plaintiff held to have relied on his own judgment, so that seller would not bear the loss when the chemical analysis turned out to be faulty); *Salisbury v. Stainer*, 19 Wend. 159 (N.Y. 1838) (plaintiff-manufacturer bought Italian hemp from defendant-merchant; plaintiff had opportunity to inspect, so seller does not bear loss); *Hargous v. Stone*, 5 N.Y. 73 (1851) (plaintiff-merchant bought cotton sheeting from defendant-merchant for shipment to Mexico; plaintiff had opportunity to inspect to see whether sheeting met Mexican import standards but plaintiff did not do so); *McCormick v. Sarson*, 45 N.Y. 265 (1871) (plaintiff sold defendant lumber after defendant had inspected it and had failed to catch obvious defect); *Gentilli v. Starace*, 133 N.Y. 140 (1892) (plaintiff-merchant sold defendant-merchant shipment of Chianti that had just arrived and was sitting on the dock; both were equally ignorant that the wine was bad). Three other cases that present similar factual situations but were decided on other grounds were *Johnson v. Titus*, 2 Hill 606 (1842) (mulberry cuttings sold by plaintiff to defendant were sufficient consideration to enforce contract, although the cuttings later died); *Muller v. Eno*, 14 N.Y. 597 (1856) (caveat emptor did not prevail because seller had made an explicit warranty); and *Hargous v. Ablon & Boyd*, 5 Hill 471 (1843) (also an explicit-warranty case, although the defendant-seller had made a mistake about the quality of the cotton cloth that he had sold).

who had only had the good in his possession a short time and a manufacturer or other large-quantity user who had generally dealt with goods of that kind many times before. The goods traded were almost always raw materials of uneven quality to be used in manufacturing, and so each shipment had to be appraised anew. Generally, too, the quality of the good was not dependent on the place of origin, something that would have given the merchant an advantage. From all of this, one can tell that the sellers here were not usually powerful relative to the buyers. They were not producers of the good but, more commonly, were merchants. Generally, the buyers had the advantage because they knew the sort of raw materials and range of quality that could be used in their particular process. And generally the losses stayed with them. In battles between merchants and entrepreneurs, then, the merchants usually won.

The number of cases presenting this sort of fact situation shrank over the century as the economy changed (see table 14.1). Fully 50 percent of the twelve cases decided between 1800 and 1819 were of this sort; only about one quarter of the cases between 1820 and 1859 were in this category; and less than 6 percent followed this pattern during the rest of the century. With the decline in situations to which caveat emptor would apply, one can see that there was good reason to believe that the rule itself was changing. It simply was not applied as often later in the century. But the principle underlying these cases stayed the same; it was the world that changed around it.

What we see in the apparent move away from caveat emptor is the rise of an economy in which products were becoming more complicated, thus giving rise to circumstances where buyers could not know as much about the goods that they bought. Coupled with this was a shift from sales through independent merchants to sales through agents of the producer. These changes increased the asymmetry of information that the seller and buyer were likely to bring to the sale, and the rules of law changed accordingly. But before we examine those changes, we will look at the exceptions to the caveat emptor rule that were built in at the start.

Food, Fraud, Horses, and Slaves: The Original Exceptions to the Caveat Emptor Rule

Even as the courts were announcing that caveat emptor ruled all sales cases, certain exceptions were recognized at the start. These exceptions fell into three categories: (1) Sellers were held responsible for the sale of rotten food, especially if the food made people sick. (2) Sellers were

Table 14.1   Defective-Product Cases in Nineteenth-Century New York

Type of Case	Who Bears Loss	1800–19	1820–39	1840–59	1860–79	1880–1900
Core caveat emptor cases	Buyer	Seixas Snell Holden Davis Sands Thompson	Swett Welsh Hart Wright Salisbury	[Johnson] [Muller] [Hargous] Stone	McCormick	Gentilli
Fraud	Seller	[Evertson] Beeker	[Fleming] Taylor		Dutchess Indianapolis RR	
Horse and slave	Seller	Schuyler* Cramer	Chapman Robert Duffee Whitney Cook	Cary		
Food	Seller	Van Bracklin		Voorhees Moses*	Parker Rust	Swain
Sample	Seller		Oneida Andrews Gallagher Beebee Boorman Waring	Beirne*	Leonard*	Brigg Argersinger Mayer Zabriskie
Executory immediate notice	Seller			Howard Hawes*	Barlett* Day Parks Dounce I	Bach Pierson Fairbank
Executory delayed notice	Buyer		Sprague	Shields	Reed Gaylord Dounce II	Kent* Norton Coplay Studer
Complex goods	Seller				Hoe Hawkins Gurney VanWyck White	Beeman Waite Carleton Bierman Hooper*
Miscellaneous		Perry	King Van Nostrand	Nelson	Stone	

Notes: 1. An asterisk next to a case name indicates that the outcome of the case is the reverse of that specified in column 2 of the table.

2. A case name in brackets indicates that the case was decided on technical grounds unrelated to the main substantive point.

also made to bear the loss if they used fraud to convince the buyer to buy the good. (3) Horse cases (and slave cases, too, in the days when New York still had slaves) were just different. Sellers of horses and slaves almost always found that the loss shifted back to them when the horse or slave got sick or died. These three sorts of transactions were unlike ordinary sales transactions of the day in that the seller in all of these cases knew more about what was being sold than did the buyer. This asymmetry in knowledge made the courts find that the seller should bear the loss.

Food

Food in early nineteenth-century America did not move very far, especially if it had to be consumed immediately in its present state. As a result, most sales of food were probably sales between the food producer and the consumer. If the person who produced the food were selling it, then one would expect to find the seller liable for selling defective food if courts were using the implicit rule that the party who had superior access to information should bear the loss of a sale gone wrong.

Such was the circumstance in New York's first spoiled-food case, *Van Bracklin v. Fonda* (1815).[30] Van Bracklin owned a cow that ate "a very large quantity of peas and oats" and "she was slaughtered for fear that she would die in consequence of her having eaten them."[31] A quarter of beef from this cow was sold to Fonda, who, with his family, was made seriously ill for two weeks after eating it. The court, in ruling for Fonda, said that the seller of provisions for domestic use was bound to know their quality; and the court laid great stress on the fact that Van Bracklin knew that the cow was sick. Clearly, this was a case where the seller knew more than the buyer.

But a later New York case, *Moses v. Mead* (1845),[32] was the exception that proved the rule. In this case Mead, a wholesale grocer, sold Moses, another wholesale grocer, 194 barrels of mess beef. Moses bought the beef not for immediate consumption but for sale to retailers. The beef was found to be unsound, but the court held that Moses was stuck with it with no redress. Rather than make Mead bear the loss for selling unwholesome provisions, Justice Bronson, writing for the court, indicated that in this sale it would have been very difficult

30. 12 Johnson 468 (N.Y. 1815).
31. 12 Johnson, 468, 468.
32. 1 Denio 378 (N.Y. 1845).

for the seller to know the quality of the goods that he sold. The seller purchased huge quantities of beef; he did not keep them long enough to know the characteristics of each barrel. The buyer, on the other hand, had the opportunity to inspect but did not take advantage of it. Caveat emptor, Bronson ruled.

Moses and *Van Bracklin* are clearly different from each other because of the seller's knowledge. Van Bracklin owned the cow and knew its condition. Mead passed along the mess beef he had bought without knowing much about it. In each case, the court shifted the loss to the party who knew the most about the good being sold, or, when the two parties were qually ignorant, the loss stayed where it fell. The other food cases arising in New York[33] demonstrated that vendors who knew about the wholesomeness of their food had to bear the loss while ignorant vendors did not. Caveat emptor only applied when the seller was a merchant who knew little about the products that passed through his hands.

Fraud

From caveat emptor's earliest days, courts found fraud on the part of the seller to merit special treatment. The seller was always judged to have acted improperly. Fraud in these cases involved demonstrating, as a matter of fact, that the seller knew that the product being sold was defective but had withheld this knowledge from the buyer. The defect could not be obvious or within reasonable reach of the buyer (or else the buyer would have access to the same information as the seller—and the law then would not shift the loss back to the seller). If the seller knew something that the buyer could not, and if the seller then did not volunteer the information, the seller would lose. This, of course, sounds just like the contemporary rule found in the cases on nondisclosure and fraud—that is, that sellers who have within their knowledge relevant information to which the buyer does not have equal access must disclose or bear the loss.

Relatively few cases in nineteenth-century New York were de-

33. *Voorhees v. Earl & Kellogg,* 2 Hill 288 (N.Y. 1842) (defendant-millers said that flour was of good quality; statement was held to be an implied warranty); *People v. Parker,* 38 N.Y. 85 (1868) (man found guilty in criminal case for selling unwholesome beef that he knew to be unsound); *Rust v. Eckler,* 41 N.Y. 488 (1869) (cheese cellar operator bore loss for cheese that had been waterlogged in operator's cellar); and *Swain v. Schieffelin,* 134 N.Y. 471 (1892) (druggist who mixed claret red for use as ice cream coloring held liable when claret red was found to contain arsenic, and to have made 200 people ill).

cided on this ground. This may be because nearly every case (whether fraud was at issue or not) produced a statement of the general rule, which asserted that caveat emptor would not apply when there was fraud or an express warranty. The legal principle may have been so clear that defrauding sellers either settled their disputes out of court or did not appeal the lower courts' rulings in this matter. One case that did find its way to the New York Court of Appeals was *Dutchess County v. Harding* (1872),[34] in which the defendant replaced the sumac in Triangle R brand bags with an inferior-quality sumac. Fraud on the seller's part allowed the buyer to recover. Although there were relatively few such cases,[35] all revealed some special knowledge on the seller's part that the buyer did not share. And, following the principle that I argue is at the core of these sales cases, judges always found that fraud should serve to turn the loss back on the seller.

Horses and Slaves

Karl Llewellyn, with his usual wit, noticed that horses got special treatment in courts of law: "Warranty, 1780–1850, divides conveniently in England, and indeed in several of the United States, into horse and non-horse. . . . (H)orse cases produce horse results. . . . There are few horses in New York, Massachusetts, Pennsylvania. But wherever they appear, the phenomenon is the same: it is *assumed* that horses call for, and get, 'express warranty'; it is (I think) therefor assumed that the *absence of express warranty,* in a trade where express warranty is usual, is queer, *and significant.*"[36]

In reading horse cases, we *do* discover that that horse cases get horse law. The cases simply find that the seller should bear the loss,

34. 49 N.Y. 321 (1872).
35. The other fraud cases are *Executors of Nicholas Evertson v. Miles,* 6 Johnson 138 (1810) (court dismissed action for breach of warranty because plaintiff should have brought action in fraud); *Beeker v. Vrooman,* 13 Johnson 302 (1816) (plaintiff bought sick horse and mare from defendant; fraud could be alleged in assumpsit action); *Fleming v. Slocum,* 18 Johnson 403 (1820) (plaintiff bought slave from defendant; demonstration of fraud requires proof that defendant knew and withheld information, but such proof could make the sale voidable); *Taylor v. Tillotson,* 16 Wend. 494 (Court for Correction of Errors, 1836) (plaintiff did not have to take back horse sold to the defendant despite agreement to do so if there was fraud by the defendant); and *Indianapolis, Peru and Chicago Railway Co. v. Tyng,* 63 N.Y. 653 (1876) (fraud by seller-defendant enabled plaintiff to void the sale of two locomotives).
36. Llewellyn, "On Warranty, Quality and Society," p. 711n (emphasis in the original).

something that does not occur in the sale of most other goods. And cases involving the sale of slaves generally have the same results.[37]

In asking why horses and slaves might be treated differently from other goods (aside from the obvious and morally relevant observation that both are living things), the legal distinction seems once again to turn on this question of relative access to knowledge. In every one of these cases, the seller had owned the horse or the slave for some time and actually knew his or her unique characteristics. The seller was, then, at a distinct advantage in these transactions, knowing more than the buyer in every case. Moreover, with the exception of one case,[38] the defect was hidden and only discoverable by someone who had been around the person or horse for some time. Here, again, the New York courts assign the losses to the party who had superior means of knowledge.

THE EXCEPTIONS TO CAVEAT EMPTOR, which held the seller responsible for the sale of food and horses (unless the defect was obvious) and which turned the loss back on the seller in cases of outright fraud, demonstrate that the unifying theme in these cases is asymmetric knowledge. Caveat emptor applied only when the buyer was at least as knowledgeable as the seller. In types of sales transactions where the seller was likely to know more than the buyer, the courts carved out exceptions.

The Rise of Sales by Sample: 1825–1900

With the rise in trade of cotton being shipped north from New Orleans, courts in New York State were confronted with yet another type

---

37. Slave cases include *Schuyler v. Russ,* 2 Caines 202 (N.Y. 1804) (defendant sold slave with crooked arm to plaintiff; defendant won because the defect was obvious); *Cramer v. Bradshaw,* 10 Johnson 484 (N.Y. 1813) (defendant sold sick slave to plaintiff; defendant held to have made express warranty). Horse cases include *Chapman v. Murch,* 19 Johnson 290 (N.Y. 1822); *Robert v. Morgan,* 2 Cowen 438 (N.Y. 1823); *Duffee v. Mason,* 8 Cowen 25 (1827); *Whitney v. Sutton,* 10 Wend. 412 (N.Y. 1833); *Cook v. Moseley,* 13 Wend. 277 (N.Y. 1835); and *Cary v. Gruman,* 4 Hill 625 (1843). What is particularly interesting in the horse cases is that the court started by making warranty a question of fact, asking whether the defendant had made any explicit guarantees of the quality of the horse (and generally found that he had done so). The court then began to assume that any statement that was made by a seller about the quality or character of the horse in a horse trade or sale could count as a warranty. Finally, by the end of this progression of cases, warranties were implied as a matter of law. But they were always found, one way or another.

38. In *Schuyler* the slave's crooked arm was completely visible to the purchaser. The court decided that the buyer should have noticed this.

of transaction, the sale by sample. Starting in 1825 with *Oneida Man-ufacturing Society v. Lawrence* (1825)[39] and continuing in a deluge[40] until the decision by the Court for the Correction of Errors in *Waring v. Mason* (1837),[41] the New York courts were hit with more cotton cases than with any other single type. And, creating an exception to the caveat emptor doctrine from the outset, the courts found that the seller should bear the responsibility when the cotton turned out to be rotten.

In the usual sale of cotton, the cotton was packed in huge bales that would have been nearly impossible to wrap up again if they were unwrapped for inspection by the buyer. Moreover, cotton merchants had worked out a method of sampling from deep inside the bales without having to open them up. Taking a device called a gimblet, which was about 15 inches long and had teeth on either side of it, the cotton merchant would plunge deep into the middle of the bale and pull out some cotton. The merchant would then take these samples around to prospective buyers who would buy on the basis of this information. Often, however, the cotton proved dry, brittle, rotten, or otherwise damaged. Chief Justice Savage, writing in *Boorman v. Johnson,* commented: "Our books show too many instances of fraud in this article."[42]

As Savage's comment makes clear, courts found exception to caveat emptor in these sales-by-sample cases because they suspected fraud. But fraud did not have to be demonstrated directly. Instead, the New York Supreme Court during this period assumed that all sales by sample gave an advantage in knowledge to the seller. In *Boorman* Savage continued: "Here is a good reason why *caveat emptor* should not apply. You cannot examine the article without opening the bales. That is never done—it would not be permitted and would be attended with great expense and inconvenience."[43]

By emphasizing that the buyer could get no reliable information on the cotton, Savage was also implying something else. By taking samples of the cotton, the merchant *could* and did find out the quality of the goods that he sold. No longer was the merchant in these cases the merchant who was merely passing goods along without inspection. It

39. 4 Cowen 440 (N.Y. 1825).

40. The Supreme Court also saw cotton in *Andrews v. Kneeland,* 6 Cowen 354 (N.Y. 1826); *Gallagher v. Waring,* 9 Wend. 20 (N.Y. 1832); *Beebee v. Roberts,* 12 Wend. 413 (N.Y. 1834); and *Boorman v. Johnson,* 12 Wend. 566 (N.Y. 1834).

41. 18 Wend. 425 (N.Y. 1837).

42. 12 Wend. 566, 575.

43. Ibid.

was the custom in cotton trading for the merchant to take samples from each bale. If the samples were good but the interior cotton was not, fraud could be presumed, even if it were not shown in each case. The seller knew what the buyer could not, and courts would rule that the seller should suffer the loss.

After the decision in *Waring*, cotton cases no longer arose. But a couple of other sale-by-sample cases did. The new Court of Appeals found no sale by sample in the sale of French blankets,[44] and the Commission of Appeals found no seller liability in the sale by sample of mixed beans.[45] In the first case, there was no evidence that the seller had actually sampled the bales of blankets sent to the buyer, and in fact there was no readily available technology for doing so without opening every bale. Again, we have the ignorant seller who is able to avoid bearing the loss. In the latter case, the sale by sample was held to indicate only the average quality of the good, not the quality of every bean in the final sale, quality that would have been as easy for the buyer as for the seller to determine.

Beginning with *Brigg v. Hilton*,[46] a case involving the sale of cotton cloakings, the Court of Appeals found itself with a series of sales by sample that also contained express warranties.[47] Presuming that when a seller expressly warrants, the seller must know something (or be willing to voluntarily assume the risk of loss that comes with knowing), the Court of Appeals held that these sales by sample were also cause for shifting the loss back to the seller. Generally, however, the sample cases illustrate that the courts look to the relative knowledge of buyer and seller to determine who should bear the loss.

Another Shift in Sales Conventions: The Executory Contract, 1840–1900

As sales cases began to show the move from an agricultural to a manufacturing economy, the New York courts dealt increasingly with executory contracts. Executory contracts occurred when the delivery of the good sold was not immediate but postponed until some date in

---

44. *Beirne v. Dord*, 5 N.Y. 95 (1851).
45. *Leonard v. Fowler*, 44 N.Y. 289 (1871).
46. 99 N.Y. 517 (1885).
47. *Argersinger v. MacNaughton*, 114 N.Y. 535 (1889) found an express warranty. *Mayer v. Dean*, 115 N.Y. 556 (1889) presented a latent defect and indicated that the buyer may have been defrauded. *Zabriskie v. Central Vermont Railroad Co.*, 131 N.Y. 72 (1892) also presented an explicit warranty.

the future. Often this meant that the good did not even exist at the time of sale but that the buyer had asked the seller to make the good to order. The rise of the executory contract generally coincides with the increasing size and complexity of manufacturing establishments, and buyers in these cases were increasingly dealing not with independent merchants who passed goods along a long chain but with manufacturers' agents, who were the sole link between the manufacturer and the purchaser. As a result, these cases involved a buyer buying directly from the manufacturer through the manufacturer's agent. Moreover, the goods bought were goods ordered, not existing goods that might be inspected before purchase.

The difficulties that the New York Court of Appeals had with these cases were substantial. Generally the court seemed to believe that sales involving manufacturers were different from sales involving merchants. In *Dounce v. Dow* (1874),[48] for example, the Commission of Appeals held for the buyer of 10 tons of XX pipe iron. The commission found that the buyer had bought the iron from a manufacturer. The iron was brittle, but the buyer did not discover this until 5 tons of it had been used. The court discovered that the quality was guaranteed in the contract, by the contract's calling the product XX pipe iron and saying that it was of a "quality suitable for use" in the buyer's manufacturing business.[49] When the case was reargued before the Court of Appeals, however, the result changed. But the Court of Appeals had suddenly discovered that the seller was not a manufacturer at all. The seller was a merchant, dealing in iron. Learning this, the court said that the seller "was not a manufacturer and was not presumed to know the precise quality of every lot of pigs bought and sold by him."[50] The manufacturer as seller would have lost the case; the merchant as seller prevailed.

The seller also prevailed in *Bartlett v. Hoppock* (1865)[51] because the seller was a merchant rather than the person who had raised the hogs in question. The Ohio hogs were allegedly corn-fed but turned out to be scalawags fed on beechnuts and acorns. The buyer and the seller were equally ignorant of this fact. Although the seller had said that his hogs were "suitable and proper" for the New York market, the court said that this was a matter of opinion and not a representation of quality. Judge Potter argued: "(W)here the vendor of an article is

48. 57 N.Y. 16 (1874).
49. 57 N.Y. 16, 19.
50. *Dounce v. Dow* (II), 64 N.Y. 411, 415 (1876).
51. 34 N.Y. 118 (1865).

not the manufacturer of the article sold, and in cases where the vendee has, as in this case, equal knowledge and equal opportunity of knowledge of the character of the articles sold with the vendor, the vendor is only liable upon an express warranty."[52]

In this case as in other, similar ones, sellers who simply pass the good along are never required to bear the loss unless there is some explicit agreement to the contrary. The buyer is presumed to know more about what he wants and to have knowledge at least equal to that of the seller, regarding the quality of the good being sold.

But the cases are not quite so simple. Many of these executory-contract cases involved buyers who used or altered the good before reporting that the good was defective, making it difficult to check on the truth of the buyer's claims. The first executory-contract case that the New York courts got was *Sprague v. Blake* (1837), an agricultural case.[53] The buyer in this case had bought a whole crop of wheat from a farmer before it was grown. The latter part of the crop delivered was alleged to be of a quality greatly inferior to that of the first batches delivered. But because the buyer had accepted the wheat and mixed it in a bin with wheat from other sources, making it impossible to check his claim, the court held that the buyer could not recover. Other cases involved buyers of manufactured goods who claimed that the goods were defective in belated counterclaims for actions to recover the price. The delay of the counterclaim raised suspicions about whether the good really had been defective on delivery.[54] The New York courts treated these delayed complaints with more skepticism than complaints made promptly, and the buyers generally were unable to recover.[55] Buyers were also unable to recover when they brought suit claiming implied warranty after waiting a long time before complaining.[56] Walking a fine line between holding that sellers should bear the loss for defective goods of their own making and holding that buyers

52. 34 N.Y. 118, 122.

53. 20 Wend. 61 (1838).

54. *Shields v. Pettie,* 4 N.Y. 122 (Court of Appeals, 1850); *Gaylord Mfg. Co. v. Allen,* 53 N.Y. 515 (1873); *Norton v. Dreyfuss,* 106 N.Y. 90 (1887); and *Coplay Iron Co. v. Pope,* 108 N.Y. 232 (1888).

55. The main exception to this general rule is *Kent v. Friedman,* 101 N.Y. 616 (1885), which involved an express warranty.

56. *Reed v. Randall,* 29 N.Y. 358 (1864) (plaintiff had bought from defendant a whole crop of tobacco alleged to be "wet and sweaty and rotten," but plaintiff then repacked the tobacco and waited seventeen months to bring suit); *Studer v. Bleistein,* 115 N.Y. 316 (1889) (plaintiff contracted with defendant to make 119 color illustrations for his book on birds of North America; after acceptance of the illustrations produced, author later decided that he did not like them).

had obligations to notify sellers immediately on discovering the defects, the court tripped itself up with a series of unworkable distinctions between warranties that did not survive acceptance of the good and warranties that did so, between contracts that incorporated warranties and contracts that were breached because the good ordered was not the good delivered. If we look at the facts that the court emphasized in its opinions, however, more sense emerges.

The fact that makes the most difference is the promptness with which the buyer reported the defect after discovering it. In *Howard v. Hoey* (1840),[57] Justice Cowen (who wrote virtually all of the court's warranty opinions between 1837 and 1843) found that the buyer of ale that turned out on delivery to be "sour, ropy and wholly unfit for use"[58] could recover from the sellers who had brewed the ale, because the buyer had notified the seller immediately. Cowen even announced that the general rule for executory contracts was not caveat emptor but caveat venditor! This was an overly expansive proclamation, however, because the cases where notice was *delayed* clearly produced different results, even though the contracts were executory.

The other fact that judges emphasize in these opinions is the seller's knowledge. In cases where a manufacturer was also the seller, the buyer generally won, as long as he complained promptly.[59] What made manufacturers as sellers different from merchants as sellers was the knowledge that the manufacturers had of both the products that they made and the processes used to make them. The New York Court of Appeals, trying to assign the loss to the party with superior access to knowledge, found that the manufacturer-seller should bear the loss unless the buyer's behavior indicated a potential fraud by the purchaser. Executory contracts generally presented a quite different distribution of knowledge among the parties to a sales transaction than earlier sales agreements had. But in all these cases, when the seller knew more about material facts, the seller bore the loss.[60]

57. 23 Wend. 350 (1840).

58. 23 Wend. 350, 352.

59. See *Parks v. Morris Ax & Tool Co.*, 54 N.Y. 586 (Commission of Appeals, 1874) (quality of manufactured steel could not be determined on inspection, so buyer was allowed to prevail over manufacturer); *Pierson v. Crooks*, 115 N.Y. 539 (1889) (another iron case in which the quality could not be immediately determined by buyers); and *Fairbank Canning Co. v. Metzger*, 118 N.Y. 260 (1890) (plaintiff bought carload of dressed beef in which the cows had been overheated prior to slaughter; only defendant could know this, so plaintiff prevailed).

60. The other executory-contract cases with immediate notification were *Hawes v. Lawrence*, 4 N.Y. 345 (1850) (failure of the product to meet buyer's expectations was due

Complex Products and the Knowledgeable Seller: 1860–1900

The final change in the nature of sales transactions which influenced nineteenth-century sales law resulted from the increasing prevalence of the complex product. Complex products are those manufactured goods about which vital information cannot be discerned from the product itself but must be figured out from a knowledge of the process used to produce the good.

In *Hoe v. Sanborn* (1860),[61] for example, the sale of circular saws was at issue. The saws, which the seller-manufacturer had made on order for the buyer (a sawmill builder), turned out to be too soft to be of any use cutting logs. But the real problem lay in the materials used and in the process employed to make the saws. On inspection, the saws looked just fine. But the seller knew the inferior quality of steel that went into making the saws that resulted from the process in which the steel was molded. All this apparently gave away the defect to anyone who knew the process. Justice Selden, writing an opinion in which he clearly set out a knowledge-based theory, stated: "The vendor is liable, in such cases, for any latent defect, not disclosed to the purchaser, arising from the manner in which the article was manufactured; and if he, knowingly, uses improper materials, he is liable for that also; but not for any latent defect in the material which he is not shown and cannot be presumed to have known."[62] The underlying logic here is clearly that the seller knew more than the buyer and had to swallow the loss as a result. Other complex-product cases bear out this observation that it is the superior knowledge of the seller that allows the buyer to recover in these cases.

In *Hawkins v. Pemberton* (1872)[63] the sale of a chemical compound known as blue vitriol (sulfate of copper) was at issue. The blue vitriol that the defendant bought turned out to have some much less valuable

---

to a factor not explicitly in the contract of sale and was held to be not a material fact; seller prevailed as a result); *Day v. Pool*, 52 N.Y. 416 (1873) (after buyer complained, seller promised to provide rock candy syrup that "would not crystallize, nor the sugar fall down" [52 N.Y. 416, 418]; after seller failed to make good on this promise, buyer was allowed to prevail); and *Bach v. Levy*, 101 N.Y. 511 (1886) (seller sold tobacco by sample but delivered the goods later, making it an executory contract; the rules that apply to sales by sample, where seller knows more than the buyer, apply here, allowing buyer to prevail).

61. 21 N.Y. 552 (1860).
62. 21 N.Y. 552, 565.
63. 51 N.Y. 198 (Commission of Appeals, 1872).

green vitriol (sulfate of iron) mixed in. The court ruled for the buyer, although this case presented the anomalous fact that the seller was a merchant and not a manufacturer. Judge Earl's opinion asked: "When a buyer purchases an article whose true character he cannot discover by any examination which it is practicable for him to make at the time, why may he not rely on the positive representation of the seller as to its character as well as to its quality and condition?" [64] Earl went on to argue that buyers could rely on positive representations of sellers and further noted that the rule of caveat emptor stated in *Seixas* was "sufficiently correct" but "not properly applied to the facts." [65]

In *Gurney v. Atlantic & Great Western Railway Co.* (1874)[66] railroad frogs were the subject of sale and in two cases, *Van Wyck v. Allen* (1877)[67] and *White v. Miller* (1877),[68] cabbage seed was found to be defective. In each case the defect could only have been known by the seller-producer who knew the process that created both the good and the defect.[69] And the buyers were allowed to prevail.

Economic and Contractarian Theories of Implied Warranty

This survey of New York State court decisions on the subject of caveat emptor and warranty shows that the underlying logic of these cases stayed the same throughout the century, even though the superficial rule appeared to change drastically. In each case, judges assessed who had superior access to knowledge about the product and let the loss fall on that party. Caveat emptor prevailed when the seller was a merchant who knew very little about the goods that passed quickly through his hands. As sellers began to know more, the courts held them responsible for the quality of their goods and for the losses caused by their defective products. Caveat emptor became riddled with exceptions.

---

64. 51 N.Y. 198, 202.
65. 51 N.Y. 198, 204.
66. 58 N.Y. 358 (1874).
67. 69 N.Y. 61 (1877).
68. 71 N.Y. 118 (1877).
69. A similar logic is visible in *Beeman v. Banta,* 118 N.Y. 538 (1890) (sale of freezer manufactured by seller); *Waite v. Borne,* 123 N.Y. 592 (1893) (wool oil made in secret process); *Carleton v. Lombard, Ayres & Co.,* 149 N.Y. 137 (1896) (petroleum that had been refined incorrectly), *reh. den.* on motion for reargument, 149 N.Y. 601 (1896) (same result); *Bierman v. City Mills Co.,* 151 N.Y. 482 (1897) (manufactured felt that was made using a shortcut process that did not work); and *Hooper v. Story,* 155 N.Y. 171 (1898) (varnishing machine; sellers prevailed because buyers did not demonstrate that the machine did not work adequately).

Even at the peak of the application of caveat emptor, however, courts in New York still admitted exceptions for food, fraud, horses, and slaves, because those transactions generally involved more knowledgeable sellers. The exceptions to the apparent rule of caveat emptor are the exceptions that demonstrate the more fundamental underlying principle.

If we think about the effects of such a principle, however, we can see that it would not necessarily be an ideal one for promoting efficiency.[70] Posner has argued that liability for nondisclosure in cases of implied warranty should rest on the seller when the purchaser cannot find out at low cost—such as when the buyer purchases the product infrequently, when the defect is not discoverable by inspection at time of purchase, when the product is very expensive, or when the characteristic is not discoverable even through repeated use.[71] This, of course, runs counter to Kronman's argument that one needs property rights to establish incentives for expensive information to be produced in the first place and especially in cases where an entrepreneur is trying to get an edge on the competition. Kronman would want the seller to keep secret any information that resulted from investment, regardless of whether the buyer could acquire it cheaply. Posner argues that the buyer's cost of acquiring of information rather than the seller's cost of acquiring the information is the standard.

Neither Kronman nor Posner seems to have captured the judicial focus in these cases; courts *compare* the buyers and sellers to see who has the *relatively* easiest time getting the information in a specific case.

70. Nor does this seem to promote the rapid growth of a manufacturing economy. Most theories of nineteenth-century American law emphasize the instrumental role that law played in creating a climate favorable to industry. Willard Hurst's well-known view that nineteenth-century common law encouraged the release of entrepreneurial energy (*Law and the Conditions of Freedom,* Madison: University of Wisconsin Press, 1960) and Horwitz's argument that nineteenth-century common law enabled the agrarian classes to be dominated by a new industrial class (*Transformation of American Law*) both rely on the strong facilitative connection between law and the ascendancy of the entrepreneur. Caveat emptor, however, seems to cut the other way. In the early part of the century, it was precisely the budding manufacturers who suffered the biggest losses under this rule; merchants and farmers went scot-free. Later in the century, manufacturers again bore the brunt of this rule, becoming the knowledgeable sellers of complex products, and responsible for selling defective goods. If anything, caveat emptor was a battleground between merchants and manufacturers in the early part of the century (with merchants winning) and between manufacturers and consumers in the later part of the century (with the consumers winning). The manufacturers were, as a group, consistent losers. It is hard to see how this let loose the entrepreneurial spirit.

71. Richard A. Posner, *The Economic Analysis of Law,* 3d ed. (Boston: Little, Brown, 1986) pp. 99–101.

Thus, how much one must disclose depends in part on the actor with whom one is dealing and in part on the features of the world that affect search costs in the particular case. It is the *relative*—not the *absolute*—search costs that make the difference in the legal rule. From an economic point of view one problem with relative search costs as a legal standard is that it does not establish clear incentives in advance; how much one has to disclose and how much of the losses of a transaction one is called on to bear depend primarily on one's position relative to one's transacting partner and not on a general rule of conduct for one's own behavior that will reliably hold in any transaction. One's property right in a piece of information depends on the condition of the person against whom one is claiming the right. One's incentive to invest, then, depends on predictions about the state of one's transacting partners and not primarily on the value of the information for one's own decision.

Incentives to search for information are skewed in strange ways by the rules that we have found in this chapter. We can see this more clearly by reexamining the sorts of sales that were at issue in the implied-warranty cases. In the complicated chain of sales common in the early nineteenth century, where the producer sold to a middleman who sold to another middleman who sold to a final consumer, the party who could produce information at the lowest cost *in the particular pair* whose sales deal was at issue was not always the economically optimal bearer of the loss *overall*. Ideally, an economically efficient result would have the person with the most knowledge in the whole chain of sales bearing the losses of deals gone wrong as long as some intervening problem did not magnify the damage. The information gatherer facing the cheapest search costs for information in a *chain* of sales, taken as a whole, is generally going to be the producer.[72] The person or firm who has grown the crop or manufactured the product will generally face much lower search costs in finding information about the crop or product than will a buyer who sees the good for the first time at the moment of sale. But the strict rules of privity of contract that prevailed throughout the nineteenth century, rules that allowed suits to be brought only against one's immediate seller and barred suits against the person who sold one's seller the good, prevented courts from achieving the result that would have been most efficient. The only person who was in a legal position to sue the

---

72. The main exception to this general rule would be when the final consumer intended the good for a specialized use that only the final consumer would be able to know.

producer was the first middleman. But the first middleman had no incentive to inspect the product, because his ignorance enabled him to prevail in a lawsuit if he sold the product quickly to someone else without inspecting it. And the next middleman had no incentive to inspect, for the same reason. Only the final buyer would have the incentive to inspect (because she would be the one using the product). If the purchase went through, that final buyer would have no recourse to collect from the person with the easiest access to information in the *chain,* the producer, because the suit would be barred by privity rules.

In the early part of the nineteenth century, then, merchants received substantial benefits from remaining ignorant of the qualities of the goods that they sold. If they moved the goods quickly and did not know much about them, they were able to avoid bearing the losses when the goods proved to be defective. This sort of incentive structure would lead rational merchants to flood the markets with defective products, a result that could hardly be said to promote efficiency. With the creation of substantial incentive effects that would reward trading partners for remaining ignorant, caveat emptor and its various exceptions seems less like a rule driven by efficiency and more like a rule guided by some other consideration.

But economists might have another argument. The implied warranties that developed in the latter part of the nineteenth century might be seen as methods for lowering transaction costs and facilitating value-enhancing exchanges as markets got more complicated. If the parties had to bargain through to every condition of every agreement (especially when many conditions were routinely taken for granted in particular markets), contracts would be very expensive to negotiate and the cost of drafting them might deter people from reaching agreements that would, were it not for the transaction costs, make everyone better off. The evolution toward implied warranties during the course of the nineteenth century might reflect the increasing complexity of sales agreements as products themselves became more and more sophisticated and likely to have hidden defects. If the legal rule were designed to maximize efficiency, we might expect the law to imply provisions that the parties would find expensive to negotiate explicitly.

That is explicitly what the law does *not* do, however. For one thing, there is not such a simple trend. The pattern of buyers having to beware sometimes and sellers having to cover the losses other times makes it hard to see how this rule would lower transaction costs. The point of such a transaction-costs argument is that the rule should be more efficient than a regime of individual negotiation in specific instances. According to Karl Llewellyn, throughout the nineteenth century the New York cases seemed to people of the time to present a chaos of conflicting rules, with the courts announcing caveat emptor as the general rule but stitching a crazy quilt of exceptions.[73] It is hard to see how this state of affairs could both increase certainty and lower transaction costs. If anything, the uncertainty of the legal rules at the time would have increased transaction costs.[74]

With incentive effects and predictability ruled out as likely explanations of the decisions, what might be going on in these cases? The contractarian would be concerned with the question, Are the two parties to the deal equally likely to find the information if they expend the same level of effort? Is there equality of access to information?

The early caveat emptor cases reveal that the buyer starts with a large advantage over the seller in being able to assess the quality of the good being bought. And the buyer bears the loss. But in the horse, slave, and food cases, where the seller has information not easily availble to the buyer, the seller bears the loss. Sales by sample, at least in those cases where the sampling procedure really does give the seller superior information, produce losses for the seller, as do executory contracts where the buyer immediately informs the seller of the defect. When the buyer delays (raising serious questions about fraud on the part of the buyer), the results flip; but by then it is no longer so clear that the buyer is blameless in causing the defect. Finally, with complex-goods cases, where the information is clearly more readily available to the seller than to the buyer, the seller bears losses because courts find implied warranties. In these nineteenth-century implied-warranty cases, courts reveal that they value equality of opportunity to acquire information. The same principle that we found in the contemporary doctrines of nondisclosure, privacy, and trade secrets can be found in nineteenth-century New York too.

But this does not answer some troubling questions. Why would a contractarian be pleased with a result that ignored valuable incentive effects and predictability? Generally speaking, those things should be valuable to a contractarian, just as they are to an economist. But the

---

73. Llewellyn, "Of Warranty, Quality and Society" and "Of Warranty, Quality and Society: II."

74. The argument in this chapter that the cases fall into a regular pattern was not made by any commentator at the time—nor, to my knowledge, by anyone since. The conventional wisdom seems to be Llewellyn's—that is, that the case law seemed chaotic at the time.

contractarian is not just worried—or even primarily worried—about getting the optimal social results among available alternatives. *How* those results are achieved is very important also.

The situation that judges confront in dealing with sales gone wrong is how to allocate losses between the parties who are in court. The person who is claiming to have been cheated in these cases is making a claim against the person who sold the good in question, not against the universe. The question that confronts the judge is what to do *in that case* and not some other.[75] Now the judge might, as the economist would probably prefer, decide the current case so as to set up incentives for the right legal rule to emerge eventually. The buyer who buys a defective good from an ignorant seller should prevail against the seller and that seller should prevail as against the seller before and so on, if the point is to have all roads lead to the person in the best position to know what would prevent the loss, the original producer. But would that produce the right result in the individual case?

In this regard, as always, the economists (and the utilitarians who share their world view) are willing to sacrifice the individual in the specific case to get the global result right. If the choice were between allocating the loss to the seller (because that would give the seller incentive to pass the loss back to the producer—even though the seller had done nothing blameworthy) and allocating the loss to the buyer (because the buyer had superior information in the specific case), justice in the economic view would require that the first option be adopted. The optimal social result would be achieved, even if it resulted in temporary losses for innocent middlemen along the way. But contractarians, with their concern for what happens to individuals as the social good is sought, would prefer the latter course of action. If the buyer were knowingly cheated by the seller or if the seller had some other advantage in knowledge, then the seller should be responsible—and courts would find her so. But when the seller and buyer are equally ignorant or when the buyer has the advantage of knowing the purpose for which the good will be used, then the buyer would seem better posi-

---

75. There may be some cases in which contractarian judges would want to challenge these backdrop rules about the organization of courts, about the focus on specific cases, and about the division of labor between courts and legislatures. If the system is not basically just, in Rawls's sense, then a judge might be morally obligated to effect such a change. But that would require that the basic injustice be demonstrated and also that the judge not do morally objectionable things in the instant case in an effort to get the institutional framework right.

tioned to be responsible for her own fate,[76] as long as there were no devious intentions on the part of the seller or special disabilities on the part of the buyer.

Assigning the loss to the party who *in the pair in court* was in the best position to know about the defect seems a sensible rule if the point is to do justice in individual cases. This might get the global result wrong—resulting in more defective goods getting into the market and establishing incentives for merchant-sellers to remain ignorant of the quality of their wares—but it is not a crazy rule if the focus is on the two parties before the court and not on just the right result in a global sense.

This is not to say that the rules about implied warranties are, from a contractarian point of view, optimal. The evolution of this rule into the proposition that sellers *should* be aware (and will be presumed to be aware) of the quality of the goods that they sell is an improvement because it addresses both the social optimality and the individual justice issues. By holding sellers to the standard that they *should* know what they sell, the law establishes incentives for them to discover such knowledge. With advance notice to potential defendants of such a standard and plaintiffs bringing these new defendants before the courts, justice also can be done in individual cases. Individual sellers can be judged according to whether their actions have been diligent as duty requires and not according to whether their actions produce globally efficient markets.

76. This sort of contractarian analysis assumes the backdrop rules and institutions that protect people against catastrophe. If the defective good does the buyer a great deal of harm, then the buyer should be able to recover, if not from the seller then at least from some social insurance scheme or from the producer of the good.

SIX
Concluding

Chapter Fifteen
The Logic of Legal Secrets

THROUGHOUT THIS BOOK, THREE THEMES have been mixed together, combined so that their distinctive outlines have merged. Those three themes, outlined at the start of chapter 1, involve the development of a sociology of secrecy, an assessment of the empirical viability and normative value of both the economic theory of law and a contractarian contender, and the search for a jurisprudence that will be informed by and in turn enrich social and political theory. Now that we have completed our tour of the detail of doctrine, it is time to assess how far we have come along each of these three paths and to inquire about where the paths may lead from here.

Toward a Social Theory of Secrecy

Social theory may be seen as the abstract description of patterns in social life, abstract description that weaves perceptions of similarity and difference into a web of interrelated concepts and concerns. Social theorizing involves seeing patterns and making meaning of them.

Most of our attention in discussing secrecy has focused on the competing claims that secrets generate, on how those who hide and those who seek justify what they do and try to attract the approval of others. But beneath this chaos of competing claims, secrets reveal a structured logic. Secrets simultaneously make possible and possess the power to undermine a number of important social forms.

Secrecy operates in a patterned way at both the individual and the collective level. At either level a secret can usefully be thought of as being a property of a relationship. A secret is kept by a specific individual or group from another individual or group, and, though it has importance and meaning to an individual in a complicated psychological sense, it exists also as an instance of a social form. As such, the secret helps to shape the definitions and boundaries of social relationships and so unites and divides people. When considering the individual level of this social form, we focus on the way in which secrets affect the relation between self and others. When analyzing the collective level, we examine the relations that secrets make possible among classes and throughout social organization.

Secrecy at the Individual Level

At the individual level, patterns of disclosure and secret-keeping can create three different sorts of social relationships:

a. *Autonomy of Self from Others.*—As is evident in claims for a right of privacy, secrets withheld by one person from others provide a basis for personal autonomy. Few thoughts are more threatening to people who value autonomy than the thought of being constantly watched, of being unable to keep or share secrets. Our literary stock of anti-utopias carries prominently the theme of continual observation. In Orwell's vision of *1984* or in Atwood's portrait of Gilead in *A Handmaid's Tale,* one feature of social life stands out: personal autonomy is almost completely curtailed through the elaboration of systems of surveillance. Without the ability to keep secrets, individuals lose the capacity to distinguish themselves from others, to maintain independent lives, to be complete and autonomous persons. The reason why the main characters in these anti-utopias can be distinct persons at all is that they try to maintain secret thoughts, secret doubts, secret criticisms of the totalitarian systems in which they live. Their autonomy, insofar as they have any, exists in their ability to have secret hopes and secret dreams. This does not mean that a person actually has to keep secrets to be autonomous,[1] just that she must possess the *ability* to do so. The ability to keep secrets implies the ability to disclose secrets selectively, and so the capacity for selective disclosure at one's own discretion is important to individual autonomy as well.

---

1. Once all one's personal knowledge has been shared, it may appear that a person possesses no possibility for autonomy anymore. But knowledge is not used up in this way. Even if one has disclosed all one's secrets to others at a particular time, it does not mean that more secrets cannot be kept later. Knowledge, even self-knowledge, accumulates bit by bit, and secrets revealed at one time, although they may make one vulnerable to attempts at control by others later, can often be counteracted with more secrets in the future.

b. *Solidarity with Others.*—Shared secrets create solidarity with others; secrets withheld from others divide and separate.[2] What distinguishes those to whom we feel close from those at greater social distance is often the amount and quality of shared information that exists in the relationship.[3] By telling others secrets we bring them closer to us, often making ourselves vulnerable in the process. By hiding secrets we push others away. We have seen this in the secrecy cases examined in the preceding chapters. Creating confidential relationships by sharing personal information brings others close and often creates special obligations among those who share information; such obligations are often enforced in American law. The failure to disclose important information relevant to a relationship, information that was formerly shared as a matter of course, is a sure sign that the closeness has ended. In American law, this can lead to a finding of fraud when the formerly confiding partner takes advantage of the trust generated by the bond of secrets once shared.

An individual's ability to reveal or hide information is crucial to that individual's ability to shape the social world in her immediate vicinity, an ability that in turn is crucial for liberty. Anti-utopias are such powerful nightmares because this ability to create individualized social worlds is lost to the people in these settings. Sharing secrets with others creates just the sort of social bonds that totalitarian regimes fear most, close contacts that resist the entry of other parties. While the individual may be able to keep a few thoughts as secrets against the world, sharing secrets in these anti-utopias is an enormously risky activity. And yet in these anti-utopias, as in social life under any political regime, sharing information that is not generally known is the primary way to reach out to others, to establish contact with them as distinct human beings, to create a world of individualized solidarity

2. Simmel made this point in his essay on secrecy ("The Secret and the Secret Society," in Kurt Wolff, ed., *The Sociology of Georg Simmel* [New York: Free Press, 1950], pp. 307–376).

3. Of course, this general statement has exceptions. Sharing secrets may drive people apart, if a secret's revelation destroys comfortable assumptions. A husband who confides to his wife that he has had an affair with someone else will not always find that this brings him and his wife closer. In those cases, keeping secrets secret may preserve and maintain the relationship (although the secret may create such tension, guilt, and hypocrisy that it will eventually damage the relationship anyway). It would be difficult, however, for the relationship to be as close as it had been prior to the existence of this secret, so revelation might be a means of repairing the invisible damage. Generally, however, shared secrets are associated with closeness, and withheld secrets are associated with social distance.

with others. Without secrets and the ability to selectively share them with others, it is difficult to establish any unique bonds of solidarity at all.

But not all sorts of solidarity rest on mutual secret-sharing. The sort of collective solidarity that comes with totalitarianism or extreme forms of communitarianism does not rest on this capacity. In fact, this sort of solidarity thrives on the publicness of the personal, on requiring that individuals live in such a way that secrets are minimized.[4] Secrecy becomes subversive when bonds of solidarity are collectively imposed because secrets present the possibility of some alternative form of social organization. Only when solidarity reflects individual choice will secrecy be vital.

c. *Strategic Manipulation of Others.*—Secrecy enables people to control others. To get another person to do one's will when that other person otherwise does not want to do so, one either can persuade the person with arguments or use physical coercion to force the person to do what one wants. But one may also hide the information that the other person would find relevant to making a decision, information that would make the decision turn out differently. This is another, powerful, invisible way of exercising control. By altering the appearance of a choice that the affected person has to make, one can often effectively determine the outcome. We have seen this throughout our examination of secrets, particularly in the fraud cases. Secrets can be used for deception, for control, and for strategic advantage.

But secrecy also can be used to evade the manipulation of others. By retaining as secret any information about oneself that would otherwise be the subject of disapproval, one can take control again and avoid the dominance of others.

SECRECY, AT THE INDIVIDUAL LEVEL, is a social form that possesses the power to destroy what it generates. Secrecy makes individual autonomy possible and also creates opportunities for solidarity. But bonds of solidarity voluntarily created through the revelation of secrets may, when affection and trust fade, make a later retreat into secrecy and its

---

4. Rosabeth Moss Kanter has shown that communes that survive often take steps to curtail the individuality and privacy of their members. The bonds of solidarity are strengthened at the expense of personal liberty, and secrecy becomes subversive. See Rosabeth Moss Kanter, *Commitment and Community* (Cambridge, MA: Harvard University Press, 1972).

associated independence difficult. This happens because secrets once revealed cannot be retracted. That another knows one's secrets can be a distressing situation indeed and may make it near impossible to re-establish one's independence. While the initial sharing of secrets may have been an expression of autonomy, the bonds that secrets create may enslave. The extreme case of blackmail illustrates the point.

Preserving secrets is an important aspect of autonomy for the individual who keeps them, but secrets withheld by others can compromise the autonomy of individual choice when the manipulative others appear to make a decision out to be something other than what it is. One person's autonomy achieved through keeping secrets may result in another's restriction when that secret influences the way in which that person sees the choices faced. The very act that serves as one person's expression of autonomy compromises another's autonomy. There need not be anything troubling or contradictory about this; after all, claims of liberty of all sorts work the same way. One person's liberty ends at the edge of another's, so the wisdom runs, and the fact that one person's liberty may interfere with another's does not make the concept of liberty internally contradictory or meaningless. In fact, some restrictions on action may actually enhance liberty. Setting the rules of a game opens up a sphere within which individuals may be free to act, a realm of action that, but for the rules restricting choices, would not exist at all.

But secrets pose a different set of challenges to autonomy. While the opportunities for manipulation that secrets create can be undermined by secret-keeping on the part of the one who otherwise would be dominated, secrecy itself can be used to hide the manipulative uses of secrets. One generally knows that one's liberty has been compromised in cases of physical coercion or intrusion on the part of others, but one does not generally know what has happened in the case of secrets. One person's expression of autonomy through keeping secrets cannot be defended against by the target of the secret when the target does not know what the secret-keeper is hiding. Restrictions on liberty that take other forms are visible; one knows that one's liberty has been affected. But in the case of secrets this very critical piece of information may itself be hidden, deepening the compromise of autonomy. In the case of secrecy it is quite possible to believe that one is operating autonomously when actually one's perceptions of the world have been undermined radically by others' manipulation of the information to which one has had access. Other compromises of autonomy do not falsely convey that one is still autonomous.

Secrecy at the Collective Level

At the collective level secrecy plays an important role in stratification, in social control, and in social structure:

a. *Stratification.*—Secrets can generate and reinforce systems of inequality. When knowledge is unequally distributed, other important resources in a social system may be unequally distributed as a consequence. When information about available jobs, for example, is made available to some but not to others, inequalities in opportunities—and then in possible income—follow. When one company possesses a trade secret unavailable to others, it may get a competitive edge. Inequality in the distribution of knowledge, of which secrecy is one important cause, ripples out into the social sea to create inequalities in other important social resources. Bacon's aphorism that knowledge is power describes this process well.

Unique knowledge may reinforce not only inequality among individuals but inequality among classes as well. When those in power retain control over unique and important knowledge, others can be excluded from entry into these exclusive groups. Law and medicine, for example, may be seen as systems of knowledge that draw sharp boundaries between insiders and outsiders, boundaries that serve to block easy mobility and that have enormous consequences for the distribution of wealth to the individuals who possess this special knowledge. By creating new social divisions secret societies also accomplish the same tasks of inclusion and exclusion based on knowledge.

But secrecy also may provide the means through which the disempowered regain their strength. The maintenance of many secrets requires little or no wealth, only acts of will. And some secrets, like those kept by the dispossessed in antiutopias, may provide chinks in the armor of the privileged, opportunities to rebel against domination by others. Secret conspiracies and secret plans may topple the powerful. If the privileged rely on information about the disadvantaged to consolidate their power, then the disadvantaged have this much more power themselves. Keeping secret what they can, the disadvantaged may be able to fight back by surprise, just as by keeping their deviance hidden they can evade the rules that apply to them.

b. *Social Control.*—Secrecy highlights the relationship between knowledge and social control. For a system of social control to be effective, the rules that are to be enforced must be generally made known to those who are expected to follow them, but, more importantly, the actions of those who are subject to the rules must be monitored. The concept of social control implies that there is some access to knowledge about the individuals who are to be controlled. To the extent that people can prevent others from learning about them, control over their actions is reduced; those who can successfully keep secrets achieve increased autonomy with respect to those attempting to control them.

Social control is never complete, if only because some kinds of deviant actions are harder to detect than others. Even if it were possible to monitor all actions, it of course does not follow that a society would want to judge or control every detectable activity. The shape that patterns of surveillance and monitoring take permeates all social relations, and the degree of knowledge that a society routinely collects about its citizens influences the forms of social life that are possible. If a person believes that she is constantly watched and will be punished for deviance, for example, she will alter her behavior to conform to expected norms. If a person believes that she is always in danger of being reported to the authorities for infractions of the rules, she will be very cautious in associating with anyone. If one's social group may be infiltrated and monitored, the group may develop an internal structure that sorts potential entrants and disguises members of the group from each other. When the monitoring necessary for social control becomes intrusive and pervasive, social life itself turns inward and loses its vibrancy.

Keeping secrets, individually or collectively, is a way of evading surveillance and monitoring. Secrets are necessary for deviance to thrive.

c. *Social Structure.*—Secrets provide the rough draft of social structure. If social structure consists in patterns of association among people, patterns that have become durable enough to be called structures, then certainly patterns of association require, first of all, shared knowledge. Moreover, that knowledge, while shared among those who are forming the association, must not be part of the general knowledge, or else it could not form a basis for exclusive association. Formal organization, for example, begins as a flow of particular knowledge among particular individuals. When that flow of knowledge settles into a pattern, the organization becomes formalized and durable patterns of association can be detected. The same process operates at the level of friendships and intimate relationships as well. Shared knowledge and mutual disclosure become the basis on which social expectations and patterns of association are built.

But the flow of knowledge is more fluid than other aspects of social organization. A preliminary form of social organization may be undercut by competing patterns of information flow. When patterns of information flow change, as they easily can when opportunities for new social interaction arise, these new patterns can be used to undermine existing institutions by providing a rough draft of an alternative social structure.

SECRETS, THEN, HAVE A DOUBLE-EDGED character. On one hand, they make stratification, social control, and social structure possible.[5] But on the other hand, they provide opportunities for undermining the existing order and creating alternative social forms. This means that all the interesting information about secrets consists in how they are being used by whom for what purposes under what set of constraints in what contexts. This is where a society's rules about secrets will matter a great deal.

Toward a Contractarian Theory of Law

Throughout this investigation of norms about secrecy as revealed in American common law, I have developed the argument that a contractarian view of law explains better than an economic view does the rules that we find. This has so far been primarily a positive claim about the fit of the theory and the logic of the cases.

Given the importance of secrecy in the organization of social life, however, it matters a great deal in both a positive and a normative sense which rules about secrets have the force of law in a particular society. Of course, the existence of rules does not foreclose the possibility of significant deviance. We cannot infer from the existence of norms what will in fact be the case in a particular social setting. But on average norms are relatively good guesses about what will happen, as well as aspirational statements about what should happen.

I have found significant support for a contractarian theory of law in the area of secrecy and have argued that the economic analysis of law does not work well to explain the legal rules that judges use. And we have already seen, through a detailed examination of four different areas of doctrine, what difference those rules make in a positive sense. What I would like to explore here is what difference it makes, in a normative sense, that we have contractarian rules rather than economic or utilitarian ones.

---

5. This is not to say that secrets are the only forces that are involved in the development of social organization. Obviously, complex social forms cannot be created unless other resources are available for the effort as well. Secrets may be necessary, but they are not sufficient conditions for social organization.

There are three critical properties of a contractarian legal system that a system based in economic principles alone would not share. First, contractarianism focuses attention on individuals as individuals, not just as units of larger social groupings. The question that contractarian analysts ask is, What social arrangements would individuals be likely to consent to, even if they were to get the least desirable outcome that the system could deal them? This question focuses attention on the plight of the worst off, and so contractarian solutions often take the form of supporting a floor beneath which one cannot fall.

Economic arguments, particularly those of the Chicago school, take floor constraints to be interferences with the operation of free markets and therefore generally undesirable from an efficiency viewpoint.[6] But in the contractarian view floor constraints are crucial for the maintenance of legitimacy. For contractarians it does not settle the issue of legitimacy to tell individuals that their sacrifice is necessary to make others better off. It would be perfectly reasonable, in such a circumstance, for the individual to ask why *she* must bear the costs of maintaining optimal social arrangements. If political systems are to be made legitimate to *individuals,* that question must have a comprehensible answer that both explains why the particular individual ought to be a willing participant in such an arrangement and convinces that individual that the arrangement is not just better on average but fair in her case. Economists who argue that individuals are *on average* better off under an efficiency-valuing scheme will generally not be convincing to a particular individual on whom the burden falls, particularly if that individual is asked to shoulder a great deal while those around her have to sacrifice nothing. A contractarian point of view involves asking what social arrangements look like to individuals, particularly those individuals most adversely affected, and not just evaluating these social arrangements from a global perspective.

Contractarians want a guarantee that individuals will be protected from the encroachment of the general good on their individual well-being. This idea is generally captured in the idea of rights. Rights may be seen as specially urgent claims of individuals as against both the collectivity and other individuals, claims that prevent others from

---

6. One place where we see these arguments worked out in some detail is in the policy debate over a minimum wage. Floor constraints on wages are shown to have adverse consequences on those whose labor value falls just below the fixed rate, and, so the argument goes, setting a floor on wages has the effect of making more people unemployed. See Richard A. Posner, *The Economic Analysis of Law* 3d ed. (Boston: Little, Brown, 1986), pp. 308–310, for a review of the arguments and evidence.

legitimately requiring that individuals fall below a reasonable condition of life. A rights claim is the mechanism through which the voice of an individual makes itself heard in a larger social forum. And a contractarian legal system will hear and act on these claims because individuals cannot be legitimately expected to tolerate any less. An economically inspired legal system will hear and act on those claims only if they serve some larger good.

A second difference between the economic and contractarian views is related to the first. Economists are concerned with legal rules as incentives. Law is a framework within which rational actors make decisions, so getting the incentives right for future decisions is, for an economist, the most important thing that the judge can do. But in this regard also the individual may be sacrificed for some larger social aim. The rule that gets the long-term incentives right may do injustice in the individual case. So, for example, the right economic result may dictate that the innocent middleman who sells defective raw materials to a savvy manufacturer be made to bear the loss because the middleman then will sue the manufacturer who sold her the good and was in the best position to prevent the loss in the first place. Shifting the loss to the middleman encourages the subsequent shifting of loss to the party who was in the best position to prevent it in the first place. And this would be the right economic result. But if the norms of trade did not encourage middlemen to inspect each lot independently and if the particular buyer were knowledgeable enough to have spotted the defects, then it is not at all clear that the right economic result in the global picture is the fair one in the individual case. A contractarian would want to say that judges need to reach the right results in the particular cases that come before them[7] and not simply treat each case as an object lesson in how to achieve efficiency.

Finally, the particular contractarian argument presented in this book forwards equality rather than efficiency as the guiding principle in the areas of legal doctrine under consideration.[8] This principle is clearly evident in the secrets examples themselves, where equality of access to information is a recurring theme. But the principle goes

7. This is not to say that contractarian judges should ignore the incentive effects of legal rules. Ideally, a contractarian judge would fashion rules that would both deal fairly with individual cases *and* create a set of social expectations that would minimize future harm. When there is a trade-off between the two, however, the contractarian judge should not make a negative example out of a particular plaintiff or defendant just to convey the right sort of social signal.

8. Of course, there may be cases in which both may be achieved simultaneously; but when there is a conflict, equality should trump efficiency.

deeper and further than this. A contractarian judge should *not* require solutions to legal problems that allow winners in lawsuits to win what they would not see as fair to lose if they had been on the other side. In the secrets examples, A should not be able to successfully demand that B disclose secrets that, if A were B, A would feel unjustly forced to disclose under similar circumstances. Equality of access to information may be the principle that explains the fairness of the judgment in the specific case of secrecy, but the deeper reason may be the connection of this specific account with a broader principle of symmetry.

A return to the logic of contractarianism can explain why symmetry matters so much. If we ask which rules people would agree to live under *if they might be anyone* in a particular society, then this requires, in the relevant thought experiments, that people try to imagine what it is like to be in other people's shoes. And when people imagine this, they ask what the best solution would be, given that they have to live their lives as individuals and not as some statistical average. We can easily see how people, confronted with that problem, would come to the view that it is unfair to require of others what one would be unwilling to do if the same request were made in return. The contractarian thought experiment limits acceptable options to those that are symmetric in this sense.

The normative argument that a legal system should embody a contractarian rather than an economic logic rests heavily on the premise that there should be a limit to what collectivities can demand of individuals. This might be interpreted to mean that contractarianism is hostile to the spirit of community. But, following the argument already made in discussing the social force of secrecy, there are two types of community to which one can aspire. One is the sort of voluntaristic community in which social ties are established by the choice of individuals and in which individuals are free[9] to alter their associations.[10] The other is the sort of all-encompassing community in which individual aspiration is subordinated to collective welfare. The main reasons for preferring the second to the first are generally thought to be that atomism and anomie come with the fragmentation of individual

---

9. Being free to alter one's associations does not mean that one is free of all obligations to those left behind who have come to rely on one's actions. See Jeremy Waldron, "When Justice Replaces Affection: The Need for Rights," *Harvard Journal of Law and Public Policy,* forthcoming.

10. A particularly attractive picture of how this sort of community might operate can be found in Georg Simmel, *The Web of Group Affiliations* (New York: Free Press, 1955).

uncoordinated choice and that the freedom to choose comes with the freedom to fail.

But in a contractarian picture of community, there is no reason to fear atomism and anomie. A contractarian society is *not* one in which individuals are isolated and faced with a myriad of anomie-producing possibilities from which they atomistically choose. And it is not a society in which individuals are free to fail so that they enter a sort of social free-fall. Rather, it is a society in which the members are routinely concerned with making social and political institutions acceptable to those who might be adversely affected by them. When individuals are guaranteed a floor beneath which they cannot fall, this requires affirmative action on the part of the community. It requires a certain empathy with others, the ability to know and feel what it would be like to be in someone else's position. It also requires that steps be taken to support those who might be in serious trouble. In such a setting community can flourish precisely because the members share a common vision of the value of individuals. And that would be a good community in which to live one's own particular, individual life.

A Note on History

Contractarianism as a normative theory of law may seem attractive to us now, but it may be puzzling to think that a contractarian spirit has driven American law for the past 200 years. While most of the evidence in this book is drawn from cases that still count as good law,[11] two centuries are represented in the materials. During this time, a complete transformation of the basic conditions of the economy, of the extent and scope of state action, of the available technologies, and of the very experience of daily life has made it quite unlikely that a single governing ideal of law would remain untouched. Certainly individual legal rules have changed in major ways, and it would be surprising if the basic principles underlying these rules had not changed also. But several arguments can be advanced to show that such stability, particularly the stability of *contractarian* ideas, might not be as strange as most would think.

First of all, the basis of American law, the Constitution, is explicitly a contractarian document, both in the way in which its process of adoption prefigures the consent that it promotes and in the way in

---

11. The conspicuous exception, of course, is the material on caveat emptor that deals explicitly with the change in doctrine during the nineteenth century and does not reflect current legal rules.

which its guarantees of rights establish limits on state action to which individuals would be unlikely to consent.[12] This is not to say that the Constitution's force has always been marshalled on behalf of the virtues of contractarianism: the second-class treatment of people not considered among those needed to consent (slaves, noncitizens, and women, for example) and the weakening of constitutional protection in times of crisis (Lincoln's suspension of crucial constitutional provisions during the Civil War, judicial approval of the incarceration of the Japanese during the Second World War, and public calls for mass violation of civil rights in times of public hysteria such as the McCarthy era, and, more recently, the AIDS epidemic, for example) indicate that the Constitution and the contractarian commitment that it represents have only limited force over some issues and at some times of political life. The presence of such a document does not magically make all violations of contractarian principles go away. But it may have a powerful influence on judicial reasoning in many areas that do not raise issues of community membership or touch concerns leading to public hysteria. The Constitution is, after all, the source of legal ideas that trumps other sources. Judges, being generalists called on to decide cases with all sorts of doctrinal bases and, as a result, being familiar with constitutional requirements, might plausibly consider the ultimate logic of American law—even in decisions that do not invoke the Constitution itself.

The contractarian underpinnings of American law may make courts receptive to arguments that point out when consent has failed. That losers in a judicial proceeding would not have consented to the rules that produced their losses is a serious charge to make against the operation of law in a consent-based regime. Here again, though, we should recall just what the claims for stability in this book have been. The claim is *not* that losers have always agreed to the fates that the courts have dealt them or that the *results* that emerge from courts are ones that those in a contractarian frame of mind would make their first choice. I have argued that the sorts of opinions that judges construct, the facts that they consider, and the way in which they marshall their arguments reflect a commitment to contractarian styles of argument.

---

12. The debt that the constitutional draftors owe to John Locke's *Second Treatise of Government* is extensive. See Edward S. Corwin, *The Higher Law Background of American Constitutional Law* (Ithaca, NY: Cornell University Press, 1955), pp. 61–89, for one discussion of this influence. Locke's contractarianism obviously differs from the conception presented here, but, in its basic insistence that government activity cannot be justified unless those affected consent to it, remains important in both conceptions.

Judges justify what they do with contractarian logic, whatever the results. And finding a consistency at the level of strategy of argument may be less surprising than finding consistency at the level of actual results—that is, who wins and who loses, over time—particularly when the type of consistency that is found has such a solid pedigree.

Second, contractarianism as a general strategy of argument does not by itself specify which *one* of a number of legal rules will be selected. As a method of political evaluation, it does not lead to single right answers either in the present or in the past. Contractarian arguments may take a variety of different forms, depending on how the contracting parties are conceived of, what they see as the problems that they are addressing, what sorts of knowledge they have, and what strategy of reasoning they adopt. Positive contractarianism makes a case in favor of a particular legal doctrine in a particular area, but there may be contractarian stories to tell about a number of different legal rules at any given moment. The way that a contractarian story goes depends crucially on features of existing social conditions and practices and on how much weight the current state of affairs has in the contractarian specification. Contractarianism, then, is not one deterministic argument about what history must have produced—and so finding *a* contractarian logic may be less difficult than finding the presence of a strategy of justification that had only one variant.

This does not mean that contractarianism produces a series of "just so" stories that can make sense of any historical development. Negative contractarian arguments rule *out* particular sorts of legal rules, and this is where we might expect contractarianism to have its strongest bite. For example, in the cases considered in this book, it would be surprising to find judges deciding that individuals with superior information could use that information to the detriment of someone else when the person about to be hurt had no way of knowing what harm would befall her. On an economic view, this rule might be permissible if the secret-keeper had ferreted out the valuable knowledge with much effort and would not have done so but for some expectation of a property right in the information. Contractarians would object, and they would not expect to find judges approving of this sort of legal argument at any time. Still, what counted as "no way of knowing" might itself vary over time, and so the surface-level legal rule, as well as which sorts of parties won and which sort of parties lost, might undergo some alteration to take this into account, even when the underlying contractarian principle remained the same.

Third, contractarian arguments may have more stability than one might imagine because they pertain to how the disputes are framed in the first place. Legal contractarians ask, What would people agree to if they were deciding on rules to govern this dispute, before the dispute arose? This question creates a thought experiment whose main function is to frame the problem in a particular way. This framing may create more stable patterns of perception than of result. In the caveat emptor cases, for example, the legal rules changed radically while the underlying principle stayed the same. What mattered continually throughout was that the party who had the superior information should bear the losses of trades gone awry. The comparative state of information was made important by asking to which rules the parties would *both* agree in advance—and, for reasons given at greater length in chapter 4, equal access to information would emerge as an important consideration. Because of the sorts of changes that occurred during the nineteenth century in the types of products being sold and because of the increased complexity of the organizations that sold them, the party generally having the superior information switched over the decades from the buyer to the seller. Saying that the party with superior information should suffer the loss from the sale of a defective good is not at all the same thing as saying that the specific rule of caveat emptor stayed the same. Of course, it did not. The results changed, if one looks only at who won and who lost. But the pattern of perception— that is, that the courts generally looked for inequalities in the parties' situations and remedied inequalities in information—remained the same.

Why would this be so? To answer this, we might look at the structural organization of courts, something that has changed remarkably little over the course of American history, at least in the sorts of settings that produce written decisions for analysis. The basic structure of the court is the triad.[13] A neutral judge, who would be disqualified if she has any special knowledge of the parties that would cause her to favor one or the other, hears arguments from both sides of a dispute and must decide between them. A logical thing for someone in such a position (who does not have anything personal to gain from one side winning) is to ask what the situation looks like from each side. This already gets the judge very close to the contractarian frame of mind. Is there any demand that one side is making that it would be unreasonable for the other side *not* to adopt? Here, reasonableness may very well be governed by the thought that if the defendant, say, were in the plaintiff's shoes, he would be making the same claim as the plaintiff is now

13. See Martin Shapiro, *Courts: A Comparative and Political Analysis* (Chicago: University of Chicago Press, 1981), for a more elaborate rendition of this view.

making and would feel outraged if the claim were not upheld. This sort of empathetic imagination, requiring the judge to see the case from both sides, frames the dispute and focuses attention on those features of each party's situation that, if faced by the other party, would produce justifiable complaint. The judge in this situation does exactly what a contractarian would do—that is, she *frames* the case in this sort of symmetric way. The contractarian logic that I have discussed in this book evinces this symmetry, with a focus on the equality of starting points for the two parties appearing before the court.

The stability of principles underlying the law is an empirical matter, and certainly more work tracing out particular areas of doctrine needs to be done before we can say that contractarianism actually does capture much of the spirit that we find behind changing legal rules. In the areas discussed here, much stability has been found. Some of this stability may come from the consonance between contractarian principles and the constitutional framework of American law. Some may come from the flexibility of contractarian arguments themselves. And some may come from the practice of judging, which reproduces in its structure the essential elements of the contractarian thought experiment.

Toward a Constitutional Jurisprudence

Having come all this way, how are we to think now about the law? Throughout this book, I have tried to develop a particular view of law and its role in social and political affairs and I have tried to rethink the boundaries of traditional jurisprudence. Let me make explicit what this process has done.

This book has proceeded from the conviction that law is a strategic research site for examining important aspects of a community's moral life. In law contemporary myths are made and stories about what *is* turn into stories of what *ought to be*. Law represents in a stylized way the concerns, the social organization, the aspirations, the political life of a particular society in a particular place and time. This is not to say that the law either perfectly reflects an ideal moral order or hides some secret wisdom. It is clearly the product of human effort, often under stress in tough times.

But just as looking at how men and women dress and act when they are trying to look their best tells us something important about ideals of beauty, so looking at legal doctrine when judges pretty it up for public display tells us something important about ideals of justice. Legal decisions probably reflect how courts actually work about as accurately as seeing people at fancy dress parties reflects how they appear in daily life. Published legal opinions are not ethnographic data about the decision-making process; instead, they embody the aspirations of legal institutions, showing us what judges do when they want to get things right for a special occasion. And there is no reason why social scientists should take legal decisions to be unimportant because they have this attenuated relation to the "real" decision-making process. If the question that one is asking is what ideals the law embodies, then one should look at those settings most likely to provide the ideal point of view. Published legal opinions do just that.

This is not to say that law invariably mirrors a consensus as to what justice is in a particular culture. Certainly that claim is naive. Making that claim implies that there is a unitary ideal of justice that is widely shared, internally consistent, and uncontroversial. Moreover, such a claim also assumes that law possesses a special neutrality that makes it either the unbiased arbiter of competing social interests or a reflection of an unproblematic consensus.

Both of these implications can be contested easily on empirical grounds, as those working in the Critical Legal Studies movement recently have been demonstrating[14] and as Marxists long have contended.[15] These scholars believe that the law is not neutral, that it tends to favor the interests of dominant social groups over those of less privileged groups. In this view there is no consensus on basic social norms.

Even if this is true, however, it does not destroy the case for law as a decent reflection of which ideals of justice exist, however partially or problematically. Even in these skeptical traditions there are some good reasons why studying the justifications in law tells us about the values that are present in a given culture, even if those values are not universally shared. For example, law operates more efficiently than threatened force as a mechanism for social control precisely because it develops and manages to maintain at least the surface plausibility that

14. See, for example, David Kairys, ed., *The Politics of Law: A Progressive Critique* (New York: Pantheon, 1982); James B. Atleson, *Values and Assumptions in American Labor Law* (Amherst: University of Massachusetts Press, 1983); Morton Horwitz, *The Transformation of American Law 1780–1860* (Cambridge, MA: Harvard University Press, 1977); Duncan Kennedy, "The Structure of Blackstone's *Commentaries*," *Buffalo Law Review* 28: 205–256 (1979); and Karl Klare, "The Judicial Deradicalization of the Wagner Act and the Origins of Modern Legal Consciousness 1937–1941," *Minnesota Law Review* 62: 265–339 (1978).

15. See Hugh Collins, *Marxism and Law* (Oxford: Oxford University Press, 1984) for a coherent and sympathetic introduction to these arguments.

the deck is not stacked against the disadvantaged. By accepting the rule of law, formal equality, and due process, dominant groups exchange limits on their abilities to use their power and privilege arbitrarily against the less advantaged for perceived legitimacy of the legal system. Law, as a result, does not automatically mirror the interests of dominant groups. The cultivation of legitimacy requires encouragement of the belief that the law is fair. And, as E. P. Thompson discovered,[16] more often than one might imagine this means *actually being* evenhanded. One of the ways in which this evenhandedness is accomplished is through using the values shared by the losers in particular cases to legitimate the decision made. The legal system may produce consistent groups of winners and losers, but that would not necessarily mean that the values of the losers are not reflected in the explanations that courts give.[17] If one focuses on explanations rather than on outcomes, as I have done in the present book, one may find values shared even by those who have lost.

This only explains how we might expect a positive fit between a population's ideals of justice and the ideals of justice revealed in law. It does not explain why we might expect a normative theory of justice to emerge from the law as we find it. For this, we might again turn to Rawls, whose method of reflective equilibrium provides a model for how this sort of process works.[18] One starts with moral intuitions and uncovers principles of justice by probing beneath these intuitions to find their underlying structure. But these deeper principles may contradict a specific intuition, or the intuitions may seem less correct once their deeper logic is exposed. A person can take a critical stance toward her intuitions once she has a set of principles against which to judge them, and she may also modify the principles if particular intuitions seem too important to abandon.

This can be done in the context of law by examining specific legal decisions, probing beneath them to find their deeper structure and then

16. E. P. Thompson, *Whigs and Hunters: The Origin of the Black Act* (New York: Pantheon, 1975).

17. Just such a strategy of judicial justification is proposed in Guido Calabresi, *Ideals, Briefs, Attitudes and the Law* (Syracuse, NY: Syracuse University Press, 1985). He notes how important it is for judges to appeal to the values of those against whom they are ruling, (so as not to alienate them from the legal system altogether) and explains how the Supreme Court's decision in the abortion case serves as a negative example. By failing to include consideration of the values of those who believe in a right to life, the Court, Calabresi contends, created a serious backlash against its own legitimacy.

18. John Rawls, *A Theory of Justice* (Cambridge, MA: Harvard University Press, 1971) pp. 48–51.

using the principles that emerge from such probing to criticize particular decisions on normative grounds. In doing this I have tried to undermine the distinction between positive and normative that has characterized much of the empirically based literature on law. Certainly our moral sense is not divorced from facts about the world, and how we see facts is not a wholly separate enterprise from having a moral point of view. The facts that courts see are framed by the values being brought to bear on a problem. In choosing among descriptions, judges reveal the values being used. With that premise in mind, I have used an analysis of the facts that judges highlight to reveal which values are implicit in the law.

How might this sort of analysis be characterized? I have called this method constitutional jurisprudence. Constitutional jurisprudence is a term customarily reserved for analyzing a particular 200-year-old document and its amendments, for examining doctrine and its interpretation, for probing the meaning of the clauses in a specific, written text. But the constitutional point of view extends beyond the boundaries of a specific set of words on paper. It is a way of thinking about political and moral and social life in general.[19]

A constitutional point of view entails the belief that positive and normative thinking are not separable. This is not the same thing as saying that there is not a useful difference between a description and an evaluation. But descriptions necessarily require principles of importance and relevance to determine what to leave out and what to put in. These principles of importance and relevance imply particular normative standards. Similarly, evaluations proceed from particular constituted descriptions. The model of the mutual construction of rules and facts shows how inseparable normative and positive questions are. It does not follow that description and evaluation are the same thing, however. One can make efforts to leave descriptions open to multiple evaluations, and one can reach the same evaluation from multiple descriptions. There must be some connection between the two, although they do not have to merge.

This point of view may be said to be "constitutional" because constitutions reveal this interpenetration of fact and value. The American Constitution, for example, both creates a particular political structure and provides principles for its ongoing evaluation and correction. The principles are embedded in the way in which the political structure is designed, just as the political structure makes possible the

---

19. I am indebted to William F. Harris II for first suggesting this line of thought.

realization of particular values. For example, the separation of powers reveals a hostility to imperial domination, and this value can be used to interpret what separation of powers itself requires. The procedures that give meaning to the term "due process" reveal the value of non-arbitrariness, and this term's deeper meaning can be used to evaluate when a process is fair. To separate the positive and normative aspects of a constitution would be an impossible operation; and such an attempt would undermine its meaning in serious ways.

The jurisprudence developed in this book is constitutional in another sense. Constitutions are texts, dialogues between words and the world. And they come with all of the interpretive dilemmas that construction implies. Framing the world in words creates a multiplicity of meanings. Debates over the meaning of texts are never-ending. There are no single right answers, although (as the earlier discussion of negative contractarianism has indicated) there may be wrong answers. As we struggle to interpret the texts of our culture, we must make meaning of meaning. The texts that we create are part of this process of cultural understanding. If we see politics and social life not as behavior that must be explained but as attempts at the construction of meaning that must be interpreted, we will have adopted a constitutional point of view. A commitment to a constitutional jurisprudence means taking the interpretive turn and being fully self-conscious that as observers of the social world we also participate in its construction.

APPENDIX

Studying the Common Law: An Introduction for Social Scientists

THIS APPENDIX DESCRIBES THE CHARACTERISTICS of the common law as a research site and the method used to locate cases for analysis.

The Common Law as a Research Site

The common law has several distinct advantages as a research site for the sort of problem tackled in this book. Before discussing those advantages, it might be helpful to review some of the critical properties of the common law that make it different from either statutory interpretation or constitutional law.

Common law is judge-made law. It gets its authority not from specific acts of legislatures or from any specific written document. Instead, it is built up from the slow accumulation of cases decided by judges over many years. The guiding principle of common-law decision making—to decide like cases alike—may appear to be an enormous constraint working against any change or flexibility in the common law, but in fact common law is highly flexible.[1] The flexibility in the common law comes from the enormous discretion that judges have in perceiving new situations as similar to or different from already settled disputes. When judges are presented with a new case, they must first decide what other past case or set of cases bears the most resemblance to the present case. Since rarely are two cases ever exactly alike, judges almost always have some flexibility in describing the present dispute and highlighting the features that make it like the case that the judge is going to use as a model.

---

1. See Edward Levi, *An Introduction to Legal Reasoning* (Chicago: University of Chicago Press, 1949); and Guido Calabresi, *A Common Law for an Age of Statutes* (Cambridge, MA: Harvard University Press, 1982).

When one studies the common law, one gets a sense of what Levi has called a moving classification system.[2] The terms and the categories shift over time so that, while at each moment the law appears not to change very much, the accumulation of small changes over time is quite substantial. Studying the common law not only provides some sense of the flexibility of rules but also allows one to see shifts in institutional perception. What count as the rules and what count as similar situations both change over time. Judges in common-law cases stress the facts that enable them to apply the rule that they think fits the case, and the rule that appears to fit depends on the choice of facts in each case. This is where the mutual construction of facts and rules is most evident.

This feature of common law provides a good reason for selecting only common-law cases for the present study. Common-law cases rest heavily on their facts. To see how rules are applied to facts, we should look to the common law because no other area of law matches facts and rules as consciously as does the common law. Because judges have to reason from case to case without the guidance of a specific legal text that provides organizing categories and because they move from case to case by reasoning from the facts of prior cases to the facts of the present case, we can acquire quite a lot of information about the precise way in which rules and facts are connected. The legitimacy of common-law decisions rests on the abilities of judges to make persuasive analogies, and analogies provide detailed information about the way in which rules apply to facts, when there is generally both the availability of multiple rules to call on and the possibility of different emphases in judges' choices of facts. In a very real sense, common-law cases are decided when the choice of relevant facts is made.

Another reason for studying the common law is that common law (particularly torts and contracts, which provide the great bulk of cases cited in the present study) is the great residual area of law. Where legislatures have not spoken and where the Constitution does not reach, the common law flourishes. This means several things. First, common law deals with very basic and general obligations that people owe each other, obligations that are diffuse and applicable to all. Refraining from harming others, whether intentionally or carelessly, and keeping agreements are examples of general obligations that common law enforces. This makes common law a good place to study if one is going to see rules that have less specialized constituencies.

2. Levi, pp. 3–4.

Second, common-law cases are *relatively* uncontroversial. If special interest groups perceive themselves to be on the short end of the legal stick in a common-law area and if those groups are capable of organizing to pressure the legislature for action on the subject, then legislatures may pass a statute to change the old common-law rule. Even those who stand to benefit from a common-law rule may pressure for legislative action when the effect of that action would be to make legal outcomes and their associated costs more predictable.[3] Those areas that remain in the common law are either those areas where interest groups find it hard to organize or where it is difficult to perceive identifiable winners and losers.[4] If we want to study an area of law as free as possible from the overt play of special interests, then we should look to the common law because it presents relatively few opportunities for judges to openly benefit some groups at the expense of others.

Common law is also overwhelmingly private law. The state does not enter as a party, at least not in its unique capacity as a political authority. States can use justifications for their actions that are not available to other actors. For example, in the case of secrecy, the justification of national security is simply not a credible claim for other actors. Since the state can make special claims, I have excluded cases involving the state from my analysis, in order to better focus on claims that private individuals can make against each other. The state presents a special case and deserves special and separate treatment.

Prior work in the economic analysis of law provides a final reason for the present study's focus on common-law cases. The economic analysis of law is the primary approach that has been used by others to explain the cases under consideration here. Over the range of common-law cases, the economists claim that theirs is a positive and not simply a normative theory of law. They claim that we might expect the common law to be efficient because inefficient rules will be litigated over and over until they strike the proper balance.[5] Since I wanted to determine whether the economic analysis of law worked as a positive theory of these cases, it made sense to examine that area of law

3. Lawrence Friedman and Jack Ladinsky, "Social Change and the Law of Industrial Accidents," *Columbia Law Review* 67: 50–82 (1969).

4. Richard Epstein, "The Social Consequences of Common Law Rules," *Harvard Law Review* 95: 1717–1751 (1982).

5. Paul Rubin, "Why is the Common Law Efficient?" *Journal of Legal Studies* 6: 51–64 (1977); R. P. Terrebonne, "A Strictly Evolutionary Model of the Common Law," *Journal of Legal Studies* 10: 397–401 (1981); and John C. Goodman, "An Economic Theory of the Evolution of the Common Law," *Journal of Legal Studies* 7: 393–406 (1978).

where the economists claim that their analysis is strongest. This gives the economists their best shot.

For all of these reasons, then, common-law cases were chosen as the subject of study. I studied justifications for secrecy because these justifications appeared in common-law cases in the areas of fraud, privacy, trade secrets, and implied warranties. These are the areas of common law that deal with the legitimacy of secrets at center stage. In addition, these areas feature disputes over the general obligations that private individuals owe each other. Other common-law areas, such as privileged communication, tend to deal overwhelmingly with special situations, such as when one may refuse to reveal in a courtroom a communication with someone else. Fraud, privacy, trade-secret, and implied-warranty cases cover general obligations on the part of individual private actors over a wide range of social settings.

Finding Cases

Each one of these areas of law contains more cases than anyone can reasonably analyze in a single work. Moreover, many of the cases add nothing new to the basic rules present in a representative subsample. Clearly, this problem called for some sort of sampling procedure if the set of cases to be analyzed were to be really representative of legal decisions in each of these areas.

In this book, I used two distinct methods for finding cases. The first method captured a representative sample of cases that still count as good law in each of three areas: fraud, privacy, and trade secrets. Although cases were drawn from a wide variety of moments in American history, they shared the feature that they still supported the rule now in effect in the relevant jurisdiction. The second method, used in the implied-warranty cases, was designed to capture the movement over time in that particular area of law in one jurisdiction, to get a clear and detailed view of the way in which the law had evolved. I will discuss each of these methods separately.

Sampling Legal Opinions

Law appears at first glance to be a sampling theorist's paradise. The *Decennial Digests* lists, by topic and subtopic, every reported case decided in every jurisdiction in the country. It is not hard to get a census of cases. In addition, computerized legal research services such as *Lexis* and *Westlaw* can search for all the cases that present select phrases. Finding all the cases is not difficult.

But law does present some sampling difficulties. Technically, because of the role of stare decisis, cases within each jurisdiction are not independent of each other. Cases cite each other and are constrained by each other. A rule used in one case is likely to reappear in another, similar case within the same jurisdiction or even in another area. Because cases are not independent, one might expect some clustering effects in any random sample.

More importantly, a strict random sample of cases will show which sorts of disputes present themselves to the courts most frequently, but it will not necessarily reveal a representative sample of rules of law. Some rules are litigated far more than others, and underlitigated rules will tend not to appear in a sample that in essence weights rules by the number of cases that bear on them. Random sampling is simply not appropriate in a legal setting.

What we need instead is some way of sampling by rules, rather by than cases. This is a more complicated puzzle, since there is no census of cases by legal rules. Instead, I have developed an alternative method that I believe accomplishes the same task. American law is summarized in two large legal encyclopedias, *American Jurisprudence 2d* and *Corpus Juris Secundum*. Each of these encyclopedias is organized by legal topic, and virtually every sentence contains a legal rule. Roughly half to three-quarters of each page contains citations to cases, citations that are attached at a minimum to every sentence and sometimes to individual words. These citations list leading cases, in a number of jurisdictions, that bear on the rule enunciated in the text of the article. Although the organizations of *American Jurisprudence 2d* and *Corpus Juris Secundum* are somewhat different, there is substantial overlap in the topics that they cover. For the three areas under consideration, I included in my sample all cases cited by *both* legal encyclopedias. This process gave me at least one hundred cases in each area.

I then read and briefed each of these cases. As it turns out, some of them (fortunately rather few) were not useful for the present study, since, although they may have mentioned my topics in passing, they were not decided on those grounds. For example, in determining whether a secret constituted fraud, the court may have had before it a defendant who both kept a secret and lied. Although the court may have commented on the existence of a secret, the case was ultimately decided on the issue of whether the defendant had lied. Regarding justifications for secrecy, nothing could be gained from these decisions, so they were later excluded from the analysis.

In addition to this base sample, I added cases from other sources. In reading the secondary literature in each of these areas, I became aware that certain cases seemed to reappear or play key roles in others' theories of the cases. Although most of the time these cases were ones that I had encountered in the base sample, occasionally they were new. I added these cases cited frequently in the secondary literature or in casebooks, on the theory that these were the cases that practicing lawyers would be most likely to know. Any theory that did not consider the cases that would most readily come to lawyers' minds would be considered implausible by lawyers not accustomed to sampling as a method of gathering data.

Once the theory began to take shape, I used two methods to check my explanations against the cases. I first went to the *Decennial Digests*. This is a series of reference books that publishes one-paragraph or often one-sentence summaries of the relevance of a particular case to each point of law. Organized by key numbers that identify legal topics, the digests offer brief accounts of each case on that point of law. These very brief summaries have their disadvantages, the main one being that one cannot always get a very good sense of the situation presented by the case. Instead, one often gets brief platitudes—which may or may not be the rule of the case—rather than descriptions of facts. In my case, it would have been preferable to have brief summaries of the facts, but the digests do not always provide this. Still, it is often possible to tell enough from the digest descriptions to know whether the case is likely to present a problem for the theory. When a case seemed to present such a problem, I would pull the case, add it to the sample, brief it, and use it to modify the theory.

The second method that I used to check my findings involved *Lexis*. Using a series of important key words and phrases that had emerged from my earlier reading of cases, I asked *Lexis* to search for all the cases presenting the same configuration of words. *Lexis* responded by printing out from each relevant opinion fifty words on either side of the target words. These brief excerpts were generally enough to see the case's relevance for my study. I added very few cases to the sample in this way, for two reasons: First, by the time that I got access to *Lexis,* I already had used all of the other methods described and had located just about everything that was important. *Lexis* turned up little that I had not already found. Second, finding just the right key words was extraordinarily difficult in this area, since situations were judged relevant to the study if they presented structural rather than linguistic similarities. Not all cases that present privacy claims involved withholding private information, and not all cases involving private information used those words to describe it. Since *Lexis* is very literal, it works much better for some legal problems than for others. When the cases that one is looking for always possess certain linguistic markers, *Lexis* is extraordinarily good at finding them; when the terminology has not settled down into a pattern, however, *Lexis* is of very limited usefulness. Unfortunately, my study was one of the latter variety.

Given my theory of interpretation—that is, that rules and facts mutually construct each other—I wanted to understand which facts were important in deciding each of these cases. I therefore undertook to code these facts for quantitative analysis. I very quickly learned that this was an almost impossible task. To code the cases one has to know in advance what is likely to matter. Since the first task in this study was to discover what facts made a difference, constructing coding categories was extraordinarily difficult.

In addition, there was another problem with coding the very specific facts characteristic of common-law cases: they are, almost by definition, quirky. If an identical case has presented itself to the courts before and a ruling already has been made, cases that all the parties will agree are similar will be settled out of court; they simply do not appear in the reporters. Cases that are litigated at the appellate-court level are almost always cases where the facts are not precisely like those in other cases. If law is, as Levi claims, a moving classification system, then we will not find a set of categories in the opinions themselves that lies still long enough for a reasonable number of cases to be coded. What I discovered was an enormous missing-data problem. Facts that mattered a great deal in one case were not even present in another; and this other case was decided on other grounds. These other grounds were not present in the first case. There were almost no variables that reliably could be coded for the majority of the cases, at least not until it was clear what the latent categories were. By the time that I figured out the latent categories that have been identified as legally relevant facts, I already knew how the courts had decided and it no longer seemed useful to code the cases.

Trends in Legal Doctrine

In the chapter on caveat emptor and implied-warranty cases, the methodology used was quite different. First, I examined only cases from New York State. New York was chosen as the site of this study for three reasons. First, the New York courts were the first to introduce the concept of caveat emptor into American law. In some senses, then, the debate was begun on their terms. In addition, New York grasped the caveat emptor doctrine more tenaciously than did other states, making it the best place to see the rule in its most severe application.

Finally, New York simply had more commercial cases than did other states.

To find the cases for this study, I used an inefficient but effective method. Starting with the earliest reported cases in 1796 and continuing until 1900, I simply went through, volume by volume, every reporter that reported cases decided by New York's highest courts. Before 1848, the Supreme Court of Judicature was in practice New York's highest court (although occasional cases were appealed to the New York State Senate, sitting as the Court for the Correction of Errors). After 1848, the Court of Appeals served as the state's highest court (with a short interlude in the early 1870s when the temporary Commission of Appeals was set up to handle the overload). Each reporter covering these courts was examined to determine whether the courts had encountered a case that involved the sale of an allegedly defective product. The study only covers the sale of defective chattels and does not touch on the companion problems of the sale of defective real property or of unreliable stocks and bonds. Indexes for each volume of each reporter helped in locating the cases, although, since the terminology and ways of classifying cases changed so much over the century, I had to look through the entire index each time. From the abstracts of cases listed in these indexes, covering a 104-year period, I was able to locate eighty-one cases involving the sale of an allegedly defective good. The first case on the subject was decided in 1804, and a steady trickle of cases occurred throughout the century.

In many ways, the approach to reading and analyzing cases that is used in this book is the approach suggested by Karl Llewellyn.[6] Llewellyn is ever mindful that not just rules but *facts* press upon judges, that judges do not do law in the abstract, but rather in the context of a specific case before them, and that one cannot hope to understand the law without knowing how the facts were seen by the judge. All of Llewellyn's urgings call attention to the facts of disputes—and to the way in which the rules and facts are woven together. The cases sampled for this book were analyzed to determine the legally relevant facts on which the decisions rested.

6. Karl Llewellyn, *The Bramble Bush* (New York: Oceana Press, 1930) and *The Common Law Tradition: Deciding Appeals* (Boston: Little, Brown, 1960).

References

Ackerman, Bruce. *Reconstructing American Law*. Cambridge, MA: Harvard University Press, 1983.

Akerlof, George. "The Market for Lemons: Quality Uncertainty and the Market Mechanism." *Quarterly Journal of Economics* 84 (1970): 488–500.

American Jurisprudence 2d, 1968, s.v. "Fraud."

American Law Institute, *Restatement (Second) of Contracts,* 3 vols. St. Paul: American Law Institute Publishers, 1979.

American Law Institute, *Restatement (Second) of Torts,* 3 vols. St. Paul: American Law Institute Publishers, 1977.

Anscombe, G. E. M. *Intentions,* 2d ed. Ithaca, NY: Cornell University Press, 1976.

Aquinas, St. Thomas. *Summa Theologica.* New York: Benziger, 1947.

Atleson, James B. *Values and Assumptions in American Labor Law.* Amherst: University of Massachusetts Press, 1983.

Beardsley, Elizabeth L. "Privacy: Autonomy and Selective Disclosure." Pp. 56–70 in *NOMOS XIII: Privacy.* Edited by J. Roland Pennock and John W. Chapman. New York: Atherton, 1971.

Becker, Gary. *The Economics of Discrimination,* 2d ed. Chicago: University of Chicago Press, 1971.

Bennett, Lance, and Feldman, Martha. *Reconstructing Reality in the Courtroom.* New Brunswick, NJ: Rutgers University Press, 1981.

Bensman, Joseph, and Lilienfeld, Robert. *Between Public and Private: Lost Boundaries of the Self.* New York: Free Press, 1978.

Bloustein, Edward. *Individual and Group Privacy.* New Brunswick, NJ: Transaction Books, 1978.

Bloustein, Edward. "Privacy as an Aspect of Human Dignity: An Answer to Dean Prosser." *New York University of Law Review* 39 (1964): 962–1007.

Bohannan, Paul. "The Differing Realms of the Law." *American Anthropologist* 67 (1965): 33–42.

Bok, Sissela. *Lying: Moral Choice in Public and Private Life.* New York: Pantheon, 1978.

Bok, Sissela. *Secrets: On the Ethics of Concealment and Revelation*. New York: Pantheon, 1982.

Bower, George Spencer. *The Law Relating to Actionable Nondisclosure and Other Breaches of Duty in Relations of Confidence and Influence*. London: Butterworth, 1915.

Breiman, Leo. "Stopping Rule Problems." Pp. 108–122 in *Applied Combinatorial Mathematics*. Edited by Edwin F. Beckenbach. New York: Wiley, 1964.

Calabresi, Guido. *A Common Law for an Age of Statutes*. Cambridge, MA: Harvard University Press, 1982.

Calabresi, Guido. *Ideals, Beliefs, Attitudes and the Law*. Syracuse, NY: Syracuse University Press, 1985.

Chow, Y. S.; Robbins, H.; and Siegmund, D. *Great Expectations: The Theory of Optimal Stopping*. New York: Houghton-Mifflin, 1971.

Coase, Ronald. "The Problem of Social Cost." *Journal of Law and Economics* 3 (1960): 1–44.

Coleman, James S. *Power and the Structure of Society*. New York: Norton, 1974.

Coleman, James S. *The Asymmetric Society*. Syracuse, NY: Syracuse University Press, 1982.

Coleman, Jules. "Efficiency, Utility and Wealth Maximization." Hofstra Law Review 8 (1980): 509–551.

Collins, Hugh. *Marxism and Law*. Oxford: Oxford University Press, 1984.

Cooley, Thomas McIntyre. *A Treatise on the Law of Torts or the Wrongs Which Arise Independent of Contract*. Chicago: Callahan, 1888.

Corwin, Edward S. *The Higher Law Background of American Constitutional Law*. Ithaca, NY: Cornell University Press, 1955.

Coser, Rose Laub. "Insulation from Observability and Types of Social Conformity." *American Sociological Review* 26 (1961): 28–39.

Cover, Robert. "Foreword: Nomos and Narrative." *Harvard Law Review* 97 (1984): 4–68.

Darby, Michael, and Karni, Edi. "Free Competition and the Optimal Amount of Fraud." *Journal of Law and Economics* 13 (1973): 67–88.

Diamond, Stanley. "The Rule of Law versus the Order of Custom." *Social Research* 38 (1973): 42–72.

Dworkin, Ronald. "How Law Is Like Literature." Pp. 146–166 in *A Matter of Principle*. Cambridge, MA: Harvard University Press, 1985.

Dworkin, Ronald. *Law's Empire*. Cambridge, MA: Harvard University Press, 1986.

Ellis, Ridsdale. *Trade Secrets*. New York: Baker, Voorhis, 1953.

Elster, Jon. "Sour Grapes." Pp. 109–140 in *Sour Grapes: Studies in the Subversion of Rationality*. Cambridge: Cambridge University Press, 1983.

Epstein, Richard. "The Social Consequences of Common Law Rules." *Harvard Law Review* 95 (1982): 1717–1751.

Evans-Pritchard, E. E. *The Nuer*. Oxford: Oxford University Press, 1940.

Fallers, Lloyd. *Law Without Precedent*. Chicago: University of Chicago Press, 1969.

Finnis, John. *Natural Law and Natural Rights*. Oxford: Oxford University Press, 1980.

Fish, Stanley. *Is There a Text in This Class?* Cambridge, MA: Harvard University Press, 1980.

Fiss, Owen. "Objectivity and Interpretation." *Stanford Law Review* 34 (1982): 739–763.

Franklin, Marc A. "Constitutional Problems in Privacy Protection: Legal Inhibitions on Reporting of Fact." *Stanford Law Review* 16 (1963): 107–148.

Fried, Charles. "Privacy." *Yale Law Journal* 77 (1968): 475–493.

Friedman, Lawrence, and Ladinsky, Jack. "Social Change and the Law of Industrial Accidents." *Columbia Law Review* 67 (1969): 50–82.

Friedman, Milton. "The Methodology of Positive Economics." Pp. 3–34 in *Essays in Positive Economics*. Chicago: University of Chicago Press, 1953.

Frolich, Norman; Oppenheimer, Joe A.; and Eavey, Cheryl L. "Laboratory Results on Rawls's Distributive Justice." *British Journal of Political Science* 17 (1987): 1–22.

Frolich, Norman; Oppenheimer, Joe A.; and Eavey, Cheryl L. "Choice of Principles of Distributive Justice in Experimental Groups." *American Journal of Political Science* 31 (1987): 606–636.

Garfinkel, Harold. *Studies in Ethnomethology*. New York: Prentice-Hall, 1969.

Geertz, Clifford. "Thick Description." Pp. 3–30 in *The Interpretation of Cultures*. New York: Basic Books, 1973.

Geertz, Clifford. "Local Knowledge: Fact and Law in Comparative Perspective." Pp. 167–234 in *Local Knowledge: Further Essays in Interpretive Anthropology,* New York: Basic Books, 1983.

Georgia Law Review, Spring 1978. Symposium on Posner's Theory of Privacy.

Goffman, Erving. *Strategic Interaction*. Philadelphia: University of Pennsylvania Press, 1969.

Goffman, Erving. *The Presentation of Self in Everyday Life*. Garden City, NY: Anchor Books, 1959.

Goldfarb, William B. "Fraud and Nondisclosure in the Vendor-Purchaser Relation." *Western Reserve Law Review* 8 (1956): 5–44.

Goodhart, A. L. "The *Ratio Decidendi* of a Case." *Modern Law Review* 22 (1959): 117–124.

Goodhart, Arthur L. "On Finding the *Ratio Decidendi* of a Case." *Yale Law Journal* 40 (1930): 161–183.

Goodman, John C. "An Economic Theory of the Evolution of the Common Law." *Journal of Legal Studies* 7 (1978): 393–406.

Hahn, Frank, and Hollis, Martin. *Philosophy and Economic Theory*. Oxford: Oxford University Press, 1979.

Hamilton, Walton H. "The Ancient Maxim *Caveat Emptor.*" *Yale Law Journal* 40 (1931): 1113–1187.

Hardin, Russell. *Collective Action.* Baltimore: Johns Hopkins Press, 1982.

Hare, R. M. *Freedom and Reason.* Oxford: Oxford University Press, 1963.

Harnett, Bertram. "The Doctrine of Concealment: A Remnant in the Law of Insurance." *Law and Contemporary Problems* 15 (1950): 391–414.

Harsanyi, John C. "Morality and the Theory of Rational Behaviour." Pp. 39–62 in *Utilitarianism and Beyond.* Edited by Amartya Sen and Bernard Williams. Cambridge: Cambridge University Press, 1982.

Hart, H. L. A. *The Concept of Law.* Oxford: Oxford University Press, 1961.

Hayek, Friedrich A. "The Uses of Knowledge in Society." *American Economic Review* 35 (1945): 519–530.

Heimer, Carol A. *Reactive Risk and Rational Action.* Berkeley: University of California Press, 1985.

Herzog, Don. *Without Foundations.* Ithaca, NY: Cornell University Press, 1985.

Hirsch, E. D. *Validity in Interpretation.* New Haven, CT: Yale University Press, 1967.

Hirschleifer, Jack. "Where Are We Now in the Theory of Information?" *American Economic Review* 63 (1973): 31–39.

Hoebel, E. Adamson. *The Law of Primitive Man: A Study in Comparative Dynamics.* Cambridge, MA: Harvard University Press, 1954.

Holmes, Eric M. "A Contextual Study of Commercial Good Faith: Good-Faith Disclosure in Contract Formation." *University of Pittsburgh Law Review* 39 (1978): 381–452.

Holmes, Oliver Wendell. *The Common Law.* Boston: Little, Brown, 1881.

Horwitz, Morton. *The Transformation of American Law 1780–1860.* Cambridge, MA: Harvard University Press, 1977.

Hurst, Willard. *Law and the Conditions of Freedom.* Madison: University of Wisconsin Press, 1960.

James, William. *Pragmatism: A New Name for Some Old Ways of Thinking* and *The Meaning of Truth: A Sequel to Pragmatism.* Cambridge, MA: Harvard University Press, 1975.

Jourard, Sidney M. "Some Psychological Aspects of Privacy." *Law and Contemporary Problems* 31 (1966): 307–318.

Journal of Legal Studies, December 1980. Symposium on Privacy.

Kairys, David, ed., *The Politics of Law: A Progressive Critique.* New York: Pantheon, 1982.

Kalven, Harry, Jr. "Privacy in Tort Law—Were Warren and Brandeis Wrong?" *Law and Contemporary Problems* 31 (1966): 326–341.

Kanter, Rosabeth Moss. *Commitment and Community.* Cambridge, MA: Harvard University Press, 1972.

Keeton, W. Page. "Fraud—Concealment and Nondisclosure." *Texas Law Review* 15 (1936): 1–40.

Kennedy, Duncan. "The Structure of Blackstone's *Commentaries.*" *Buffalo Law Review* 28 (1979): 205–256.

Kerr, W. W. *W. W. Kerr on the Law of Fraud and Mistake,* 7th ed. Revised by Denis Lane McDonnell and John George Monroe. London: Sweet and Maxwell, 1952.

Kitch, Edmund W. "The Law and Economics of Rights in Valuable Information." *Journal of Law and Economics* 9 (1980): 683–723.

Klare, Karl. "The Judicial Deradicalization of the Wagner Act and the Origins of Modern Legal Consciousness 1937–1941." *Minnesota Law Review* 62 (1978): 265–339.

Knapp, Steven, and Michaels, Walter Benn. "Against Theory." Pp. 11–30 in *Against Theory: Literary Studies and the New Pragmatism.* Edited by William J. T. Mitchell. Chicago: University of Chicago Press, 1985.

Knight, Frank. *Risk, Uncertainty and Profit.* Chicago: University of Chicago Press, 1971.

Kronman, Anthony. "Mistake, Disclosure, Information and the Law of Contracts." *Journal of Legal Studies* 7 (1978): 1–34.

Labor Relations Reporter, Fair Employment Practices Manual. New York: Bureau of National Affairs, Looseleaf Service.

Law Commission. *Breach of Confidence.* Working paper no. 58. London: Her Majesty's Stationery Office, 1974.

Levi, Edward. *An Introduction to Legal Reasoning.* Chicago: University of Chicago Press, 1949.

Llewellyn, Karl N. "On Warranty, Quality and Society." *Columbia Law Review* 36 (1936): 699–744.

Llewellyn, Karl. "On Warranty, Quality and Society: II." *Columbia Law Review* 37 (1937): 341–409.

Llewellyn, Karl N. *The Bramble Bush.* New York: Oceana, 1930.

Llewellyn, Karl. *The Common Law Tradition: Deciding Appeals.* Boston: Little, Brown, 1960.

Loftus, Elizabeth. *Eyewitness Testimony.* Cambridge, MA: Harvard University Press, 1979.

Luce, R. Duncan, and Raiffa, Howard. *Games and Decisions.* New York: Wiley, 1957.

Mackie, J. L. *Ethics: Inventing Right and Wrong.* New York: Penguin, 1977.

Malinowski, Bronislaw. *Crime and Custom in Savage Society.* London: Routledge and Kegan Paul, 1926.

Meikeljohn, Alexander. *Political Freedom.* New York: Harper, 1960.

Merton, Robert K. *Social Theory and Social Structure.* New York: Free Press, 1968.

Merton, Robert K., and Barber, Elinor. "Sociological Ambivalence." Pp. 3–31 in *Sociological Ambivalence.* By Robert K. Merton. New York: Free Press, 1975.

Miller, Arthur R. *The Assault on Privacy: Computers, Data Banks, and Dossiers.* Ann Arbor: University of Michigan Press, 1971.

Miller, George. "The Magic Number Seven Plus or Minus Two." *Psychological Review* 63 (1956): 81–97.

Mitchell, William J. T., ed. *Against Theory: Literary Studies and the New Pragmatism.* Chicago: University of Chicago Press, 1985.

Montrose, J. L. "The *Ratio Decidendi* of a Case." *Modern Law Review* 20 (1957): 587–595.

Montrose, J. L. "*Ratio Decidendi* and the House of Lords." *Modern Law Review* 20 (1957): 124–130.

Moore, Michael. "Moral Reality." *Wisconsin Law Review* 1982 (1982): 1061–1156.

Moore, Michael. "A Natural Law Theory of Interpretation." *Southern California Law Review* 58 (1985): 277–298.

Murphy, Walter; Fleming, James; and Harris, William F. II. *American Constitutional Interpretation.* Mineola, NY: Foundation Press, 1986.

Nader, Ralph. *Unsafe at Any Speed.* New York: Grossman, 1965.

Noonan, John. "The Passengers of Palsgraf." Pp. 111–151 in *Persons and Masks of the Law.* New York: Farrar, Strauss and Giroux, 1976.

Oliphant, Herman. "Facts, Opinions and Value Judgments." *Texas Law Review* 10 (1930): 127–139.

Olson, Mancur. *The Logic of Collective Action.* New York: Schocken, 1965.

Pomeroy, John Norton. *A Treatise on Equity Jurisprudence as Administered in the United States of America,* 3 vols. San Francisco: Bancroft-Whitney, 1901.

Posner, Richard A. "The Right of Privacy." *Georgia Law Review* 12 (1978): 393–422.

Posner, Richard A. "Privacy, Secrecy and Reputation." *Buffalo Law Review* 28 (1979): 1–55.

Posner, Richard A. "The Uncertain Protection of Privacy by the Supreme Court." *Supreme Court Review* 1979 (1980): 173–216.

Posner, Richard A. *The Economics of Justice.* Cambridge, MA: Harvard University Press, 1981.

Posner, Richard A. "Statutory Interpretation in the Classroom and in the Courtroom." *University of Chicago Law Review* 50 (1983): 800–822.

Posner, Richard A. *The Federal Courts.* Cambridge, MA: Harvard University Press, 1985.

Posner, Richard A. *The Economic Analysis of Law,* 3d ed. Boston: Little, Brown, 1986.

Pratt, Walter F. *Privacy in Britain.* Lewisburg, PA: Bucknell University Press, 1979.

Prosser, William L. "Privacy." *California Law Review* 48 (1960): 383–423.

Prosser, William L. *Torts,* 4th ed. St. Paul: West Publishing, 1971.

Raiffa, Howard. *The Art and Science of Negotiation.* Cambridge, MA: Harvard University Press, 1982.

Rawls, John. *A Theory of Justice.* Cambridge, MA: Harvard University Press, 1971.

Ricoeur, Paul. "The Model of the Text: Meaningful Action Considered as a

Text." Pp. 73–102 in *Interpretive Social Science: A Reader*. Edited by Paul Rabinow and William Sullivan. Berkeley: University of California Press, 1979.

Rubin, Paul. "Why Is the Common Law Efficient?" *Journal of Legal Studies* 6 (1977): 51–64.

Rule, James B. *Private Lives and Public Surveillance*. New York: Schocken, 1974.

Rule, James B.; McAdam, Douglas; Stearns, Linda; and Uglow, David. *The Politics of Privacy*. New York: New American Library, 1980.

Ryave, A. Lincoln, and Schenkein, James N. "Notes on the Art of Walking." Pp. 265–274 in *Ethnomethodology*. Edited by Roy Turner. London: Penguin Books, 1974.

Samuelson, Paul. "The Pure Theory of Public Expenditure." *Review of Economics and Statistics* 36 (1954): 387–389.

Sarat, Austin, and Festinger, William L. "Law and Strategy in the Divorce Lawyer's Office." *Law and Society Review* 20 (1986): 93–134.

Scanlon, T. M. "Contractarianism and Utilitarianism." Pp. 103–128 in *Utilitarianism and Beyond*. Edited by Amartya Sen and Bernard Williams. Cambridge: Cambridge University Press, 1982.

Schauer, Frederick. "Easy Cases." *Southern California Law Review* 58 (1985): 399–440.

Schelling, Thomas C. *The Strategy of Conflict*. Oxford: Oxford University Press, 1960.

Schelling, Thomas C. *Micromotives and Macrobehavior*. New York: Norton, 1978.

Scheppele, Kim Lane. "Patterns in Fear of Crime on Manhattan's West Side." Senior thesis, Barnard College, 1975.

Scheppele, Kim Lane, and Soltan, Karol Edward. "The Authority of Alternatives." Pp. 169–200 in *NOMOS XXVI: Authority Revisited*. Edited by J. Roland Pennock and John W. Chapman. New York: New York University Press, 1987.

Schwartz, Barry. "The Social Psychology of Privacy." *American Journal of Sociology* 73 (1967): 741–752.

Shapiro, Martin. *Courts: A Comparative and Political Analysis*. Chicago: University of Chicago Press, 1981.

Shils, Edward A. *The Torment of Secrecy*. Carbondale: Southern Illinois University Press, 1956.

Shils, Edward A. "Privacy: Its Constitution and Vicissitudes." *Law and Contemporary Problems* 31 (1966): 281–306.

Shils, Edward A. "Privacy and Power." Pp. 317–344 in *The Intellectuals and the Powers*. Chicago: University of Chicago Press, 1972.

Shiryayev, A. N. *Optimal Stopping Rules*. New York: Springer, 1978.

Simmel, Georg. "Quantitative Aspects of the Group." Pp. 87–177 in *The Sociology of Georg Simmel*. Edited by Kurt Wolff. New York: Free Press, 1950.

REFERENCES

Simmel, Georg. "The Secret and the Secret Society." Pp. 307–376 in *The Sociology of George Simmel*. Edited by Kurt Wolff. New York: Free Press, 1950.

Simmel, Georg. "The Triad." Pp. 154–162 in *The Sociology of Georg Simmel*. Edited by Kurt Wolff. New York: Free Press, 1950.

Simmel, Georg. *The Web of Group Affiliations*. New York: Free Press, 1955.

Simon, Herbert. *Models of Bounded Rationality: Behavioral Economics and Business Organizations,* vol. 2. Cambridge, MA: MIT Press, 1982.

Simpson, A. W. B. "The *Ratio Decidendi* of a Case." *Modern Law Review* 20 (1957): 413–415.

Simpson, A. W. B. "The *Ratio Decidendi* of a Case." *Modern Law Review* 21 (1958): 155–160.

Smith, Robert Ellis. *Compilation of State and Federal Privacy Laws*. Washington, DC: Privacy Journal, 1981.

Southern California Law Review 58, No. 1 & 2 (1985). Symposium on Interpretation.

Sowell, Thomas. *Knowledge and Decisions*. New York: Basic Books, 1980.

Spence, Michael. "Job Market Signalling." *Quarterly Journal of Economics* 87 (1973): 355–374.

Stigler, George. "The Economics of Information." *Journal of Political Economy* 69 (1961): 213–225.

Stinchcombe, Arthur L. *Theoretical Methods in Social History*. New York: Academic Press, 1982.

Stinchcombe, Arthur L.; Adams, Rebecca; Heimer, Carol A.; Scheppele, Kim Lane; Smith, Tom W.; and Taylor, D. Garth. *Crime and Punishment: Changing Attitudes in America*. San Francisco: Jossey-Bass, 1980.

Stone, Julius. "The *Ratio* of the *Ratio Decidendi*." *Modern Law Review* 22 (1959): 597–620.

Story, Joseph. *Commentaries on Equity Jurisprudence as Administered in England and America,* 12th ed. Revised by Jairus W. Perry. Boston: Little, Brown, 1877.

Taylor, Charles, "Interpretation and the Sciences of Man." *Review of Metaphysics* 25 (1971): 3–51.

Terrebone, R. P. "A Strictly Evolutionary Model of the Common Law." *Journal of Legal Studies* 10 (1981): 397–407.

Texas Law Review, Spring 1984. Symposium on Law and Literature.

Thompson, E. P. *Whigs and Hunters: The Origin of the Black Act*. New York: Pantheon, 1975.

Tuchman, Gaye. *Making News*. New York: Free Press, 1979.

Tushnet, Mark. "Following the Rules Laid Down: A Critique of Interpretivism and Neutral Principles." *Harvard Law Review* 96 (1983): 781–827.

Unger, Roberto Mangabeira. *The Critical Legal Studies Movement*. Cambridge, MA: Harvard University Press, 1986.

Verplanck, Gulian. *An Essay on the Doctrine of Contracts: Being an Inquiry How*

*Contracts Are Affected in Law and Morals by Concealment, Error or Inade-
quate Price.* New York: G. & C. Caruill, 1825.

Vickrey, Alan B. "Breach of Confidence: An Emerging Tort." *Columbia Law
Review* 82 (1982): 1426–1468.

Waldron, Jeremy. "What Is Private Property?" *Oxford Journal of Legal Studies*
5 (1985): 313–349.

Waldron, Jeremy. "John Rawls and the Social Minimum." *Journal of Applied
Philosophy* 3 (1986): 21–33.

Waldron, Jeremy. "When Justice Replaces Affection: The Need for Rights."
Harvard Journal of Law and Public Policy, forthcoming.

Warren, Samuel, and Brandeis, Louis. "The Right of Privacy." *Harvard Law
Review* 4 (1890): 193–220.

Westin, Alan F. *Privacy and Freedom.* New York: Atheneum, 1967.

Westin, Alan F., and Baker, Michael A. *Databanks in a Free Society: Computers,
Record-Keeping and Privacy.* New York: Quadrangle, 1972.

White, James Boyd. *The Legal Imagination.* Chicago: University of Chicago
Press, 1973.

White, James Boyd. *When Words Lose Their Meaning.* Chicago: University of
Chicago Press, 1984.

White, James Boyd. *Heracles' Bow.* Chicago: University of Chicago Press,
1986.

Wilson, Edward H. "Concealment or Silence as a Form of Fraud and the Relief
or Redress Afforded Therefor, Both in Law and in Equity." *Counsellor* 5
(1895): 230–238.

Woito, Linda, and McNulty, Patrick. "The Privacy Disclosure Tort and the
First Amendment: Should the Community Decide Newsworthiness?"
Iowa Law Review 64 (1979): 185–232.

Table of Cases

Index of Names

Ackerman, Bruce, 92n
Adams, Rebecca, 74n
Akerlof, George, 28n
American Law Institute, 127n, 128n, 152n, 155–156n, 158n, 186n, 212n
Anscombe, G. E. M., 13n
Aquinas, St. Thomas, 57n
Atleson, James B., 317n
Atwood, Margaret, 302

Baker, Michael A., 183
Barber, Elinor, 182n
Beardsley, Elizabeth L., 184n
Becker, Gary, 38
Bennett, Lance, 98n
Bensman, Joseph, 181n
Bloustein, Edward, 181–182, 211n, 213n
Bohannan, Paul, 59n
Bok, Sissela, 22n, 111n
Bower, George Spencer, 112, 138n, 143n, 144, 148, 156
Brandeis, Louis, 185n
Brandon, Mark, 96n
Breiman, Leo, 27n
Brown, Michael E., 14n

Calabresi, Guido, 318n, 321n
Chamberlin, John, 76n
Chow, Y. S., 27n

Coase, Ronald, 29n, 38, 163–164n
Coleman, James S., 183
Coleman, Jules, 24n
Collins, Hugh, 60n, 317n
Cooley, Thomas McIntyre, 186
Corwin, Edward S., 313n
Coser, Rose Laub, 182n
Cover, Robert, 4n

Darby, Michael, 52n, 164
Diamond, Stanley, 59n
Durkheim, Emile, ix
Dworkin, Ronald, 4n, 85n, 93n, 105n

Eavey, Cheryl L., 73
Ellis, Ridsdale, 240n
Elster, Jon, 121n
Epstein, Richard, 323n
Evans-Pritchard, E. E., 58n

Fallers, Lloyd, 58n
Feldman, Martha, 98n
Festinger, William L., 97n
Finnis, John, 57n
Fish, Stanley, 88n, 105n
Fiss, Owen, 88n
Fleming, James, 4n
Franklin, Marc A., 212n
Fried, Charles, 182, 184n
Friedman, Lawrence, 323n

Subject Index

355